# A MANUAL

OF

# CHRISTIAN EVIDENCES

FOR

# JEWISH PEOPLE

BY

A. LUKYN WILLIAMS, D.D.

*Vicar of Guilden Morden and Hon. Canon of Ely Cathedral, formerly Tyrwhitt Hebrew Scholar in the University of Cambridge*

VOLUME 1 OF 2

WITH A PREFACE BY

DR. H. L. STRACK

*Professor of Old Testament in the University of Berlin*

And Indices

*Wipf & Stock*

PUBLISHERS

*Eugene, Oregon*

*First issued by*
MESSRS. HEFFER & SONS,
in 1911.

Wipf and Stock Publishers
199 West 8th Avenue, Suite 3
Eugene, Oregon 97401

Christian Evidences for Jewish People-2 volumes
By Williams, A. Lukyn
ISBN: 1-57910-197-6
Publication date 11/27/1998
Previously published by SPCK, 1911

2 Volumes in 1

שנים שהיו יושבין ועוסקין בדברי תורה שכינה ביניהם שנ׳ אז
נדברו יראי יהוה איש אל רעהו וגו׳:

*Pirqe Aboth* iii.

*Two that sit together and are occupied in the words of the Law have the Shekinah in their midst, for it is said, Then they that feared the LORD spake often one to another, etc.*

Mal. iii. 16.

## AUTHOR'S PREFACE

THE presentation of the truth of Christianity to those who do not accept it changes from age to age, in accordance with the fresh knowledge of it attained by Christians, and with alterations in the mind and attitude of those to whom they would present it. No defence therefore is required for attempting to restate the evidences of our religion.

But in doing so it is necessary to define the standpoint from which such an attempt is made, and to distinguish those to whom in particular it is addressed.

They who are on the extreme "left" of Judaism not only reject the Oral Law and the greater part of the Prayer Book, but also regard the Hebrew Scriptures as little more than a collection of fables, and think that miracles were never performed, and that prayer can expect no answer. In fact, they are only so far Jews as to observe circumcision, because it is a national sign, and to hope much from "the Mission of Israel" in its proclamation of Monotheism, and are not very far removed from the position of Unitarians. For them many recent and most excellent books on the Evidences of revealed religion, and especially of Christianity, already exist.

But the Orthodox Jews, who form the large majority of the Jews (say ten millions out of the eleven and a half), are in a very different case. They accept, more or less, the Oral Law, the Prayer Book, and, as the foundation of all, the

Law of Moses, with, as they hold, the less fully inspired books of the Former and Latter Prophets and the Holy Writings. These books of Scripture are for them the final court of appeal, however much certain Talmudic sayings appear to the less educated of Jews, or even to the less instructed of Gentiles, to place the Oral above the Written Law. For these, it is true, many books in defence of Christianity have been written (of which Justin Martyr's *Dialogue with Trypho* is the earliest that has come down to us in a fairly complete form), but none, so far as I am aware, of recent date, and of comprehensive character. It is then for Orthodox Jews, diverse though they are in degrees of western culture and of Jewish practice, that the following pages are written.

The plan of the whole work is as follows. In this, the first volume, the arguments of R. Isaac of Troki, in the First Part of his *Chizzuk Emunah* ("Strengthening of Faith"), are examined, generally in the order in which he adduces them. In the second volume, God willing, the Second Part of the same book, dealing with the New Testament, will be discussed. And in the third volume other difficulties will be considered which are not contained in either part of the *Chizzuk Emunah.*

The reasons why this restatement of Christian Evidences for Jewish people has taken its present form are: first, the author of the *Chizzuk Emunah* collected all the difficulties he could find, and combined them into one handy volume; secondly, being a Karaite his standard of appeal was much more definitely the Hebrew Scriptures than any treatise written by a Rabbinic Jew could have been; and, lastly, although a few of his arguments are rather grotesque, and have lost much of their weight with most Jews of the present time, the greater number are still considered valid, and are reproduced almost daily. It is in fact almost im-

possible to take up a Jewish paper, or religious book, without recognizing on nearly every page one or other of the arguments adduced in R. Isaac's famous work.

The outlook from which the following pages are written is, speaking generally, conservative. The author cannot indeed hope that his explanations of scriptural passages will commend themselves in every case to all his readers. Where the accepted Jewish opinion, as seen in its standard authorities, has seemed to him to be right against that of many, or even most, Christian writers, he has not hesitated to say so. For his one aim has been to set before his readers arguments for Christianity from the point of view of sound modern scholarship as well as of faithful membership of the Church of England.

For the Church of England teaches that the one and only source of Christian doctrine is Holy Scripture, in both the Old and the New Testaments: "Whatsoever is not read therein, nor may be proved thereby, is not to be required of any man, that it should be believed as an article of the Faith, or be thought requisite or necessary to salvation" (*Thirty-nine Articles of Religion*, Article vi.). Hence attention has been called again and again in the following pages to the mistake made by R. Isaac of Troki in supposing that certain practices or doctrines are a part of Christianity, although they are not contained in either the Old Testament or the New. This is the more important in that most Jews have lived, and still do live, under very imperfect forms of our holy religion, and can hardly be blamed for identifying them with Christianity itself.

The writer has been obliged to work independently, and has not been able to derive any great assistance from other books or pamphlets dealing directly with the subject under consideration. Yet he would be ungrateful indeed if he did not acknowledge his indebtedness to Gousset's elaborate answer in Latin to the *Chizzuk Emunah* (Amsterdam, 1712), lent him by the London Society for Promoting Christianity amongst the Jews; J. Z. Lichtenstein's reply to the Second Part only, printed in Hebrew of almost microscopic characters, a copy of which was lent him by Prof. Strack (חזוק אמונת אמת, Leipzig, no date, but 1879); and Pastor Carl Becker's reply to the First Part, in German manuscript (1873), lent by Pastor Bieling, of the Berlin Society for Promoting Christianity amongst the Jews. From these he has gleaned many suggestions in details. He has also received much encouragement from Dr. W. O. E. Oesterley, Secretary of the Parochial Missions to the Jews, the Rev. H. Heathcote, Secretary of the East London Fund for the Jews, the Rev. C. T. Lipshytz of the Barbican Mission to the Jews, and, last but not least, the Rev. A. Bernstein, Editor of the Yiddish paper *Qôl M'bassēr*, in which the greater part of this volume originally appeared.

English quotations from the Bible are generally taken from the Revised Version, unless there is some reason for the employment of a more literal translation. Where the numbering of chapter or verse differs in the English Versions from that in the Hebrew, the first reference is to the former, and the second, in brackets, to the latter.

Some passages of the Old Testament, which are quoted in the New, are considered in the second volume, and some, no doubt, which are nowhere adduced by R. Isaac, will be found in the third volume.

The addition of a Glossary for non-Jewish readers, and of Indices, will, it is hoped, be of service.

A. L. W.

GUILDEN MORDEN,
*November 30th*, 1910.

# PREFACE TO THIS VOLUME

BY

DR. H. L. STRACK,

*Professor of Old Testament in the University of Berlin.*

OF what matter to us are the charges and objections brought against Christianity by a Lithuanian Jew who lived three centuries and a half before our own time, a Jew who did not even know Greek, and therefore was not able to read the New Testament in the language in which it was written?

This is a question which many of our Christian readers will ask.

Let me remind them in the first place that the *Chizzuk Emunah* ("Strengthening of Faith"), written by R. Isaac ben Abraham (commonly called R. Isaac of Troki, from the town where he lived), at any rate *was* of great influence, and ranked as a high authority among the Jews of the last three centuries, and that not a few Christians felt it to be their duty to write works in confutation of it.

To name but two of the earliest of those who wrote against R. Isaac; Brandanus Henricus Gebhardi, Professor of Theology in Greifswald (Pomerania), wrote: *Centum Loca Novi Testamenti, quae R. Isaac ben Abraham, in suo* חזוק אמונה *i.e. Munimine Fidei depravaverat, vindicata*, Gryphiswaldiae, 1699 (pp. 234 quarto). Also the famous Jacobus Gussetius (Gousset), Professor of Theology in Groningen (Holland), who died November 4, 1704, was the author of

שֶׁמֶשׁ צְדָקָה וּמַרְפֵּא בִּכְנָפֶיהָ

*sive Jesu Christi Evangeliique Veritas Salutifera, demonstrata in confutatione Libri Chizzouk Emounah, a R. Isaco scripti. Amstelodami*, 1712 (pp. 522 folio).

We may also mention that R. Isaac's book has been translated not only into Latin, but also into Yiddish, Spanish, English * and German.

Secondly, to-day, at the present time, the *Chizzuk Emunah is* in great repute among the Jews. Dr. Isaac Broydé in the *Jewish Encyclopedia*, xii. p. 265 styles it "epoch-making," and Orthodox Jews in their discussions with Christians, or when they desire to strengthen themselves in their faith, often, either consciously or unconsciously, make use of the arguments adduced by R. Isaac of Troki.

For these reasons I hoped more than twenty years ago to publish in my *Nathanael, Zeitschrift für die Arbeit der evangelischen Kirche an Israel* (Berlin), a series of articles written by a friend, on the exposition, and refutation, of the *Chizzuk Emunah*, but, not receiving the promised manuscript, and being myself overburdened with other work, I was able to issue only an introductory article (*Nathanael*, 1889, pp. 52-69).

I have therefore been very glad to see that an excellent Hebrew scholar and earnest Christian has devoted himself to this task, and it gives me now great pleasure to add a few words in recommendation of his book. It will prove useful to Christian readers who may be at a loss how to answer the objections raised in the *Chizzuk Emunah*, when they are brought forward by a Jew, or encountered in books. Jewish readers also will see that the much-lauded arguments of this Karaite of old are not irrefutable, but are often either weak in themselves or rebutted by the history of the Christian Church, especially the Church of the nineteenth century, the first missionary century of modern times.

It would have been an alluring task for Mr. Lukyn Williams to have criticized R. Isaac's work from general points of view

* Moses Mocatta, חזוק אמונה or *Faith Strengthened*, London, 1851.

only. He might, for example, have shown that the delineations of the future given by the prophets of the Old Testament were necessarily liable to some limitations as to time, land and nation; for otherwise they could not have made the intended impression on the contemporaries of the prophets, whose primary task was not to satisfy human curiosity as to future events, but to influence the religion, the life, the morals, of the then living generation. Or he might have pointed out that the prophets were bound by the ideas of their own time; or that all the prophecies, promises as well as threatenings, were conditional (*e.g.* Jer. xviii. 7, 8). Or he might have demonstrated at length that the Old Testament expresses much in figurative language, and that the Holy writers love to employ tropes and parables.

All this will, in fact, be found in the present book, but the author has done wisely, in my opinion, in accompanying R. Isaac from point to point, from paragraph to paragraph, lest any one should say: He has talked only about general subjects, because he was not able to enter into a discussion of the details.

The preparation of this volume has been both difficult and laborious, but may He who has promised to bless all conscientious work send attentive readers, who are earnestly enquiring after truth, and may He grant that by their reading of it not a few of God's ancient people may find Him who has said, "I am the way, and the truth, and the life," to be indeed the Messiah of God, and experience in their own hearts the truth of His utterance.

HERMANN L. STRACK.

BERLIN, GROSSLICHTERFELDE W.
*October*, 1910.

## CONTENTS

CHAPTER II.—JEWS AND CHRISTIANS AS THE OBJECTS OF GOD'S AFFECTION (parr. 72-104).



CHAPTER III.—A CONSIDERATION OF CERTAIN PASSAGES IN THE LAW (parr. 105-179).



CHAPTER IV.—A CONSIDERATION OF CERTAIN PASSAGES IN THE PROPHETS (parr. 180-275).

# INTRODUCTION

# INTRODUCTION.

## R. Isaac of Troki and the *Chizzuk Emunah*.*

1] When in the end of the 14th century the Lithuanian Grand Duke Witold settled, as we are told,† in Lithuania some Karaites from the Crimea, placing some of them in the city of Troki not far from Wilna, he can hardly have supposed that the new comers would add considerably to the fame of that city. Yet it is probable that the greater part of those who have ever heard of Troki owe their knowledge of its existence to the fact that one of the descendants (as may be presumed) of those Karaites, and himself a Karaite, wrote a book which has become famous among all Jews, and among all those who take much interest in the welfare of Jews. For that the author of the famous *Chizzuk Emunah* was R. Isaac b. Abraham of Troki, and a Karaite, may be regarded as certain.

It was first published by the German scholar J. C. Wagenseil, with other Jewish anti-Christian writings, in his *Tela Ignea Satanæ*, 1681. Wagenseil tells us in his preface that while paying a flying visit from Spain to the little town of Ceuta on the North African coast, he so interested the Jews there by what he told them of their brethren in Europe, that not only did they give him in return information about their own affairs, but one of them also made him a present of a manuscript of the *Chizzuk Emunah* (previously quite unknown to him) with words of high commendation of it. Scholars long supposed that R. Isaac belonged to Cracow, and was a strict Rabbanite, but later investigations have shown that both

* The Hebrew text used is that of D. Deutsch, published with a German translation, second edition, Sohrau, 1873. Geiger's essay, valuable for its information about the sources used by R. Isaac, published originally in 1853, has been reprinted in his *Nachgelassene Schriften*, 1876, pp. 178 sqq.

† *Jewish Encyclopedia*, vii. 444. xii. p. 263.

these suppositions were wrong. He quotes indeed Rabbinic authorities not infrequently, but he no doubt does this after the spirit of an earlier Karaite teacher, Nissi b. Noah, a Persian of the eleventh century, who said that it was obligatory on the Karaites to study early Rabbinic literature, as the larger part of their teaching was based upon the true national tradition.* And if further the question be asked why, as it seems, Isaac never quotes Karaite authorities, the answer is presumably that, as he wished to put a book into the hands of Jews of all kinds and classes, he could attain his object better by omitting all reference to those writers whom the bulk of Jews would refuse to accept.

What else we know of Isaac may be put into very few words. He was born in 1533 and died in 1594. He was the pupil of a Karaite writer of repute, Zephaniah b. Mordecai, and it is said that he composed a few "liturgical hymns and compendiums of the religious laws in Aaron ben Elijah's 'Gan Eden.'" He had also some knowledge of Latin. †

Poland at that time was in even a greater ferment than were most countries in the sixteenth century. It had become the common receptacle for all sorts and conditions of religious enthusiasts; turbulent or original spirits that found no congenial home elsewhere. Every branch and sect of the Christian Church found liberty of speech in Poland, and obtained more or less following. It was inevitable that Jews also should be exposed to controversy, and it was typical of the time and place (would that it were more typical of every time and place!) that they were able to argue for their faith openly without fear of consequences.

Hence it is no great matter for wonder that Isaac tells us that he had frequent discussions with persons of every faith and rank, and that he had kept some records of these discussions.

Upon the basis of these notes he arranged his book, referring to them not infrequently, and incorporating them as

* *Jewish Encyclopedia*, vii. p. 442.

† *Ibid.* vii. p. 444. xii. pp. 265 sq.

need occurred. His book was finished (save part of the list of contents) only the year before he died (*i.e.*, in 1593), he giving it in charge to his pupil Joseph b. Mordecai (Malinowski), also of Troki, who added a preface of his own and a more complete list of contents, without, as it seems, actually printing the work.

**2**] It is confessedly a famous book, but the date at which it was written makes us pause and ask ourselves whether it is worth reading in these days. Much water has flowed under the bridge since 1593. Is it the case that Jews can still depend upon it for a defence of Judaism against Christianity, and can still venture to use it for an arsenal of weapons whereby to attack Christianity? Or is it not altogether too old-fashioned a book, too wholly out of date, for either Jews to use or Christians to reckon with?

Of course in many ways this is the case. It is old-fashioned; it is out of date. But not altogether. Many of its arguments are in fact very well suited to the Jewish mode of thought existing to-day, and many, it must be confessed, are well worth the consideration of Christians.

It is indeed not original. There is hardly a trace of originality in it. But this makes it none the worse for Jews, who are more accustomed to look to the repetition of ancient teaching than to the enunciation of new truths, and has in fact tended towards its permanence. For what was original three hundred years ago must long since have ceased to present any charm in that respect to-day, and the absence of any claim to originality has no doubt helped to secure its better preservation and respect among so conservative a race of religious thinkers as the Jewish nation.

But its charm lies in its clearness and its comprehensiveness. It is absolutely clear. There is very seldom any doubt at all what the author means. He was in no sense a great man. But to write a summary of other people's thoughts, and record them in a clear and convenient form, does not require greatness as we understand the term. He thinks clearly, knowing his own mind, and he expresses his thoughts clearly. Also he is comprehensive; he has gathered his material as widely as possible, and has collected together all the arguments in favour of Judaism and against Christianity that he can find. He has too, in the second part of his treatise, gone through the New Testament writings *seriatim*, dealing with each point that arises there. Hence his work has always been a very convenient storehouse from which weapons may be picked with ease, to meet the arguments adduced by Christians, or to confirm the wavering faith of a member of the Jewish community. That Jews have found such a work useful to them from their point of view is not surprising.*

**3**] Yet it is not too much to say that the *Chizzuk Emunah* shows but a very superficial acquaintance with Christianity. Jews think that by using it they are using arguments against Christianity which are sound and good. But in reality this is far from being the case. R. Isaac evidently had some acquaintance with the various sects and forms of Christianity, but he never seems to have grasped its real character and teaching, and is often (so at least it seems to me) very unfair in his reasoning.

Do I hear a Jew say in his heart, That does not matter if the end is reached, freedom from the snares of a false religion? Nay, my Brother. It can never be well for our soul's life to make use of the help of a lie. And if R. Isaac all unwittingly (that I fully grant, for he seems to have been a perfectly honest man at heart, however unfair he was in some of his arguments) let himself adduce reasons that will not hold the light of candid and fair examination to-day, our souls suffer if we are deceived by him. For it may be that if he is wrong on some points he is wrong also in others. And it may even be that if he gives a wrong impression, because he himself is wrongly informed, about either the New Testament or the Lord Jesus, he turns away from fuller light souls that otherwise would perceive it.

The various errors into which R. Isaac falls will appear

* "Il a rassemblé toutes les difficultés que les incrédules ont prodiguées depuis. Enfin les incrédules les plus determinés n'ont presque rien allegué qui ne soit dans le Rempart de la Foi du rabbin Isaac" (Voltaire, *Mélanges*, iii. 344 in the *Jewish Encyclopedia*, xii. 266).

in detail as we proceed. Suffice it now to say that they centre round the following subjects :—

(1). He forgets, or is not aware, that the New Testament was written by Jews, and must be judged in its arguments by Jewish methods. R. Isaac argues as though he thought that the New Testament was written, for example, by a learned and logical Pole of his own time. In other words R. Isaac fails to judge the New Testament by the same standard as that which he would apply to the writers of the Talmud.

(2). He misunderstands the Christian doctrine about Jesus. He forgets, whenever at least he can score a point by doing so, that Jesus was not only God but also man, with a manhood perfect and complete in every respect.

(3). He fails to see the attractiveness of the character of Jesus, and confines his argument much too exclusively to the relation that Jesus holds in word and work to the prophecies of Messiah contained in the Old Testament.

Faults, you say, these of the time when R. Isaac wrote! Yes, undoubtedly to a great extent. And so far he himself is not to be blamed. But the strange thing is that he still holds the ears of so many; that so many of his readers still fail to see that his book is far behind the time in numberless respects, and thus shut their eyes to Jesus as He is portrayed in the New Testament, to Jesus as He really is.

**4**] May I call the attention of all those who read these pages to an excellent saying that R. Isaac himself quotes from "the greatest of philosophers"?

אם סוקר"אט ואפלטון אהובינו האמת יותר אהובה אצלנו.

"If Socrates and Plato are dear to us the Truth is dearer still" (p. 10).* Let us then act on this. We love wise men and their writings, heathen or Jews, but we love the Truth very much more, and are determined to follow it at all costs. I myself shall try to carry out this principle. I hope to be absolutely candid, and shall not hesitate to say when the argu-

* By "the greatest of philosophers," R. Isaac certainly means Aristotle. The saying, however, is a proverb found in various forms, and is doubtless derived ultimately from only a misunderstanding of Aristotle (*Ethics*, I. vi. I.).

ments of the *Chizzuk Emunah* appear to me to be right (and they often are right); and again, on the other hand, I shall endeavour to show where and why they are wrong, and only ask the reader to weigh fairly, and without prejudice, such arguments as may be adduced. We both want the Truth, and nothing less than all the Truth. May the One God whom Jews and Christians serve guide us into it.

# CHAPTER I

## PRELIMINARY OBJECTIONS TO CHRISTIANITY

# CHAPTER I.

## PRELIMINARY OBJECTIONS TO CHRISTIANITY.

### i. ITS RELATION TO HEATHENISM.

#### R. Isaac's Preamble (ההצעד).

5] BEFORE beginning his book R. Isaac writes a short Preamble, in which he places from the very first the whole of Christian teaching under a cloud. He gives such a tone to all his book that any Jew who reads it will say, It is of course quite useless studying Christianity at all after what this learned Rabbi says here, for he has shown the absurdity of it at once. R. Isaac is in fact like those lawyers who, while professing to plead in a case, begin by raising a demurrer that the case itself ought never to have been brought forward, because there is a fatal flaw in the whole of it. Yet we must not blame R. Isaac overmuch. He is quite above board in stating that his purpose is not to consider the truth of Christianity, but only to shew that it is utterly and entirely wrong. Only let no reader of the *Chizzuk Emunah* come to it with the impression that he is beginning the study of Christianity under an unprejudiced and scrupulously fair guide. Intentionally or not, and we think unintentionally, R. Isaac is very far from being that.

The Preamble is likely to make every Jewish reader have a deeper prejudice against Christianity than ever.

For R. Isaac says that he could not understand how Christians could believe doctrines so contrary to reason until he read in a certain Polish Chronicle some account of the beliefs of the heathen before the birth of Jesus. He read, for example, that the heathen believed that one god was born from a virgin; that another was born from a virgin's head; that a king killed his own son, and cooked him, and set him before the gods to eat; that they however refused to eat him, but restored him to life; and many other nonsensical tales like the nonsensical tales that are now found in the writings of the Christian faith:

וכן שאר דברי שגעונות ושבושים אחרים הרבה דומים לשבושים הנמצאים עתה בספרי אמונתם.

Does R. Isaac really think for a moment that the doctrines of Christianity have any common ground with the filthy stories of Greek and Roman mythology?

Further, having made this unseemly remark, he explains the phenomenon at which he wonders by saying that as Christians had been accustomed from their childhood to hear such tales they came to regard Christian doctrines as natural, "For habit is second nature" (ההרגל טבע שני).

But in saying this he seems to forget who it was that composed the books contained in the New Testament. He implies that these were written by Christians who had been heathen. But every one knows, unlearned and scholars alike, that out of all the writers of the New Testament, not more than one, St. Luke (and even in his case there is room for doubt), can possibly have been a Gentile by birth. All of them, save one, were Jews, and apparently as strict Jews as ever R. Isaac himself was. They had, that is to say, no more been accustomed to hear heathen tales than had R. Isaac. They had all been trained carefully in the Jewish faith, and been taught, as it seems, in deeply religious homes, and, if they came to believe on Jesus, it was because their hearts could not resist Him, as they recognized in Him the Saviour of their souls.

**6**] Perhaps, however, some may feel that it is not necessary to point out this blunder on the part of R. Isaac; he is dead and gone, why recall his errors? It certainly would not be worth noticing if a thought did not lie at the back of it which still hinders Jews in their examination of Christianity. It is urged by many Jews (quite without reason, as I myself believe), that some Christian doctrines have been derived from heathenism, and it is urged that these doctrines are therefore not true.

(1). Let us take the last point first. What right have we to say that because a doctrine has been derived from heathenism it is therefore not true? Have we ever thought how many of the practices and laws and even doctrines of the Jews themselves would stand if this were the case? What, for example, of the customs on New Moons? They are not mentioned in the Bible. But these, it may be urged, are mere details. What then even of circumcision itself? Oh, it is said, that was given to Abraham by God! Certainly, but not before it had been practised by heathen. Long before Abraham's time circumcision had been a common practice among the heathen. But, a Jew will say, our circumcision is not like heathen circumcision; there are details of difference. I know well enough that there are details of difference now. But there is no evidence that these details are anything more than plans of human devising to differentiate Jewish from heathen circumcision. Circumcision as such is a heathen practice. Again, take the Jewish Law. No educated man to-day is ignorant of the fact that long before the time of Moses, and the coming of the children of Israel to Mount Sinai, many of its laws were in existence. I refer in particular to the great Code made by Khammurabi, who is almost certainly to be identified with the Amraphel mentioned in Gen. xiv. His Code, which dates therefore at least as early as the time of Abraham, long before the Exodus, contains many of the laws that were given at Mount Sinai. In origin therefore they were heathen. But they are none the less true because of that. So with the doctrine of Angels. It existed in some form long before the books of the Bible were written, and in its present developed form is to be traced much more to heathen sources than to the Bible. And yet some Jews turn round and say that doctrines taken from heathenism are *ipso facto* to be rejected!

It is very hard to escape from the notion that God, the

One Holy God whom Jews and Christians worship, is only the God of the Jews, and not also the God of the whole earth. He has indeed been the God of the Jews in a very special sense, far be it from me to deny it; but He is also the God of the whole world. He has from time to time taught even the heathen some truths, and if He has guided either Jews or Christians to take over some of these truths from the heathen, it is not very fitting that either Christians or Jews should turn round and say, Lord, we will have nothing to do with these, because they come from the heathen. If Jews were to do this to their own faith, and to their own Books, they would lose a very great deal of what they now rightly hold sacred.

**7**] (2). But is it true that Christian doctrines have been derived, indirectly at least, from heathen sources?

I am not concerned to attempt to defend all so-called Christian doctrines, much less all Christian practices, for there are several doctrines and practices against which we who are members of the Church of England most heartily protest. I am concerned only with those practices and doctrines which are upheld in the New Testament. Neither shall I attempt to discuss in detail now any one such doctrine or practice. I ask the reader at present to notice only the great outstanding points of difference between the practices and doctrines of heathen religions and those of Christianity, *i.e.*, of the New Testament. For, as we must remind ourselves again and again, it is not a question of the Christianity of England or of Russia or of Germany or of America, but of the New Testament that is before us.

There are two great differences easy to be remembered. First, the teaching of Christianity is always moral, while Heathenism pays very little regard to morals. Even Socrates, the greatest of the ancients, defended practices utterly and abominably immoral. But the teaching of Christianity, the Christianity of the New Testament, is in every case moral and pure. Jews, speaking generally, will acknowledge this. Even in spite of all that they have, alas, suffered at the hands of Christians, they know that the actions of their persecutors have been wholly against the teaching of Jesus Christ.

Secondly, Heathenism is very often utterly irrational and contrary to reason. But I have myself never yet heard of a single Christian doctrine contained in the New Testament (I am not thinking of strange additions to Christian doctrine made in later ages) that is not both consistent with the purest reason and the most advanced thought and philosophy, and at the same time based upon the Old Testament. Jewish readers will smile at this. I can only ask them now to withhold their judgment until we have considered more questions together. For I entreat them not to be turned away from the study of the New Testament, *i.e.*, the study of the Lord Jesus, by *primâ facie* difficulties in Christian doctrines.

### ii. Supposed proofs that Jesus of Nazareth cannot be the promised Messiah.

#### *a.* His Genealogy. §§ i. 45; part ii. § i.

**8**] R. Isaac begins his Treatise by saying that he will postpone to the Second Part his objections to the use made in the New Testament of the Prophecies found in the Old, but he has several weighty proofs that Jesus of Nazareth was not Messiah at all.

The first of these refers to His Genealogy, according to which, R. Isaac says, *first*, Jesus Himself was not a descendant of David, for He was not, according to Christian teaching, the son of Joseph, and we know nothing of Mary's ancestry; and *secondly*, even if He were the son of Joseph the Genealogy of the latter is most uncertain, for the two witnesses to it, Matthew and Luke, contradict each other. In Part ii. §i. R. Isaac returns to the same subject, and repeats, with some enlargement, the same objections, so that it is convenient for us to consider both passages together.

**9**] (1). Let us take the second objection first, the untrustworthiness of the evidence for the genealogy of Joseph.

R. Isaac finds three difficulties :—

*A*—According to Matthew, Joseph's father is Jacob and his line comes down through Solomon ; according to Luke, Joseph's father is Eli and his line comes down through Nathan the son of David.

*B*—According to Matthew there were forty-two generations from Abraham to Jesus ; according to Luke fifty-six.

*C*—Matthew makes an evident error (טעות מפורסמת) in saying that Joram begat Uzziah, for he thus omits Ahaziah, Joash, and Amaziah (*cf.* 1 Chr. iii. 11, 12).

**10**] (i). Now candidly, I do not think much of the difficulties raised in *B* and *C*. Indeed, if the truth must be told, they seem to me to be more fit for a Gentile than a learned Rabbi. Has R. Isaac never heard of mnemonics and Midrash? Has he never noticed that Matthew divides his series into three times fourteen, presumably for the sake of memory, and that fourteen equals by Gematria דוד, while three is the number of the letters themselves in that word? * But, if Matthew purposely arranged his names thus, was it not almost necessary that he should leave some names out? "What!" it is said, "in a Genealogy?" Yes, even so. Does not Ezra leave out names in a Genealogy? See Ezra vii. 1—5 where the names from Amariah to Johanan, six in all, are omitted ; compare 1 Chr. vi. 7—11. (=*Heb.* v. 33—37). The learned Dr. Schechter, now President of the Jewish Theological Seminary of America, is a wiser man than R. Isaac, when he says (*Jewish Quarterly Review*, xii. April, 1900, p. 418): "the impression conveyed to the Rabbinic student by the perusal of the New Testament is in many parts like that gained by reading an old Rabbinic homily." And then he goes on to remark upon the thoroughly Rabbinic character of the Genealogy contained in Matthew. Compare also *Pirqe*

* Gfrörer, *Die heilige Sage*, ii. p. 9, note (see Mr. G. H. Box's important article on the Gospel narratives of the Nativity and the alleged influence of heathen ideas, in the *Zeitschrift für die N. T. Wissenschaft*, 1905, p. 85.).

*Aboth*, v. 2 and 3, where we are told, first, that there are ten generations from Adam to Noah, where Adam is included, and, secondly, that there are ten from Noah to Abraham, where Noah is excluded. Mere exactness in numerals easily gives way in Jewish writings to mnemonics and hortatory instruction. No really learned Jew will dream of blaming the Genealogy in the First Gospel for this.

**11**] (ii). His first difficulty (*A*) with regard to the genealogy of Joseph is however more worthy of consideration.

(*a*). I freely grant that the difficulty cannot be got over by saying that Luke's form is not the genealogy of Joseph, but of Mary. For Luke gives not a trace of a hint that this is the case. We may assume that both are Joseph's.

(*b*). I grant also that all such explanations as the following are extremely improbable: (1) Jews of rank had more than one name. (2) The two sons of Matthan were Jacob the elder and Eli the younger; Joseph was the son of Jacob, and Mary the only child of Eli; then by marriage with his cousin Mary, Joseph becomes Eli's son as well as Jacob's. This explanation is ingenious in that it both explains the two genealogies as Joseph's, and yet shows that in fact Luke's is also that of Mary. But it is quite too ingenious to be admitted without proof.* (3) Jacob died without children, and Eli marrying his widow, according to Jewish usage, became by her the father of Joseph, who hence would be called Jacob's son, that the elder brother's line might not die out. This too seems to be highly conjectural.

(*c*). But there is one other explanation which is possible, and, in view of the statements made, even probable: *viz.*, that Luke gives the true descent through private persons, and Matthew the line of succession of heirship, largely through kings. In favour of this explanation is the fact that he places Jehoiachin, who, as he very well knew from Jer. xxii. 30, was to have no child of his own worthy of the name, among the ancestors of the Messiah.

* John Lightfoot's supposition that the notice in T. J. *Chagigah*, ii. 2. (77 d.) of Miriam the daughter of Eli refers to the mother of the Lord Jesus seems to be quite unwarranted.

The result therefore of our consideration of this first question as to the Genealogies is that they both refer to Joseph, and that there is no sufficient reason to doubt the general trustworthiness of them both, each in its own way.

**12**] (2). We now come to the further and still more important question as to the Davidic origin of Jesus if the two genealogies are those of Joseph, it being presupposed that according to the Christian belief He was born of the Virgin Mary alone.

(i). I grant that there is no clear and definite statement in the New Testament that Mary was descended from David.

(*a*). Yet there are several passages in the New Testament which point to this belief. In Luke i. 32 the angel who addresses Mary at the Annunciation tells her that God shall give unto her son "the throne of his father David," and in *v.* 69 Zacharias says that God "hath raised up a horn of salvation for us in the house of his servant David." So too in Acts ii. 30 St. Peter speaks of God swearing to David that "of the fruit of his loins He would set one upon his throne," and applies this promise to Jesus. St. Paul's evidence is most convincing of all. He, as a learned Jew, knew perfectly well that the Messiah was to be of David's line, yet, though after his conversion he mingled much with Christians who had known the Lord Jesus in the flesh, he never shows the slightest hesitancy in attributing to him Davidic descent. He writes for example in Rom. i. 3 of Jesus "who was born of the seed of David according to the flesh." Besides, we have numerous examples in the Gospels of Jesus being addressed as Son of David, and nowhere is there the least hint of any objection being raised against His claim to Messiahship on the ground that He was not of David's line.

(*b*). But while it is true that the New Testament may just leave room for doubt as to the origin of Mary herself, the Christians of the next generation had no doubt at all. In other words they who had seen Apostles (and others who had known Jesus in the flesh) accepted the Davidic origin of Mary as a fact. See in particular Ignatius (A.D. 110), who says (*To the Ephesians*, 18, 2), "For our God Jesus the Christ was conceived of Mary according to the appointment of God, of the seed of David and of the Holy Ghost." *

There is therefore every probability, according to the evidence before us, that Mary, as well as Joseph, was descended from David.

**13**] (ii). It must however be borne in mind that the question is not of such vital importance as at first sight it might seem to be. Imagine what Jews would have said, and certainly a learned Rabbi like R. Isaac would have caught up the cry at once, if the genealogy of Mary had been given in the N. T. and not that of Joseph. "We do not reckon a genealogy by the mother! You have produced no proof at all that he was descended from David! You ought to have produced the genealogy of Joseph if the evidence was to weigh with us who are acquainted with Jewish customs! We say, "The father's family is called 'family'; the mother's is not" (T.B. *Baba Bathra*, 109*b*). †

משפחת אב קרויה משפחה, משפחת אם אינה קרויה משפחה.

There was therefore no special object in giving the genealogy of Mary, though she was of David's line.

(iii). The fact is that according to every human law Jesus was reckoned legally as Joseph's son. No other father could be found or was known. ‡

Listen to the words of one who of all Gentiles living is perhaps the most learned in matters of this kind:

"The descent from David is attested by the evangelists with regard to Joseph only, and not Mary, in accordance with the view that descent on the mother's side does not carry with it any right of succession, and that her husband's recognition of Mary's supernatural child conferred upon it the legal rights of his son. Lichtenstein § recalls the fact in this connexion that all property acquired

* ὁ γάρ θεὸς ἡμῶν Ἰησοῦς ὁ Χριστὸς ἐκυοφορήθη ὑπὸ Μαρίας κατ' οἰκονομίαν θεοῦ ἐκ σπέρματος μὲν Δαυίδ, πνεύματος δὲ ἁγίου. See also *To the Trallians*, 9.

† The second clause is absent from the Munich MS., and is doubtless an explanatory gloss, but the sense remains the same.

‡ Indeed we may say in all truth that no fatherhood of any kind, human or Divine, produced in Mary the birth of Jesus. Jesus Himself, according to the teaching of the New Testament, took human nature in her, she being strictly a virgin.

§ *Hebrew Commentary on Mark and Luke*, 1896, 13[a] sq.

by a spouse becomes uniformly the possession of the husband according to *Keth.* vi. 1, and that in the case of any question as to one's origin, common opinion was, in point of law, the decisive consideration T.B. *Kidd.* 80*a.* * Nevertheless, neither of these points touches the right of succession. The criterion for this, according to *Baba-Bathra*, viii. 6 [האומר זה בני נאמן=T. B. *Baba-Bathra*, 134*a*] is whether the father is willing to recognise anyone as his son. A case such as that of Jesus was, of course, not anticipated by the law ; but if no other human fatherhood was alleged, then the child must have been regarded as bestowed by God upon the house of Joseph, for a betrothed woman, according to Israelitish law, already occupied the same status as a wife. The divine will, in the case of this birth, conferred upon the child its own right of succession, which, once Joseph recognised it, would not have been disputed even by a Jewish judge." †

The conclusion then at which we arrive with regard to this difficult subject is that, although it is true that we have no direct evidence as to the Davidic origin of Mary, R. Isaac does not deal with the question accurately, for the balance of probability is very greatly in favour of her being a descendant of David ; also that in any case, according to Jewish law, Jesus himself must be pronounced to be a descendant of David.

### *b.* The Actions of Jesus.

§ 1 continued; compare Part II. §§ 13 and 21.

**14**] The first of the learned Rabbi's grave difficulties, namely that concerning the Genealogy of our Lord Jesus, was, as we have seen, a very real difficulty, and well worthy of being raised. It was a perfectly fair objection to make, even though we could not find that it was ultimately valid. But this his second difficulty is of a very different character. He solemnly affirms (for there is no sign that he means it other than seriously, even if joking were at all in place in the discussion of so solemn a subject) that Jesus cannot be the Messiah because of His own description of His work. First, He says that He came to bring not peace but a sword, and divisions in families

* D. Deutsch rightly rejects this argument in his edition of the *Chizzuk Emunah*, 1873, pp. 426 sq. (A.L.W.).

† Dalman, *Words of Jesus*, xii. 2, pp. 319 sqq.

(Matt. x. 34, 35); whereas we read of the true Messiah, "He shall speak peace unto the nations" (Zech. ix. 10), and "they shall beat their swords into plowshares, and their spears into pruninghooks" (Isa. ii. 4); and again we find that in the true Messiah's time Elijah the prophet "shall turn the heart of the fathers to the children" (Mal. iv. 6). Secondly, He says (Matt. xx. 28), "The Son of man came not to be ministered unto, but to minister"; whereas of the true Messiah we read (Ps. lxxii. 11), "All kings shall fall down before Him: all nations shall serve Him"; and (Zech. ix. 10), "His dominion shall be from sea to sea, and from the River to the ends of the earth"; and (Dan. vii. 27), "All dominions shall serve and obey Him."

It is, I repeat, very hard for a Christian Englishman to think that these objections have been made seriously, but, as there is no reason to doubt this, we must take them into consideration.

**15**] (1). Let us consider the second objection first.

To R. Isaac it seems unworthy of Messiah that He should serve. What! Is it not a graceful and most king-like action for a king sometimes to serve? I do not suppose that R. Isaac was able to read English, learned man though he was, but he had plenty of histories in Polish or German which might have told him about our own Edward the Black Prince, who died in 1376. Did the Prince think it a disgrace to wait upon the French King whom he had made a prisoner? Did he not then, or at some other time, take as his motto the words *Ich Dien*, "I serve"? And does not the Prince of Wales to this very day have them for his own, even though he stands next to the King of England, Emperor of India and of the Britains across the sea? How can the fact that Jesus says that He serves invalidate His position as king? For is not Jesus king? What is a king but one who rules? And does He not rule over men to a most extraordinary degree? Was there ever one born of woman to whom men in all ages since His coming, and in all countries where His name has been proclaimed, have yielded and are yielding such willing homage? See also parr. 27, 79.

What has been the reason? Is it not this in no slight

measure, that when He was on earth He was always ready to do His very uttermost for the bodies and souls of others, willing to serve them to the extremest limit of His power?

**16**] (2). R. Isaac's other objection is that Jesus said that He had come to bring not peace but a sword.

What does the Rabbi mean by this objection? Does he seriously suppose that Jesus came to make men fight? If he did he would be as amusing, or as irritating, if you prefer it, as those critics of the Talmud who take everything *au pied de la lettre*, and forget that hyperbolical and figurative language is natural to one born in the East. Surely R. Isaac knows that Jesus expressly says that He left His disciples peace: "Peace I leave with you; my peace I give unto you: not as the world giveth, give I unto you. Let not your heart be troubled, neither let it be fearful" (John xiv. 27). Again, in John xvi. 33 He says: "These things have I spoken unto you, that in Me ye may have peace. In the world ye have tribulation: but be of good cheer; I have overcome the world." And not only does He promise His disciples peace in their hearts, but He also urges them to do everything in their power to bring about peace with others. What else is the effect of His command that they should love one another, and that they should love their enemies? To read R. Isaac's words it might be supposed that Jesus was a firebrand urging His followers to strife and war. Whereas everyone who reads the New Testament knows that the very reverse was the case.

**17**] What then did Jesus really mean when He said that He came to send a sword? Surely it is not so very difficult to understand His parable. Does it not mean this—I speak as to wise men—that His doctrine would have, as its immediate effect, a separating power; that whenever a person accepted Jesus and His words, and took Him as his Saviour and endeavoured to carry out His commands, he would become different from others round him, and they would necessarily feel that he was different, and would act accordingly?

**18**] Does not the experience of all who read these pages bear out what I say? Have you ever known a Jew become a Christian? If so, what has been the effect upon his family?

He says that he himself still loves his family. But do they still love him? I dare say they do, but they show their love in a very strange way. For is it not the case that they feel deeply the estrangement that his conversion to Christianity has brought about, and even in many cases refuse to have anything more to do with him? Have you never heard of a Jewish mother refusing to see her son who has become a Christian? Have you never heard of a Jewish father turning such a son out of his house? Have you never heard of a whole Jewish family mourning for a baptized member, a son or a daughter, a brother or a sister, as though dead, and never mentioning even the name of the one who has been baptized, save with a shudder?

I do not ask whether such an action of the father, the mother, the family, is right or wrong. I desire only to point out that whenever members of a family do this they are unconsciously fulfilling the prophecy of Jesus, and helping to prove the truth of His sayings, that He came to bring a sword and to divide households.

**19**] But someone will say: How can such a separation, such a sword (to keep up the imagery employed by Jesus), be consistent with the idea of Messiah, who, as we read in Isaiah ix. 6, was to be "Prince of Peace"? Let us imagine for a moment what the effect would be if a perfectly holy Messiah were to come into the world. Would not the revelation of so much goodness and holiness necessarily make a division among those to whom He came? Would it not necessarily distinguish people into higher and lower; into those who gladly and thankfully try to follow Him, and those to whom, at first, the immediate change in the life of such followers appears as something exceedingly curious, and condemnatory of their own unchanged behaviour? Do we not read in the Bible that the coming of God Himself is to produce just such an effect? For in Isaiah lxv. 6—10 (to take but one passage), you will see that the manifestation of God has this very result. Some are marked out as those who oppose Him, and others as those who are His. In other words, the revelation of God Himself produces division, brings (in Jesus' imagery) not peace, but a sword. If Jesus was the Messiah it is hard to understand how His appearance could fail to produce just such a separation as He said it would produce, and as, in fact, we see it does produce.

**20**] But if the question be raised whether the coming of Jesus has upon the whole made for peace or war, there is no doubt what the answer must be. Everyone will admit that in spite of all the faults of His followers (and alas, they have been many) the general result of the coming of Jesus has been to diminish war, and the horrors of war. It will be acknowledged that Christian nations have gradually been learning to desire peace, and to try to bring about peace between nation and nation. The teaching of Jesus has always made for peace, in spite of opposition stirred up by evil passions. In other words, we must confess that R. Isaac has taken one of Jesus' sayings out of its proper surroundings, and has not tried to understand its real meaning.

### *c.* The Time of the coming of Messiah.

§ I CONTINUED.

**21**] R. Isaac argues that the time when Jesus came does not correspond with that in which, according to the prophets, the true Messiah appears.

He says first that the Prophets affirm that Messiah shall come באחרית הימים ("auf die spätesten Tage," "in the last days," as Deutsch translates, fully in accord with R. Isaac's views), and that therefore Jesus cannot be the true Messiah. To prove his point he quotes Isa. ii. 2, Ezek. xxxviii. 8 (where however the phrase is not באחרית הימים but באחרית השנים), Hos. iii. 5, and Dan. ii. 28. As however this last passage would prove too much for his purpose, for strictly it indicates the whole of Nebuchadnezzar's dream, he says that it really refers only to *v.* 44, the kingdom which shall never be destroyed. We consider *v.* 44 in parr. 25-30, but it does not contain באחרת הימים or its Aramaic equivalent, and therefore does not in all fairness belong to our immediate discussion.

**22**] With regard to the Rabbi's contention that these passages show that Jesus cannot be the true Messiah because they say that the latter will come באחרית הימים, observe:

(1). Of the four passages three contain no reference to Messiah Himself at all. It is only in Hos. iii. 5 that He is spoken of ("David their king"), and even there, many commentators find no reference to Him. But personally I think that R. Isaac is right in understanding "David" there to mean Messiah. In the three other passages however the time indeed is Messianic, but if Messiah Himself is not mentioned we have no right to regard this as a mere accident, but rather to see if there be not a hidden meaning in this omission. May not the omission of all mention of Messiah, in these passages that speak of the Messianic time, have been purposely made in order to hint to us that the time spoken of is not so strictly limited to the actual period of Messiah's appearance as the Rabbi thinks?

**23**] (2). R. Isaac appears to assume that the phrase באחרית הימים means "in the very latest days," "in the end of the days," in such a sense that there is no time to come after. But is this the Scriptural meaning of the phrase? How is it used in the very first passage where it occurs, in Gen. xlix. 1? ויקרא יעקב אל בניו ויאמר האספו ואגידה לכם את אשר יקרא אתכם באחרית הימים׃ Does it mean there, as R. Isaac would pretend it always means, "in the very end of time," after which there is to be no more? This is impossible. It does not there even mean "in a time that continues to the end of all things." For the history of Jacob's children which the Patriarch unfolds to them in the following verses has long since come to an end, so far as regards the character and separate history of each tribe. The passage shows clearly enough what the phrase properly does signify, viz, the latter part of any specific time. It may in itself be a long time or a short time; it may also be short or long in comparison with that part which has preceded it, but it is only the after as contrasted with the former part. Thus אחרית is used of the latter part of Job's life (Job xlii. 12), and lasts 140 years, in contrast to the earlier part of his life, before his terrible sufferings came upon him.

Here then we see the true meaning of the phrase in the utterances of the Prophets. It affirms that in a period of time which is later than that in which they were actually prophesying, Messiah shall appear, or the Messianic work and influences shall take effect. But the phrase does not contain the slightest hint that time shall cease to be, immediately that Messiah has come, or that a long period of time may not elapse between the inauguration of the Messianic period and the final establishment of all things upon a Messianic basis.

This objection, therefore, brought by R. Isaac against the Lord Jesus (a merely verbal one at best), seems to be invalid.

**24**] (3). Probably, however, he did not desire to lay so much stress upon this verbal argument itself as upon the presence or absence of the signs and tokens that are to be the outcome of the true Messiah's advent. For he next proceeds to deal with these in detail, considering them formally under a fresh head. But here, unfortunately, the Rabbi loses some of his usual clearness of argument. For he considers them in two separate lists, and repeats himself not a little. His first list is in § 1, and his second in § 6, and several of the items occur in both lists. His reason for this treatment of them is that in § 1 he argues that because these signs have not taken place, therefore Jesus cannot be the true Messiah, and in § 6 that the Captivity of the Jews is to last until Messiah has brought about all these signs, and therefore the Messiah cannot come until the end of the present Captivity. But his arguments run so much into one another, and there is so much in common between the two lists, that I shall consider them together.

## *d.* The Signs of the coming of Messiah.

### *α.* One Kingdom and One King.

§ 1. i., compare § 6. xi.

**25**] R. Isaac argues that when the true Messiah comes there is to be one Kingdom and one King, viz, Messiah, and he quotes Dan. ii. 44. וביומיהון די מלכיא אנון יקים אלה שמיא מלכו די לעלמין לא תתחבל ומלכותה לעם אחרן לא תשתבק הדק ותסף כל אלין מלכותא והיא תקום לעלמיא:
" And in the days of those kings shall the God of heaven set up a kingdom, which shall never be destroyed, nor shall the sovereignty thereof be left to another people ; but it shall break in pieces and consume all these kingdoms, and it shall stand for ever." He says that now, on the contrary, we see many kingdoms, each with its own laws, and each with its own king, and therefore it is plain that Jesus is not the true Messiah.

**26**] (1). To us Christians however this does not seem a very strong argument. For the mere fact of many kingdoms existing is quite compatible with their all acknowledging the sovereignty of one over-lord, and, besides, there is nothing in the text to show that such a oneness of rule (even if intended in such a sense as to exclude altogether the existence of other kingdoms) was to be the immediate result of the establishment of this kingdom. I ask whether it is God's usual method to bring about great changes, especially changes in the social fabric of mankind, by one act immediate in its effects ? Look at all past history. "The mills of God grind slowly," and therefore they "grind exceeding small." But they grind slowly, yes much more slowly than R. Isaac ever thought. For we in these days are in a very different position from R. Isaac when enquiry is made into the nature of God's ways and methods. R. Isaac did not know of the great age of this world in which we live, and of the exceeding slowness with which

God has brought about changes in sea and continent, and plant and living creature. R. Isaac had never heard of Evolution. This was not his fault. But he was in a far worse position than we are for estimating the probable method of God's dealings with this world. To R. Isaac one thousand, or two thousand, years doubtless seemed a very long period. To you and me they represent a very short time indeed compared with the ages of the world's history, while to God they surely appear as mere drops in the ocean of time. The fact that an universal kingdom is not visible to the naked eye proves little or nothing against the claims of Jesus to be the true Messiah.

**27**] (2). But may it not be the case that such a supreme kingdom has already begun? In par. 15 it was pointed out that the kingship of Jesus is something very real indeed, if by kingship we mean actual rule over the hearts and lives of men, for never has a person received such homage and obedience as Jesus Christ is now receiving. His kingship is acknowledged by no less than five hundred millions of the human race. See also parr. 15, 79.

Further, His kingdom is growing in extent every day. Fresh lands are being won to Jesus Christ. His heralds are going into all countries proclaiming Him as King, and where they go men are acknowledging the justice of the proclamation and yielding obedience. All Europe has long ago submitted; all North America, Australia, and most of the Islands in the Southern Seas, have acknowledged Him. India, China, and large parts of Africa, are now in the very act of learning to bend the knee to Him. See also par. 31.

His rule too is becoming more powerful where He is acknowledged. In other words, His laws are permeating civilisation. Slowly, I grant, for it is only natural that men should perceive but gradually the meaning of ordinances which they accept, and little by little understand the ways in which these are intended to mould their lives.

**28**] (3). A Jew may answer: "This that you say is all very well, but is beside the point. I expect to see a visible King and a visible Kingdom." But may he not be in error in thinking that all the time a king reigns he must be visible? Consider the analogy of ordinary beings. Is it necessary that a king should always be visible to his subjects? On by far the greater part of his dominions King Edward VII. never set foot as king. But did this take away from the reality of his rule over, for example, India, Canada, Australia? There is no need for a king to be visible in order for him to rule. Jews of course consider Jesus to be a dead man. We do not. We hold that He is alive; that He ascended up into glory at the right hand of the Father; and it is not in the least surprising to us that we cannot see Him now, even though He is reigning as King all the time, yes and ruling more than mortal man as such ever ruled.

**29**] (4). Yet it does not follow that because our King is now invisible He will always remain so. It may well be the case that a long time of preparation is required before it is fitting for Him to appear, but we Christians expect His coming, and many think that He will in some sense rule visibly upon the earth, for a period to be measured by human time. Whether this will be so or not, I cannot say. But He will certainly appear, reigning in glory. We hope for this complete fulfilment of the idea of a King, and base our hope partly upon such Old Testament promises as R. Isaac brings forward, and still more upon the teaching of the Lord Jesus Christ Himself, and upon what He has already done towards the fulfilment of His promises.

**30**] (5). Consider His words briefly.

(i). He claimed to be King. Speaking of Himself in a parable He says, "Then shall the King say unto them on His right hand, Come, ye blessed of my Father," &c. (Matt.xxv. 34.). Again, "My kingdom is not of this world: if my kingdom were of this world, then would my servants fight;" and when Pilate asks Him if He is a king, He acknowledges that this is the case (John xviii. 36, 37). Similarly, in the vision given to His favourite disciple St. John, He is seen with His name written upon Him, "King of kings, and Lord of lords" (Rev. xix. 16).

(ii). He spoke of His kingdom in three relations: (*a*) He says that it has come: "If I by the Spirit of God cast out devils, then is the kingdom of God come upon you" (Matt. xii. 28); "The kingdom of God is come nigh unto you" (Luke x. 9). (*b*) He describes it by parables as increasing. Recall to mind only one of His parables, that of the mustard seed, where He says "the kingdom of heaven is like unto a grain of mustard seed, which...when it is grown,...becometh a tree" (Matt. xiii. 31, 32). (*c*) He says that one day hereafter it will come in its fulness: "I appoint unto you a kingdom, even as my Father appointed unto Me, that ye may eat and drink at my table in my kingdom; and ye shall sit on thrones judging the twelve tribes of Israel" (Luke xxii. 29, 30). So also: "When the Son of Man shall come in His glory, and all the angels with Him, then shall He sit on the throne of His glory" (Matt. xxv. 31). Hence it is that we Christians pray every day the words "Thy Kingdom come," and, as we pray them, think not only of Christ's kingdom now spreading over the whole earth, but also of that glorious day when He shall return, with those who sleep in Jesus, to be worshipped and obeyed by all.

### β. One Religion and that the Religion of Israel.

§ 1. ii., *cf.* §§ 6. vi. vii. viii. x. and 44.

**31**] R. Isaac affirms that when the true Messiah comes there is to be but one religion in the world and this the religion of Israel, and he quotes several passages from Scripture in support of his contention, to the more important of which we shall presently refer.

(1). I ask however, first, whether it is not a curious thing that at the present rate of increase there will be in a few centuries only one religion acknowledged in the world. Christianity is spreading so fast, so very much faster than any other religion,* that we are already in measurable distance of seeing part, at least, of the Rabbi's statement actually carried out. It is not of course surprising that this fact did not strike the Rabbi himself. For he lived in days long before the extraordinary missionary activity (extraordinary, I mean, as compared with the work done in the more immediately preceding centuries) that has marked the last hundred years. To R. Isaac Christian missions were things of the past, and things of the unknown future. He knew little of them from history, and could have no knowledge of the development that they would begin to make some two hundred years after his death. But now every reading man can acquaint himself with the spread of Christianity, and it is great and wonderful. There is, I repeat, every sign that the religion of Jesus Christ will, in a few centuries more, have spread over the whole world, and, as we have already seen in par. 26, the gradual accomplishment of God's purpose is more in accordance with His methods than a sudden change. He is actually bringing about before our very eyes, and more quickly than at any previous time in history, one of the texts quoted by R. Isaac, Isa. xlv. 23, לי תכרע כל ברך תשבע כל לשון "Unto Me every knee shall bow, every tongue shall swear."

**32**] (2). But R. Isaac urges that the one religion which is to prevail must be the religion of Israel, and he quotes Zech. viii. 23 :

יחזיקו עשרה אנשים מכל לשונות הגוים והחזיקו בכנף איש יהודי לאמר נלכה עמכם כי שמענו אלהים עמכם:

"Ten men shall take hold, out of all the languages of the nations, shall even take hold of the skirt of him that is a Jew, saying, We will go with you, for we have heard that God is with you."

Certainly! That is the very thing that has happened, and is still happening. For there is no denying the fact that

* I am not forgetful of the fact that Mohammedanism has wrested certain lands in nearer Asia and northern Africa from Christianity, nor that it threatens to spread faster in middle Africa at the present moment. The demands that it makes upon the conscience and the life are so much lower that no surprise can be felt at its gaining a temporary victory in some quarters.

Christianity came from men of Israel, or that every one of the writers of the New Testament, with the possible exception of St. Luke, was a Jew. It is to Jewish teaching that men come when they learn of Christianity.

**33**] (3). But R. Isaac objects that Zech. xiv. 16, and Isa. lxvi. 23, speak of the Nations coming up to Jerusalem to worship, and keeping the feasts there.

I am not sure that there would be nothing at all in the argument if I were to reply that, in fact, a good many Gentile Christians do go to Jerusalem even now on a kind of religious pilgrimage, and that there are many signs that, with the increasing improvement in communication, even far larger numbers of Gentile Christians will go there in the future than in the present. But I would rather ask whether the outer covering of religion is of such supreme, such final, importance? Is it not, in reality, the spirit of Judaism that is the all-important thing? We see this even in the Judaism of to-day, much more, surely, in the Judaism of the Prophets. We all accept, I feel certain, the ancient saying that "a Jew is not a Jew who is one outwardly, but he is a Jew who is one inwardly." Surely, in other words, it is the religion of Israel that is now spreading so much, when Christians believe and practise the great truths contained in the Old Testament.

**34**] (4). Of course R. Isaac does not agree to this, for he quotes triumphantly Zech. xiv. 9:

והיה יהוה למלך על כל הארץ ביום ההוא יהיה יהוה אחד ושמו אחד׃

"And the LORD shall be king over all the earth: in that day shall the LORD be one, and His name one." Yet this is in the completest possible agreement with our teaching. For we hold that when Jesus is acknowledged over the whole earth, then indeed will the LORD be king in a way in which He has never yet been, for Jesus' teaching was ever of His Father in heaven, and of the complete obedience that men ought to render to Him. It must not be forgotten that the New Testament distinctly says that "when all things have been subjected unto him, then shall the Son also himself be subjected to him that did subject all things unto him, that

God may be all in all" (1 Cor. xv. 28). Further, the statement that He is one and His name one is exactly in accordance with our Faith. We acknowledge no difference in essence between Jesus and the LORD, so completely Divine is Jesus. This statement touches, I know, on deep and difficult questions, which must find a place in our enquiry later on. They do not properly come under treatment here. It must suffice here to point forward to later paragraphs (*e.g.* 105-125), and to affirm once more the conviction of the Christian that R. Isaac's objection to the Messiahship of Jesus, on the ground that the true Messiah brings in One Religion and this the Religion of Israel, is virtually pointless, in view of the facts that the Religion of Jesus is spreading so fast, and that this Religion is essentially due to Israel.

### γ. THE ABOLITION OF IDOLS.

§ 1. iii., *cf.* § 6. ix.

**35**] R. Isaac argues next that when the true Messiah appears the idols of the heathen are to be utterly abolished, and he quotes in favour of his statement several passages, of which perhaps the most important is Isa. ii. 18:

והאלילים כליל יחלף: "And the idols shall utterly pass away."

Yet is not this the very thing that Christianity is bringing about to a marvellous degree? Judaism as such has done little or nothing towards the abolition of idols. For reasons into which we need not now enter, Jews have not thought it well to try to propagate their religion directly, and have left missionary work to Christians. But where Christians go idols flee. Look around. Where are the gods of Europe and their accompanying idols? The idols of Rome and Greece used to be numbered by thousands. When, for example, a famous Jew visited Athens in the middle of the first century of the

Christian era, "his spirit was provoked within him, as he beheld the city full of idols" (Acts xvii. 16), and Athens was little more than typical of the state of every town in Europe at that time. Britain, to look still nearer home, had its idols, though not, as it would seem, of so permanent a character. Where are they now? Look away to the distant Isles of the Southern Seas. Had any of us visited them a hundred years ago he would have been exceedingly fortunate to have escaped alive, instead of being dragged before some horrid image of a false god, slain before it as a propitiatory offering, and his body consumed in a sacrificial feast. But now! It is now comparatively difficult to find an island upon which a man cannot land in safety, and hear in part of it Christian hymns to the Lord Jesus, and it is difficult to discover any of the idols which but a few years ago were worshipped so openly and so enthusiastically.

Do you answer that there are still many thousands of idols of false gods remaining in the world, as, for example, in India, in China, in Japan, in Africa? Of course there are. But it is unnecessary to repeat once more that God's methods are to bring about results slowly. Upon that I have already spoken.

No! as we look around, and see how idols have disappeared from many countries, and how they are disappearing from others just in proportion as Christianity itself is spreading, is it not only fair to say that the argument which the Rabbi adduces is in reality an argument not against but for our Lord Jesus Christ? It is due to the followers of Jesus that the idols of the false gods are disappearing, and, humanly speaking, in a few centuries will all be gone.

**36**] It may however be replied that Mohammedanism has a similar effect. I gladly acknowledge the help of Mohammedanism in this matter. But I am not afraid that any thoughtful Jew will put Mohammedanism into serious competition with Christianity. Jews are far too keen on ethical purity, and on progress in every direction, to think the teaching of Mohammed worthy to be compared with the life of Jesus. R. Isaac however does not touch in this passage upon this point, and I need not therefore further allude to it. Where the teaching of Jesus comes the idols of the false gods are abolished, and the prophecies of the Old Testament are surely, in this respect, being fulfilled in Jesus.

### δ. Freedom from Sin.

§ 1. i., *cf.* § 6. xiv.

**37**] R. Isaac's next argument against the Messiahship of our Lord Jesus is that when the true Messiah comes there will be no sins committed in the world, especially among the people of Israel.

We can all sympathize with the longing of R. Isaac for the coming of that day when we shall be free from sin. Sin does so spoil our own lives, and those of our friends, that we cannot help longing with an intense desire for the time when we shall all wholly escape from it. The Lord of His mercy deepen in us this desire, and enable us to obtain as much of that freedom as is possible even now!

It is however to be remarked that in § 6. xiv. R. Isaac modifies his statement to the extent of saying that he expects the coming of the true Messiah to set men free from sins, "except sins committed by chance" (כ"א במקרה). But that is a very serious difference. For either the Rabbi identifies "chance" sins with merely physical impurities, the sinfulness of which we in these days hardly acknowledge, or he is not contemplating the absolute, but only the comparative, abolition of sin when the true Messiah comes. If the latter is really his meaning it would not be difficult to show that the coming of Jesus has at the least reduced sins to a large extent, so far as regards their grosser forms. But in truth, I suppose, the Rabbi only intends to say that at the coming of the true Messiah the set of men's minds will be for good, and no longer for evil. Let us then examine his words.

**38**] (1). He says that this will be the case in the world generally. But of the seven different passages that he quotes only one touches upon this point, *viz.*, Jer. iii. 17, where we are told that the nations shall be gathered to Jerusalem in the name of the Lord, and shall no more walk in the obstinacy of their evil heart.

ונקוו אליה כל הגוים לשם יהוה לירושלם ולא ילכו עוד אחרי שררות לבם הרע׃

But this is no more than to say that the nations will have the religion of Israel, a subject with which we have already dealt. I shall not therefore say more about this passage so far as regards the Gentiles.

**39**] But it does claim our attention for what it says as regards the Jews, and it may fairly be considered with the next passage quoted by R. Isaac, namely Jer. l. 20, "The iniquity of Israel shall be sought for, and there shall be none; and the sins of Judah, and they shall not be found."

יְבֻקַּשׁ את עון ישראל ואיננו ואת חטאת יהודה ולא תמצאינה׃

These are beautiful promises, and I do not wonder that they appeal to R. Isaac. He would be hard-hearted indeed who was not moved by them. But what, strictly speaking, have they to do with the coming of Messiah? They do not mention Him. Neither are they necessarily even Messianic, so far as anything in the context shows. What they say is that when Israel repents, then this good thing will happen to it. That surely is just what we Christians say. We too are expecting the time to come when Israel will repent. For then Israel will receive unnumbered blessings, both spiritual and material, and their conversion to God will so influence the Gentile nations that these in their turn will receive blessing. But, alas, why does not Israel repent now, and enjoy these blessings and procure them for others?

**40**] (2). Deut. xxx. 6 is also quoted by R. Isaac: "And the LORD thy God will circumcise thine heart, and the heart of thy seed, to love the LORD thy God with all thine heart, and with all thy soul, that thou mayest live."

ומל יהוה אלהיך את לבבך ואת לבב זרעך לאהבה את יהוה אלהיך בכל לבבך ובכל נפשך למען חייך׃

But where is the reference to the time of Messiah here? The verse is speaking of the time of Israel's repentance, and there is nothing in it to show whether this takes place before Messiah comes, or when He comes, or long after He has come.

**41**] (3). R. Isaac also quotes Isa. lx. 21: "Thy people also shall be all righteous" (עמך כלם צדיקים). That is exactly what the New Testament says (see Rom. xi. 26), "So all Israel shall be saved." He quotes also Zeph. iii. 13: "The remnant of Israel shall not do iniquity, nor speak lies."

שארית ישראל לא יעשו עֽוְלה ולא ידברו כזב׃

But what is there here about Messiah, unless R. Isaac is writing as a Christian and sees in the 15th verse ("The king of Israel, even the LORD, is in the midst of thee.")

מלך ישראל יהוה בקרבך.

a reference to the Messiah of the Christians? But I fear that the Rabbi was not prepared to recognise in these words a reference to the Messiah at all, though we Christians would welcome such an interpretation.

**42**] (4). Then he quotes Ezek. xxxvi. 25—27, that glorious promise of the sprinkling of clean water and the giving of a new heart and a new spirit, and then xxxvii. 23, 24, where the prophet says: "neither shall they defile themselves any more with their idols, nor with their detestable things, nor with any of their transgressions: but I will save them out of all their dwelling places, wherein they have sinned, and will cleanse them: so shall they be my people, and I will be their God. And my servant David shall be king over them; and they all shall have one shepherd: they shall also walk in my judgements, and observe my statutes, and do them."

ולא יטמאו עוד בגלוליהם ובשקוציהם ובכל פשעיהם והושעתי אתם מכל מושבתיהם אשר חטאו בהם וטהרתי אותם והיו לי לעם ואני אהיה להם לאלהים׃ ועבדי דוד מלך עליהם ורועה אחד יהיה לכלם ובמשפטי ילכו וחקותי ישמרו ועשו אותם׃

Yes, here indeed is Messiah mentioned, I grant it gladly. But how does it help R. Isaac's argument? The words suit admirably the Christian position, that a time will come when

Israel will repent and turn to God and Messiah, and once more live in full communion with God. But there is not a hint that their repentance will be synchronous with the appearance of Messiah, and therefore it proves nothing for R. Isaac's opinion.

**43**] (5). How comes it that R. Isaac quotes this, and the other similar passages, when most of us find them so curiously outside the subject under discussion? I imagine that there are at least two reasons. First, he was writing in a day when most Christian expositors of Scripture explained, or rather explained away, the frequent references in the Old Testament to the glorious future of the Jews, as though they referred to the Christian Church. It is very easy for Christian commentators to fall into this habit, especially if they have been accustomed to Jewish modes of interpreting the Scriptures midrashically. But to do so does grave injustice to the proper meaning of the inspired word, and prevents a right understanding of the future history of the Jewish nation, to which the words indubitably refer in their primary significance. In consequence of this pernicious Christian custom of R. Isaac's day he thinks it necessary to adduce texts that certainly refer to blessings to be enjoyed by Israel in the future. But to the mind of most thoughtful Christians to-day there is no question as to this. We agree with R. Isaac so far. But we desire to point out to him their equally primary meaning that this blessing is to be Israel's only when it repents.

**44**] (6). Secondly, the Rabbi cannot imagine it possible that the true Messiah can come to Israel and be rejected. But why not? What is there against the possibility of this? Let us examine our own experience. What do we find in our own hearts, or in what we see around us? Suppose, only suppose, that God were to make a perfectly full revelation of His goodness and holiness, and offer this to us and our neighbours? Are we so very sure that we and they would be attracted by it, and thankfully receive it? Is there no possibility that we should each say in our heart of hearts: "This is more than I want; if I accept this I shall be obliged to give up certain sins, to remodel my opinions on many parts of religion, to accept a much lower place for myself in the judgment of those around me?" Or if we ourselves are, by God's mercy, so inclined to God and the things of God that we can have no doubt about ourselves, are we so sure about our neighbours? And if not of our neighbours, can we be sure about those who lived some nineteen hundred years ago? Is it not possible, to say the least, that they, having no better hearts than we have, may have been so taken up with the things of this world as to reject the true Messiah? R. Isaac evidently holds this to be impossible. But wherein does the impossibility consist?

Would you expect anything better from the accursed brood of Annas, High Priest in the days of Jesus of Nazareth? You remember what is said in *Pesachim*, 57*a* (Munich MS.). "Woe! for the house of Annas! woe! for their curses! woe! for their serpent-like hissings!"*:

אוי לי במית חנין אוי לי מאלתן אוי לי מלחישתן.

No reader of Talmud or of Jewish history can be surprised that the High Priests did not acknowledge Jesus of Nazareth if He was only half so good as the Gospels declare Him to be. They could have nothing in common with holiness. But what if the Divine saying, "Like people, like priest" (Hos. iv. 9) were true of that time? Would not then the rejection of a really holy person be a matter of course, and the holier he were the more certain and thorough would be his rejection! Surely, we can hardly escape facing the possibility that if God did give a supreme revelation of Himself in the person of Jesus Christ the men of the time would reject it. A few, as we know, did turn to Him in meekness of heart. These repented, and found, as they affirmed, the Messiah. Can it be that they were right, and it was, after all, their repentance that opened the eyes of their heart to recognise Jesus as Messiah? If so, what would be the result of a wide-spread repentance to-day?

* For this phrase *cf. Aboth*, ii. 10 (14).

### ε. Gog and Magog.

§ i. v. and § 6. ii. and xii.

**45**] Another sign which R. Isaac affirms is closely connected with the coming of the true Messiah is the destruction of Gog and Magog with their hosts (Ezek. xxxviii. and xxxix.; Zech. xiv. 1-3, 12-15; Isa. lxvi. 19), and the cessation of wars ever after (Isa. ii. 4; Ezek. xxxix. 9, 10; Hos. ii. 18 (20); Zech. ix. 10; Mic. iv. 3).

I am not concerned to examine each of these various passages in order to see whether the Rabbi's quotation of them is always justified by their proper meaning. I am content to assume that he is right. For, strictly speaking, we Christians have no quarrel with him upon this subject. If he believes in this great war, between the forces of evil and those of good, that is to take place in days still future, so also do we. Our holy Book itself tells us that this is to be the case. In Rev. xx. 7-9 we find it stated that "Satan...shall come forth to deceive the nations which are in the four corners of the earth, Gog and Magog, to gather them together to the war: the number of whom is as the sand of the sea. And," adds the Seer in his vision, "they went up over the breadth of the earth, and compassed the camp of the saints about, and the beloved city." They perish, and after this final attack all war ceases, and there is peace.

It is indeed true that we Christians, of the present time at least, are not altogether prepared to say whether that great war will be wholly literal (*i.e.*, solely between bodily presences arrayed in material armour), or rather spiritual, against the forces of evil as such, armed with weapons all the more deadly because they can pass into the very mind and heart. Such a battle, between spiritual foes, a war between evil powers and good powers, would be a far more awful thing than any such material fight as the Rabbi himself seems to contemplate. But whether the war is literal or solely spiritual seems to us Christians to be a very secondary question. We leave this for the future to unravel. In any case, according to Christian belief, there comes after it the full and final manifestation of Messiah's kingdom. We are ready to grant the position of R. Isaac generally, the only difference between him and us being that he thinks it impossible that the Messiah can have already come without at once taking upon Himself this war. But, as we have said before, so now we say again, our interpretation of what God considers the flight of time in its relation to the various events in the Messianic work and progress is so uncertain, so moulded by the brevity of our own lives, that we are not justified in saying that the fact that two or three thousand years may elapse between one act performed by Messiah and another is any hindrance to the two acts being described in Scripture as virtually concurrent. Prophecy, being the message of God conditioned by human modes of thought, must, surely, often place close together two events, which in fact are separated by a long time in history. To a traveller in Switzerland two peaks of a mountain range often seem to be very near to each other, whereas in truth they are separated by many weary miles.

We both then, Christians and Jews, are expecting a great war in the future, when Messiah shall triumph fully and finally over His enemies.

**46**] But each one of us ought to ask himself whether, if such a war were to begin at once, he would be found fighting upon the right side. For I assume that every one of us is not satisfied with the expectation of the coming of a mere worldly Ruler, in earthly pomp and glory. Each of us is looking for a rule wherein dwelleth righteousness, whence every thought of evil, and every desire of unrighteous gain, are utterly banished. But would this suit us? I ask this in all seriousness. How should we like so perfect a kingdom? Should we find ourselves really enjoying it, or a little conscious that we have not been preparing for so perfectly good a state? On which side should we each be? If He came now, and suddenly bade us fight upon the side upon which we had been fighting when He came, which side would that be? Do you say, "Certainly upon the side of Messiah"? Why so? His side must be that of the good. Are our lives so decided now that we are sure we should at once be found upon His side? Does any reader answer "I am a Jew, and therefore sure to be upon the right side in the great battle between the forces of good and evil described as the war against Gog and Magog"? Alas, have even Jews always been on the side of right and goodness? Were the majority of those who were alive when a very perfect Person, according to the admission of almost all Jews of our own time, came into their midst, decidedly ready to uphold Him against fraud and trickery and open violence? That very holy Person was rejected by many, because, as it seems, His demands for holiness were greater than they could bear. Are we quite sure that if such a demand were made upon us now we should respond to it properly?

We can see, if we will, what in fact our own answer would be. If we do really desire what is good above everything else; if we do hate sin and everything approaching sin; if we are endeavouring to spread and encourage the knowledge of God by our words and actions, filled with an intense desire for His glory, even though we are conscious that in many things we all offend, then we may confidently expect that a fuller unveiling of God to our souls will find us responsive to His light, and we may humbly hope that He will not only deepen in us the longing after Him, but will satisfy that longing with increasing power to find Him. May it be so with each of us. May the Lord be very gracious to us, and fit us for that day when He shall reign in righteousness, and triumph gloriously.

### ζ. Wild Beasts.

§ 1. vi. and § 6. xiii.

**47**] R. Isaac next argues that Messiah cannot have come already because it is said that in His days Wild Beasts shall not injure domestic animals or men, and he adduces in favour of this Isa. xi. 6-9, lxv. 25; Ezek. xxxiv. 25 and 28; Hos. ii. 18 (20).

(1). Now to an Englishman this objection against the Messiahship of the Lord Jesus seems so curious that he is hardly able to sympathise with it, or to realise the force that it evidently has for minds like that of R. Isaac. For we English have been taught to regard the mention of beasts in these passages either as mere details in a picture of general happiness which are not intended to be pressed, or as merely figurative. In favour of this latter interpretation we can claim no less a person than Maimonides (*Hilkoth Melakim* xii. 1):

אל יעלה על הלב שבימות המשיח יבטל דבר ממנהגו של עולם׳ או יהיה שם חידוש במעשה בראשית׳ אלא עולם כמנהגו נוהג׳ וזה שנאמר בישעיה וגר זאב עם כבש ונמר עם גדי ירבץ משל וחידה׳ עניין הדבר׳ שיהיו ישראל יושבין לבטח עם רשעי אומות העולם׳ המשולים כזאב ונמר׳ שנאמר זאב ערבות ישדדם ונמר שוקד על עריהם׳ ויחזרו כולם לדת האמת׳ ולא יגזלו ולא ישחיתו׳ אלא יאכלו דבר המותר בנחת בישראל׳ שנאמר ואריה כבקר יאכל תבן׳ וכן כל כיוצא באלו הדברים הכתובים בעניין המשיח׳ הם משלים׳ ובימות המלך המשיח יודע לכל לאי זה דבר היה משל׳ ומה עניין רמזו בהן: (Amsterdam Edition 1702. iv. 307).

"Let no one imagine that in the days of Messiah anything in the course of Nature will be altered, or that there will be any new thing in Creation. The course of the world will go on as before. Isaiah's words, 'And the wolf shall dwell with the lamb, and the leopard shall lie down with the kid' (xi. 6) are a parable and figure of speech, and the meaning is that Israel will dwell safely among the more wicked of the nations of the world, who are compared to the wolf and the leopard, as in Jer. v. 6, for they shall all turn to the true religion, and shall not plunder or destroy, but eat lawful food quietly in Israel, for it is said, 'And the lion shall eat straw like the ox' (Isa. xi. 7). And so all similar statements with regard to Messiah are parables, and in the days of King Messiah all shall know the exact meaning of each parable and what each signified."

If Maimonides is right, and his interpretation appears to be very sensible (*cf.* also Saadiah's *Emunoth w'Deoth*, viii. § 19, *ed.* Fürst), then in so far as the coming of Jesus of Nazareth has tended to diminish war, &c., and to gather the nations into one religion (on both of which topics we have already spoken), so far does R. Isaac's objection fail.

**48**] (2). If, however, we are to understand the term "wild beasts" literally, as many Jewish teachers suppose, and if also the matter is of real importance, I would ask you to consider the curious fact that in proportion as Jesus is accepted as Messiah wild beasts do, in fact, cease to do harm.

Among the heathen it is evidently not so. A Hindu, for example, speaks with the greatest respect of his majesty the tiger, and will not injure him in any way unless he is obliged to do so. A Mohammedan again will do but little. His feeling of fatalism is far too strong. If a tiger injures any of his friends, or carries off his wife or his child, he says *Kismet*, and regards the accident as the result of an inscrutable and unavoidable fate. But with Christians it is far otherwise. Christians see in wild beasts the ever present possibility of injury to men and to harmless animals, and a serious hindrance to the development of a country. And Christians, with their deep conviction that it is their duty in the name of God to bring a country to its greatest possible perfection, and to secure by all means in their power the safety of every man, woman and child dwelling in it, do their best to prevent the possibility of wild beasts injuring other more useful creatures, and especially human beings. Wild beasts do cease to injure wherever Christianity spreads. The fact cannot be denied. May there not be a very real connexion between this fact and these prophecies? *

* Another argument is contained in parr. 51, 56, sqq.

### η. In Israel all Troubles are to cease, and Lives to be long and happy.

§ 1. vii. and § 6. xv.

**49**] R. Isaac next argues that when Messiah comes those who live in the land of Israel are to have no troubles or sorrows, but will live long and happy lives, and he quotes in support of his argument Is. lxv. 16 and 19-22. But R. Isaac ought to have pointed out, what is very often pointed out both in Scripture and in the sayings of the rabbis, viz.: that all God's promises are conditional. No one can expect this blessed state of things to take place in Israel if Israel refuses to acknowledge the Messiah when He comes. We have seen that such a refusal on Israel's part is not impossible. We Christians believe that it is a fact, and that therefore this difficulty of R. Isaac's is no difficulty.

### θ. The Shekinah is to return to Israel, and there is to be much Prophecy, Wisdom, and Knowledge of God.

§ 1. viii. and § 6. xvi.

**50**] We here come to something of greater interest and of more importance. R. Isaac says that in the time of King Messiah the Shekinah is to return again to Israel as at the first, and Prophecy, Wisdom, and Knowledge shall be great among the people of Israel, as it is written in Ezek. xxxvii. 26-28, and in several other passages of Scripture, which he quotes at length. Among them may be mentioned Joel ii. 27, 28; iii. 17, 21 (*Heb.* iii. 1; iv. 17, 21).

(1). Now it is no part of my duty in these pages to

investigate the Jewish doctrine of the Shekinah. A good deal has been written upon the subject, and a good deal yet remains to be written. The term is used to express the Presence of God among men, occasionally under the visible light in the Holy of Holies (see R. Isaac, § 6. xviii.), but more often in a less defined way. So, for example, in *Aboth*, iii. 3, "Two that sit together and are occupied in words of Thorah have the Shekinah among them."

שנים שהיו יושבין ועוסקין בדברי תורה שכינה ביניהם.

It is in this latter sense, as it seems, that R. Isaac uses the term here. He means that in the days of Messiah the Presence of God will be very near, and will manifest itself particularly in abundance of Prophecy, Wisdom, and Knowledge, presumably Knowledge of God.

(2). But here is a remarkable thing. We Christians entirely agree with the learned Rabbi as to this. We say with him that in the days of Messiah there must be a special Presence of God, and an abundant outpouring of the spirit of prophecy and of wisdom and of the knowledge of God, and that among the Jews. But where we differ from him is in further saying that this blessed promise has already been largely fulfilled, and is on its way to complete fulfilment.

**51**] (i). For, in the first place, we must again remind him that in arguing against Christianity he is not at liberty to pick out this or that doctrine, and to forget, when he is attacking them, that there are other doctrines supplementary to them. In this way any religion, and any doctrine of any religion, can be triumphantly proved to be absurd. R. Isaac may not, as in the case in point, forget that we Christians hold, at least as strongly as do Jews, that Messiah is yet to come. We believe that He came, but we believe also that He is to come again. Hence a great many of the Rabbi's arguments against our holy faith appear to us to be one-sided and unfair. In this case we also, as well as he, are expecting, when Messiah returns, a great manifestation of the Presence of God, and an abundant outpouring of spiritual gifts. Yet we also hold that the prophecy has been already fulfilled in a most remarkable degree.

**52**] (ii). In what way do we all expect to see the Presence of God? It is not the same thing as a bright light; that we have already noticed. We do not expect, again, to see anything special with our natural eyes. At least, if it were God's will that we should do so, we would say that this was not necessary to the idea of the Presence of God. We expect to know that He is very near, in quite a different way from that in which we know anything with our mortal eyes. For we all recognize that God is a spirit, and has neither form nor fashion of any kind. How do we expect then to recognize the near Presence of God? I suppose chiefly in the perception of an awful holiness, in the realization that a Love, a Righteousness, is near, before Whom we feel ourselves unworthy to stand, and in Whose Presence we feel utterly abashed. We have indeed already seen that this does not necessarily imply that even with this awful perception of Holiness, and Love, and Righteousness, we submit ourselves to Him, and follow where He leads. There can be no compulsion, even towards good, exercised upon us by God, if we are to remain the free creatures that He has made us. The fear of God, say the Wise, is the one thing that is not determined by God. הכל בידי שמים חוץ מיראת שמים (*Berakoth* 33*b*.).

**53**] (iii). But, I ask, how is God to make us feel His presence in Holiness, and Love, and Righteousness? Presumably only through our senses in some way. And would it not be at least a possible way for God to do this if He were to give His Presence in a special degree to one person, and then, through the life and actions of that person, were to show what Holiness, and Love, and Righteousness really could be? Of course you see the trend of my remarks. But I do not want you to think for one minute that the Presence of God could manifest itself very thoroughly by, so to speak, joining Itself to a sinful man. A man, as we know men, would be an extremely imperfect medium for such a manifestation of God's Presence. But what if something utterly different were done? What if, instead of the Presence of God joining

Itself to a man, It were to take the constituent parts of human nature—body, soul, and spirit, including, of course, the will and the ability to suffer—and then to show by the life of this perfect representative of human nature what the Presence of God could produce; what Holiness meant amid a world of sinners; what Love meant, not sparing itself in any degree if only others might be helped; what Righteousness meant in the observance of all the will of God? Do you not think that by this means God might make such a revelation to men of what He really desired of us (of what, in other words, He really is in His inmost being as regards Holiness, Love, and Righteousness), as to bring about, among those who accepted this revelation of Himself, a complete change of thought and life, and to enable them to receive from Him power for Prophecy, Wisdom, and the Knowledge of Him?

This is indeed but an unworthy description of the Presence of God with man, for who am I that I should declare to you the marvels of His Presence, ineffable as they must be? But I hope that my description is at least better than R. Isaac's mere parody of what Christianity is—a parody of the Christian doctrine of the Incarnation. It is a subject which will very frequently come before us, for the Rabbi is never tired of holding up to ridicule the Christian belief in the Lord Jesus, while in reality he is only exposing his own ignorance of what Christian belief is.

I ask again whether you can imagine a higher and better form by which the Presence of God can manifest Itself than that of clothing Itself, if I may use such an expression, with human nature, nature that had never sinned and possessed no trace of sin, and shining through this human nature in a life of Holiness, Love, and Righteousness? Such a manifestation we Christians affirm to have taken place in Jesus the Christ. The Shekinah, we affirm, was to be seen in Him. (See also parr. 245-250).

**54**] (3). Lastly, a few words on Prophecy, Wisdom, and the Knowledge of God. It will hardly, I think, be disputed by those who attribute any historical worth at all to the New

Testament that the time of the Lord Jesus was marked by these gifts. Many Jews of that time possessed them in a very remarkable degree, and one, in answer to enemies, actually quoted one of R. Isaac's passages to explain what this phenomenon meant: "This is that which hath been spoken by the prophet Joel; And it shall be in the last days, saith God, I will pour forth of my Spirit upon all flesh: and your sons and your daughters shall prophesy, and your young men shall see visions, and your old men shall dream dreams: yea and on my servants and on my handmaidens in those days will I pour forth of my Spirit; and they shall prophesy" (Acts ii. 16. *sqq.* from Joel ii. 28, 29, *Heb.* iii. 1, 2). The experience of those days was wonderful. But it was hardly more wonderful than the experience that has often been repeated. For the perception of the near Presence of God in Christ has frequently produced the same kind of spiritual results. When Christ is accepted the Holy Spirit often pours out upon the soul not only an intense desire to serve Him, but also ability to speak for Him, and to show forth His marvellous love; or gives a deep insight into the things of God; or leads to deep knowledge of God; and, we must remember, in not a few cases these results go far beyond what we might have expected from the mental position of the convert. Is it not wonderful how spiritual are the prayers of many a Chinese Christian; and how earnestly a Uganda convert will plead for the spread of the Gospel; and how a poor cottager in England, with almost nothing of this world's joys, will rejoice in God and thank Him for innumerable mercies? No Jew living would grudge that such wonderful results should be poured out upon the Gentiles, and that, as we Christians believe, the prophecy of Joel should be fulfilled before his eyes? For it is just the same whenever a Jew turns to the Lord Jesus. He too then receives spiritual insight, and is surprised at his former state of ignorance of the Lord Jesus. He, like those Jews of nineteen hundred years ago who ventured to trust in Jesus, finds that what God has promised He is able also to perform. Every believer in Jesus, be he Jew or be he Gentile, finds that Jesus is the very Presence of God, and in Him receives spiritual gifts, sometimes of Prophecy, sometimes of Wisdom, sometimes of Knowledge.

### ι. THE MOUNT OF OLIVES IS TO BE DIVIDED IN HALF.

§ 6. iii.

**55**] We have now examined all the signs that R. Isaac adduces in § 1. as proofs that Messiah has not yet come, and have referred to those parts of § 6. where he mentions them again for practically the same purpose (see par. 24). But in § 6. he brings forward certain additional signs to prove his contention, and it will be convenient to deal with these at once. To avoid, however, unnecessary length of discussion here, we shall postpone (a) to parr. 86 sqq. the subject of the Restoration of the Jews to Palestine, together with the accompanying destruction of Christians and Mohammedans; (b) to parr. 99 sqq. the subject of the Restoration of the Ten Tribes; and (c) to parr. 269 sqq. the subject of the coming of Elijah foretold by the prophet Malachi.

**56**] In Zech. xiv. 4, 5, we read, "And his feet shall stand in that day upon the mount of Olives, which is before Jerusalem on the east, and the mount of Olives shall cleave in the midst thereof toward the east and toward the west, and there shall be a very great valley; and half of the mountain shall remove toward the north, and half of it toward the south. And ye shall flee by the valley of my mountains." This is confessedly a curious and interesting passage, but it is not very easy to see what it exactly means. R. Isaac understands it in the most literal sense: that the Mount of Olives shall actually be divided in half. But evidently he does not take the whole verse literally. For, if so, what does he understand by "his feet"? Whose are the feet here mentioned? Certainly they are the LORD'S, for the preceding verse has said, "Then shall the LORD go forth," &c. Let R.

Isaac be consistent, and acknowledge that "the feet" of the LORD are really feet, and mean therefore the feet of Him who is both man and God. In this case Christians will not quarrel with him, and will say that if the whole passage is to be understood in a literal sense, its fulfilment will take place at a late period in the Messianic time.

But we are far from wishing to press the learned Rabbi on this point. For to our mind the whole passage is a description of the result of the coming of the LORD, expressed figuratively. There is not even anything directly to say that "the LORD" here refers to the Messiah. It probably does not, and rather describes in parabolic terms the coming of God to avenge His people.

But if the cleaving of the Mount of Olives is figurative, what does it mean? Kimchi says that it indicates the cleaving of the Nations who have come against Jerusalem, and their falling hither and thither.
ומשל האות הזה שיבקעו הגוים הבאים על ירושלם ויפלו הנה והנה.
Others think it means that the difficulty is broken down which stood in the way of the Jews escaping from Jerusalem when it is besieged. But I do not know that I am called upon to decide what exactly the figure is intended to represent. We shall know some day. In any case it is exceedingly precarious to base the argument that Messiah has not yet come on the fact that the Mount of Olives is still standing intact. If the cleavage be literal it can well take place at the Second Coming of Christ; if it be spiritual or metaphorical *cadit quæstio.*

### κ. THE DIVIDING AND DRYING UP OF THE RIVER OF EGYPT, AND OF THE RIVER EUPHRATES, FOR ISRAEL TO PASS THROUGH.

§ 6. iv.

**57**] We will accept R. Isaac's paraphrase of Isaiah xi. 15, 16, even though it be verbally inexact (he seems to understand והחרים as though it were והחריב). But we would again ask whether this passage stands in any contradiction to the Christian religion? For if it be understood literally, then, once more, its fulfilment can very well take place in the future, when the Lord Jesus returns; and if it be understood metaphorically, it is of course fully consistent with Christian teaching.

Is it not probable that the great event of the redemption of Israel from Egypt, by bringing them through the Red Sea, would be used to express in figurative language the marvellous way in which God would redeem Israel out of all lands? Is it not also probable that Isaiah, writing long before the Babylonian Captivity, would use language which had a primary fulfilment in the return from Babylon? Many interpreters have even understood the expression here, "He... shall smite it (Euphrates) into seven streams, and cause men to march over dryshod," to refer to "the drying up of the Euphrates, which Cyrus diverted into the enlarged reservoir of Sepharvaim, so that the water fell to a foot in depth, and one could go over dryshod on foot (Herod. i. 189). This made it possible both for the conquerors to cross and the exiles to issue forth from the prison of the imperial city, girt as it was with both natural and artificial lines of water, xi. 15" (Delitzsch on Isa. xliv. 27). But, in view of what the Inscriptions tell us about the conquest of Babylon by Cyrus, this interpretation is very doubtful. It is safer to understand the passage to refer to the removal of hindrances to the return of the Jews to their own land, without attempting to define as yet the precise form that this will take.

We Christians therefore cannot attribute much weight to this difficulty adduced by R. Isaac.

### λ. The Life-giving Stream.

§ 6. v.

**58**] R. Isaac next urges that when Messiah comes there must issue from the Temple at Jerusalem a spring of living water, of which half shall turn to the eastern sea, and half to the western, on the banks of which trees shall produce their fruit every month, as it says in Ezek. xlvii. 1-12, Zech. xiv. 8, Joel iii. 18 (*Heb.* iv. 18).

(1). Now I believe that here again I may fairly urge much the same argument as I urged in the two preceding cases, that if the Prophets speak of a literal stream of water issuing from the Temple, this prophecy may be fulfilled in the future, when Christ returns. But I do not care to dwell on this interpretation.

(2). For why should we suppose that the Prophets are here speaking of material things? I know that the Talmud understands these passages literally (T. B. *Sanhedrin* 100*a.*), but no Jew of any education accepts the verdict of the Talmud, or rather of one or two of the many speakers in the Talmud, as decisive in a question of exegesis, and of literal as contrasted with spiritual meaning. If it were a question of Halakah it would be different, but there is no Halakah here. On this matter the Talmud is of no weight at all.

**59**] (3). The book of Zechariah itself can teach us how to understand the description. At least it is significant that shortly before xiv. 8 mention has been made of a spring opened in Jerusalem for sin and for uncleanness (xiii. 1). Does the Rabbi think that a stream of literal water is of much use in taking away sin and uncleanness? Will he not agree with me in saying that undoubtedly the prophet is there thinking of a stream which washes the soul clean, and therefore must itself be spiritual and not material? But if in the thirteenth chapter the prophet is thinking of a spiritual stream, is it not at least very probable that in this fourteenth chapter he is thinking of a spiritual stream also? And if this is the thought in these chapters in Zechariah, is it not probable that it is the same in both Ezekiel and Joel? Are we for ever to be so hampered by our crass western ideas as to be unable to rise to the finer imaginations and more poetical heights of those who have always lived in eastern lands? Is the Bible for ever to be so understood as though its writers did not love to employ trope after trope, parable after parable?

**60**] (4). Consider too how beautiful and significant such a figure is. You remember how Jeremiah (vi. 7) compares Jerusalem to a cistern, "As a cistern keepeth her waters cool, so she keepeth her wickedness cool" (כהקיר בור מימיה כן הֵקֵרָה רעתה)? * May it not have been in contrast to this that the other Prophets speak of a fountain of fresh spring water issuing from her, spreading not wickedness but spiritual life? Or, again, we know that, for an eastern town, Jerusalem was well supplied with water, so that in all its sieges we never hear that it suffered from thirst, and yet that outside it the stream, very small indeed in size, ran through severe wildernesses down to the Dead Sea.† What so suggestive to a thoughtful and spiritual-minded man? Would he not say to himself, as he looked forward to the Word of the Lord going forth from Jerusalem, "Now indeed the spiritual waters that we enjoy are limited to ourselves, as these streams and streamlets that water only Jerusalem and its immediate suburbs, but then, in those days, her spiritual life shall flow out from her far and wide, and all nations shall be blessed through her teaching"? Is not this a far more glorious, and far more probable, interpretation of this marvellous life-giving stream than any literal body of material water could ever be? ‡

**61**] (5). Let us then assume that the picture is of the spread of spiritual blessings beginning at Jerusalem, and let us join in thanking God that it has already begun to flow.

* See R.V. margin.

† See especially Pusey on the passage in Joel.

‡ So the newly discovered *Odes of Solomon* (dating as it seems from about 100 A.D.): "For there went forth a stream and became a river great and broad; for it flooded and broke up everything and it brought [water] to the Temple: and the restrainers of the children of men were not able to restrain it, nor the arts of those whose business it is to restrain waters; for it spread over the face of the whole earth, and filled everything: and all the thirsty upon earth were given to drink of it; and thirst was relieved and quenched: for from the Most High the draught was given" (*Odes of Solomon*, 6, *ed.* Rendel Harris, 1909).

If it be urged that the prophet "pictures a fountain in Jerusalem, providing a continuous supply of water for the removal of all [ceremonial] impurity from the people," it may be replied that such a physical stream would be nothing new.

It is not as if Christians claimed to be independent of Jews. Far from it. All the spiritual life that we possess has come to us through the Jews. From them the stream of life has flowed out. Why grudge it flowing on till it reached our shores? Nay, I am sure that Jews do not. For there is nothing inconsistent with their position, if they rejoice that to us Gentiles the stream of religious life has spread. Yet do they, in fact, thank God for this? Do they consciously thank God for the wonderful way in which He is still directing the course of this river of life ever to fresh lands and districts? I wish that I could think that they do. For then they would be daily thanking God for the signs of His life-giving grace among us Gentiles, and would be daily learning more of His ways in His government of the world and in His revelation of Himself.

### μ. The New Temple, and the New Division of Palestine.

§ 6. xviii. & xix.

**62**] R. Isaac mentions next among the prophecies that have not yet been fulfilled those in Ezek. xl.-xlviii., which speak of the building of a new Temple, when the Jews are restored, and the Division of the land. The latter is a comparatively unimportant subject, and it is so dependent upon the building of the Temple that we shall consider the two subjects as one.

But what shall we say of these chapters generally? If every Jewish commentator were sure of the meaning of them, the task would not be so difficult; or if Christian commentators were at all agreed, the task would be comparatively easy. But now! When no single writer, either Jewish or Christian, is able to say for certain what their precise meaning is—unless of course he be one of those excellent and enviable persons who know everything—it is extremely hard to be quite sure how best to deal with the Rabbi's difficulty.

But let us look at the matter. Fourteen years have passed away since the city of Jerusalem was given over into the hands of her enemies, and the fair-speaking promises of her false prophets were exposed (Ezek. xl. 1). During that time Ezekiel has been faithfully continuing his work of encouraging his fellow-exiles to remain true to God and to the words of His law. He has handed on to them the Lord's assurance that He will not leave His people in captivity for ever, but will one day restore them to the land of their fathers. But now he is bidden clothe his message of consolation in fairer and more glorious colours. He sees in vision a new temple arise, and hears ordinances given affecting both it and those who are to care for it. The vision is confessedly great and glorious, but the details are often curious, and sometimes not quite what we should have expected from a priest like Ezekiel. Two things at least are clear, which in fact all expositors of this difficult part of the Bible will be ready to acknowledge, that the thought of holiness runs through all the vision and its enactments, and that the holiness is to be such as will permeate every part of the national life. Whatever interpretation we give to Ezekiel's vision of the Temple, and of the division of the land, we must confess that he looks forward to a time when holiness shall become the ruling principle of the nation of Israel.

**63**] But what does the vision mean?

(1). We are all aware that the system of interpretation fashionable at the present day, acquiesced in not only by many Christian theologians, but also by many who deservedly stand high among Jews for their learning and religion, is that Ezekiel knew nothing of the greater part of the Pentateuch (all that part in fact which describes the Tabernacle and the ordinances closely connected with it and the Priesthood), for the simple reason that it did not as yet exist. They go on to say that Ezekiel thought much about Solomon's Temple, and longed earnestly for its restoration, when the Jews should have returned to their own land, and that he desired it to be hedged round, both literally and figuratively, in such a way as to increase the holiness of the people. When indeed the people returned to Palestine, they were able only to make a Temple which corres-

ponded in some little degree with the one that he proposed. But his vision was not wasted. Far from it. It became the starting point for a description of a service of God even more ideal than it was itself, in which the vision was thrown backwards instead of forwards, and the people were told in so many words that plans and ordinances, either identical or at least similar, had been seen and heard by Moses in the Mount, and had been carried out by him into material and real existence. Yet in fact, say these theologians, the Tabernacle never existed, and the description of it was but a pious adumbration of the way in which, when the narrative was spiritually understood, the LORD intended His people to have all their lives, secular and religious, interwoven with holiness.

Of course, if this interpretation of the Temple described by Ezekiel is right, the Rabbi's arguments, that such a Temple must be actually built before Messianic times, fall to the ground. But speaking for myself, and I should suppose for most of my readers, I find it very hard indeed to believe that such an interpretation can be true. A parable on so large a scale as this would be, a parable which has been misunderstood for sober fact during a period, *ex hypothesi*, of some two thousand five hundred years, has no parallel in history. I cannot believe that Ezekiel's Temple is a mere programme of legal enactments carried out partially in the Return, much less that it is a parable which served as an introduction to that greater parable of the Mosaic Tabernacle.

**64**] (2). Is Ezekiel's Temple then merely a prophecy of the Christian Church, or, to put it otherwise, a poetic idealisation of great truths which are already finding their fulfilment in Christianity? Not a few Christian interpreters, both in the past and in the present, have thought so. The Temple in this case, of course, does not mean a literal Temple, but the Society of Christian people, which towers up above all other forms of religion, and is the direct outcome of the earlier faith of the Jews. If this interpretation of the prophecy be accepted, it is again clear that R. Isaac's objection falls to the ground.

**65**] (3). But what if, after all, there be some measure of truth in his opinion that in the future there will be a Temple, imposing in size and majestic in external worship, set up in Palestine? It is well to remember that this opinion has been held by very many Christians, and is not at all inconsistent with Christianity. It must be confessed that it is quite possible that a Temple answering in some degree to that presupposed by R. Isaac may yet be built.

Even so, however, there are grave difficulties in accepting all that R. Isaac seems to see in it. Let us suppose that the Temple will be built. Will not a very different kind of worship be found there from that which was rendered in the days of the Monarchy, or after the return under Zerubbabel and under Ezra? What of the sacrifices? I know indeed that the majority of Jews to-day still repeat in the Synagogue services the prayer that the Temple may be rebuilt and the sacrifices restored. But is it likely that even if the Temple be rebuilt the sacrifices will be restored? Is not a feeling spreading day by day that the time for animal sacrifices has gone by, that they were very well in the days of man's comparative ignorance as an expression of duty towards God, and of the sacrifice of the heart that He requires, but are worse than useless now? Is it not true that even Jews have been influenced, and are being influenced in ever increasing measure, by the Christian doctrine that the blood of bulls and goats can never take away sin? Is it not probable then that, even if the Jews do rebuild their Temple, the more thoughtful among them will determine that the slaughter of innocent animals shall form no part of their worship? For men's prayers and praises are worth far more in the sight of God than any sacrifices.

**66**] (4). But suppose that some such glorious building be built in Jerusalem by the Jews after they have recognized the Messiahship of Jesus. Suppose it, I say, only suppose it! The time within which Ezekiel's Temple is to be built is nowhere stated, and the date at which it is to be built will, according to this supposition, altogether fall within the Messianic period. For there is no hint that it is to be built immediately after the coming of Messiah. Suppose it be a Christian building that is here shown in vision to Ezekiel? "What," say you, "with its slaughter houses and arrangements for the offering of material sacrifices?" This is hardly a difficulty. For Ezekiel naturally was bound by the ideas of his own time. But Jews and Christians alike have gone past those ideas now. If it be the Lord's will that such a great Christian Temple some day be built in Palestine, with all the wealth and beauty, both in material and worship, that wealthy members of the house of Israel can lavish upon it, will this be a wholly unnatural fulfilment of the vision unfolded to Ezekiel?

For consider the glory that it would mean for Israel! Picture to yourselves a building surpassing St. Peter's in Rome for fame and beauty, in which rise daily from Jewish lips hymns to God and His Anointed, a building built and maintained by a restored Israel which has repented of its sin! But as you gaze you see not only Jews worshipping there! It is the scene of spiritual worship by all portions of the Christian Church, who come to do honour to the God of the Jews in the Jews' own land. In that blessed time the Christian Church will itself be purified from its sins and inconsistencies, and be glad to worship at the ancient centre of its faith. What if, when the true religion of the Jewish nation has spread over the whole earth, each nation gladly sends its representatives to worship at Jerusalem, to show forth there the praises of God for His mercies vouchsafed in the Lord Jesus? The Lord hasten it in His time!

לשנה הבאה בירושלים!

### *v*. The Resurrection of the dead.

§ 6. xx.

**67**] Another proof adduced by R. Isaac, in evidence of his belief that the Messianic promises have not yet begun to be fulfilled, is that the Resurrection of the dead has not yet taken place. In support of his claim he quotes Deut. xxxii. 39, and Isa. xxvi. 19, and Dan. xii. 2. I am not going to quarrel with the learned Rabbi for his use of his texts, even though there is not a little to be said in favour of the opinion that neither of the two first passages really refers to the subject of the resurrection, save perhaps by way of allusion. I am content to share with him the full belief in the resurrection of the dead.

**68**] Yet when we examine the matter further, it seems that the Rabbi looks forward to a very different kind of resurrection of the dead from that which the majority of Christians are expecting. For I suppose that by the resurrection of the dead most Christians understand the resurrection at the last day, when the end of the world shall have come, and the newly risen shall depart at once to everlasting happiness or woe. But it is probable that the Rabbi means something very different. Indeed, if he meant what we mean, his argument would be somewhat useless. It would be in effect—evidently the last day has not yet come, for we are still on earth, therefore Messiah has not yet come. But this would be to mistake the Rabbi's opinions.

**69**] (1). These may be learned from the famous work of Saadiah, entitled *Emunoth w'deoth*, which gives a very clear account of the more important beliefs of the Jews. It was indeed written in the 10th century, but orthodox Jews have always virtually accepted it as giving a true summary of the creed of Judaism—if we may dare use such a word as "creed" without incurring the reproach of purists, who, looking to the letter rather than the spirit, tell us that Judaism has never been bound by the shackles of a creed. There is however little doubt that R. Isaac would have professed himself quite ready to abide by what Saadiah tells us of the resurrection of the dead. To put his statement briefly, the resurrection is something quite different from participation in the existence of the future world. It means that in the Messianic time all the righteous and repentant are to rise again (*i.e.*, practically all Jews, because "nearly all of them will repent before their death") and will live again on earth. They will be recognized by those who are still alive; the blind, and others who have died with some deformity, being raised blind, &c., and being afterwards restored to sight, &c., by a special miracle. They will live the same kind of life that they lived before, eating and drinking (Chap. vii. §§ 14-16, edn. Fürst). Saadiah indeed does not touch on the question whether these risen men and women will marry, as well as live in other respects like ordinary human beings. But R. Berachya Ha Nakdan, in the 12th century, is very explicit. For he says the man who had two wives in his ordinary earthly life will, in this new resurrection-life on earth, probably have only the wife of his youth (*Masref*, § 13, *ed.* Gollancz, p. 320). It is not impossible that it was some such gross materialism as this which on the one hand led to the objection of the Sadducees against the doctrine of the Resurrection, and on the other drew forth the spiritual answer of the Lord Jesus, " In the resurrection they neither marry, nor are given in marriage, but are as angels in heaven " (Matt. xxii. 30).

**70**] (2). R. Isaac evidently expects that the righteous will rise before the wicked and will continue to live on earth, and represents in his opinion the statements of many other Jews. But in itself, and so far, this is not necessarily opposed to the belief of Christians, at least when it is shorn of its grosser features. There always have been many Christians, among others Justin Martyr and Tertullian, who have believed in what is called the First Resurrection as literally as R. Isaac himself.

It is no doubt a difficult subject from the Christian point of view, for we Christians are apt to give undue weight, it may be, to the spiritual side of Scripture. Hence it is not surprising that a great teacher like Augustine should have considered that the First Resurrection is but "the spiritual awakening which began to work in mankind after the coming of Christ, *i.e*, the resurrection in its mystical aspect; and that the millennium of Rev. xx. is the period from that awakening onwards" (See Chancellor E. H. Bernard in Hastings' *Bible Dict.* iv. 236). Of course if this interpretation be right, R. Isaac's objection is valueless, nay it would even act against himself, for a resurrection in a very real sense would be already past. But we should be sorry to insist that this spiritual interpretation is right.

**71**] (3). Personally, we are inclined to believe that there will be two resurrections from the dead—the first, that of the righteous; the second, that of all. But there does not seem to be sufficient evidence that between the two any appreciable interval of time will elapse. Even if this were the case—even if a period, answering, as we measure time, to a thousand years, were to elapse between the First Resurrection and the Second—what weight would this fact add to the Rabbi's arguments? In not one of the texts that he quotes is there any close connexion indicated between the resurrection of the dead and the coming of the Messiah, much less any hint that the resurrection is to take place directly He appears. Again, we must insist upon the fact that we Christians are looking for the coming of Messiah at least as earnestly and as strongly as do the Jews. Nay, more; we venture to affirm that in these days, when so many Jews are leaving the faith of their fathers for philosophical ambiguities, Christians expect the coming of Messiah a great deal more firmly and wistfully than Jews. The Messiah is to us a great reality. We do not weaken the conception of Him to mean only a Messianic time, as do so many Jews; though we do expect the Messianic time as much as they. But we expect Him who once came down to earth, and lived and moved among us as Man (being Man in the very fullest sense, though also God), to return to us in glory. Then His saints who now sleep in their graves will be caught up to meet Him in the air, and afterwards—be the time long or short—all the dead shall arise, and the Judgment be set, and the books be opened. God grant, my dear friends, that you who read, and I who write, may be accounted worthy to rise in that First Resurrection!

# CHAPTER II

## JEWS AND CHRISTIANS AS THE OBJECTS OF GOD'S AFFECTION

# CHAPTER II.

## JEWS AND CHRISTIANS AS THE OBJECTS OF GOD'S AFFECTION.

### i. THE ASSERTED REJECTION OF ISRAEL AND THE CHOICE OF CHRISTIANS.

§ 2.

**72**] In this section R. Isaac charges Christians with the assertion that God rejected Israel because they disbelieved and crucified His Messiah, but that He chose the Christians and let Messiah suffer for their salvation because they received Him and believed on Him. He then argues that this assertion is untrue, because, before the coming of Jesus, the Christian nations were confessedly heathen, and, after He came, not only did they not believe upon Him at once, but they in fact persecuted His apostles and followers, as may be seen from many historical examples. He also adds that there are still many Christians who practise heathen rites, worshipping serpents, trees, stones, fire, in accordance with their old heathen customs, and also many who still have idols in their churches, especially idols of bread (פסילי הלחם), all this being diametrically opposed to the teaching of Jesus. Christians also, he says, generally disobey the New Testament in their use of foods and their neglect of the Sabbath. Therefore it cannot be asserted with any truth that Christians have been chosen because they have received and obeyed the teaching of Jesus.

**73**] (1). Now I freely grant that in the main contention of this section R. Isaac is right. It is certainly absurd for any Christian to argue that God chose Christians because of their goodness, and it is hard to think that any Christian could have brought forward such an argument unless he had given undue weight to human merit. But no Christian man can argue (at least in any agreement with the New Testament) that his own good deeds, or even his own faith in Christ, secured God's choice of him, or again that the good actions of his nation, or of Christian nations generally, secured God's choice of them. The New Testament tells us clearly that men are not chosen for their good deeds, and if not men, then not nations.

**74**] But this is not the reason why R. Isaac rejects the assertion of his opponent ; he endeavours to prove his opinion by the evil actions of Christian nations. Now I am not careful to answer him in this matter, for though I should be sorry indeed to say that he is accurate in all his details (in some he makes gross mistakes), yet his statement of the facts generally is sufficiently true for the purpose. The Gentile nations which have become Christian were of course at first heathen, and did in fact bitterly persecute the followers of Jesus. But what then ? Were the heathen nations so much to blame even for this as were the Jews for their similar action, who after the long and special preparation by God that they had received, the long-standing and intimate knowledge of His teaching that they possessed, yet rejected (as many of them now confess) the holiest example of human life that the world has ever seen ? For the Jews thus to sin against the highest teaching of their moral nature was tenfold worse than for the Gentiles to sin against their comparative ignorance.

**75**] (2). It is however possible that R. Isaac misunderstood the argument of his Christian opponent. It is possible that the Christian meant to say only that the prosperity in worldly things of Christian nations (including their civilization) is due to their reception of Jesus Christ ; that because they listened to the New Testament (as a whole) they made progress even in the things of this world ; that, in other words, God blessed them in temporal things because they served

Him in spiritual things. If this is the real meaning of the Christian's argument, I doubt whether even R. Isaac could have found much fault with it. For it is little more than a truism in view of the facts of history past and present. Whatever we may think to be the reason, the fact stands good, that it is only Christian nations that have made progress in civilization and material prosperity. Those nations that have remained heathen, or have become only Mohammedan, have made hardly any progress at all.* Belief in the Lord Jesus Christ, on the other hand, has invariably produced energy in all directions of human life, and the development of all human powers.

**76**] (3). But R. Isaac makes much of the disobedience of Christians to the teaching of Jesus and the New Testament. He uses, in fact, the statement of his Christian opponent as a peg whereon to hang his attack on Christianity for its disregard of things that are contrary, the Rabbi holds, to the right worship of the living God.

(i). May I first of all be allowed to remind you once again that I hold no brief for the Christians of our own or of any other day? If at any time Christians act contrary to the teaching of the Lord Jesus and His apostles, so far they are wrong. It is the Lord Jesus to whom I would that my readers should be attracted; it is His teaching, His teaching too as interpreted by His apostles in the New Testament, to which I would they should yield obedience. The followers of the Lord Jesus have never yet been free from faults, and never will be, I suppose, until His return; but Jesus is perfect—"His mouth is most sweet: Yea, He is altogether lovely" (Cant. v. 16. חכו ממתקים וכלו מחמדים:), and again, "Thou art fairer than the children of men; grace is poured into thy lips" (Ps. xlv. 2 יפיפית מבני אדם הוצק חן בשפתותיך:) —and the object of these pages is ultimately to draw both writer and readers nearer to Him.

(ii). Therefore I confess that there is much to be said for the Rabbi's attacks on Christians. But yet he ought not to

* Japan is so far an exception in that she has deliberately adopted the external results of Christian civilization.

be so ready to confuse heathen sects, or, if you will, semi-heathen sects, with Christians who deserve the name. I have however no word in defence of the heathenism that still cleaves to some professed Christians, any more than I should expect an earnest Jew to defend such heathen superstitions as the Evil Eye, the wearing of amulets, &c., still current among some Jews.

(iii). Neither again have I a word in defence of the worship of idols in Christian churches, or, in particular, of the worship of the Host, the consecrated bread of the Sacrament of the Lord's Supper. We who are members of the Church of England have specifically rejected all such errors, and though, alas, it is true that large portions of the Christian Church still accept them, such Christians hardly attempt to defend their action from the teaching of the Lord Jesus and of the New Testament. And if these practices cannot be defended thus, as they cannot, they fall out of the range of our discussion, as I have already stated.

(iv). Lastly, the Rabbi's difficulties about Food and the Sabbath are, I confess, difficulties which he may quite fairly and properly adduce. But he himself deals with them at length further on in his book, and it is only fitting that I should imitate him, and leave the discussion of these two subjects for later pages (see parr. 152-159 and 166-171).

## ii. The reason why the Jews have not a King.

### § 3.

**77**] R. Isaac informs us that a Greek once argued with him that the Jews no longer had a king of their own race over them because they rejected Jesus their true King; and that he had replied that it was indeed true that their many sins had deprived them of a king, but this deprivation took place as far back as the time of Nebuchadnezzar, four hundred years before the birth of Jesus; further, that Jesus was never a king at all; and lastly, that Christians were not really in a position to say anything, first, because the Roman kings who put Jesus to death remained to that day, and, secondly, because many Christian nations, including that of Greece to which his interlocutor belonged, had themselves lost their own kings and were under the sway of Mohammedan rulers.

R. Isaac is evidently very well pleased with his answer, but it appears to me to be singularly weak.

**78**] (1). I say little about R. Isaac's chronology, for he is never strong in history, but it seems a pity that he should parade his ignorance. For it is not by any mere slip of the pen that he allows only four instead of six hundred years to the period between Nebuchadnezzar and the birth of the Lord Jesus, for he repeats the date in § 14. But apart from this his argument is poor. Granting, of course, that the kingdom in its independent form (though in fact it had hardly been independent for at least a hundred years before Nebuchadnezzar's time), ceased with the capture of king Zedekiah and the accompanying destruction of Jerusalem, yet the learned Rabbi ought not to have omitted all mention of the Hasmonaean kings after the Maccabean revolt. Neither ought he to have omitted all mention of the famous king Herod the Great, for, although he was of Edomite stock, yet the Jews, by their leading representatives, accepted him as their king. But Herod the Great died about the very year that the Lord Jesus was born, and since that date the Jews have never had a king to reign over them as a united nation.

The coincidence is very remarkable, to say the least, and is to be reckoned with by all Jews who wish to understand the reasons for their present state of national degradation.

**79**] (2). R. Isaac however raises a demurrer to the effect that at any rate Jesus never was a king. He asks in a tone of triumph, Who made Jesus king, and Where did He rule?

(i). Who made Jesus king? R. Isaac means that no man or body of men formally acknowledged Him as an earthly ruler, leading Him in solemn state to a material throne, crowning His temples with a crown of gold, and anointing Him with sacred oil. Be it so; we do not deny it. But even R. Isaac will grant that Messiah was to be a king. But where can he find in the Old Testament, in so many words, that a man, or a body of men, would one day formally anoint and crown and enthrone Him? If he can find no such statement, why does he attempt to browbeat us Christians by insisting on so carnal and material a view of coronation? Or perhaps the Rabbi would point us to the second Psalm, and say that the sixth verse speaks of God setting His king Messiah on the holy hill of Zion, for this would be fully in accord with the interpretations of ancient Rabbis. But to this the answer would be, that, if it is God that so appoints Messiah, we dare not say that God is tied to any visible inauguration of His reign. Directly we have to consider the way in which God will perform any predicted action, we are at once confronted with the possibility that He may act only in a spiritual way, without directly employing the material methods that we commonly associate with the particular act. To put it otherwise, God's inauguration of the Messianic kingdom need not be with blare of trumpets and human processions, but in a purely spiritual manner.

(ii). Where then did Jesus rule? asks R. Isaac. Alas, I reply, has R. Isaac here condescended to quibble? For to us Christians it appears to be a matter of very slight importance whether Jesus did or did not reign over a particular portion of this earth's surface. Material kingship is, to our minds, of almost no importance at all compared with kingship over men's hearts and lives. And surely the Rabbi will not deny that Jesus held and holds this? But those who have read the earlier pages of this work will doubtless remember that I have dealt already with this question (parr. 15, 27). It is unnecessary to discuss it here also. One who is King over men's hearts and consciences, and has His subjects, as even R. Isaac will confess, in all parts of the inhabited world, is far more truly a King than ever was David or even Solomon.

**80**] (3). We now come to the Rabbi's appeal to History, that God is not on the side of the Christians.

(i). He argues that the Roman king killed Jesus, and yet the Roman kingdom has lasted until now. As for the extremely interesting and important question who, whether

Romans or Jews, were really responsible for the death of Jesus, I do not propose raising any discussion now. The subject will come up in a later volume. But it is really little short of absurd on the part of the Rabbi to argue that the Roman kingdom had lasted until his own day, the very end of the sixteenth century. Rome was sacked by Alaric in 410; the Western Roman Empire perished in 476, and the Eastern shared its fate in 1453 A.D. It is of course true that a so-called Holy Roman Empire existed from 962 to 1806 A.D., but this was a German Empire, and had little more than the name in common with Rome. Rome as a sovereign State perished in the fifth century, punished, we Christians would say, for its failure to obey ordinary precepts of God's Law, whether Jewish, Christian, or natural, and receiving the due reward of its deeds.

(ii). R. Isaac also says that Christians cannot in all fairness accuse the Jews of losing their kingdom through lack of faith in Jesus, because even many Christian nations have no king of their own race, but are in bondage to Mohammedan rulers. I venture to think that this is a different thing altogether. Where will the Rabbi find in the Scriptures that Gentile Christians are to have a king of their own race over them? But with the Jews this is expressly the case. Promise after promise was given to the Jews that they should always have a king, and that a king of David's line. It is therefore a very serious matter for the Jews if this promise has not been fulfilled. But let him notice what exactly the Christian argument is. We Christians do not say that the Jews have no king of their own race, but that although they possess Him they do not acknowledge Him; and that because they do not acknowledge Him therefore their present condition as a nation is so miserable. We affirm, upon, as we believe, the strength of many prophecies, both in the Old Testament and in the New, that when the Jews turn to God in true contrition of soul, and acknowledge Jesus as their King, they will then regain a position of independence among the nations of the earth, inheriting the land promised to Abraham. We believe, I say, that the acceptance of our King, the Lord Jesus

Christ, as their King, will be rewarded by temporal and national, and, blessed be God, even spiritual eminence.

For God is wont to link, though by no means inseparably, temporal with spiritual blessings. And this may well suggest an answer to the Rabbi's difficulty that Mohammedan nations have sometimes triumphed over, and in many cases have long ruled over, professedly Christian nations. For in the Mohammedan conquests thoughtful readers of history, whether they be Jewish or Christian, perceive the all-ruling hand of God. Christians, whether individuals or nations, who leave the simplicity of their faith, who add manifold errors of doctrine and practice to the simple teaching of the New Testament, are often punished for their sin. The New Testament itself proclaims this. We Christians acknowledge that as God dealt with Jews, correcting them for unfaithfulness, so does He deal with us. But in both cases repentance for sin brings restoration to favour. Would indeed that both Christians and Jews acted on this principle.

## iii. THE PERMANENCE OF CHRISTIANITY.

### § 4.

**81**] R. Isaac tells us that a certain nobleman who was a Lutheran by religion urged in argument with him one day the need of due attention to the words of R. Gamaliel as quoted in Acts v. 38, 39. For he there bids the Council "Refrain from these men, and let them alone: for if this counsel or this work be of men, it will be overthrown: but if it is of God, ye will not be able to overthrow them; lest haply ye be found even to be fighting against God." The Lutheran bids R. Isaac notice that the Christian religion has lasted very many hundreds of years, and consider whether it be not therefore true.

R. Isaac says that he replied that this saying of R. Gamaliel was not accepted as true by the Jews, and that, in any case, it was not spoken by him as a prophet (for he was no prophet), but was only a remark based upon his experience of false leaders. R. Isaac also says very plausibly that mere length of time is no criterion of truth. For otherwise the palm must be given to idolatry, which has lasted many more ages than Christianity. Even Mohammedanism, if duration of time were alone taken into consideration, would also be proved true. He proceeds to argue that false religions are permitted to continue in order that the fools who accept them may one day give account, and he says also that idol-worship will not cease until the true Messiah comes.

With this last point I have already dealt (parr. 35, 36), and I shall therefore confine my remarks to the chief thought of this section.

R. Isaac's reply, I say, is plausible. But he hardly goes to the root of the matter.

**82**] (1). Observe that it is of extremely little importance whether the saying attributed to R. Gamaliel is authentic or not. There does not appear to be any valid reason for rejecting it, and it agrees with what we know of the shrewd but kindly character attributed to him in the Talmud.* In any case the saying is remarkable, and suggests thought.

**83**] (2). Observe also that the argument of R. Gamaliel, to call it by his name for convenience' sake, was never intended to be conclusive. It was the prudent advice of a lawyer to do nothing rashly, but to wait and see what God's providence should determine. Yet surely it is not wrong for us Christians to urge this argument with superlatively increased force now. No one can deny that God's providence has been on the side of Christianity, or that His providence has been exerted in behalf of Christianity in a very different manner from that in which it was shown in the case of Heathenism and of Mohammedanism. Had idol-worship any opposition? We have no reason to suppose so. Did

* It is sometimes difficult to know whether the sayings there reported under his name refer to R. Gamaliel the elder or to his grandson, but this hardly affects our present discussion.

Mohammedanism use the same peaceful weapons that the Christians of the first four centuries employed when they were conquering the Roman world for their Master? We all know that Mohammed himself enforced his religion at the point of the sword, and that his followers always imitated his example. R. Isaac surely forgets the poverty and lowly origin of the first preachers of the Gospel, the countless persecutions they endured, and their faithfulness under distresses of all kinds, when he ventures to compare the success of idol-worship and of Mohammedanism with that of the religion of Jesus. Its triumph in spite of so many obstacles, by the use of only spiritual weapons, raises a presumption in its favour that is wholly absent from those false religions with which he compares it.

It is true, of course, that mere length of time in the existence of a religion proves little or nothing in its favour; so far R. Isaac is right. But he is wrong in hiding the fact that Christianity prevailed by the use of only ethical and moral means, notwithstanding the bitter and unscrupulous opposition of powerful adversaries. Would indeed that Christians were able to say that in later times they had always maintained the purity of their early methods!

## iv. The Humiliation of the Jews.

### § 5.

**84**] The same Lutheran nobleman said to R. Isaac: When you served God you prospered, but since you sinned all dominion is taken from you, and has passed over to other nations. Your present humiliation is a proof of your evil deeds, and of the imperfection of your faith.

R. Isaac replied: The argument is wholly untrue, because in this world the wicked often prosper and the righteous are in misery; Nebuchadnezzar, for example, and Alexander ruled over the whole world, but no one would assert that the religions professed by them were true. Witness too, he says, the present prosperity of Mohammedans, and their dominion over a great part of the world. No! Scripture says, "Wherefore doth the way of the wicked prosper" (Jer xii. 1. מדוע דרך רשעים צלחה)? and "Whom the Lord loveth He reproveth" (Prov. iii. 12. את אשר יאהב יהוה יוכיח).

At first sight R. Isaac's answer would seem to be complete, for, moreover, not only does the Old Testament, followed by the New, insist upon the loving correction inflicted by the Lord upon His true servants, but also, as D. Deutsch points out in his notes to the *Chizzuk Emunah*, Christ warned His followers to expect poverty and misery, and Himself died upon the Cross. Christians therefore, it is argued, ought to be the very last persons to say that distress in this world is a proof of wrongness of faith.

**85**] Yet two considerations must not be overlooked.

(1). The history of nations, and our experience of the lives of individuals, tend to show convincingly that upon the whole God does so determine life that earthly prosperity follows a faith which is true in itself and has a real effect on its adherents; that if there is trial it is only for a short time, after which the success and prosperity of those who have been tried is more conspicuous than ever. Hence it is to be expected that if Judaism is the truest of all faiths, and is faithfully observed, its followers will be in greater earthly prosperity, generally speaking, than others. But this is not the case. It is therefore not unreasonable to think that Judaism, in so far as it differs from Christianity, is not as true as it.

(2). Earthly prosperity is distinctly promised in Scripture to the Jews if they are faithful to God, and, on the other hand, Jews are distinctly warned in Scripture that if they are unfaithful to God terrible calamities will come upon them. See, for example, Deut. xxviii. But to non-Jews no such general promises and warnings are given. In other words, earthly prosperity is not so closely bound up with non-Jews by the promises and warnings recorded in

Holy Writ as it is with Jews. It seems therefore to be only reasonable that Jews should ask themselves what is the cause—for cause there must be—why the warnings have been fulfilled upon them, if, as they assert, they have on the whole been faithful to God.

The argument of the Lutheran nobleman is not to be so lightly dismissed as R. Isaac supposes.

## v. THE RESTORATION OF THE JEWS AND THE DESTRUCTION OF THE NATIONS.

§§ 6. 17.

**86**] A Christian scholar said to R. Isaac that he could find in the Prophets no reference to the present Captivity of the Jews under Rome, and to the Restoration from it, and that therefore there was no need for Messiah to come hereafter (as the Jews supposed), seeing that all the promises connected with Him had been already fulfilled in the time of the second Temple.

R. Isaac replied that it was no wonder that a Gentile could not find such prophecies, for God "sheweth His word unto Jacob, His statutes and His judgments unto Israel" (Ps. cxlvii. 19).

מגיד דברו ליעקב חקיו ומשפטיו לישראל׃

R. Isaac then adduced passages from the Prophets referring to (1) this strange present captivity, in which one nation is scattered to the ends of the earth; (2) the continuance of the Jews in this captivity for a very long time, even until "the end of the days"; (3) their redemption from it; (4) the fall of Rome and other Gentile kingdoms, including the Mohammedan; and, lastly, many details that must be fulfilled before Messiah comes.

We have already considered these details, and now turn to say something upon the other subjects.

**87**] (1). The prophecies of the present Captivity. We agree with R. Isaac in this, that the Old Testament contains such statements (though he may be wrong in some of the particular passages that he adduces), and therefore we have no need to discuss the matter here.

**88**] (2). We have already examined the meaning of the phrase "in the end of the days," and shown that R. Isaac does not understand it correctly (parr. 21-24).

**89**] (3). The Restoration of the Jews from this Captivity. R. Isaac speaks as though in defending this belief he were attacking Christianity. But let him attack Christianity as it is, not as he thinks it is. This is important here. For Christians have always believed in two comings of Messiah, and are, for the most part, ready to accept with the Rabbi the belief that many things prophesied of the times of Messiah are yet to take place. Thus a large number of Christians (probably the majority in these days) believe in the Restoration of the Jews as much as do the Jews themselves. We are indeed looking forward to it with no little intensity of expectation. For to our minds the Restoration of the Jews to Palestine is closely bound up with that event for which we daily hope, for which we daily pray, the return of our Master, the Second Coming of the Lord Jesus Christ. It is true that, if we are wise, we do not pretend to know the order of the scenes in the great drama to be enacted when He returns, but, so far as we can understand His own words and the words of the Prophets, His Coming and the Restoration of the Jews to their own land are bound closely together. If the Jews return to Palestine first the Lord Jesus will return soon after; if the Lord Jesus comes first He will hasten their return thither. In any case the Rabbi is not justified in using the truth of the future restoration of the Jews as a rod wherewith to smite Christians of to-day.

**90**] (4). He however goes further than this and connects the restoration of the Jews with the destruction of the Gentile nations, in particular with that of Christians and Mohammedans.

(i). He finds the connexion of these two subjects partly in Num. xxiv. 17 to 19, 24. (*cf.* also Obad. 21 and Ezek. xxv. 14), where he sees not only the triumph of Israel but also the overthrow of the other nations, especially Rome, which, as he believes, is intended by the terms "Edom" and "Kittim" (*cf.* Dan. xi. 30). For Rome he also quotes Obad. 18 and Isa. xxxiv. 5, 6, 8. For the Mohammedans he quotes not only Joel iii. 19, where, according to him, Egypt means Ishmael, on the strength of Gen. xvi. 1 and xxi. 21, but also Isa. lxvi. 17. He says that this last passage refers to both Rome and the Mohammedans, so that it is perhaps worth while to quote it here at length: "They that sanctify themselves and purify themselves to go unto the gardens, behind one in the midst, eating swine's flesh, and the abomination, and the mouse; they shall come to an end together, saith the LORD."

המתקדשים והמטהרים אל הגנות אחר אחד בתוך אכלי בשר החזיר והשקץ והעכבר יחדו יספו נאם יהוה:

On this the Rabbi remarks that the phrase "they that sanctify themselves and purify themselves" means the Mohammedans, who are always cleansing themselves externally (he refers to their ceremonial washing before prayer), while they allow themselves unclean things; and "eating swine's flesh" refers to Edom, *i.e.*, the Christians.

(ii). Now we have no objection, in one sense, to the belief that hereafter those who refuse to obey God shall be destroyed. Both the Old and the New Testament speak of this judgment in plain terms. But we fail to see that R. Isaac has the right to see in Scripture any indication that the Mohammedans and Christians, as such, are expressly included among these evil nations. His discovery of Mohammedans in Isa. lxvi. 17 and Joel iii. 19, rests on so far-fetched a method of interpretation that it may safely be disregarded by every thoughtful student of to-day.

**91**] (iii). Is he any better off in his discovery of the mention of Christians? No doubt he can find many passages in the Old Testament that foretell the destruction of Edom. Well and good: Edom has been destroyed. But he identifies Edom with Rome, *i.e.*, with Christians. How does he arrive at this equation? His process of thought appears to have been somewhat as follows: In the first place, he thinks that Christians have their headquarters at Rome, so that Rome may fairly be taken to represent them. But even if it were true in the Rabbi's days (as it was not) that Christians had their headquarters at Rome, it certainly is not the case now. One would suppose that the Rabbi, living though he did in Poland, had never heard of the Greek Church, which would warmly, and rightly, have repudiated the notion that it had received its Christianity from Rome. But in these days, after the great development of the English-speaking races, who, generally speaking, owe and give no allegiance to Rome, it is plainly absurd to say that Christianity is represented by it.

**92**] Secondly, there are ancient tales, which R. Isaac repeats as though he believed them, to the effect that the founders of Rome came from Edom, and again that the founders of Christianity were Edomites who went to Rome.* But no scholar of the present day, either Jew or Gentile, believes these tales for a moment. They are in fact quite worthless for historical purposes.

**93**] Thirdly, he found the frequent use of the word "Edom" in Rabbinic literature to represent "Rome." R. Isaac had been accustomed to this from his earliest youth, and he doubtless regarded the usage as a proof of the identity of meaning. But anyone can see how the usage arose. It was not convenient in either imperial or papal times for Jews openly to teach or write that Rome would perish, and they therefore substituted another word for it, the connotation of which was well known to their readers, though not to the uninitiated. Sometimes they spoke of Rome as Babylon (see reff. in Zunz, *Lit. der synag. Poesie*, pp. 100 sq.; *cf.* 1 Pet. v. 13), when they were thinking of the power and glory of the empire; but sometimes, and much more often in papal times, simply as Edom (*cf.* Buxtorf *Lex. loc. cit.*).† For the substitution was so neat. They had only to presuppose (in Obad. 8 for example) an *al-tiqri* of "d" (ד) to "r" (ר), and "Edom" became practically "Rome." But we do not base dogmas on Haggadoth, as Jews will be the

* Compare also Buxtorf *Lex.* s.v. Edom.

† See additional references in Schechter, *Some Aspects of Rabbinic Theology*, 1909, pp. 99 sqq.

first to acknowledge, and if this is all the evidence that R. Isaac has (and it seems to be all) for finding references to the destruction of Christians within the writings of the prophets his argument is worth nothing.

To put the matter otherwise. His appeal to the statements of the prophets that Christians are to be destroyed in the future rests on mere fancy, and a misapprehension of the use of the word "Edom" by earlier Jewish writers. There is, in fact, no indication in the Old Testament that either Mohammedan or Christian nations, as such, are included amongst those adversaries of the truth who are doomed to perish.

## vi. The Length of the Present Exile.

### § 7.

**94**] It is strange how, as the years roll on, difficulties that troubled our fathers lose their force for us. Few Christians of to-day, for example, would bring forward the argument in favour of Christianity that is adduced in this chapter of R. Isaac's book, and, if they were to do so, few Jews would answer it in R. Isaac's manner. Many of the arguments on either side are in fact antiquated. Yet, as we shall see, there underlies the discussion something that is at the very core of the differences between Jew and Christian.

(1). Christians are represented as saying (and there is no reason to suppose that the Jew was not reproducing arguments often addressed to him) that while the Egyptian Captivity lasted four hundred, and the Babylonian seventy years, this present exile has already lasted more than fifteen hundred, or, in fact, now more than eighteen hundred years. Also that the date of the end of those captivities was made known beforehand to Abraham and to Jeremiah, but no date has been assigned to this. The reason of this, say the Christians, is doubtless because it has no end, because God does not purpose restoring the nation of Israel to His favour once again. Lev. xxvi. 38, say the Christians, will certainly be fulfilled: "Ye shall perish among the nations, and the land of your enemies shall eat you up." Lastly, say the Christians, even Reason teaches the hopelessness of the expectation of the Jews, for if God has not delivered them in fifteen (eighteen) hundred years, He is very unlikely ever to do so.

(2). The Rabbi evidently feels the force of this argument more than we should to-day. Our ideas of God's time in His management of the world are much enlarged (*cf.* par. 26). He therefore thinks it his duty to state at length his reasons why the dates were made known to Abraham and to Jeremiah. The former was told because it was advisable for his own faith, and that of his descendants in Egypt, that they should not be too impatient. R. Isaac also makes an elaborate calculation by which he shows that, notwithstanding the date fixed for the Egyptian captivity, its years were actually exceeded by thirty (Ex. xii. 40), because of the sinfulness of the Israelites in Egypt. Again, Jeremiah was told of seventy years, because in this way Israel was informed that a definite sin, that of neglecting the sabbatical years, had to be worked off by the seventy years of exile.

**95**] But why is it that no date has been assigned to this present exile? Here the answer of the Rabbi is so important that I must quote it in its entirety. "This exile," he says (p. 69), "has been decreed to atone for the iniquities, transgressions, and sins, which Israel sinned from the day of their entrance into the Land until they came into captivity. For iniquities are a grievous uncleanness for the souls of sinners, and separate between them and God, and they need washing and purification by the many strokes and cruelties done to them during the long time of their captivity. For in the Captivity of Babylon they were not cleansed properly. Only the sin of not keeping the years of release in Palestine was atoned for. But the iniquities, transgressions, and sins, *e.g.*, immorality, idolatry, bloodshed, &c., were not atoned for in the Captivity of Babylon, because of the shortness of the time, therefore Divine wisdom decreed that Israel should come into this captivity, and that they should stay in it a very long time, until the end of the days, to receive their punishment, to destroy the transgression of idolatry, to annihilate the sin of immorality, and to atone for the iniquity of bloodshed, as it is said in Ezek. xxii. 15 and Lam. iv. 22."

"But in Babylon," he continues, "not only were their iniquities not effaced (except their sin about the years of release), but they sinned still more. Therefore they were obliged to go into captivity again to atone for all iniquities and sins. For after our iniquities are atoned for, and our uncleanness effaced by the chastisements of this bitter and hard captivity, then we shall no more sin, and then Deut. xxx. 6 will be fulfilled: 'The LORD thy God will circumcise thine heart, &c.' So also Ezek. xxxvi. 26, 27 will be fulfilled: 'A new heart, &c.'; and similarly with other prophecies. Further, in that God determined to prolong the days of this captivity for the abundance of our iniquities, transgressions, and sins, and that the complete and perfect redemption from it depends upon our repentances, His wisdom determined to hide the date of the future redemption even from the Prophets (Deut. xxxii. 34), and not even Daniel was allowed to know it (Dan. xii. 9). For the knowledge of the distance of the time would have been a hindrance and would have brought harm. Jews in this exile would be tempted to despair, and to break off the yoke of the law, as indeed has happened to many."

Further (p. 73), "Our redemption from this captivity depends on complete repentance (see Deut. xxx. 1—6), and repentance depends upon our own choice and will. Therefore it is not possible to set a fixed time, seeing that we are able to shorten the time of the end if we turn to Him with all our heart in perfect repentance. For God's knowledge of the time does not do away with the freedom of our will."

**96**] (3). How much good there is in what the Rabbi writes! As Christians read his expressions of longing for the repentance of the Jewish nation, and still more as they read the fervent utterances of the Jewish heart in the cries contained in the Hebrew Prayer Book, they are moved to their very depths, and join earnestly in the prayers for the outpouring of God's divine gift of true repentance upon His chosen people.

And yet they cannot but think that they see at least part of the reason why this Repentance so long desired is so long withheld, as they read upon the very same page the reason for the length of this captivity, which the Rabbi has recorded, and the authors of the Synagogue Prayers have also made their own.

What is the reason adduced by R. Isaac for the long continuance of the present exile? What but that Israel may atone for its sins committed in Palestine by suffering and persecution? See how the natural pride of the human heart makes itself known! The sufferings of the Jews are to work out their atonement! Where did the Rabbi learn this? Not from Scripture. Nor from Reason. How is it possible for suffering, endured, if you will, for thousands of years, to make up for a single sin, much less for sins committed, as the Rabbi says, during all the time that Israel was in Palestine? It is astonishing to find that Jews have so little due perception of the love of God. They talk about it, and appear to assume it, and then think that God is not to be propitiated unless a man suffer, on behalf of himself or another. A Jew will say, "I have sinned, therefore I must suffer for my sin, and, when I have suffered long enough for it, then God will forgive me." Or else he will say, "I have sinned, and at any rate some one else must suffer for me, and when he has suffered long enough then God will forgive me." All such reasoning is abhorrent to Scripture, and to Reason also. It is altogether too much akin to the thought of him who supposes that the LORD is pleased with thousands of rams, or with ten thousands of rivers of oil; who wishes to give his first-born for his transgression, the fruit of his body for the sin of his soul (Mic. vi. 7.). No! the way of pardon lies in the humble acceptance of the Lord's love.

**97**] But possibly some Jewish reader may be thinking in his inmost heart: "Surely Christians are always insisting on the value of the sufferings and death of another man for them!" No; that is not the case. No Christian believes that the death of any man, however good and holy, is of the least value in securing salvation. Christians hold that the very Presence of God gave Himself up, by taking human nature, to be a self-sacrifice for human sin, and, whatever may be the difficulties of this belief, it is at all events very different indeed from a belief that the suffering of a man as such can at all atone for sin—yes, utterly opposed to it and contradictory. The Jew makes much of man; the Christian makes much of the Presence of God. There is all the difference in the world between the two conceptions.

**98**] (4). Lastly, I must mention one or two matters of less importance. (i). The Rabbi is doubtless right when he declines to accept the use made of Lev. xxvi. 38 by the Christians whom he quotes at the beginning of this chapter. He is right in saying that that passage is no valid argument for the destruction of the Jews during this present exile. (ii). He is also doubtless right in refusing to see that the length of time that has elapsed is of any weight at all. But I wonder that he did not insist on the remarkable fact of the preservation of the Jews during all these centuries. It would be extraordinary indeed if, after preserving the Jews through untold hardships during all this time, God were to allow them to perish, without fulfilling His gracious promises towards them. It is incredible that He who has done so much should not do more. (iii). Finally, in the course of his argument (p. 72), the Rabbi makes an objection against the Lord Jesus which I must not altogether pass by, lest it be thought that there is no answer to give to him. He quotes Acts i. 6, and, after pointing out that the Apostles expected the establishment of the Kingdom (which no one denies, though perhaps there may be a difference of opinion as to the nature of the Kingdom expected), urges that the answer of Jesus shows that He was not the Messiah, for He did not say that He was the one who would establish it, but said that God alone knew the end of this exile. A strange explanation indeed! It is all bound up with that primary error of the Rabbi, which we have so repeatedly pointed out, that when Messiah comes He must do everything at once. For if one does but assume that Jesus is the Messiah,

His answer contains no difficulty at all. It is but reminding the Apostles that they must not expect to have everything revealed to them ; that God's purposes are to be worked out in their own time, and are not to be subjected to human curiosity. It would be well for many of us, whether Jews or Christians, if we took the warning of that passage to heart.

## vii. The Return of the Twelve Tribes to the Holy Land.

§ 8.

**99]** In this section the Christian is represented as expressing his astonishment that the Jews can expect to return to Palestine and receive the Land as once more divided among the Twelve Tribes, when they do not even know to what Tribe they severally belong.

(1). R. Isaac answers :

(i). There is no difficulty in the case of the Ten Tribes who were carried away by Shalmaneser (had he lived in these days the Rabbi would have known it was Sargon, and praised the accuracy of Scripture, which only tells us that it was "the king of Assyria," 2 Kings xviii. 11) to Chalah and Chabor, for they still dwell in one place, and all know their own tribes, as may be learned from the descriptions of those who have seen them, and from the narrative of Benjamin of Tudela.

(ii). There is also no great difficulty in the case of the two Tribes of Judah and Benjamin. For all the Jews who are now scattered among Christian and Mohammedan nations belong to one or other of these two tribes (most no doubt belong to Judah), with the addition of a few Levites and descendants of Aaron, both of whom are known, as in fact are those who are of the line of David. It is indeed true, says R. Isaac, that at present the two tribes of Judah and Benjamin are so mixed that whether a Jew belongs to Benjamin or Judah no one knows, but this is a point which will be made clear by Elijah when he returns. For he will separate the members of the two tribes. The Rabbi adds that even the proselytes shall then know to which tribe they really belong. For it is said in Ezek. xlvii. 23, "And it shall come to pass, that in what tribe the stranger sojourneth (or the proselyte is proselyte), there shall ye give him his inheritance, saith the LORD God."

והיה בשבט אשר גר הגר אתו שם תתנו נחלתו נאם אדני יהוה׃

**100**] (2). In earlier paragraphs I have already stated my complete willingness to accept the belief in a future Return of the Jews to the Holy Land. Not only is this by far the simplest explanation of the many prophecies that apparently proclaim it, but the fact of the preservation of the Jews as a separate people during these nineteen centuries, in spite of the greatest trials and, alas, the bitterest persecutions, is most easily explained by the existence of a reason in the counsels of God connected with some great work in the future which they shall yet perform. We all indeed know that their preservation enables them to be a standing witness to the world of the general truth of the Bible, in both the Old Testament and the New, yet this alone would not appear to be cause sufficient for so unique a miracle as their preservation. On the other hand, grant that the Bible demands, if it be fairly interpreted, that the Jews have yet a future before them in proclaiming the Kingdom of God—a future connected in some way, as it would appear, with their Restoration to Palestine—and then it is not at all surprising that God, the God of Abraham, Isaac and Jacob, continues to preserve them until the time is ripe for the accomplishment of their special task.

I grant then to the full that the Jews will yet be restored to their own land.

**101**] But how we are to understand the details by which that restoration is described by the Prophets is a wholly different matter. For example, in this very question of the division of the Land to each Tribe, it is extremely perilous to make any dogmatic statement. Personally, I think that the literal fulfilment is very improbable (with the curious parallelograms described in Ezek. xlv., reminding the modern reader of a map of the back blocks in Canada in 1910), but in any case the question is of no importance for our present subject. It is no part of my task to decide what is the exact meaning of prophecies that deal with the future of the Jews, especially in their details. Both Jews and Christians agree or differ, as the case may be, with regard to the interpretation of such problems, which are probably insoluble with our present knowledge, and therefore the problems are not such as really enter into our discussion. But I cannot help adding that if the division of the Land to each Tribe requires, as the Rabbi says, such a strange miracle as the return of Elijah to inform any Jew of his lineage, the improbability of the literal interpretation is greatly increased. For the subject of the return of Elijah see parr. 269-275.

**102**] Similarly, the return of the Ten Tribes is a question that is more curious than important in our present discussion. I should probably not have touched upon it at all if R. Isaac had not already said in § 6 that the fact that the Ten Tribes have not returned is an argument against the truth of the belief that Messiah has already come.

In one respect we know much more about the Ten Tribes than the Rabbi knew. We know now that they do not exist as such, distinct and separate. Eldad the Danite in the ninth century, by adding real Haggadic knowledge to a very fertile imagination, was able to describe in detail the manners and customs of the Ten Tribes in Abyssinia or Ethiopia; Benjamin of Tudela again in the twelfth century recounted at length the tales told him by a certain R. Moses about the Ten Tribes in Samarcand; Prester John about the same time spoke of them in India, recounting from far older sources how "a river which comes from paradise, passes between us and the great country of the mighty Daniel, King of the Jews. This river flows all the week days, but remains quiet on the sabbath day"; * but we in this twentieth century, to whom there is no longer any part of the surface of the earth unknown, except

* Neubauer, "Where are the Ten Tribes?" (*Jewish Quarterly Review*, i. p. 192).

the South Pole, know that in no country whatever, however far from civilisation it may be, do the Ten Tribes dwell. The "travellers' tales" have been proved to be false; the Ten Tribes as such do not exist.

It is indeed possible that they may have been ancestors of certain nations or tribes possessing features or customs like those of the Jews, as for example the Afghans, but even this is highly conjectural, and proof there is none. If there were, we should not find (as we do find) that almost every nation existing at the present day has been thought to represent the Ten Tribes.* Even the British nation is no exception, but the presuppositions of this strange theory, and the arguments by which it is supported, come hardly within the bounds of sober criticism.

**103**] There are, in short, only two theories about the Ten Tribes which seem to deserve consideration. First, out of those who remained in Palestine some attached themselves to the Jews, while, in spite of the silence of the Books of Ezra and Nehemiah, some at least of the others returned with the Two Tribes. In favour of this opinion is the mention in St. Luke ii. 36 of a certain Anna the daughter of Phanuel, belonging to the tribe of Asher; also, as it seems, a person from the tribe of Dan, and another from the tribe of Zebulun, are mentioned in T. B. *Pesachim* 4*a* בדקו ואשכחו דאתי מדן and בדקו ואשכחו דאתי מזבולן (in the Munich MS.). If this theory is adopted we may perhaps say that the union of the Ten Tribes with the Two has already taken place.

Secondly, the Ten Tribes are so merged in the Gentiles as to be quite unrecognizable by any means yet at our disposal. In this case it may be assumed that the prophecies of their return as distinct and separate tribes are not to be understood literally. In either case, the Rabbi's objection to the belief that Messiah has come, based upon the fact that the Ten Tribes have not returned, is untenable.

**104**] I may conclude with quoting Neubauer's words at the end of his illuminating articles in the first volume of the *Jewish*

* A convenient summary may be found in the *Jewish Encyclopedia*, s.v. "Tribes, Lost Ten" (xii. pp. 249—253).

*Quarterly Review* (p. 422): "Where are the Ten Tribes? We can only answer, Nowhere. Neither in Africa......nor in India, China, Persia, Kurdistan, the Caucasus, or Bokhara. We have said [p. 15] that a great part of them remained in Palestine, partly mixing with the Samaritans and partly amalgamating with those who returned from the Captivity of Babylon. With them many came also from the cities of the Medes, and many, no doubt, adhered to the Jewish religion which was continued in Mesopotamia during the period of the Second Temple. As to the prophetical promise that they will be gathered together in the Messianic time, we follow R. Akiba, who said that they will never return. Why should we be more orthodox than the great R. Akiba?" *

עשרת השבטים אינן עתידין לחזור שנ' (דברים כ"ט כ"ז) וישליכם אל ארץ אחרת כיום הזה מה היום הזה' הולך ואינו חוזר' אף הם הולכים ואינם חוזרים' דברי ר"ע.

* R. Aqiba's opinion is recorded in the Mishna, *Sanhedrin* x. 3 (6).

# CHAPTER III

## A CONSIDERATION OF CERTAIN PASSAGES IN THE LAW

# CHAPTER III.

## A CONSIDERATION OF CERTAIN PASSAGES IN THE LAW.

### i. Gen. i. 1, 26. THE DOCTRINE OF THE TRINITY IN UNITY.

§§ 9, 10.

**105**] R. Isaac tells us at the end of the eighth section of his work that he will now begin to discuss the Christian interpretation of various passages in the Bible which are adduced by Christians in confirmation of their opinions. Therefore in § 9 he considers the first verse of Genesis, and in § 10 he considers the 26th verse of the same chapter. But as in these two sections he is in reality dealing with the whole question of the Christian doctrine of the Trinity in Unity, it will be well for us to imitate him.

But let me say at the outset, that if it were not that the Rabbi has brought forward this subject so early in his book I should not myself have done so. For it seems to me that it is unreasonable to expect a Jew to understand, in any satisfactory degree, the Christian doctrine of the Trinity in Unity. Jews are ready enough to tell us Christians that no Christian can understand Judaism. We, with at least equal right, may retort that no Jew as such is able to understand Christianity. For the doctrine of the Trinity is not a doctrine independent of others, but rather is the final result and apex, or, to change the figure slightly, the connecting arch, of all Christian truths. They lead up to it; they do not start from it. This will become more clear at the end of our consideration of the subject. Sufficient to say now that if a person regards the doctrine of the Trinity in Unity as mere theory he will fail to understand either it or the reasons for its formation, and that the necessity for it will be appreciated only by him who approaches it from the standpoint of his own personal need.

We shall first consider R. Isaac's attacks upon the doctrine, and then state briefly why we Christians accept it.

**106**] (1). R. Isaac argues that the Christian doctrine of the Trinity has no support either in Gen. i. 1 or in Gen. i. 26.

(i). Gen. i. 1, "In the beginning God created." All know that the plural form *Elohim* is here found with the singular verb *bara*, and that although there are a few cases where *Elohim* is found with a plural verb or adjective, yet the singular is the regular construction when *Elohim* is used of the one true God. Christians, however, have often urged that this is due to the existence of more than one "Person" in the Godhead. R. Isaac argues, on the contrary, that it is only an example of the Plural of Majesty, like the royal "We" in English and other languages. Whether, however, this "Plural of Majesty," in the strict sense, exists in Hebrew is more than doubtful, and, if that explanation of the meaning of the plural were all that could be adduced against the Christian interpretation, the latter would hold the day. But essentially the Rabbi is right. The plural of intensity (*e.g.* מֵישָׁרִים "uprightness"; see many other examples in Gesenius-Kautzsch, *Hebrew Grammar*, § 124. *e.*) is very common, and the plural *Elohim* is best explained as an indication of the fulness of power and might contained in God. It is, at any rate, impossible to see in Gen. i. 1 any proof of the doctrine of the Trinity. So far the Rabbi is right.

**107**] (ii). Gen. i. 26, "And God said, Let us make man in our image." Similarly in this case Christian controversialists have often claimed (compare even the Epistle of Barnabas § 5, written between 70 and 137 A.D.) that the words were addressed by the Father to another "Person" in the Trinity. But there is nothing in the context to suggest this. The Rabbi may be right in his assertion that the words were addressed to the Angels that ever surround the throne of God, and necessarily take the deepest interest in all that

He does. At the same time it is strange that God should associate Himself in work with angels, upon, as it would seem, terms of equality; and indeed the supposition is contrary to Isa. xl. 14, "with whom took He counsel?" and xliv. 24, "I am the LORD, that maketh all things; that stretcheth forth the heavens alone; that spreadeth abroad the earth; who is with Me?" Possibly, as in the former case, the plural indicates the fulness of power and might in the Godhead. Yet, after all, if the doctrine of the Trinity is true, the phrase does fit in exceedingly well with it. The verse cannot be adduced as a proof of it, but it is strange that in the very beginning of the Bible two passages occur which strikingly illustrate it.

**108**] (2). R. Isaac also asserts that the Old Testament altogether contradicts the Christian belief in the Trinity. For, he says, "Scripture is opposed to the belief in more than one God." Of course it is. Who denies it? We grant this quite as heartily as does the Rabbi. But this is a very different thing indeed from opposition to the Christian doctrine of the three-fold personality in the one Godhead. Scripture contradicts in the strongest possible language all belief in the duality or the plurality of Gods. The heathen might say, for example, that there is one God of light and another of darkness; one of good, another of evil. But it stands written in the Book of Isaiah (xlv. 6, 7), "I am the LORD, and there is none else. I form the light, and create darkness; I make peace, and create evil; I am the LORD, that doeth all these things." And it stands written even more plainly in Deut. xxxii. 39, "I, even I, am He, and there is no god with Me." But, as I have already said, Christians accept these statements as heartily as does R. Isaac himself. There is no Christian believer who says that there is more than one God. On the contrary, every Christian believes in one God, and in one God only, accepting with all his heart and soul the words signed by every clergyman in the Church of England, "There is but one living and true God, everlasting, without body, parts, or passions; of infinite power, wisdom, and goodness; the Maker and Preserver of all things both visible and invisible." Out of all the many texts of Scripture which R. Isaac quotes there is not one which insists upon the supreme truth of the Unity of God more strongly than do these words. But neither they, nor any of his passages, touch the question whether there be, or be not, that ineffable plurality in the One Godhead, which for want of a better name we call the Trinity.

**109**] (3). R. Isaac also affirms that Reason itself is opposed to the Christian doctrine of the Trinity in Unity. So far from this being the case we shall see further on in our consideration of this subject that Reason itself demands the doctrine. But meantime let us see what the Rabbi says under this heading. He knows his Maimonides and uses his arguments well. He also combines an attack on the doctrine of the Incarnation with that of the Trinity. He is not to be blamed for this. For it is only through the Incarnation that men have come to perceive the Trinity. In other words, the essential Trinity, God in Himself, in His three-fold Personality, is only known to men through His action upon men, culminating, as Christians hold, in the Incarnation. It was therefore a true instinct that led the Rabbi to connect the two doctrines, separate though they might appear to be at first sight.

**110**] (i). He denies that the One God can be compounded of two or more parts. If He is, he says, He does not come up to the highest idea of unity that human intelligence requires. If indeed by "compounded" the Rabbi means compounded of distinct parts, we Christians agree with him. There are, as I have said, no parts in God. If, on the other hand, he means that, as an abstract principle, the idea of a bare Monad, containing in Himself nothing answering to the idea of the Trinity, is in itself a finer and more philosophical conception than the Christian belief, he is begging the question. We have no experience of a bare monad of any kind in Nature, and our Reason does not in any way compel us to a belief in its existence. So far from this, as we shall see, Reason itself is against such a doctrine. Of course if Christians held that One is Three and Three are One they might well be accused of believing a statement contrary to reason, and D. Deutsch would be right in his foolish remark, "If three can be one, so can a hundred" (Können drei eins sein, so auch hundert, *Chizzuk Emunah*, p. 361), and would be right in his ensuing deduction that we are thus brought to belief in polytheism. But I cannot believe that any thoughtful Jew really supposes that this is Christian doctrine. The doctrine of the Trinity is an extremely philosophical conception, which is only parodied by saying that it means that three are one and one is three. To misinterpret a statement and then to laugh at it may be good controversy, but it is very poor honesty.

**111**] (ii). The Rabbi also affirms that it is unphilosophical to believe in the Incarnation, for we cannot believe in a being who is compounded both of divinity and flesh, and also we cannot imagine God becoming incarnate. Yet we may point out that human thought is advancing more and more to the position that God comes into the closest possible contact with the creatures that He has made; that He has not that horror of matter which R. Isaac's words imply; and that if He were to manifest Himself in a supreme degree under the limitations of human life (supposing that great ethical and moral results could best be brought about by His doing so), this would be in accordance with what we know of Him in other ways. The Incarnation does not presuppose, as the Rabbi fancies, change in God (if it did, it would indeed be incredible), but only a more complete manifestation of Himself than He has already shown in Nature. The Incarnation, if it be a fact, is indeed a stupendous fact, but it is not, as R. Isaac says, contrary to Reason and Philosophy. It is rather the top stone to the slowly mounting edifice of the manifestation of God. God had shown Himself in the physical life, but far more stupendously in the moral life, and when the time came He showed Himself, as Christians believe, in the same sphere but more completely, when His very Presence came down and lived out all the requirements of His moral law, exhibiting in human nature a perfect example of a life that fulfilled all its demands. Is this in reality contrary either to our experience of God and His work, or to our highest and most philosophical conception of Him? I think not.

**112**] (4). Rabbi Isaac also affirms that the New Testament itself often contradicts the Christian doctrine of the Trinity. We shall later consider more fully the teaching of the New Testament upon this subject, but it is fitting that even here we should not altogether pass by the passages adduced by the Rabbi to prove his point.

**113**] (i). He quotes St. Matt. xii. 32 (with the parallel passages St. Mark iii. 28, 29, and St. Luke xii. 10) where our Lord says: "Whosoever shall speak a word against the Son of man, it shall be forgiven him; but whosoever shall speak against the Holy Spirit, it shall not be forgiven him, neither in this world, nor in that which is to come." The Rabbi argues that these words show that the Holy Spirit and the Son are not One, therefore the Three are not One. Yet we Christians have never said that the Son and the Spirit are One in such a sense as to obliterate all distinctions between them, as the Rabbi assumes. Next, he argues that the words show that Jesus is the Son of man, and not God. I presume that he means that if Jesus were God then an offence against Himself would be as great as that against the Holy Spirit. But this is a misinterpretation of the passage. If the Christian belief in the Incarnation is true, the passage means something very different, and is not hard to understand. Jesus is speaking of Himself as the Son of man, *i.e.*, is speaking about the human side of His existence. And He says that it is a much smaller sin to speak against Himself as man than to deny the all-powerful and holy work of God the Holy Spirit in the world, as the Pharisees had just been doing, when they refused to recognize goodness and holiness, and attributed the expulsion of demons to Satan himself. The Rabbi, like only too many controversialists, takes the passage out of its context, and makes it say what it was never intended to say.

**114**] (ii). He also quotes St. Mark xiii. 32 (parallel passage St. Matt. xxiv. 36): "Of that day or that hour knoweth no one, not even the angels in heaven, neither the Son, but the Father." The Rabbi urges that this shows, first, that the Son and the Father are not One (to which we would reply as above), and, next, that the Son is not God, because He does not know the future. Yes, we grant that Jesus says that His knowledge is limited. What of that, according to Christian doctrine? For if, as we Christians hold, Jesus was perfect man as well as perfect God, must He not, as man, have been ignorant of many things? Elsewhere in the New Testament He is said to know all things (St. John xvi. 30).* So He both knew all things, and was ignorant of some things! Yes, as God He knew all things, as man He did not. Why should not this be so, if the Christian doctrine be true? The Rabbi has failed to prove his point that this passage of the New Testament is contrary to Christian teaching. Observe further, that the Rabbi ought, surely, to have avoided quoting this passage, for in it Jesus places Himself above the angels. Who then is He? And what can that Person be who is above them? Scripture knows of no being above the angels but God Himself. The very passage that the Rabbi adduces against the Divinity of Jesus testifies to it.

**115**] (iii). R. Isaac further says that the New Testament contains no clear proof of the doctrine of the Trinity, especially in that Jesus never calls Himself God, but regards Himself as the messenger of God, and as man, and bids His disciples pray not to Himself but to the Father. But we have just seen that He implies He is God, and no Christian denies that He was God's messenger, much less that He was man. In fact the Rabbi never seems to understand that according to Christians Jesus was a true man. It is therefore useless of him to tell us that Jesus calls Himself man. Of course He did. Why should He not, if, as we Christians hold, He was man? But it is said that in the Lord's Prayer He bids His disciples pray not to Himself, but to "Our Father." Why not, according to the Christian doctrine? For we Christians usually address our prayers to the Father, pleading to be heard for the merit of Jesus Christ the Son. When he gave this prayer to His disciples He was walking among them. He did not want their hearts to be tied to the visible.

* Compare St. Matt. xi. 27, "all things have been delivered unto me of my Father: and no one knoweth the Son, save the Father; neither doth any know the Father, save the Son, and he to whomsoever the Son willeth to reveal Him."

He wanted them to look up to His Father in heaven with much more simplicity and faith. Whatever He Himself was, even if, according to the Christian belief, He was true God all the time, it was surely more natural and fitting for Him to direct their hearts to the invisible than to Himself. His claims, recorded in other passages of the New Testament, as we shall presently see, were quite sufficient to lead them to a true understanding of His own Divine nature.

**116**] (5). The Rabbi also urges the fact that there have always been among Christians opponents of the orthodox Christian doctrine of the Divinity of Jesus and the Trinity in Unity, and that in his own day there were still such opponents. Had the Rabbi lived until our time he could have said the same. But what of this? Does any orthodox Jew care for the errors of a Boethus or an Elisha ben Abuyah, or for the fancies of Moses de Leon or Sabbathai Zebi, or even for the heresy of the Baalshem? All truths have their opponents, and the fact that there is opposition to them proves absolutely nothing. There are still persons who say that the earth is flat, and there are still blind men who cannot see the sun. But the sun still shines, and the earth is round, in spite of their failure of vision or their incredulity. This last argument of the Rabbi is worthless.

**117**] (6). It would not, however, be treating those many Jews whom R. Isaac represents with that courtesy which is due to them if I did not attempt to place before them, very briefly indeed, some of the reasons why we Christians accept the doctrine of the Trinity in Unity. "In Unity," I repeat. For the Unity of God is the most fundamental of all the Christian doctrines. "Hear, O Israel, the LORD our God is one LORD" is the foundation of our Christian faith. God forbid that anything we say or believe should conflict with that. We Christians humbly believe that our faith in the Trinity is fully consistent with our faith in the Unity, yes, and is, as we shall see, a necessary deduction from it.

**118**] (i). In the first place it seems to us that the Old Testament itself requires it. I quite agree with the Rabbi that the Old Testament does not teach the doctrine of the

Trinity in so many words, and also that some of the separate texts upon which Christians have been accustomed to lean for the support of their doctrine are frail and broken reeds. Yet even these, as we have seen, fit in well with the doctrine, and there are other considerations to which I must refer. I can only refer to them shortly, and in a summary way here, for most, if not all, of them will recur at different times in our study of the Rabbi's book.

**119**] (*a*). Is not the Scriptural teaching about Angels very curious if God is the bare Monad that the Jews affirm? How is it that when the Angel of the LORD is mentioned there is often so much doubt whether the words are those of the angel in his own person, or of the angel as messenger reciting God's message, or of God Himself and not the angel? I am well aware that in each case it may be argued that the difference between God and the Angel is clearly defined, yet, notwithstanding all subtleties in refining away language, there still remains an impression upon our minds that there is something unique in the relation of the Angel of the LORD to the LORD Himself. The Angel of His Presence, as He is sometimes called, suggests to every Christian reader a strange similarity to Him who, as Christians hold, took human flesh and lived among us. In other words, the Old Testament in this particular is readily susceptible of a Christian interpretation.

**120**] (*b*). Similarly the doctrine of the divinity of Messiah, though perhaps not to be proved with mathematical certainty from isolated passages of Scripture, is, to say the least, easily to be seen in many. I refer in particular to Isa. ix. 6 (5), where he is called "Mighty God, Everlasting Father."

אל גבור אבי עד.

True that in this passage He is not distinguished from the first Person in the Trinity with the precision that belongs to Christian times. But He is described as "everlasting" and as "God." The terms are often explained away, and the passage will come before us again (parr. 195 sq.); but it is singular how easily it fits in with Christian truth. Other passages which resemble this in directness of teaching are

Jer. xxiii. 6 and Micah v. 2 (1). I grant that they cannot convince a man who is not convinced already. But they do confirm his opinion if it is already derived from elsewhere. Probably we have no right to demand more.

**121**] It is the same with regard to the divinity of the Holy Ghost. Look at Isa. lxiii. 9-14. Is it not at least remarkable that the phrases "His Holy Spirit" and "the Spirit of the LORD" are there used as equivalent, as it seems, to "the Angel of His Presence"? Is there not, in fact, a suggestion that there is something personal about the Spirit, and that He is in the truest sense Divine? Observe again, I say, that this cannot be proved mathematically. The impression that this and the other passages quoted leave upon the mind will be different in different cases. But if the Jews are right in saying that God is a bare Monad it is very strange indeed that Scripture should have used such language as would suggest, when the due time came, a plurality in the Godhead.

It cannot, however, be too often repeated that Christians do not base their belief in the doctrine of the Trinity upon the statements of the Old Testament. We say only that the Old Testament contains not a word that is opposed to this doctrine, and that its language is best satisfied if that doctrine is true. We base our belief in the doctrine of the Trinity in Unity upon other grounds.

**122**] (ii). Reason itself suggests to us such a doctrine as the Trinity in Unity. Let me here quote the eloquent words of the present Bishop of Birmingham, Dr. Gore: "The reasons which lead us to believe in God at all, lead us to think of Him as an eternal and spiritual being. Now the life of spirit, the highest life we know, is made up of the action of will and reason and love. In God then, we imagine, is a perfect and eternal life, of will and reason and love. But must not this be a life of relationships? Most surely love is only conceivable as a personal relationship of a lover and a loved. If God is eternal love, there must be an eternal object for His love. Again, the life of reason is a relationship of the subject which thinks to the object thought, and an eternally perfect mind postulates an eternal object for its contemplation. Once more, the life of will means the passage of will into effect: there is no satisfaction to will except in production; an eternally living and satisfied will postulates an eternally adequate product. Thus it is that our upward-soaring trains of thought lead us to postulate over against God in His eternal being, also an eternal expression of that being, which shall be both an object to His thought and a satisfaction to His will and a repose to His love, and this is St. John's doctrine of the Logos, the eternal expression of God's being in fellowship with Himself: 'The Word was with God, and the Word was God'" (*The Incarnation of the Son of God*, 1898, pp. 134 *sq.*).

Or consider the thoughtful words of another recent writer:

"A person is primarily and essentially a self-conscious subject; and if we are to think of God as personal, He too must be, metaphysically speaking, a subject. But a subject means a subject of experience, one who undergoes experience, or for whom experience exists, and therefore implies as his correlative an object or objects of experience. And the metaphysician is compelled to ask, what can this object be, in the case of God? For if we suppose the universe to be this object, we must either regard God as dependent for His realisation upon something which is other than Himself; and, in that case, His absoluteness vanishes; He ceases to be God: or we must view the universe as a mode of Himself, in a way that leads to Pantheism, in which personality is lost. We are driven, therefore, to the conclusion that, if there be an absolute, eternal subject, He must have a correspondingly absolute object, an eternal experience, if His proper absoluteness is to be maintained" (J. R. Illingworth, *The Doctrine of the Trinity, apologetically considered*, 1907, pp. 136 *sq.*).

**123**] (iii.) The Lord Jesus Christ, in whose every act there was no trace of sin, and in whose words no untruth has ever been detected, claimed to be Divine. R. Isaac has adduced certain passages in which He spoke of being man. Be it so. We have dealt with these already. He was undoubtedly man. But He also claimed to be God. For what did He claim? To forgive sins (Mark ii. 9, 10); to be lord even of the sabbath

(Mark ii. 28); to come hereafter in the glory of His Father (Mark viii. 38); to be the only Son of the Divine Owner of the Vineyard (Mark xii. 2—7); to be the recipient of all things from the Father, for "All things have been delivered unto Me of My Father: and no one knoweth the Son, save the Father; neither doth any know the Father, save the Son, and he to whomsoever the Son willeth to reveal Him" (Matt. xi. 27); and again, "All authority hath been given unto Me in heaven and on earth. Go ye therefore and make disciples of all the nations, baptizing them into the name of the Father, and of the Son, and of the Holy Ghost" (Matt. xxviii. 18, 19), Christ thus putting, as you will observe, Himself and the Holy Spirit on an equality with the Father. Further, the fourth Gospel is permeated through and through with His claims to Divinity, as, for example, where He says "Before Abraham was, I am" (John viii. 58), or again "I and the Father are One" (John x. 30). It is hardly possible for any one who reads the New Testament to doubt that Jesus claimed to be divine, even if he is not prepared to accept the theory that the New Testament was inspired. If he takes it up only as a book of ordinary history, the fact of Jesus' claim is clear.*

We Christians then accept the doctrine of the Divinity of Jesus, the all-important step to the doctrine of the Trinity in Unity, largely upon the evidence of the words of Jesus Himself. His character and His mental sobriety are above suspicion, and His words agree with what we have already seen to be the dictates of our Reason.

**124**] (iv). The doctrine of the Trinity in Unity contained in the Gospels is confirmed by the teaching of the rest of the New Testament. I repeat that I do not care whether or not you regard the Book as inspired. I am content if you regard it as ordinarily trustworthy. What does it tell us about the belief of those who were alive during the time that Jesus lived

* I am aware that some writers are of opinion that the words and assertions mentioned in this paragraph were only put into the mouth of Jesus by His followers and were not spoken by Him, for it is impossible (they say) that any man, even Jesus, can have made so high a claim. But this is prejudice in the strictest sense of the word, not criticism.

on earth, and wrote to their friends within, say, five and twenty, or thirty, years after His death, not a long period for any middle aged man to throw back his memory? What, above all, does St. Paul say in the earliest of his Epistles, written only some twenty-one years after the Crucifixion? "Paul, and Silvanus, and Timothy, unto the church of the Thessalonians in God the Father and the Lord Jesus Christ" are his opening words. "Ye turned unto God from idols, to serve a living and true God, and to wait for His Son from heaven, whom He raised from the dead, even Jesus," are found in the ninth and tenth verses of the first chapter. The whole Epistle is in the same strain, placing the Lord Jesus on an equality with the Father. Or look at the end of his second Epistle to the Corinthians, written some twenty-five years after the crucifixion: "The grace of our Lord Jesus Christ, and the love of God, and the communion of the Holy Ghost, be with you all." How do you account for these statements? The man who wrote them was once as strict and orthodox a Jew as any who does me the honour to read this book. Yes, he was as strict a monotheist, with a perfect hatred of anything like the worship of more than one God. Had he given up his monotheism? God forbid! But he was only one out of many Jewish believers in the Messiahship of Jesus. Did these other believers oppose and contradict his belief in the Divinity of Jesus? There is not a sign of any such opposition. He was opposed bitterly enough on other points, but, so far as our evidence goes, never on this point. All the many Jews who acknowledged Jesus as Messiah acknowledged also His Divinity. Later on, I grant, there was a sect of Jewish Christians who denied it, but there was no such denial among the early believers. These, who ought to have known Jesus best, and ought to have had the most accurate acquaintance with His teaching, were (so far as our evidence goes), firmly convinced that He was God in the highest sense, and placed Him on an equality with the Father and the Holy Spirit. It was, I fully grant, an amazing thing for Jews to believe. But they could not help themselves. The facts of Jesus' life, and the plain meaning of His words, were too clear for them to do otherwise.

We in these days who study history cannot but give weight to their opinion, backed up as it was by their readiness to endure all things out of love for Jesus, who (as they wrote) had loved them, and given Himself for them.

**125**] (v). This leads me to speak of the last reason for our faith in the doctrine of the Trinity in Unity with which I shall trouble you. It satisfies the ethical sense. This, as is apparent from history, knows nothing of a love on God's part which is able to forgive sins without an offering. Of course in the vast majority of cases the belief in the need for such an offering has taken strange forms quite unworthy of the living God, not the least strange being the common notion that something which we do can satisfy the justice of an angry God. But man's ethical sense has always required an offering of some kind. Is our ethical sense wrong? Is the opinion that, after all, God can forgive out of His own love without any punishment of sin, or satisfaction in some form, really right? Neither you nor I can think so. Love standing alone, apart from principles of righteousness and justice, seems to you and me to be unworthy of the name of Love, to be a mere invertebrate parody of the Holy God. Love and Righteousness must be inseparable. If so, an offering must be made, and since sin is in itself an eternal thing (for a man's sin is no mere breaking of a rule, independent in itself, but something affecting his whole relation to the living God), it would seem that the offering on behalf of it must be eternal also. In other words, no man can offer it. He who makes it must be the very Presence of God Himself, able to bridge over the chasm between God and man.

But if the Saviour must be Divine, then we are brought rapidly to the full doctrine of the Trinity in the one Godhead.

Thus not Reason alone, but Practical Need also, together with the study of the life and words of the Lord Jesus, and of the belief in Him held by the Apostles, together with the fact that such a doctrine fits in remarkably with the teaching of the Old Testament, lead us to accept with all our hearts the doctrine of the Trinity in Unity, and in accepting it to adore, crying "Holy, Holy, Holy, is the LORD of hosts"; "Unto Him that loveth us, and loosed us from our sins by His blood; . . . . . to be priests unto His God and Father; to Him be the glory and the dominion for ever and ever. Amen."

## ii. GEN. ii. AND iii. THE FALL AND ITS EFFECT.

### § 11.

**126**] R. Isaac is not at his best in this section. He shows indeed much learning and much acquaintance with Christian thought of a kind, and many of his details are undoubtedly right, as, for example, where he shows the folly of those Christian controversialists who identify Sheol (Hades) with Gehenna, but he does not arrange his matter clearly and his argument as a whole leaves a very confused and blurred impression. He no doubt intends to attack the Christian doctrine of Original Sin, but he states the consequences of it in their most extreme, not to say bizarre, form. For instance, knowing Christianity chiefly under the form of Roman Catholicism, he speaks of the Roman Catholic doctrine of the effect of original sin upon the Old Testament saints as though this were the doctrine of all Christians, and even then he does not state it correctly. For he says that we Christians believe that these saints went to Gehenna until Christ came and released them. But even the Romanists do not say that they went to Gehenna, but to the *Limbus Patrum*, a place between hell and purgatory. Protestants, as for example members of the Church of England, believe in no such place or state. We affirm that the Old Testament saints were saved even as we ourselves, by living faith on God, and that their salvation was procured by Christ, the effect of His death being attributed to them beforehand. Our Thirty-Nine Articles say: "Both in the

Old and New Testament everlasting life is offered to Mankind by Christ, who is the only mediator between God and Man, being both God and Man. Wherefore they are not to be heard which feign that the old Fathers did look only for transitory promises." So also St. Paul speaks of "the passing over of the sins done aforetime, in the forbearance of God" (Romans iii. 25).

The chief points in the Rabbi's argument appear to be the following.

**127**] (1). The effect of the Fall was much less than Christians think. They often argue that the words, "Thou shalt surely die" (מות תמות), Gen. ii. 17, imply death of soul as well as death of body. He answers: Not death of soul but only physical death, and probably physical trials and illnesses, if indeed the extra word מות means anything additional, and is not only a common grammatical expression. Here R. Isaac's Karaitism may be plainly seen. For if he had been a Rabbinic Jew he would hardly have hesitated to allow that the additional word must have some additional meaning. R. Akiba put his stamp on all Rabbinic exegesis far too firmly to admit of any doubt being expressed about that. But of course, as a mere matter of grammar, R. Isaac is right. In strict exegesis according to grammatical rules מות only intensifies the certainty of death.

He grants however that by Adam's action the lust of the flesh was increased in Adam and his seed (p. 92),

תאוה הבשרית אשר נתוספה באדם ובזרעו מאכילת עץ הדעת,

yet he still refuses to allow that it brought death to the soul. He says indeed (if I understand him aright) that the action as such brought death of soul to Adam and Eve, for an evil action in itself means death (p. 88); but he appeals to Ezek. xviii. 20 for his belief that a person can bring death upon his own soul only, and cannot bring it upon another. He forgets that Ezekiel's words were intended to summon to fresh courage those Jews who were becoming disheartened by the pressure of that other truth stated clearly in Scripture, viz., that God visits the sins of fathers upon their children. He forgets too that the race of men is so entirely one and united that it must share in the effect of its great progenitor's action. The solidarity of the human race is however more clearly perceived by us to-day than was the case in the Rabbi's time.

**128**] (2). He says that even before the giving of the Law it was possible to live a holy life. For Enoch, Noah, Abraham, Isaac, and Jacob, conformed to the will of God. Adam's sin, he argues, did not in any case affect them with death of soul, for Enoch "was not, for God took him." They were delivered also even from bodily sorrows, for Noah was to comfort his father from the curse laid upon the ground. Abraham too enjoyed such special privileges that he was given circumcision, whereby to diminish the lust of the flesh that had been increased, as we saw, by Adam's sin. He and other Old Testament saints were saved with an everlasting salvation by their own merit, and they did not need any other merit than their own to save their souls, as Christians imagine. But, in saying this, he forgets that these early fathers nowhere show any sign of such a thought of their own righteousness as the Rabbi here supposes, and that Moses is far from attributing it to them. Moses expressly writes, not that Abraham obeyed God and thus stored up merit for his own salvation (much less for the salvation of others also, as too many Jews think), but that Abraham "believed in the LORD; and He counted it to him for righteousness" (Gen. xv. 6). This is not Judaism, but Christianity.

Further the Rabbi urges (p. 90) that in no case can Christ's death be of any effect in removing the harm brought by the Fall, for "one sin cannot be atoned for by a greater sin, viz., the slaying of the body of their God" (הריגת גוף אלהיהם). But he forgets that the same deed may be a sin on the part of those who perform it, and a glorious act of self-sacrifice on the part of the sufferer. If it were otherwise, where would be the meritoriousness of the sufferings of the Jews themselves, according to common Jewish teaching? Their sufferings are, from one point of view, the sins of the Gentiles, though they may be the outcome of self-sacrifice on their own part. The

Rabbi can hardly have considered the meaning of his words. The sin of crucifying Jesus cannot militate against the nobility of His death (see also par. 289).

**129**] (3). While R. Isaac affirms that even before the giving of the Law men were able to live holy lives, he further claims that the effect of the Fall was altogether counteracted by the Law itself.

(i). There are commands in the Law which expressly meet the words of condemnation in Gen. ii. and iii. For example, Lev. xviii. 5 ("Ye shall therefore keep my statutes, and my judgements: which if a man do, he shall live in them") meets Gen. ii. 17 ("In the day that thou eatest thereof thou shalt surely die"). Again Lev. xxvi. 3, 4 ("If ye walk in my statutes......the land shall yield her increase") meets Gen. iii. 18 ("Thorns also and thistles shall it bring forth to thee"). For the Rabbi harps again and again on the thought that the true tree of life, of which Adam and Eve were not allowed to partake after the Fall, was restored to them in the Law, quoting for his purpose Prov. iii. 18, "She is a tree of life to them that lay hold upon her." But this is only a pretty *D'rash*, certainly not the *P'shat* of the passage, which is not speaking of the Law as such, but of the Wisdom of God revealed in all His word and work.

(ii). He even claims that St. Paul himself bears out his statement that the effect of the Fall lasted only until the Law. He quotes Romans v. 14 to prove his point. But here the Rabbi unexpectedly becomes extremely interesting. For he ventures upon the ground of Textual Criticism. There is in this passage a well known various reading. The usual text, supported by all the Greek manuscripts except three late "cursives," and by nearly all the Greek fathers, is "Death reigned from Adam until Moses, even over them that had not sinned after the likeness of Adam's transgression." But the Rabbi, following Pseudo-Ambrose, and also, though he knows it not, Origen himself (in two or three places), leaves out the word "not." He thus makes St. Paul say that Death as the effect of the Fall was only upon those who imitated Adam by expressly disobeying God; whereas the other and common reading makes him say that it was also on all who were born, apart from their committing actual sin. This last reading we must accept, for there is no reason to suppose that all the old manuscripts are wrong, and the very few and late manuscripts and Origen are right. The fact is that St. Paul feels strongly that the Law has brought death, not life, and he adds that so great was the effect of Adam's sin that even before the Law came, death reigned, even on those who might have been thought to be free from it. St. Paul, that is to say, in reality is arguing in a sense precisely the opposite to that which the Rabbi attributes to him. He is showing the terrible effect of the Fall.

**130**] (4). But I cannot leave this subject without indicating very briefly indeed why we Christians believe that the sin of Adam has affected all his descendants so deeply that they may be said to have suffered death of soul in consequence. The Jew, as we know, does not hesitate to say, in his daily morning prayer, " My God, the soul which Thou hast placed in me is pure" (T. B. *Berakoth*, 60*b* :אלהי נשמה שנתת בי טהורה),* but the cry of the Psalmist is very different : " I was shapen in iniquity, and in sin did my mother conceive me" (Ps. li. 5[7]):

בעוון חוללתי ובחטא יחמתני אמי

meaning that from his very birth, before he knew how to do wrong or right, and even before birth, he possessed an evil bias towards sin. Where then is the purity which Jews so readily claim? Surely "Unclean ! Unclean !" much more truly expresses the feelings of every man who looks at his fallen nature in the same way as did the Psalmist. Can we imagine it otherwise? Can we, who live in this age, when the awful power of heredity is so frequently brought before us, imagine that the first act of the human pair committed consciously in opposition to the will of God should not both place them out of communion with Him, and exercise an enormous influence for evil upon all their children? The Rabbi grants that the lust of the flesh was increased, and yet does not seem to

* See also Singer, *Authorised Daily Prayer Book*, p. 5, and other references in the *Jewish Encyclopedia*, xi. 473.

realise what his admission involves. It can surely mean nothing less than that every individual person born afterwards stands in an abnormal relation to God, and therefore is out of communion with Him. But to be out of communion with God is to be separated from the source of Life, and to be in death. The Christian himself says no more than this. For more cannot be said.

Whether the Law restored all who accepted it to their right relation to God is another matter. Rabbi Isaac says that it did. The Psalmist would not agree with him, for he prays, "Enter not into judgement with thy servant: for in thy sight shall no man living be justified" (Ps. cxliii. 2). The Law itself only says that those who perform it shall live by it, and no one has ever yet heard of any one who kept it perfectly, save One alone, with Whom even His enemies could find no fault.

No! The evil tendency, which implies a wrong relation to God, marks us all, and we need a miracle to be performed in each of us before that wrong relation, and that evil tendency, are overcome. The Law cannot do this. It must be the work of the Holy Spirit of God.

## iii. The Seed of the Woman.

### § 12.

Gen. iii. 15. "*And I will put enmity between thee and the woman, and between thy seed and her seed: it shall bruise thy head and thou shalt bruise his heel.*"

ואיבה אשית בינך ובין האשה ובין זרעך ובין זרעה הוא ישופך ראש ואתה תשופנו עקב׃

**131**] R. Isaac tells us that Christians believe that this verse refers to Jesus, who was to kill Satan, *i.e.*, the being who is the cause of sin. The Rabbi raises the objection that if this were so then believers in Jesus would not sin, but they confessedly do; and also that if Satan were slain he could not have caused, as he did, the deaths of Jesus and the Apostles; further, that even St. Paul says that Satan is not slain, for in Rom. xvi. 20 he writes, "The God of peace shall bruise Satan under your feet shortly," and in 1 Thess. ii. 18, "We would fain have come unto you, I Paul once and again; and Satan hindered us." It is therefore a mistaken supposition on the part of Christians that the verse means that Jesus has put Satan to death.

**132**] Now in the first place I am glad to see that Rabbi Isaac acknowledges the existence of Satan. For to-day very many Jews are far from saying this. They are too apt to suppose that Satan is a mere figment of the imagination, without any real existence. But R. Isaac takes his stand on Scripture, and he is wise in so doing.

But, secondly, the Rabbi's argument as a whole is not very impressive. The difficulties that he raises are trivial, and are rather a play upon words than sober argument. For Christians never say, never have supposed, that Satan is killed. They believe that Christ gave him his death-blow by His own death and resurrection, but did not entirely destroy him; the final "death" of Satan will take place only hereafter. They hold also, in contradiction to the Rabbi's travesty of their opinions, that if Satan bruised the heel of Jesus this was not after his own "death," but before, at the cross. Thus, too, it is evident that it is quite possible for St. Paul to speak consistently of hindrances still brought about by Satan, and also of the final "bruising" of him as lying in the future.

But the real interest of the subject lies, not in the consideration of the Rabbi's somewhat weak arguments, but in the question whether the passage refers to a personal Deliverer from Satan and his power, and whether Jesus of Nazareth is that Deliverer. Let us consider these two points. And may the Lord of His mercy give us a right judgment as we do so.

**133**] (1). What is the real meaning of Gen. iii. 15? *

(i). Some suppose that it speaks only of the perpetual

* The exact meaning of the root שׁוּף used, twice in this verse, is not of great importance for our discussion, though the commentators discuss it at some length. The usual rendering is "bruise," for which see Job ix. 17.

hatred that there is between men and snakes. That the enmity exists no one denies. Men naturally, unless their mind is perverted by some strange religious motive, or moved by an unusual love of science, kill a snake whenever they see it. We find something loathsome in snakes, and we also fear their bite. But it argues a strange ignorance of early religious thought and of the motives that led men to incorporate such an incident as that of Gen. iii. in their holy writings, to think that their aim was only to mention, or even to account for, this natural enmity. Early religion never occupied itself with material objects, no, not even with snakes, as such, but with them as representing spiritual powers behind them. Primitive man was intensely religious, but never seems to have worshipped a single stock, or stone, or animal, or star, for itself and itself alone, but as being the representative, and generally the embodiment, of some spiritual power. To see in Gen. iii. 15 a description and prophecy of the undying hatred of men for snakes, and presumably *vice versâ*, is inconsistent with our present knowledge of the religion of primitive man.

**134**] (ii). A second interpretation has much more in its favour, and may indeed be right. It is that the words tell us of a long struggle between man and temptation to sin, and of his ultimate victory, notwithstanding the damage that he receives from his awful foe. For "the poisonous serpent, with its glistening, rainbow colours, its tortuous windings, its duplicity and its bewitching gaze," * is a fitting representation of the devil, with his manifold wiles, and subtle temptations. But "as the serpent pierces with its poison-fang the heel that crushes it, so man, in spite of painful wounds, must grapple with temptation. But the struggle will end in victory. Man will plant his foot on the venomous head of the serpent, temptation, and crush it to death." †

Yet it must be observed that with this second interpretation the reference to Jesus is by no means excluded. For even if the promise is to man generally, yet it is quite possible that

* Orelli, *Old Testament Prophecy*, 1885, p. 88.

† Schultz, *Old Testament Theology*, 1892, ii. p. 345.

there may be One man who is the leader of his race in the battle, and the first and final instrument in the defeat of Satan. And in this connexion it may not be out of place to notice that it is not merely the head of the serpent's seed that is to be smitten, but the head of the serpent itself—"it shall bruise thy head." It is in accordance with this view of the matter that in this passage the Targum of Jerusalem I. (Pseudo-Jonathan) says, "When the sons of the woman keep the commandments of the Law they shall be ready to smite thee on thy head, and when they leave the commandments of the Law thou shalt be ready to smite them on their heels, but for them there shall be healing, and for thee there shall not be healing, and they (the sons of the woman) will make agreement (or "peace") in the end of the days of King Messiah":

כד יהוון בנהא דאתתא נטרין מצותא דאוריתא יהוון מכונין ומחין יתך על רישך וכד שבקין מצותא דאוריתא תהוי מתכוין ונכית יתהון בעיקביהון ברם להון יהי אסו ולך לא יהי אסו ועתידין הינון למעבד שפיותא בעקבא ביומי מלכא משיחא:*

135] (iii). Yet perhaps there is more to be said for the old Christian interpretation of the verse—that it refers directly

*The last clause is expressed more fully in the Targum of Jerusalem II. (Fragment-Targum):

ברם עתידין אנון אלין ואלין למעבד שפיותא בעקבא בסוף עקב יומיא ביומוי דמלכא משיחא:

"But they (the sons of the woman) will make agreement, one with another, in the end, in the close of the end of the days, of the days of King Messiah."

The text of both Targums is taken from Dalman, *Aramäische Dialektproben*, 1896, p. 6, based on the best manuscripts. For the meaning here assigned to שפיותא see Jastrow, *Dictionary of the Targumim, etc.*, 1903, *sub verbo;* also Dalman, *Aramäisch-neuhebräisches Handwörterbuch*, 1901. For עקבא see Levy, *Chaldäisches Wörterbuch*, 1868, and Jastrow. Observe that both the Targums play on the words תשופנו and עקב. I should add that my friend and neighbour, Mr. G. H. Box, while agreeing with the above interpretation of Targ. Jer. II., thinks that this itself is an attempt to force the older Targum Jer. I. from its proper meaning, which is: "But they (the sons of the woman) shall effect a crushing with the heel in the days of King Messiah," *i.e.*, the curse shall be annulled, the heel (no longer a vulnerable part which the serpent may bruise) shall then tread on and crush the serpent. For this translation of שפיותא see Dalman, *Aramäische Dialektproben*, 1896, and Buxtorf, *Lexicon*, 1640, col. 2493, "facere conculcationem in calcaneo in diebus regis Messiæ."

to the work of Messiah—than is sometimes thought. We must ask ourselves what meaning was attributed to it when it was written down as Holy Scripture. Many scholars say that this was in the latter part of the Exile. If this date be accepted, then it would be at a time when indisputably the doctrine of the coming of Messiah * was known and accepted by all religious Jews, and therefore readers would naturally have seen in it a promise of His coming.

But if Moses wrote down these words, the same inference would be true. Merodach was the great God of the Babylonians in the time of Abraham, and he was worshipped as the destroyer of Tiamat the great world-serpent. Now if, as is quite possible, the prophecy of Gen. iii. 15 came down to Moses through Abraham, it is at least likely that Abraham was accustomed to see in it a prophecy of One to come who should be greater than Merodach, in that He would destroy the serpent that was far greater than the legendary world-serpent, as being the principle of evil and sin in the world. Further, we may assume that, if Abraham believed this, the belief would be handed on to his descendants, including Moses. I grant indeed that it cannot be proved as yet that Abraham and his successors were influenced in this point by the Babylonian worship of Merodach, but evidence is tending that way.

If Abraham thus looked forward to a personal Messiah (compare St. John viii. 56), and if Moses shared his hope, we should indeed expect to find a trace of this doctrine of a personal Redeemer, who was to appear in the future, elsewhere in the Pentateuch. So, I venture to think, we do, notably in Gen. xlix. 10, as we shall see when we come to the consideration of that passage.

On the whole then it is quite possible that that interpretation is right which sees in Gen. iii. 15 a promise of the coming of One who shall slay the great representative of sin, while receiving in Himself slight damage of some kind.

* Whether the *word* "Messiah" was used so early to designate specifically the expected Deliverer is an entirely different thing, into the discussion of which I do not enter.

There is to be war between Satan and Messiah, but Messiah is to be victorious.

**136**] (2). We can consider only very briefly the next question, whether Jesus of Nazareth does correspond to the hope of the coming Deliverer.

(i). Every believer in Jesus says so, whatever his interpretation of this verse may be. His experience, and the experience of all true believers in Jesus, is that He has not only set the sinner free from guilt, but also is daily giving him a good measure of success against the power of sin. He does not say that Jesus has set him free from the power of sin altogether. That is not, at any rate, his actual experience, even though he is ready to confess that the power of sin over him would be greatly diminished if he placed his affection wholly on Jesus, and trusted Him more completely with his daily life. But the believer has found so much already in Jesus that he is quite prepared to trust Him for the future and to expect that the complete deliverance from sin, the complete subjugation of Satan, will certainly take place at the last day, in accordance with the promises contained in the New Testament.

(ii). For the death and life of Jesus do correspond strangely with the words of our passage. Jesus was bruised in His heel, figuratively speaking, when He was put to death upon the Cross, and knew in some very awful sense (far beyond the comprehension of people like ourselves, who have been accustomed to the presence of sin within us) the power of sin to separate from His Father. But He rose triumphant from the grave, thus giving a fatal blow to Death, and to sin, the sting of death. R. Isaac no doubt would reply that he did not believe that Jesus rose from the dead. This is another question, and indeed, if the Jewish denial of Jesus' resurrection were true, Jesus would not fulfil the idea of the Deliverer mentioned in Gen. iii. 15, for He would be bruised not in the heel, but in the head. But if Jesus never rose we Christians would not think it worth while to discuss Christianity with the Rabbi at all. For Christianity without the resurrection of Jesus is not Christianity in the historical sense of the word.

Christianity as it has existed for nineteen hundred years is based on the resurrection of Jesus. We shall be quite prepared to discuss later the subject of Jesus' resurrection. But, according to the testimony of believers from the very earliest times, Jesus, the Christian Jesus, by His death and resurrection won the battle over death, and sin, and the devil, for Himself and for all who believe on Him, although the complete victory, when sin shall have lost all power, and death have yielded up its captives, and the devil have been destroyed, will take place in the future, at the Return of Messiah in glory. Jesus of Nazareth, we believe, does correspond to the promise of Gen. iii. 15.

### iv. The seed of Abraham, and the blessings through it.

§ 13. Part ii. § 90.

Gen. xxii. 18. "*And in thy seed shall all the nations of the earth be blessed; because thou hast obeyed my voice.*"

והתברכו בזרעך כל גויי הארץ עקב אשר שמעת בקלי.

**137**] R. Isaac begins this section by saying that Christians see in this passage a reference not to any of the seed of Abraham, but to Jesus only, for He is the most important part of the seed of Abraham. In Jesus alone therefore is the promise fulfilled, and by Him alone are all nations blessed, because by Him they come to the knowledge of God, and to their soul's salvation.

The Rabbi replies to this argument by saying that Christians always disregard the context in their arguments from prophecy, and accordingly do so here. For the preceding verse shows that God was thinking of the whole race of Abraham, and not of any particular person in it. Further, as the Rabbi states at length, the promise was repeated to Isaac and Jacob, showing that as Abraham, Isaac and Jacob were themselves the means of winning some Gentiles to the true knowledge of God, so would their descendants be. Indeed, Scripture frequently says that only through the people of Israel shall Gentiles come to know God, and in fact individual Gentiles have thus come to know Him.

It is hard to realize to-day the intellectual state of many of the Christians with whom R. Isaac held his discussions. Their simplicity must have been great, their ignorance greater. But surely R. Isaac, as a reader of books, ought to have arrived at a truer conception of what learned Christians believed. The only reason that suggests itself for his treatment of the subject is that he wrote his book for Jews who mixed with unlearned Christians, and that he wished to arm them against all possible objections and misbeliefs.

Let us consider, first, the true meaning and fulfilment of the passage, and, secondly, the alleged Christian explanation that it refers to Jesus only.

**138**] (1). The meaning of the verse and its fulfilment. We may fully accept the Rabbi's argument that the word "seed" refers to the seed of Abraham generally. There is nothing in the verse or the context to suggest anything else. The verse means, that is to say, that the Gentiles are to be blessed, or bless themselves (the exact translation is of no importance for our present purpose), in the seed of Abraham, *i.e.*, in the nation that sprang from Abraham.

But at this point, and not before, Jewish and Christian scholars differ.

**139**] (i). R. Isaac and other Jewish scholars say that the Gentiles are blessed in Jews as Jews are at present, *i.e.*, in Jews as anti-Christians; in Jews, whether Karaites, as R. Isaac, or in Talmudic Jews as the bulk of Jews, or even in Reform Jews; in Jews as the upholders of what we mean to-day by Judaism, whatever precise form that may now take. The Rabbi, in other words, insists on the present mission of Judaism (to put his language into modern terms), that "mission of Israel" which provides so much material for oratory and seems to have so little power for work. For, speaking candidly, the so-called mission of Israel has very little to show for itself. Jews, as Jews, are doing almost nothing to spread the knowledge of the true God among the Gentiles.

It cannot be affirmed too often, or too strongly, that Jews are worthy of all admiration for their perseverance, their temperance, and, in the majority of cases, their faithfulness to their creed. But, just as it is not their religion which is the cause of anti-semitism, but their success in business and their ostentation, so also it is not their religion which influences Gentiles for good, but certain qualities of their character. Jews are always saying that the Gentiles are, and are to be, blessed in and by Judaism. We can only reply that we can see no traces of this blessing as yet, and cannot find any reason either in Scripture, or in the probabilities of the case, to expect it in the future.

**140**] (ii). Yet the Gentile world owes all to Jews. This we acknowledge gladly. Gentiles have accepted the God of the Jews and the Book of the Jews, and profess to have accepted also the spiritual side of the religion of the Jews. Prophecy, that is to say, is already being fulfilled; Gentiles are already being blessed in large numbers in and by the Jews. But the Jews who have brought this blessing are those few Jews who were born about the first year of the Christian era. Gentiles have been led to a faith in the true God not by anti-Christian, but by Christian, Jews. They have, it is true, become blessed in the seed of Abraham, but it has been through the efforts and assistance of those members of the seed of Abraham who themselves believed on Christ, not of those who have systematically opposed Him. We do not attempt to deny that God's words to Abraham have had, and are having, a glorious fulfilment, but the fulfilment is to be seen in the way in which the great truths given to the Jews in the Old Testament have been made known to the Gentiles by the Founder of Christianity and His disciples. It is Judaism as seen in the Christian Church, not Judaism as seen in the Jewish synagogue, through which the Gentile world has come to know God, and to bless itself in the seed of Abraham.

**141**] (2). It is however alleged that Christians understand the verse to refer only to Jesus, and to be fulfilled only in Him. What R. Isaac no doubt means is that St. Paul seems to say so in Gal. iii. 16: "Now to Abraham were the promises spoken, and to his seed. He saith not, And to seeds, as of many; but as of one, And to thy seed, which is Christ." In Part II. § 90 the Rabbi deals with this passage, and, by saying that the Hebrew word for seed (וזרע) is used in the singular to express descendants or progeny as a whole, thinks he has entirely vanquished St. Paul.

**142**] What a convenient thing it is to be a Karaite! One can then so easily ignore the ways of Rabbinism, *i.e.*, the methods of using Scripture that are adopted by the greater part of learned Jews. I say unhesitatingly that, in spite of all that has been said above, St. Paul's language is quite defensible from the standpoint of Jewish learning, and quite intelligible if we only grant that St. Paul was a learned Jew.

For example, suppose a friend asked you to consider the full force of the word דמי (literally "bloods") in Gen. iv. 10, saying that the plural certainly had a special meaning, either Abel's own blood and that of his descendants, or Abel's blood dashed on the trees and on the stones. Would you tell him that דמי ("bloods") is regularly used in Hebrew to express blood shed by violence, and that his argument of a special meaning in Gen. iv. 10 is absurd, and only due to ignorance of the Hebrew language and of Jewish learning? He would reply that it was not his own argument at all, but that of the Mishna in *Sanhedrin* iv. 5 (=T. B. *Sanhedrin* 37*a*), and that the author of the Mishna might be credited with a knowledge of Hebrew, and with the ability to quote the Old Testament in a Jewish way. Or again, your friend might turn to Deut. xxv. 2 and argue that certain lessons were to be learned from רשעה ("wickedness") standing there in the singular and not in the plural. Would you reply with a sneer that this word is always found in the singular, and that therefore it is unscholarly, and the mark only of an ignoramus, to argue that it has a special meaning there? Most assuredly you would not, for, if you had any spark of Hebrew learning, you would know that such an argument derived from the use of the singular is thoroughly Jewish, and that this example is taken from T. B. *Kethuboth* 37*a*. No one supposes that the scholars of the Mishna or the Gemara thought that these were the literal and simple meanings of דמי ("blood") or רשעה ("wickedness") in those passages. They only saw in the use of these terms further meanings, not altogether unintentional on God's part.* So also with St. Paul. He knew as well as any of us what was the literal and simple meaning of Gen. xxii. 18, but he wished to call attention to the fact that God has not caused a plural word to be recorded, as for example בנים ("children"), but זרע ("seed"). He means that there is something in the selection of a word used only in the singular (*i.e.*, of human progeny) which, speaking midrashically, not only excludes Ishmael but even suggests that all Abraham's descendants may be summed up in one Person, even the Messiah, in whom all are to be blessed.

It is, of course, an argument that does not appeal to us who live in this twentieth century of universal knowledge, but it was, as we have seen, just such an argument as learned Jews were fond of using, and it did appeal to Jews if they were learned; nay, it does appeal to Jews even to-day if they are learned only with strictly Jewish learning, and have not received the benefits of western culture. It is, to put it briefly, not a *P'shat*, but a *D'rash*, and must be treated as such.

We however content ourselves with the *P'shat*, the literal meaning, however much we may admire the ingenuity of Rabbinically trained Jews like the authors of the Mishna and of the Gemara, and St. Paul. To say that "seed" in Gen. xxii. 18 refers to Jesus is a pretty *D'rash*, but no Christian scholar believes it to be more.

**143**] The literal meaning of the passage is sufficient. But we say also that history tells that the promise of Gen. xxii. 18 has been fulfilled in Jesus to a degree incomparably outweighing its fulfilment in any other way; and that through the Lord Jesus masses of Gentiles (not merely individuals here and there)

* See Surenhusius, *Biblos Catallages*, pp. 85 sq.

have been brought to the knowledge of the one true God. We claim therefore that, as a historical fact, Jesus alone has brought about the fulfilment of the verse, and that Jesus alone is so far the fulfilment of the whole expectation of the Old Testament that through Him, and Him alone, the Gentiles are being brought to God. In a word, the Old Testament belongs now more to Christians, Gentile and Jewish, than to Jews.

## V. Shiloh.

### § 14.

Gen. xlix. 10. "*The sceptre shall not depart from Judah, nor the ruler's staff from between his feet, until Shiloh come; and unto him shall the obedience of the peoples be.*"

לא יסור שבט מיהודה ומחקק מבין רגליו עד כי יבא שילה ולו יקהת עמים:

**144**] A very famous passage, frequently adduced by Christians in controversy with Jews, although it is hard to see why so much stress should have been laid upon it by either side. The cause is probably that controversialists are apt to read more into passages than legitimately may be found there, or else to deny the real contents of a passage if these are against them. But may both writer and readers of these pages be always kept from forcing the Word of God to mean either less or more than it properly does mean.*

In the short space at our disposal we shall not attempt to follow the Rabbi's arguments step by step. It would be impossible to do so, without making a very much longer study

* For the various interpretations of this verse see the elaborate monograph by Adolf Posnanski, *Schiloh, ein Beitrag zur Geschichte der Messiaslehre*, Erster Teil, die Auslegung von Genesis xlix. 10 im Altertume bis zu Ende des Mittelalters, Leipzig, 1904.

of the subject than is here possible. The more so, as, after giving the opinions of other Rabbis as if they were right, he ends with stating what are really his own. To these last we shall return. Now we consider the passage itself.

**145**] (1). Observe that the general meaning of it is to show the superiority of the tribe of Judah, by means of its ruler, over the other tribes, and, as it seems (though this is not so certain), over other peoples. For doubtless the strange word יקהת, found elsewhere only in Prov. xxx. 17, really means "obedience," in accordance both with Hebrew tradition, and the cognate roots in Arabic and Assyrian. Further, the verse says that this succession of rulers is never to fail until the great ruler appears. For I assume that the words שבט and מחקק are parallel expressions, and I cannot see that it is of any importance for our present purpose whether מחקק be translated "ruler" or "ruler's staff."

The verse seems to say plainly that a great ruler is to come, and that until he is come Judah shall be supreme. There may be, nay, there are, differences of opinion about details, but with very few, not (I confess) unimportant, exceptions (see below), Jews and Christians alike agree in this general interpretation of the verse. They differ as to who this ruler is.

**146**] But, before going any further, one common Christian argument must be ruled out of court. The Rabbi, of course, so rules it, and we have no hesitation in saying that he is right. It is impossible to lay such stress on "until" as to say that it precludes the superiority of Judah after the Ruler has come. Also, it is impossible to prove historically that Judah was superior until the coming of Christ, and then ceased to have superiority. No doubt it is true that the nation of the Jews ceased to have a local habitation soon after His coming, but Jews have not perished, and, above all, the superiority of the tribe of Judah has not ceased. From the days of David until the Exile Judah was supreme (for the Schism of the Northern Kingdom was but an interlude), and after the Exile it was the tribe of Judah into which the other tribes were merged, and which carried on the succession. It has been the same from the destruction of the second temple onwards; the Jews of to-day are, to all intents and purposes, the tribe of Judah. Of a truth, whether we are Jewish or Christian expositors, we must confess that the prophecy has had a wonderful fulfilment; Judah has proved to be superior to all his brethren.

**147**] (2). What, however, is the exact meaning of "Shiloh?"

(i). We all know that some writers, among them two Christian scholars, whom all of us, whether Jews or Christians, reverence both for their Jewish learning and their deep love for the Jews, Professor Franz Delitzsch and Professor Strack, believe that the right translation is "until he come to Shiloh," *i.e.*, Judah is to be supreme until Canaan is taken by the twelve tribes. Delitzsch's words are: "Jacob promises to Judah the leadership of the tribes of his people as an inalienable right, won through his lion-like courage, until, on his coming to Shiloh, his dominion of the tribes should be enlarged to a dominion over the world" (*Messianic Prophecies in Historical Succession*, 1891, § 9.). In this case Shiloh will have been chosen for mention because it became the spot where the tabernacle was set up. But we have extremely little evidence that Judah took at all a prominent place so early as that; and it is quite certain that for the greater part of the time of the Judges it was far in the background, not in the front, or it could not have been passed over in the Song of Deborah.

**148**] (ii). I shall now, therefore, assume that "Shiloh" has some direct reference to the Ruler. This, and this alone, is in accordance with Jewish tradition, even though that tradition differs as to the way in which the reference is made.

(*a*). Onkelos translates "until Messiah comes, whose is the kingdom."

עד דייתי משיחא דדיליה היא מלכותא.

The Targum of Jerusalem II. (Fragment-Targum), "until the time when the King Messiah comes, to whom the kingdom belongeth."

עד זמן דייתי מלכא משיחא דדידיה היא מלכותא.

The Targum of Jerusalem I. (Pseudo-Jonathan) translates

"until the time when the King Messiah, the youngest of his sons, shall come."

עד זמן די ייתי מלכא משיחא זעיר בנוי.

So too in a list of names given to Messiah in T.B. *Sanhedrin* 98*b*, the school of R. Shelah, a Rabbi of the third century, says, "Shiloh is his name, as it is said, Until Shiloh come."

דבי רבי שילא אמרי שילה שמו שנאמר עד כי יבא שילה.

**149**] (*b*). But how do they get the meaning of Messiah from the word itself? The key is probably to be found in Ezek. xxi. 27 (*Heb.* xxi. 32), "Until he come whose right it is."

עד בא אשר לו המשפט.

So in fact some of the manuscripts of the Septuagint translate our verse, *ἕως ἂν ἔλθῃ ᾧ ἀπόκειται*; while others read "Until that which is his shall come," *ἕως ἂν ἔλθῃ τὰ ἀποκείμενα αὐτῷ*, meaning, apparently, that Judah shall be supreme until he gets that which really belongs to him. In either case the relative is expressed by ש and לה stands for לו. Probably Ezekiel referred directly to our passage, and understood it to mean that Judah should be supreme until He should come to whom all rightly belongs, and that to Him should "the obedience of the peoples be."

**150**] (*c*). R. Isaac, however, gives another explanation. He follows Kimchi, and, as we have seen, the Targum of Pseudo-Jonathan, in connecting "Shiloh" with שליה, Deut. xxviii. 57, understanding it to mean "the youngest son." He then says, first, that it refers to David, the youngest of the sons of Jesse, and afterwards that it refers to Messiah Himself, "who shall arise from David's seed in the end of the days." This explanation is very improbable, but that is of no matter for our present purpose. What is really important is that R. Isaac, like nearly all Jewish scholars, sees in the word a direct reference to Messiah, not indeed as His title, but as descriptive in some way of His position or His work. This is what I said at the beginning, that Jews and Christians alike are agreed, with very few exceptions, that the passage refers to the coming of a great Ruler, whom, for the sake of brevity, we may call the Messiah.

**151**] (3). The only dispute is whether Jesus is the Messiah, the Shiloh, or whether we must look for another. It resolves itself, in other words, into the great question, which in reality this text does nothing to solve, whether Messiah has or has not come. We Christians do not say that He has come because we think that this text says that He has. Our reasons are quite independent of it. There is one fact with which men must reckon. A Person of the line of David has appeared, to whom peoples are obedient in a most extraordinary degree. Is He not Messiah?

But we strongly urge all our readers not to be satisfied with discussing the prophecies of the Old Testament. Read the life and history of Jesus of Nazareth for yourselves. See what sort of a person He was. Then, when you have read all that you can about Him in the New Testament (for nowhere else is there more than the merest trace of tradition, so that everything outside the New Testament is practically worthless for learning of Him), then, I say, turn back to your Old Testament, and see if its words do not wonderfully confirm the portraiture of Jesus. Learn to know Jesus, first, as He is described in the New Testament, and then you will have no difficulty in seeing Him portrayed also in the Writings, the Prophets, and the Law itself.

## vi. The Dietary Laws. Deut. xiv. 3, 4, and elsewhere.

§§ 15, 49, 50, Part II. § 72.

**152**] Christians, as we all know, claim liberty to eat and drink whatever they like. They are restricted only by considerations of health, or of effect on others, or of self-discipline. To this liberty of ours R. Isaac of Troki raises several objections.

(1). In the course of his argument he mentions one which is so important that, if it is granted, there is no need of further discussion, viz., that if a command is plainly given in the Law no subsequent statement, for example in the Gospels, can overthrow it. But, notwithstanding its importance, it is not an objection to which all Jews would give their assent. At least in the past all Jews have not assented to it. For some have acknowledged that when Messiah comes He will give a new Law. "The Law which man learns in this world is vanity compared with the Law of Messiah" (*Midrash Qoheleth* on Eccles. xi. 8).

תורה שאדם למד בעוה"ז הבל היא לפני תורתו של משיח.

So also *Midrash Tehillim* on Psalm cxlvi. 7, says: "'The LORD looseth the prisoners' or 'the forbidden.' What is this? Some say that every beast which was made unclean in this world the LORD, blessed be He, makes clean in the world to come."

מתיר אסורים מהו מתיר אסורים יש אומרים כל הבהמה שנטמאת בעולם הזה מטהר אותה הקב"ה לעתיד לבוא.

Therefore the idea of alteration of the Law is not contradictory to the fundamental belief of strict Jews. If Messiah and His times have come, then change in the Law may be expected. Thus the objection really becomes the primary question whether or not Jesus is the Messiah.

**153**] (2). Another argument urged by the Rabbi is more curious than profound. It is that God forbade certain foods to the Israelites because His people were too precious to eat such common and low things as were allowed to Gentiles. For it is said in Lev. xi. 8, "they are unclean unto you," *i.e.*, to you only (טמאים הם לכם). So that, he proceeds to argue, if these things are allowed to Christians, it is because Christians are inferior to Jews. Well, well, let the Rabbi have his joke; a saving sense of humour lightens up many a weary page. But the Rabbi can hardly have intended his words to be taken seriously in view of the appeals in the New Testament to Christians to live holy lives, and the way in which they are told that except their righteousness exceeds that of the leading religionists among the Jews they will in no case enter into the kingdom of heaven (Matt. v. 20). God, speaking through Jesus Christ, expects greater holiness from Christians than ever He demanded of Jews through Moses.

**154**] (3). The Rabbi spends some little time in attacking our Lord's saying recorded in Matt. xv. 11 (parallel passage Mark vii. 15): "Not that which entereth into the mouth defileth the man; but that which proceedeth out of the mouth, this defileth the man."* He asserts that the statement is altogether mistaken. For unclean food does defile the body, and not the body alone, but also the soul. For Scripture says: "Neither shall ye defile yourselves," literally "your souls" (Lev. xi. 44).

לא תטמאו את נפשתיכם.

But do these words bear out what the Rabbi implies? Can food as such really defile? Is it not the fact that God saw everything which He had made, and behold it was very good? And can a very good thing in itself defile? Yet, "lest ye defile your souls!" Yes, nothing is easier. For if a man breaks the commandment of God in order to please himself he most certainly defiles his soul, and even his whole personality, for this term better expresses the meaning of the Hebrew. However good a food may be in itself, it may not be partaken of with impunity, if God has forbidden it. Christian teaching fully accepts this, and goes indeed even further than this, when it says that "He that doubteth is condemned if he eat, because he eateth not of faith; and whatsoever is not of faith is sin" (Rom. xiv. 23). But this, we Christians hold, takes us into a sphere of ethical morality much higher than that from which the Rabbi draws his weapons.†

* Observe the right reading, and translation, of Mark vii. 19, "*This he said*, making all meats clean" (R.V.).

† R. Isaac uses one argument here and in Part II. § 18, which seems hardly worth mentioning, but is still used even by intelligent Jews. It is to the effect that our Lord's saying: "Not that which entereth into the mouth defileth the man," is contradicted by the fact that too much strong drink will do this, as in the case of Noah and Lot. But such an argument rests on forgetfulness of the occasion of our Lord's words. He was showing the error of insisting on ceremonial washing, and of the scrupulous care taken to prevent the eating of certain foods.

**155**] Suppose however that God were so to order the affairs of this world that the reasons for which He forbade certain foods (and surely He must have had reasons for doing so, whether they are discoverable by us or not) ceased to be; that there were such alterations in the conditions and circumstances of His followers as to make such prohibitions no longer necessary, or in some cases render their observation impossible; may we not then consider that the prohibitions have been abrogated by the providence of God? What kind of reasons come under consideration? Maimonides in his *Moreh Nebukim*, iii. 48, asks why God gave these prohibitions. He answers that all, or nearly all, of the forbidden foods are unhealthy, and also that other rules were probably due to the fact that the things forbidden formed part of some heathen cultus; and investigators of our own day have added very largely to the examples that he gives of this kind of reason. He also points out that in any case the discipline of self-denial was most valuable in forming the character of the Israelitish nation. Do all these reasons hold good now? In so far as the forbidden foods are unhealthy no one wants to eat them. But all connexion of them with heathen rites has long ago ceased, just as Christians of the Anglo-Saxon race no longer need to have horse-flesh forbidden as food on the ground that, as horses are sacred to Odin, the chief god of Scandinavian mythology, the eating of them is a participation in heathenism. There is to-day no danger of either Jew or Gentile being drawn back into heathenism by eating any of the animals forbidden in the Law. Lastly, as regards abstinence from them being a means of discipline, we surely ought to have learned after all these years that materials upon which to discipline ourselves surround us on all sides. The discipline of abstinence from food may be needed for some natures, but hardly belongs to that higher state of spiritual life to which Christians as such are called. Even if there are, as undoubtedly there are,

The childish questions of whether lawful foods could be eaten to excess, and whether greediness in food was sinful and produced evil effects, were not before Him. Every thoughtful and unbiassed person knows what He would have said in reply to these.

survivals of this insistence upon abstinence from food still remaining in the customs and regulations of the Christian Church, these do not pretend to justify themselves upon commands expressed in the New Testament, but are to be regarded as the advice of those who have found them helpful to their own souls. Fasting in Lent, for example, is not actually binding upon the Christian, however useful experience shows it to be in many cases. Self-discipline indeed is binding during Lent and always, for only through it can we maintain communion with God, but it has no necessary connexion with abstinence from food.

**156**] (4). There is no occasion to do more than mention the reference of the Rabbi to Zech. ix. 7, a passage which in reality only says that in the time to come heathen sacrificial feasts shall cease, but which is forced by him to mean that Gentiles shall cease to eat unclean foods.

**157**] (5). Naturally however R. Isaac makes much of the letter of the Apostolic Council held in A.D. 49 at Jerusalem, recorded in Acts xv. It will be remembered that the Christian Church was then agitated by the demand that Gentile converts should be compelled to be circumcised, and to keep the Law. Some of the many Jewish believers in Jesus (for there were many) urged it. They could not bear the idea of Gentiles coming in to receive equal privileges with themselves unless they first became Jews, by being circumcised and living under the claims of the Jewish Law. But the Council decided absolutely against these Pharisaic Christians, and said so in a letter that they sent forth. Yet at the end of it they said that the Gentile Christians should, because of the Jews, keep themselves from four specified things, meats offered to idols, fornication, things strangled, and blood.

The passage is difficult; I fully acknowledge it. Yet there are some considerations which must not be overlooked, for they certainly modify the *primâ facie* view of the matter.

The whole tone of the letter is to set the Gentile converts free, without requiring them to be bound by the Law. It would be strange if, after all, the Council laid upon them a binding regulation, which should half undo their declaration of Christian liberty. Probably therefore they never intended their statement to be a command binding upon their readers. That this view of the matter is right, appears not only from a consideration of the letter generally, but also from St. Paul's position. He had had to fight hard at the Council for his converts, fearing lest, as he puts it, they should be brought into bondage. Yet he cordially accepted the letter. Also, writing to the Corinthians some eight years later, he insists very strongly on Christian liberty as regards foods: "Whatsoever is sold in the shambles, eat, asking no question for conscience sake; for the earth is the Lord's, and the fulness thereof. If one of them that believe not biddeth you to a feast, and ye are disposed to go; whatsoever is set before you, eat, asking no question for conscience sake" (1 Cor. x. 25—27). Here St. Paul leaves it open to a Christian to eat, if he likes, things that may have been offered to idols, and things strangled, and even flesh containing blood. It seems impossible that he should have written like this if he had understood the Council to mean that their letter was binding on believers with the force of a law.

**158**] Above all it must be remembered that the items mentioned in that letter of the Council are not derived from the Law of Moses as such. They are earlier. They therefore cannot supply an argument for the observance of the Law, to which in fact the Rabbi wishes to bring us. "These four precepts" writes Dr. Hort, perhaps the most learned of recent English theologians, "were meant as concrete indications of pure and true religion, not of Judaism in the exclusive sense. There was a real risk that Gentile converts admitted freely into full communion without having to submit to a painful and in many eyes disgraceful rite, as Jewish proselytes had, might misinterpret and misuse their liberty...... There was much to be said for laying this emphatic stress on certain well-chosen abstinences or restraints held to have a close connexion with purity of religion, and they were none the worse for being coincident with hallowed Jewish laws or traditions, though this was not the source of their authority. It was a clear gain that their agreement with the inherited moral associations of Jews should make the whole arrangement more acceptable to the Jewish party in the Church, since they were not of a nature to suggest any kind of obligation on Gentile converts to obey any part of the Mosaic Law. They were no doubt biblical, but they were of pre-Mosaic origin." *

**159**] Thus the regulations of Acts xv. 20, 29 were advisory, not compulsory, and were given, no doubt, in view of the immediate circumstances of those for whom they were first written, not for Christians of every time and every place. Hence they were not contrary to the words of the Master, when He affirmed that it is not what enters into the mouth that in itself defiles, but the evil thoughts and plans and words that come out of it. We are right in our claim to freedom from the bondage of the Dietary Laws.

## vii. THE LAW: ITS DEMANDS AND ITS PERMANENCE.

**160**] The Law (and the Old Testament generally) does not limit its doctrine of rewards and punishments to the body and to this life. R. Isaac's arguments in § 18 are quite sound, considered as a whole. Would that all Jews and Christians were as free from Sadducaic tendencies as he!

### *a.* ITS DEMANDS GENERALLY. § 16.

Deut. xxvii. 26, "*Cursed is he that confirmeth not the words of this law to do them.*"

ארור אשר לֹא יקים את דברי התורה הזאת לעשות אותם:

Gal. iii. 10, "*For as many as are of the works of the law are under a curse: for it is written, Cursed is every one which continueth not in all things that are written in the book of the law, to do them.*"

* *Judaistic Christianity*, 1894, p. 71.

**161**] (1). In the verses that precede this passage from Deuteronomy various sins, some open, others secret, have been named, and after each the people have been told to say "Amen" to the curse pronounced. Here Moses sums up all these and any other enactments, whether positive or negative, contained in either Deuteronomy or the whole Law, and says that if a man does not give effect to each so as to fulfil it, he is cursed. It is self-understood that only such commandments are included as are presented to him to observe. R. Isaac, that is to say, is of course right in presupposing that those laws, for example, which can be performed only in the land of Palestine are not expected of Jews who live elsewhere, and that these are therefore not to be considered "cursed" because they do not perform them. It is also, of course, self-understood that repentance of any transgression of these laws may lead to the abolition of the curse, though, as we have already seen in par. 125, there is no reason to think that repentance possesses in itself any real remedy against the curse. Thus the verse means that the Law if disobeyed brings a curse on him who disobeys it.

R. Isaac, however, puts a gloss upon this statement. He urges that no man is perfect, and that every man sins sometimes, and that therefore the verse cannot be meant absolutely; that in reality it means that if a man does not purpose keeping a certain law, then, and only then, he is cursed (unless he repent), and the Rabbi strains the Hebrew to make it fit in with his gloss. But in vain. For the word translated "confirmeth" (קום in the Hiphil) nowhere means "to purpose keeping," but, when employed in a metaphorical sense at all suitable to this passage, "to carry out," "to give effect to," a word or command or promise; compare Gen. xxvi. 3, Lev. xxvi. 9, 1 Sam. xv. 11, 13.

St. Paul therefore, in the passage quoted above, rightly takes the passage in its simple and plain meaning (legitimately adding "all" from Deut. vi. 25, xxviii. 1), and he argues from it that every one who has failed lies under a curse, whether he be Jew or Gentile (see below).

**162**] (2). How are we to account for the grave difference between the two interpretations of the passage, that of the Rabbi, and that of St. Paul? It is due to the way in which each regards the Law. It is not, as has been argued, that R. Isaac has a high, and St. Paul a low, conception of it. It is not, again, that St. Paul thinks that the Law was given in anger, and the Rabbi thinks that it was given in love. The difference lies deeper. The Rabbi regards the Law as a collection of separate items, St. Paul regards it as a whole. The Rabbi thinks that a man is saved by his performance of a number of individual laws, and, if this opinion is right, then indeed his gloss upon our passage in Deuteronomy is necessarily right also. But if the Law is to be regarded as St. Paul regards it, not as a collection of laws, whether ceremonial or moral, but as a whole, as a revelation of God to man, and a revelation of what God expects man to be (so that even though a man is only a Gentile he does, when he knows the Law, incur the responsibility of knowing it), then St. Paul's interpretation is not too strong. The Law by the vastness and depth of its vision of God, and by the awfulness of the claim that it makes on man, brings every man under failure to keep it, and therefore under the curse that attaches to that failure.

**163**] This explains that attitude of St. Paul to the Law which Jewish writers find so extraordinary. He claims (the claim is allowed by all) to have been trained in the best Rabbinical learning of his time, and yet he regards the Law in a way that is as far distant from the Rabbinical way of regarding it as pole is from pole. For the Rabbis, as Jewish writers are never tired of telling us (though the fact is patent to every one who has read any of the Talmudic or the Rabbinical writings), rejoiced not only in the Law as such, but also in each new law which they could discover to be contained in the Law, and in each opportunity of observing any law that came before them. For by keeping it there was an increase of merit. "Therefore it was," says R. Isaac in this section (p. 109), "that Moses our Teacher was desiring and longing to enter into the Holy Land, that by means of keeping the commands which could only be kept there he should attain to a higher position in the world to come."

ולזה היה מרע"ה כוסף ותואב להכנס לארץ כדי שע"י קיום המצות התלוית בארץ יזכה למעלה יותר גדולה בעה"ב.

"'The more the merrier,'" writes Mr. Claude Montefiore, "is the Rabbinic attitude towards the number of legal enactments. Because God loved Israel, therefore He gave them so many commands. From a lower point of view these commands were the means by which the Jew could earn reward—the reward of the future life. From the higher point of view they were the ornaments of Israel, his crown of glory, his links of union and communion with the God who gave them." *

A still later writer, Dr. Moritz Güdemann, of Vienna, after quoting some remarkable ancient and modern examples of this joy even in the accidental observance of an enactment in the Law, continues as follows: "What to the superficial critic appears as fear of offending against the Law, as busying oneself with minutiæ, as a belittling of the religious spirit, or as a legalistic treatment of religion, for such is the representation in Christian writings—this, when looked at in a right light, is rather a deep plunge of love into the word of God, which brings up thence ever new pearls, by which to be sure, the subtlety of one's thought enhances the joy of the Mitzvah." †

**164**] St. Paul on the contrary says that the Law brought him death! "I was alive apart from the law once: but when the commandment came, sin revived, and I died" (Rom. vii. 9). While the Rabbis look at the Law as a bundle of laws by which to acquire merit, St. Paul looks at it as the one great

* *Jewish Quarterly Review*, Jan., 1901, pp. 189, sq.

† "Was dem oberflächlich Urteilenden als Furcht, gegen das Gesetz zu verstossen, als eine Beschäftigung mit Minutien, als eine Verkleinerung des religiösen Gedankens, oder als eine juristische Behandlung der Religion erscheint, wie man dies in christlichen Darstellungen ausgedrückt findet, das ist in richtiger Beleuchtung vielmehr die liebevolle Versenkung in das Gotteswort, die immer neue Perlen daraus hervorholt, wobei denn allerdings der Scharfsinn die Freude an der Mizwa noch erhöht" (*Jüdische Apologetik*, 1906, p. 193).

demand made upon him, as the one great revelation of holiness required from him by God, and through it he is convinced of sin. He speaks in the spirit of the Psalmists, when they say: "If thou, LORD, shouldest mark iniquities, O Lord, who shall stand?" (cxxx. 3); "And enter not into judgement with thy servant; for in thy sight shall no man living be justified" (cxliii. 2).

**165**] It may, however, be urged that God has no right to expect such holiness from us sinners. But may it not be the case that He wants to bring home to us the fact that we are sinners; and that He desires to reveal to us more of the extent of our moral weakness than we usually perceive; that He wishes to disclose to our shrinking eyes somewhat of the ravages made in our nature by sin, in order that by this we may be brought nearer to Himself? Most certainly the Law was given in love, as R. Isaac insists, but we contend also that it was given that we might pass through the process of self-condemnation and thus come to the enjoyment of God's love. Love was its motive, and Love its aim; but the aim could be attained only by man knowing his need of God.

Is not, in reality, St. Paul's view of the Law infinitely higher than that of R. Isaac, which represents, we fear only too truly, that of the majority of Jews to-day? The Rabbi lowers the Law by bringing it down to meet the possibilities of present human nature. St. Paul exalts the Law and makes it honourable, in order that through it man may be humbled, and may exalt God and look to Him and His grace alone. This, and nothing less, is what St. Paul means when he writes, "I through the law died unto the law, that I might live unto God" (Gal. ii. 19). The effect of the Law is to humble us in the dust, and to make us flee to the God whom the Law reveals, for there is none other than He.

### *b.* SABBATH OR SUNDAY.

### § 19.

**166**] R. Isaac speaks of the Sabbath as one of the details in which Christians do not keep the Law, and it is convenient to deal with this one question here before passing on to the wider subject of this chapter in the *Chizzuk Emunah*, the permanence of the Law generally.

(1). He says that Jesus kept the Sabbath. Certainly He did. But the Rabbi might have added that He did not keep it in the manner in which the more religious Jews of His day kept it. In fact He directly set His followers free from the painful observance of it, defending them when they plucked ears of corn as they passed through a corn-field on a Sabbath, and rubbed them in their hands and ate them (Mark ii. 23—28). On Sabbath too He healed the man with the withered hand (Mark iii. 1—5), and also a woman who had been bent double for eighteen years (Luke xiii. 10—17). He said on one or other of these occasions that it is lawful to do kind actions on the Sabbath, that man is superior to the Sabbath, and that the Son of Man is lord of it.

**167**] I know full well that modern writers claim that these words of Jesus were but echoes of older Rabbinic sayings. If so it is strange indeed that the Rabbis of His time evidently did not think so, and were enraged with Him both for what He said and for what He did. Besides, the Rabbis into whose mouth these utterances upon the Sabbath are put by the compilers of the Mishna and the Talmudic writings lived some time after Jesus (*e.g.* R. Simeon b. Menasya, c. 180 A.D., quoted in the Mechilta on Ex. xxxi. 13), and it is therefore more in accordance with historical probability that they borrowed from Him than He from sources of which we know nothing.

**168**] (2). The Rabbi also says that the Lord's Disciples

observed the Sabbath. No doubt they did, for they attended the synagogue services on a sabbath in the different towns which they visited (Acts xiii. 14 and often). But the point is that they also observed the first day of the week, the day we call the Lord's day or Sunday. Take for example Rev. i. 10, written probably about 90 A.D., but perhaps as early as about 65 A.D., where the author says: "I was in the Spirit on the Lord's day." *

Again, in Acts xx. 7, of an event that took place about 56 A.D., the author writes: "Upon the first day of the week, when we were gathered together to break bread, &c.," a hint that the first day of the week was specially observed for religious observances. And in 1 Corinthians xvi. 2, written a year or so earlier, say in 55 A.D., we find St. Paul giving the direction: "Upon the first day of the week let each one of you lay by him in store, as he may prosper, that no collections be made when I come." This suggests a certain solemnity, to say the least, about the first day in the week, making it suitable for so religious an act as setting aside money for the Lord's people.

**169**] (3). Thus for a time, as it seems, both Sabbath and Sunday were observed, especially by Jewish Christians. But it may be doubted whether Gentile Christians ever observed the Sabbath as a day of special devotion. It must be remembered that they as heathen had not been accustomed to have any fixed day in the week as a day of rest. It is therefore probable that on first becoming Christians they could not, even if they wished to do so, set aside either Sabbath or Sunday for this purpose. But there was nothing to prevent their regarding one day in the week as especially suitable for assembling for prayers and other religious observances, and the day which they did so observe appears to have been not Sabbath but Sunday. Thus we read in the Didaché (? 110 A.D.): "Being gathered together on the Lord's day of the

* It is just possible that by "the Lord's day" is here meant the great day of the Lord's appearing hereafter, with which some of the visions in the Revelation are certainly concerned. But the nearly contemporary use of the term (see further on in the text) makes the reference to Sunday almost certain.

Lord, break bread and observe the Holy Communion, confessing beforehand your sins, that your offering may be pure." *

So Ignatius writes at about the same time, "No longer keeping the Sabbath, but living according to the Lord's Day, in which too our life sprang up by Him and His death." †

So also Dionysius, Bishop of Corinth, writing about 175 A.D. says, "To-day, therefore, we spent the Lord's holy day." ‡

And the Talmud itself implies that very soon after this, say about 200 A.D., the first day of the week was recognized as the special day held sacred by Christians. §

**170**] It is thus plain that by the end of the second century, and without any express rule or law having been laid down either by the Apostles or by any secular power, Christians observed Sunday and had gradually ceased to observe Sabbath. The laws of Constantine (321 A.D.) ordering rest from work upon Sunday, and of the Emperor Leo 469 A.D., extending this rest to all forms of work, were only the natural result of the religious observance of the day, when persons came into power who were able to make such laws for a Christian State.

**171**] (4). How came it about that so much honour was paid to the first day of the week? It was evidently considered to be a more important day than the Sabbath. For the claim of the Sabbath was so strong that only a still stronger claim on the part of the Sunday could displace it. Why was this? There can be only one answer. Christians believed that something had happened upon it which was of overwhelming

* *κατὰ κυριακὴν δὲ κυρίου συναχθέντες κλάσατε ἄρτον καὶ εὐχαριστήσατε, προεξομολογησάμενοι τὰ παραπτώματα ὑμῶν, ὅπως καθαρὰ ἡ θυσία ὑμῶν ᾖ* (§ 14).

† Ad Magnes. ix. *μηκέτι σαββατίζοντες, ἀλλὰ κατὰ κυριακὴν ζῶντες, ἐν ᾗ καὶ ἡ ζωὴ ἡμῶν ἀνέτειλεν δι' αὐτοῦ καὶ τοῦ θανάτου αὐτοῦ.*

‡ *τὴν σήμερον οὖν κυριακὴν ἁγίαν ἡμέραν διηγάγομεν*, quoted by Eusebius, *Church History*, iv. 23.

§ See Deutsch's learned notes on Aboda Zara 6*a*. and 7*b*. in his edition of the *Chizzuk Emunah*, 1873, p. 386.

importance. Why should it be called the Lord's day, and consecrated especially to Him, unless something had occurred to make it ever memorable in connexion with Him? In other words, those early Christians observed it for the same reason for which we observe it now, that on it they believed that Jesus rose from the dead. Christians were convinced the Lord Jesus Christ rose upon that day; they were determined to observe the day at all costs, even if its observance did displace that of the Sabbath.

**172**] (5). Here, however, comes the question—How could they, nevertheless, think of neglecting the command of the Law to keep the Sabbath? This is the wider question of this chapter in the *Chizzuk Emunah*, to which we now turn.

### *c.* THE PERMANENCE OF THE LAW.

§ 19 continued, § 49 & Part II. § 10.

**173**] R. Isaac and all other Jews are amazed that we Christians do not observe the Law of Moses. Why do we not observe it, or rather, why do we not observe the laws contained in it?

(1). Briefly, because Christianity is the very opposite, the very antithesis, of laws; because to Christians the Law is abolished as a collection of laws, and this in all its parts, ceremonial and moral alike, in so far as they are laws. This will seem strange to many Jews. They will suppose, for example, that the reason why we do not steal is because the eighth commandment says, "Thou shalt not steal." But it is not so. The reason why we do not steal is not because we are told not to do so, but because stealing is contrary to the character of God, and to the first principle of love to God and man. In the same way all laws as such in the Law, including those commanding the observance of the sabbath, are swept away for those who believe in Christ. Hence we Christians do not acknowledge that the Law of Moses is binding upon us in any of its parts considered as laws.

**174**] (2). R. Isaac however has many objections to bring forward.

(i). Jesus said that He came to establish the Law (Matt. v. 17, 18). Of course He did, in its true character and aim. Jesus would have been no true Prophet of God if He had done otherwise. For it must not be supposed for a moment that His work was only negative. Not only did His words lay the axe at the root of the dietary laws (Mark vii. 14-19, see par. 154), and also free men from over-scrupulous observance of the Sabbath (see par. 166), but He brought out higher meanings in the Law than had ever been perceived before, both in His Sermon on the Mount (Matt. v.) and in His other teaching, as, for example, in His parable of the Good Samaritan (Luke x. 25—37). He thus "glorified the Law and made it honourable" beyond what had ever before been done. This He did, it will be observed, without adding to it, as the Talmud in the true text of *Sabbath* 116*b* affirms He said: "Not to take from the Law of Moses am I come, but to add to the Law of Moses am I come."* His object, in other words, was not to set the Law aside, much less to ignore it, but to establish it in its full and true meaning; as Bishop Martensen writes: "How can He say that not a tittle shall pass from the Law, since the development of the Church shows that the ceremonial law, that the whole Mosaic dispensation, has been annihilated by the influences proceeding from Christ? We answer: He has fulfilled the Law, whilst He has released it from the temporary forms in which its eternal validity was confined; He has unfolded its spiritual essence, its inward perfection. Not even a tittle of the ceremonial law has passed away, if we regard the Mosaic Law as a whole; for the ideas which form its

* אנא לא למיפחת מן אורייתא דמשה אתיתי אלא לאוספי על אורייתא דמשה אתיתי.

So in the Munich MS., though the common text of the later printed editions reads "nor" (ולא) instead of "but" (אלא).

basis, as the distinction between the unclean and the clean, are confirmed by Christ, and contained in the law of holiness which He teaches men" (*Christian Ethics: General*, § 125).

**175**] (ii). St. Paul, says the Rabbi, often urged his converts to keep certain of the laws of Moses. No doubt. But to keep them as laws because they were parts of the Law of Moses? Assuredly not. St. Paul realized to the full that Christian people are expected to be the holiest men and women upon earth, and therefore he could not but urge them to be holy in word and deed, and remind them that those who walked in the sins of the heathen, which were contrary to the known will of God as expressed in the Old Testament, had no share in the kingdom of heaven. A great teacher of morals like St. Paul could not fail to urge his converts to keep those great expressions of the will of God in which the laws of morality are conveniently summed up.

**176**] (iii). But, says the Rabbi again, the Law itself states that it is permanent, and is to be obeyed by all Jews and all who have joined themselves to the Jews, as Christians have. Here, too, I might satisfy myself with replying that Christ Himself taught the permanence of the Law, in the true sense of "permanence," as I have already done. But there is more to be said.

**177**] (*a*). Can it be that the Rabbi, a Karaite, was having a sly hit at Rabbinism when he speaks of the permanence of the Law? In any case it is certain that he must often have felt sore at the way in which Rabbinic Jews treated the Law. For they have never found the Law of Moses, in the sense in which R. Isaac used the term, sufficient for them. To R. Isaac the Oral Law was an abomination, tending, as it did, to supplement, and even explain away, the written Law which alone he accepted. He, as a Karaite, clung to the letter of the Law, and would never, for example, have admitted that interpretation of Qorban, by which money dedicated only in form to God became free from use for one's own parents, an interpretation scathingly rebuked by Jesus. Nor surely could he, as a Karaite, have allowed the Prosbul, by which the collection of debts over a Sabbatical Year was permitted in spite of the plain utterance of the written law on the subject (Deut. xv. 1—3). The fact is that Rabbinic Jews have altered the Mosaic Law immensely. I am not blaming them; I am only pointing out that it is only by exceeding subtlety that many of the practices of Rabbinic, and therefore of most modern, Jews, can be brought within the four corners of the written Torah. Rabbinic Jews have no right to complain if some go further than they in following not the letter of the Law of Moses, but its spirit.

**178**] (*b*). The passages quoted by the Rabbi were doubtless necessary for the time when they were written. It would have been disastrous to true religion if the Jews had cast off the shell of ceremonies, and the legal habit, before something better had been presented to them. But the end and object of the revelation of God is to make men holier and better, more like Himself, and there are signs that even the writers of the Old Testament looked forward to a time when the externals of Judaism should be of quite secondary importance. Consider the words of Jeremiah (iii. 16, 17), "In those days, saith the LORD, they shall say no more, The ark of the covenant of the LORD; neither shall it come to mind: neither shall they remember it; neither shall they visit it; neither shall that be done (or made) any more. At that time they shall call Jerusalem the throne of the LORD; and all the nations shall be gathered unto it, to the name of the LORD, to Jerusalem."

בימים ההמה נאם יהוה לא יאמרו עוד ארון ברית יהוה ולא יעלה על לב ולא יזכרו בו ולא יפקדו ולא יעשה עוד: בעת ההיא יקראו לירושלם כסא יהוה ונקוו אליה כל הגוים לשם יהוה לירושלם.

Jeremiah seems to contemplate a time when religion will be a heart-religion, independent of ceremonies and laws. This Christianity is. When accepted in the heart (not otherwise) it becomes a new law, but a law of wholly different kind from that of precepts and separate rules. (See further parr. 222-231 sq).

**179**] (iv). For thus we come to a fourth objection adduced by the Rabbi. He quotes triumphantly a saying of a Socinian that Jesus never gave a new Law. Assuredly He did not, in the sense in which the Rabbi uses the word "Law."

(*a*). The many laws of Moses press heavily. But heavier still is the moral claim of the Law of Moses as a whole. Heaviest of all is the moral claim of the life of Jesus, as a revelation of what man can be. Yes, sinners we are when tested by the laws of Moses; greater sinners when tested by the Law as a whole; greater sinners still when tested by the life of Jesus. Yet from all this pressure and weight did Jesus the Christ set us free, because by faith we are united to Him the Risen and Ascended Lord.

(*b*). Is this to destroy the Law? Is it not rather to bring it into full power and effect? St. Paul was right when he said (Rom. iii. 31), "Do we then make the law of none effect through faith? God forbid: nay, we establish the law." "The Gospel," says a writer of growing reputation, "is the power to fulfil the Law," * by the royal law of nearness to Christ and union with Him. This is the "law of Christ" mentioned by St. Paul in Gal. vi. 2; not one laid down by Him in precept upon precept, and line upon line, fit only for babes in spiritual things; but one learned in union with Him, the law of love to God and man, a law not reducible to rules in black and white, but understood by His servants, who have ventured their all—not on a Law but on a Person, and have found not even "Christianity," but Christ.

* Du Bose, *The Gospel according to St. Paul*, 1907, p. 25.

# CHAPTER IV

## A CONSIDERATION OF CERTAIN PASSAGES IN THE PROPHETS

# CHAPTER IV.

## A CONSIDERATION OF CERTAIN PASSAGES IN THE PROPHETS.

### i. THE LAW FROM ZION.

§ 20.

Is. ii. 3. "*Out of Zion shall go forth the law, and the word of the* LORD *from Jerusalem.*"

Is. li. 4. "*A law shall go forth from me.*"

**180**] R. Isaac tells us that Christians affirm that while the Law of Moses was given from Mount Sinai these passages speak of a Law being given from Mount Zion, and therefore this is a different Law from that, and was, no doubt, the Law which was given there by the Lord Jesus Christ.

**181**] (1). The Rabbi answers this rather crude argument in two ways. First, he replies that he has shewn in § 19 that no second Law was to be expected. We have already investigated his statement, and shewn how much truth, mixed with no little error, there is in it. Secondly, he explains these two passages in Isaiah. He says that they do not speak of another Law, but of one and the same Law, and that they mean that the teaching, or instruction, about the Law of Moses shall go forth from Mount Zion. He defends this by pointing out that although the word *Torah* is used, this does not always mean a Law as such, but in some cases, as, for example, in the Book of Proverbs, teaching or instruction. Thus in i. 8 we read, "My son, hear the instruction of thy father, and forsake not the law (*torah*) of thy mother." And again in

iv. 1, 2 the writer says, "Hear, my sons, the instruction of a father, and attend to know understanding: for I give you good doctrine; forsake ye not my law (*torathi*)." Thus then the passages in Isaiah mean that teaching about the Law of Moses is to proceed forth from the centre of Judaism, Jerusalem, the hill of Zion.

Further, he says, they mean more than that. This teaching is to be brought to all peoples by means of Messiah (naturally the Rabbi is thinking of a Messiah yet to come!), for "He will teach us of His ways, and we will walk in His paths" (Isa. ii. 3). The Rabbi urges strongly that the words refer to Messiah, for there is added, "and one shall judge among the nations." He explains this by the well-known grammatical principle that when the person is not defined separately he is defined by the verb itself. Thus, for example, in Gen. xlviii. 1, "That one said" really means "That the sayer said," and in xlviii. 2, "and one told" is really "and the teller told." So here, "one shall judge" means in reality "the judge, namely, King Messiah, shall judge."

Thus the Rabbi concludes that Christians are quite wrong in deducing from these two passages in Isaiah that a new Law was to be given from Mount Zion.

**182**] (2). Let me first of all grant freely that the Rabbi has much the better of his opponents as regards the merely verbal controversy. It is indeed absurd to think that Isaiah is prophesying that another Law will go forth from Mount Zion. I have also shewn in par. 179 that Jesus never gave another Law. Nothing indeed was further from His thought. It is a conception of Christianity which could only arise in a time when the nature of the religion of the Lord Jesus was beginning to be forgotten, and overlaid with notions derived in part from Rabbinic Judaism, and in part from heathenism. Jesus never came to give a new Law. He who says that He did, weighing seriously the meaning of his words, shows his misapprehension of what Christianity is.

Yet the words of the Rabbi explain why it is that we Christians so readily adduce these passages from Isaiah in support of our holy religion. R. Isaac himself says that

Messiah, when He comes, shall, by His teaching, spread the Jewish Law among the nations of the world. This is just what we Christians affirm has been done, and is being done, by the Lord Jesus. We say that whereas Jews as such have done nothing, or next to nothing, to promulgate the Jewish Law among the Gentiles, Jesus and His followers have carried, and are carrying, it far and wide. To our minds, therefore, it is not unfitting to adduce these passages from Isaiah in support of our belief that Jesus of Nazareth is the true Messiah.

**183**] (3). It is no doubt to be expected that any Jewish reader who does me the honour to study these pages will remark that, after all, Jesus of Nazareth and His followers have not spread the Jewish Law, but Christianity. I fully grant, as I have explained on earlier pages, that Jesus did not spread the Jewish Law as a collection of precepts and rules. But can it be denied that He has spread it in its most important features? Of course we Christians go much further than this, and affirm that He has spread it in all its details, if these are regarded as having a fuller and better meaning than their merely external performance. We Christians accept fully, as I have already shewn, the saying of Jesus that He came not to destroy the Law, but to fulfil it, ensuring that not a tittle of it should perish. But I speak not now of details. Is it not the case that He has spread the Jewish Law in its chief and most essential features?

What should we all, Jews and Christians alike, say are the most important parts of the Law? Are they not these—the Unity of God, and the duty, yes, the absolute necessity, of Love to God and man? Is not the whole Law contained in these principles? Are they not the special and unique glory of the Law as found in the Old Testament, and as confirmed and taught in the New? Is not the whole of the teaching of Jesus and of the writers of the New Testament books dependent on these truths? Are they not the very substance of their message?

**184**] It is possible indeed that many Jews will reply that Christian teachers do not teach the Unity of God. I cannot believe this. All the Christian teachers whom I have ever heard, all the Christian books which I have ever read, insist upon this fundamental truth. We Christians believe that we teach the Unity of God in a far more consistent and logical way than do Jews, much more than do Mohammedans. To us the Unity of God is the truth of all others that is dear to us, and we place no man, no woman, no angel, no power, in any sense on an equality with Him. It is true, of course, that in the Unity of God we believe that there are three permanent forms and modes of being, as already explained in parr. 105-125, but this, as it seems to us, is the only logical result of belief in One Living and Loving God; and we are of opinion that this belief is not only not contrary to the teaching of the Old Testament, but is the true and proper deduction from it. In any case it is the earnest endeavour of Christians to preach the truth that there is One God, and One God only.

**185**] Similarly we insist upon the need, the absolute necessity, of Love to God and to man. I read many Jewish books and papers, and I am amazed at the ignorance that is sometimes indicated with regard to Christian teaching upon this subject. Jews sometimes seem to imagine that Christianity teaches salvation by a kind of magic. Alas, some Christians do come very near to teaching this, just as there are some Jews who think that the mere performance of circumcision practically ensures the salvation of a Jew. But thoughtful Jews and thoughtful Christians, who endeavour to understand the true meaning of the religions which they profess, know well that merely external rites are powerless, unless there is something answering to them in the heart of him who performs them, or of him on whom they are performed. The thoughtful Christian insists upon the fact that there must be a heart-relation to God, a conscious attitude of reverence and love for Him. But this brings the believer into touch with God, the living God, so that it is impossible for a man to be a true believer without acquiring some of the character of God, and feeling something of the same thoughts with which He regards men. It is, in other words, impossible for a man to love God without at the same time loving men. And the nearer we come to God the more do we love Him and those who are made in His image. For to us a man is, in a very real sense, the representation of God, and, as the saying has it, "Thou hast seen thy brother; thou hast seen thy Lord!" (Tertullian, *de orat.* 26; cf. Resch, *Agrapha*, 1889, p. 296).

Is not this the essence of the Jewish religion? Is it not also the essence of Christianity? But this is the teaching spread by Jesus the Messiah from Mount Zion. Is it not the fulfilment of the words of Isaiah the prophet?

## ii. THE VIRGIN. Isaiah vii. 14.

§§ 21, 45. Part II. § 2.

Is. vii. 14. "*Behold, a virgin shall conceive, and bear a son, and shall call his name Immanuel.*"

הנה העלמה הרה וילדת בן וקראת שמו עמנו אל׃

This famous passage has been, and is likely to be for some little time yet, the subject of much discussion between Jewish and Christian writers.

**186**] (1). It must be granted that the word translated "the Virgin" (העלמה) does not, if its etymology be considered, strictly mean "virgin," but rather, as it would appear, one sexually mature. But the etymology of a word is not decisive. The real question is: What is its usage? In this case it is impossible to show that עלמה is ever used in the Old Testament of any one not a virgin. This is the case even in Prov. xxx. 19. (דרך גבר בעלמה), and much more in Cant. vi. 8, where virgins (עלמות) are contrasted with queens and concubines. There is in fact no Hebrew word to which Jews would not have brought an objection if Christians had urged that it meant "virgin." For even if בתולה had been employed they would at once have remembered that in Gen. xxiv. 16

a further definition was required in order to ensure the meaning of "virgin," and they would certainly have quoted Joel i. 8, "Lament like a virgin girded with sackcloth for the husband of her youth" (אֱלִי כבתולה חגרת שק על בעל נעוריה׃). We may rest easy therefore in accepting the interpretation that עלמה in usage, though not in etymology, meant "virgin." It must be remembered that the "Seventy" Jewish pre-christian translators of the passage rendered it by *παρθένος*.

**187**] (2). Did Isaiah however use it here in this sense of "virgin"? Was he not thinking of his own wife (viii. 3), especially as in viii. 4 (as in vii. 16) the limit of time for the destruction of the enemies is bound up with the early age of the child? This is hardly possible, for surely it is excluded by viii. 8, where the child Immanuel of vii. 14 is addressed, and the land is said to belong to him: "Thy land, O Immanuel." As Kimchi says, this cannot apply to the son of Isaiah and his prophetess-wife.

**188**] (3). But was it possible for Isaiah to use עלמה in this passage of a virgin? Why not? His language implies that he is thinking of a coming Redeemer. But "born of a virgin"! Who ever heard of such a thing? It is probable that Isaiah had. It was, as it seems, no new idea. The Jews were not so isolated from the rest of the world as not to come in contact with the beliefs of other nations. Scripture teems with instances in which the Jews were influenced, both for evil and for good, by the religious opinions of their neighbours, and this in all ages of Israel's history. But nations round them were, it appears, expecting the coming of a Redeemer who was to be born of a virgin. "If people had known," writes Pastor A. Jeremias of Leipzig, "the circle of ideas current in the ancient East, they would never have doubted that a son of a virgin was certainly in the mind of the author of Isaiah vii." *

The evidence that he gives is indeed taken more from Egyptian sources, and from the religion of the primitive

* "Wenn man den altorientalischen Vorstellungskreis gekannt hätte, würde man nie daran gezweifelt haben, dass im Sinne des Verfassers von Jes. vii. wirklich ein Jungfrauensohn gemeint sei" (*Babylonisches im Neuen Testament, 1905, p. 47*).

Greeks, than from the Babylonians, who would have influenced Israel more than they, but there are few persons living who are better acquainted with Eastern mythology than Pastor Jeremias, and he has probably more evidence for his statement than he has actually adduced. It seems probable therefore that Isaiah, in looking forward to the coming of a Redeemer, clothed his prophecy in language taken from current beliefs, and so made these his own.

**189**] (4). But how then was it a sign to Ahaz? For in some way surely it was intended that the king should himself see the result of this prophecy. I should suppose that Isaiah's words contained a higher and a lower meaning; one, which was all that Ahaz would understand, that a girl standing by, who was as yet unmarried, should, in the ordinary course of nature, bear a son within the year. It is even possible, as some have thought, that she became the wife of Ahaz. But in any case the son who was born could not be Hezekiah, as some have rather foolishly supposed, for he was already nine years old, when his father Ahaz came to the throne. Kimchi points this out plainly enough.

That may have been what we may call the lower sense of the prophecy. But to Isaiah himself, looking forward as he did to higher things, not shrinking even from adapting the language of the current belief that the coming Redeemer would be fed on the Divine food of butter and honey*—to him, I say, the words meant far more, and implied the coming of One who should not only redeem mankind, but also be born of a virgin.

One thing is clear. We cannot limit the meaning of the words of an inspired prophet like Isaiah to the understanding of a dense unspiritual person like Ahaz. It must not be forgotten also that Micah, the contemporary of Isaiah, takes up the thought in the fifth chapter of his prophecy, and expands it still more clearly, as we shall see when we come to consider his words.

* See Gressmann, *Der Ursprung der Israelitisch-jüdischen Eschatologie*, 1905, pp 211 sq., 291.

**190**] (5). Can we wonder that the writer of the first Gospel used our passage (Matt. i. 22)? If he accepted on quite other grounds the fact that Jesus was born of a virgin, was it not only natural that he should see in that fact the fulfilment of the ancient Hope which was incorporated in the Book of Isaiah? He did not, it will be observed, take it from Gentile sources. There it was, and there it is, contained in the books sacred to every Jew. He, who believed in Jesus as the Messiah, and who knew that Jesus was, in fact, born of a virgin, did, in quoting our verse, but claim the fulfilment of the Hope, which, whatever its final sources (and God is God of the world as well as of the Jewish nation), was for him enshrined in what we call the Old Testament. The Jewish leaders and teachers in the eighth century B.C. appeared to have expected such a Redeemer. St. Matthew in the first century A.D. acclaimed the fulfilment of their expectation. Granting that the fact about Jesus was as he believed, was he not right in doing so?

**191**] (6). In Part II. § 3. R. Isaac objects that Jesus is never called by the name "Immanuel" in the New Testament. But to make an objection of this kind is surely only to trifle with the subject, in a way unworthy of a thoughtful and candid mind. Jesus is, as a matter of fact, often called Immanuel in Christian parlance, and, whether He is called by this name or not, the word ("God with us") does correspond exactly to the nature and personality of Jesus according to the evidence of the New Testament, the only evidence which we possess.

## iii. The Child in Isaiah ix. 6, 7 (*Heb.* 5, 6).

§ 21 continued.

**192**] (1). Aben Ezra says:

יש אומרים כי פלא יועץ אל גבור אבי עד הן שמות השם ושם הילד שר שלום והנכון בעיני כי כל אלה שמות הילד.

"Some say that פלא יועץ אל גבור אבי עד are the names of God, and the name of the Child is שר שלום, but the right opinion to my mind is that all are the names of the Child."

This, which also is the opinion of all modern scholars, makes it unnecessary to discuss R. Isaac's strange construction: "And He who is the Wonder-Counsellor, El-Gibbor, Father of Eternity, called the Child the Prince of Peace." For this, though found in the Targum and some well-known Rabbinic commentaries, and not absolutely impossible in itself, probably would never have occurred to any one unless he were trying to escape the pressure of Christian arguments. We shall therefore assume that all the titles are descriptive of the Child.

**193**] (2). But who is the Child?

(i). The Rabbis say, with one voice, as it seems, that he is Hezekiah, and by some little straining of the titles they make them fit in with events in his life. But it is strange that the Child should be Hezekiah, for, as we have already seen, he was nine years old already when his father Ahaz came to the throne, and our verses plainly describe joy at the birth of one yet unborn when the prophet wrote. No, the Child cannot be Hezekiah.

(ii). Who is he? Is he perhaps Zerubbabel? Poor Zerubbabel! For he is one of those convenient people of whom we know almost nothing, and to whom therefore we can attribute anything we please. But if the prophet did mean Zerubbabel his words were singularly ill chosen, for Zerubbabel did not accomplish much more than lead the first caravan of returning exiles home to Jerusalem, and play a rather dilatory part in rebuilding the Temple. There are no such incidents in his life as will warrant us in referring to him the titles descriptive of this Child.

(iii). Who then is He? Surely the Messiah. So the Targum (משיחא דשלמא יסגי עלנא ביומוהי). And so the alternative explanation of R. Isaac himself. It is the Messiah who is to be the Wonder-Counsellor, the Mighty God, the Everlasting Father, the Prince of Peace.

**194**] (3). R. Isaac however argues that if the passage refers to Messiah it cannot refer to Jesus.

(i). פלא יועץ.* How could Jesus be termed Wonder-Counsellor, when His own disciple Judas brought His counsel to nothing and betrayed Him? Truly a deep argument! It had been more just if the Rabbi had recalled the fact that Jesus knew of Judas' treachery before it took place (Matt. xxvi. 24), and had stated that Jesus therefore included even His betrayal by Judas in His far-reaching plan. If Jesus' death was necessary, as He said it was, for the accomplishment of the purpose for which He lived, it is hard to see how the fact that He was brought to His death by another shows, as the Rabbi asserts, that His plan was frustrated. See further par. 289.

**195**] (ii). אל גבור. R. Isaac says that this phrase could not be used of one slain, as Jesus was. Why not, in whatever sense the words be understood? If they mean "Mighty Hero," has not Jesus shown Himself so? Are the actions of any one else so lauded as His? Is the self-sacrifice of any hero so admired as that of Jesus? Or what if they do mean "Mighty God"? Luzzatto was so impressed with the fact that they must mean this that he twisted all the titles into one long name of Messiah descriptive of God's dealings with Him: "The Mighty God, the Everlasting Father, the Prince of Peace, counsels wondrously." But this was because Luzzatto thought "Mighty God" was too high a title for Messiah. Probably here again it was the pressure of Christian interpretation that drove him to this unnatural explanation. In any case it does not appear that any scholar of note has followed him. Rather "Mighty God" is, and, if a right translation, was intended to be, a paradox when used of the Messiah whose birth has just been mentioned. Yet if it is true of Messiah surely it may well be true of Jesus, I mean the Jesus of the New Testament, who answers most truly of all persons to such an appellation, for His whole life and

* One of the most recent and suggestive investigations into the meaning of this and the following terms is to be found in Dr. W. O. E. Oesterley's *Evolution of the Messianic Idea*, 1908, pp. 212—226.

death and triumph over death correspond to the deepest moral and ethical conceptions of what a Messiah-God would be and would do.

**196**] (iii). אבי עד. How can "Everlasting Father" be a title of Jesus, when He was slain before He had attained half the allotted span of human life? I grant freely that the argument is true enough if the Jewish opinion of Jesus is right, that He was a mere man and died as such. But it is of no weight at all against the Jesus of the New Testament, who died and rose again. Of course every one knows that for some years a wholly different translation was much in vogue: "Father of booty." But עד is used very rarely in this meaning, but often in that of "eternity," and, moreover, very few recent scholars accept an interpretation which is so contrary to the spirit of the other attributes of the Child. There can be but little doubt that it describes the protective and fatherly care exercised by the Child over the people committed to Him, and states that this care will continue for ever. A more beautiful picture of the work and character of Messiah it would be hard to find, and it sums up with extraordinary fulness the work attributed to the Jesus of the New Testament.

**197**] (iv). שר שלום. The Prince of Peace! When Jesus Himself said that He came not to send peace, but a sword! The Rabbi loves to harp on this, just as his successors do still. We have however already dealt with this rather foolish argument in parr. 14-20. Here it is enough, first, to quote that other saying of Jesus found in John xiv. 27: "Peace I leave with you; my peace I give unto you: not as the world giveth, give I unto you. Let not your heart be troubled, neither let it be fearful;" secondly, to point out that even His enemies confess that if His precepts are followed they will bring peace; thirdly, that Jesus, according to Christian teaching, brought about peace between God and the sinner. Thus the title fully suits the Jesus of the New Testament, the only Jesus whom we know.

**198**] (v). R. Isaac objects to our laying stress on the phrase לםרבה המשרה ולשלום אין קץ—"of the increase of His government and of peace there shall be no end," though it is plain how extraordinarily well this suits the Christian doctrine of Messiah, for he says that it is a hyperbolical description of the reign of an earthly king. But it is evident how hard pressed the Rabbi feels himself to be. He can take language literally enough when he chooses, as may be seen from the very next clause. For he goes on to say that "the throne of David" is not metaphorical but literal, and he pictures Messiah as sitting one day on David's material throne governing a realm of this world. Perhaps the prophet did use these words in a more literal sense than that in which Christians generally understand them, for he was obliged to use terms and thoughts current in his time; but even so they suit the Lord Jesus, who, as the great descendant of David (see parr. 8-13), has succeeded, not merely in a metaphorical but in a real sense, to David's power, increased a thousand fold.

Yes, we Christians are right in seeing in the Child of Isa. ix. the Messiah, and in believing that Jesus of Nazareth, as He is described in the New Testament, corresponds to the picture of Messiah drawn in the Child and in the titles that are given to Him.

## iv. The Servant. Isa. lii. 13—liii.*

### § 22.

**199**] Every truly Christian reader feels humbled as he reads this portion of Scripture, because he sees in it a description of his Saviour, and the cost of his redemption; almost every Jew is likely to feel lifted up, because he sees in it a description of the value of Israel to the nations of the world, and of his own sufferings as a means of peace and

* The student of Jewish interpretation of this passage will find almost complete materials in Pusey, Neubauer and Driver's *The fifty-third chapter of Isaiah according to the Jewish Interpreters.* Texts and Translations, 1876, 1877.

prosperity to Gentiles. There is thus a fundamental difference in the two interpretations of this chapter, answering to the fundamental difference that there is between Judaism and Christianity, the one a religion which magnifies human efforts, the other one which makes humiliation of soul necessary to true exaltation.

The Rabbi's arguments are of two kinds: first, those which are intended to show that the wording of the chapter is inapplicable to Jesus, and, secondly, those which are intended to show that they directly refer to the nation of Israel. We propose to consider first the former class of arguments, and secondly the latter, afterwards examining briefly the doctrine of a suffering Messiah.

**200**] (1). R. Isaac and others urge that the language of this chapter does not correspond with what we know of Jesus.

(i). God speaks throughout it of "My servant." But how can Jesus (if he is God Himself, as Christians assert) be called a servant? We reply, Why not? What Christians affirm on the strength of the New Testament is that Jesus, though very God, took also the nature of man, and as man could of course be servant.

(ii). No, replies R. Isaac, that will not do at all, because I have already shown in § 10 that according to Jesus' own words He was not God. If so, the Rabbi ought not to raise any objection to the application of the term "servant" to Him. But we do not for a moment grant the truth of his argument. For we, on the other hand, have shown in parr. 113, 114, convincingly to our own mind, that the terms employed by Jesus (to which the Rabbi refers) are quite consistent with knowledge on His part that He was God, and also with other terms used by Him which expressly claim this. The Jesus described in the New Testament, the Jesus for whom men have laid down their lives, the Jesus in whose name Christians have lived, is man in the fullest sense, as well as also God in the fullest sense.*

* A recent writer curiously misunderstands Christianity when he speaks of Christians believing in a "semi-human saviour," and can allow himself to write of the Christian doctrine of the Atonement "that one god should have died an

**201**] (iii). "He shall be exalted and lifted up, and shall be very high" (ירום ונשא וגבה מאד). This, it is urged, cannot be true of Jesus, for He was condemned to death, and died like one of the lowest of the people. Once again, the description may not suit the Rabbi's idea of what Jesus was, but confessedly it does suit the representation of Him found in the New Testament, the only one with which our discussion is concerned. For, according to this, Jesus is now indeed exalted, and is seated at the right hand of God.

**202**] (iv). "He shall see his seed" (יראה זרע). This phrase is more difficult. The Rabbi urges that זרע always means children of the flesh, not spiritual children, such as disciples and followers, and that as Jesus had no children the phrase contradicts the New Testament description of Him. Yet in Gen iii. 15, God says to the serpent: "thy seed" (וזרעך), and we have already seen in par. 133 that the verse can hardly refer to a literal serpent and its brood. It is much more likely that God's words refer to the old serpent, the Devil, and his followers, *i.e.*, that זרע is used not of natural but of spiritual offspring. Besides, may not we Christians argue fairly that the word זרע is really on a par with other words of similar import, such as בנים, בכור, ילד, which are undoubtedly used in a spiritual sense in the Bible,* and that therefore even if we cannot point to any parallel usage of this very word we may still take it so here? Further, we must not forget that post-Biblical Jewish teachers did not find that difficulty in using זרע in the spiritual sense which R. Isaac finds. R. Aqiba, for example, interprets the phrase in Eccles. xi. 6, "In the

ignominious death to appease the implacable fury of another god." We can only reply that it would be well to learn what Christianity does teach before speaking so inaccurately about it. We have never heard of any Christians who believe in a saviour who is half man and half God, nor, in modern times, of any who regard Jesus as one God appeasing the wrath of the Father, another God. To say this is a mere parody of Christianity and of the teaching of the New Testament. The Christian conception of Jesus is of One who is fully and wholly man, and yet fully and wholly God, and of His atonement as involving no manner of contradiction between what we (in our poverty of diction to express eternal truths) call the two Persons in the one Godhead.

* *e.g.* Hos. ii. 1; Jer. xxxi. 20; Ex. iv. 22.

morning sow thy seed, and in the evening withhold not thine hand," by "If thou hadst disciples in thy youth get disciples also in thy old age" (*Bereshith R.* § 61, on Gen. xxv. 1). And R. Judan b. Shalom explains the promise to Abraham, "In Isaac shall thy seed be called," by "Whosoever believes in two worlds shall be called thy seed, but whosoever does not believe in two worlds shall not be called thy seed" (*Bereshith R.* § 53 on Gen. xxi. 12). If then we find the word זרע used by post-Biblical writers in the sense of spiritual seed, and if we find that this rests on at least some firm support in the Bible, we cannot affirm that in itself the word is contradictory to what we know of Jesus, who has indeed had multitudes of sons and daughters in the faith.

**203**] (v). Connected with this is the difficulty felt by the Rabbi in the next clause: "He shall prolong his days" (יאריך ימים). It is urged, first, that this term cannot refer to Jesus as God because it would be no mark of triumph to God that He should prolong days, seeing that He necessarily lives for ever; and secondly, that if we apply it to Jesus as man, then also it does not hold good, for Jesus died at the early age of thirty-three. How then on either consideration does Jesus satisfy this promise? To the second part of the objection it may fairly be answered that what is here said of the Servant is expressly placed by the prophet after, and not before, His death. He is said in the eighth and ninth verses to have been put to death, and this tenth verse says that if He offers atonement with His own life He shall prolong His days and see seed. The Servant is described as living after death and prolonging His days. Is there any contradiction here to the New Testament picture of Jesus?

If we turn to the first part of the objection; that if the term "He shall prolong his days" is applied to Jesus as God it becomes meaningless, we see that this also rests upon a misunderstanding of Christian teaching. Jesus, according to us Christians, is not merely God as such, but God who has become incarnate and has thus placed Himself in some sense under the limitations of time and space. As such, as God incarnate, He can receive the reward of His self-sacrifice by obtaining in a special sense length of days, not being overcome by the mortal combat to which He subjected Himself, but triumphing over it, and prolonging His days as God incarnate for ever and ever. R. Isaac does not understand the meaning of the Christian doctrine of the Incarnation.

**204**] (vi). "Therefore will I divide him a portion with the great, and He shall divide the spoil with the strong."

לכן אחלק לו ברבים ואת עצומים יחלק שלל.

How does this suit Jesus? Who are "the great" and "the strong"? Let the Rabbi himself supply the answer. For later in this section he says that "the great" are the prophets. If so, Jesus may assuredly take His place among them, for no prophet has had so many followers as He. "The strong" too, he says, are the nations. But according to the New Testament, the only authority on Jesus whom we can recognize, it is precisely the nations who in the time to come will carry their wealth into His kingdom (Rev. xxi. 26), sharing, as it were, their spoil with Him.

**205**] (vii). Lastly, there are the words, "He......made intercessions for the transgressors" (ולפשעים יפגיע).

The Rabbi asks: to whom, when He was Himself God? Once more I repeat that, at any rate, this forms no contradiction to the New Testament, the point which we are now considering. Jesus is pictured there again and again as praying to His Father in heaven, and interceding for men. For as the Incarnate One He can pray to His Father in heaven for everything He needs. Nay, more than that, the truly Christian idea of Jesus is that of one who never exercises His divine power for Himself, but rather lives day by day, both physically and spiritually, as one who is dependent on His Father. This may seem strange to a Jew, and no doubt it does, but it is clear that he may not turn round and argue that because the Servant in Isa lii., liii. prays to God he is therefore acting unlike Jesus. The Jew would do well to face the question of the extraordinarily close correspondence between the language of the prophet and the description of Jesus given in the New Testament.

**206**] (2). R. Isaac and others urge that this chapter refers directly to the Nation of Israel. This indeed was the reply given so far back as the time of Origen in the third century by a Jew with whom he conversed,* and it is certainly made to-day by ninety-nine Jews out of every hundred. This is not surprising. Not only is it a very easy solution of the difficulties surrounding the existence of the Jewish nation, but it falls in with the self-complacency, which, latent in every man, is developed in none more strongly than in a Jew. He never fails to reckon himself the object of the Lord's favour, and to expect that God will work great things through his means.

There are too some arguments for it derived from the passage itself which are attractive at first sight.

**207**] (i). Appeal is made to the very forms of some of the words. In the eighth verse we read: "For the transgression of my people was he stricken" (מפשע עמי נגע למו). It is said that למו is really a plural form, and should therefore be translated "were *they* stricken"; or that, at the very least, the servant is not to be regarded as a single individual, but rather as containing within himself several units; that, in fact, although the servant is spoken of in the singular throughout the chapter, yet here the true thought of the Prophet is seen, for he cannot help using a term that implies plurality.

So it is said, but the fact that in Phoenician, which is almost identical with Hebrew, the suffix for the third person singular ends in ם makes the argument doubtful. Besides, we find in the Bible, and even in the very part of it containing our chapter (the second half of the Book of Isaiah) a passage (Isa. xliv. 15) where the word occurs in the singular: "he maketh it a graven image, and falleth down thereto" (ויסגד למו).

**208**] (ii). But it is further urged that even though there be nothing decisive in the chapter itself, when considered by itself, the phrase "the Servant of the LORD" has already been used several times in this Book to designate the nation,

* *c. Celsum*, i. 55. I cannot recall another example for several centuries.

and that therefore it must be used here in the same sense.

I grant that in many places the phrase "My Servant" refers to the nation, *e.g.*, xli. 8, 9. But in some places this is not the case. Consider xlii. 1—6, where the Servant is said to be "for a covenant of the people," as well as "for a light of the Gentiles," and xlix. 5—8, where the Servant is plainly distinguished from the nation of Israel whom He is to raise up and restore, and to whom He is to be made "a covenant of the people." The nation cannot be said to be its own covenant.

**209**] (iii). How are the Sufferings explained by Jews who understand the chapter to refer to the Nation, or even to a part of the Nation, the true Israel?

That all Jewish writers emphasize the importance of these sufferings goes without saying. Yet only comparatively few writers allow themselves to accept the full meaning of the Prophet's language. Most whittle away the force of his words, and refuse to give the full weight to the sufferings that these describe. Let me speak first of the few and then turn to the many.

(*a*). Aben Ezra says that the sufferings mean that "the sins which the Gentiles ought to have borne Israel has borne" * And Rashi says, "Israel has been chastised in order that all the nations should be atoned for by Israel's chastisements." † It will be observed that in these quotations there is at least this fact recognized, that the sufferings endured by the Servant of the LORD are described by the Prophet as vicarious. But Scripture nowhere else mentions such a doctrine with regard to the sufferings of Israel. Its language is rather that of Amos, when he writes: "You only have I known of all the families of the earth: therefore I will visit upon you all your iniquities" (Am. iii. 2).

**210**] (*b*). Most Jewish teachers however do not consider the sufferings as strictly vicarious, but regard them in much

* on *v.* 12, בעבור צערם היה שלום לכל הגוים והחטא שהיו ראויים הם לשאתו היה ישראל נושאו.

† on *v.* 4, מיוסר היה ביסורין להיות כל האומות מתכפרות בייסוריהן של ישראל.

the same manner as Christians regard the sufferings of St. Paul, necessary means whereby he was able to accomplish his task of preaching the knowledge of God to others. "To enable Israel," says Deutsch, "to accomplish its mission, the Infinite Wisdom found it good to scatter it in the whole world, and to let it suffer there. It is just in suffering that Israel takes courage, and holds fast to God and His teaching. The nations, in whose midst it suffers, are through it becoming acquainted with the true knowledge of God and the teaching of Revelation, and turn to these ever more and more. Consequently, strictly speaking, Israel suffers only through and for the sins of the Gentiles, namely, to make them free from sin in order to be able to bring them true salvation and healing from delusion and error......*vv.* 4, 5 mean that Israel must suffer because we Gentiles are sinners, in order to fulfil his mission with reference to us." *

As we read such remarks do we not feel that, however truly they may express some of the terms of this chapter, if these stood alone, yet they come very far short of the intention expressed by its language as a whole? It is all very well to say the Prophet means only to speak of suffering endured in the process of bringing God's message to a world, or even to the ungodly of one's own nation, but the terms are far too strong for us to water them down like this. Consider, for example, "Surely *our* sickness He hath *borne*, and as for *our* sins He *carried* them." For few would venture to imitate a respected Jewish writer, who translates: "Surely he hath borne griefs caused by us, and carried sorrows caused by us;" †

* Um Israel daher die Ausführung seiner Mission zu ermöglichen, fand es die Allweisheit für gut, dasselbe in alle Welt zu zerstreuen, und dort leiden zu lassen. Gerade im Leiden ermannt Israel sich, und hält fest zu Gott und seiner Lehre. Die Völker, unter denen es leidet, werden durch dasselbe mit der wahren Gotteserkenntniss und Offenbarungslehre bekannt, und wenden sich denselben immer mehr und mehr zu. Demnach genau genommen leidet Israel *durch* und *für* die Sünde der Völker, nämlich um sie sündenfrei machen, um ihnen wahres Heil und Heilung von Wahn und Irrglauben bringen zu können......*vv.* 4, 5. d.h. *er* muss leiden, weil wir Sünder sind, um seine Mission in Rücksicht auf uns erfüllen zu können (*Chizzuk Emunah*, 1873, *Anmerkungen* p. 397).

† Dr. Michael Friedländer, *The Jewish Religion*, 1891, p. 224.

a rendering which appears to be completely opposed to the plain meaning of the words, and to be merely the result of controversial exigencies.

**211**] (iv). Lastly, have we any right to attribute to the Jewish nation such meekness in the face of persecution as is here described? Dr. Kohut could bring himself to write of the Jews: "We have suffered much and murmured less; the annals of history teem with the atrocious crimes of cruel Torquemadas, but fail to reproach us with even a breath of remonstrance... We whispered sweetly of our wrongs, not imprecations of revenge, but hope-fraught hymns of glad release."* But meekness is not, and never has been, a characteristic of Jews, and they have not hesitated to call down the vengeance of God upon their enemies in their private or their public devotions. So for example in the Service for the Festival of the Dedication: "When Thou shalt have prepared a slaughter of the blaspheming foe, I will complete with song and psalm the dedication of thy altar," † and, at the end of the same piece, though omitted by Dr. Singer: "Lay bare Thy holy arm, and bring the time of salvation near. Take vengeance for the blood of Thy servants from the wicked nation." ‡

**212**] Nor do we ever see in the history of the Jewish nation that its energy in propagating the faith has brought upon it suffering. Can a single example, we ask the question in all sincerity, be shown of persecution being brought upon the Jews because of their earnestness in endeavouring to spread the knowledge of the true God? Jews, of course, have often borne martyrdom because they would not sacrifice their own faith at the bidding of so-called Christians. But it is almost impossible to find any occasions in their history since the rise of Christianity when they made even any serious endeavour to spread the knowledge of God among others. Their temper

* Dr. A. Kohut, *Discussions on Isaiah lii. 13—liii. 12.* 1893. pp. 3 sq.

† לעת תכין מטבח מצר המנבח אז אגמור בשיר מזמור חנכת המזבח.
(*Authorised Daily Prayer Book*, 1892, p. 275).

‡ חשוף זרוע קדשך וקרב קץ הישועה, נקום נקמת דם עבדיך מאומה הרשעה.
(Seder *Derek ha Chajjim*, Vienna, 1877, ii., p. 96*b*).

and purposes have been utterly different from those of the Servant of the Lord described for us here. If the Prophet intended his picture to be that of the Nation of Israel, either as a whole, or in any large part, he has certainly drawn it very badly.

I doubt not then that the Prophet in this chapter describes a personal Messiah as making atonement for others through His sufferings.

**213**] (3). A suffering Messiah! This seems to many Jews, I am well aware, a contradiction in terms. The ordinary Jewish conception of Messiah is that He is a king, triumphant in worldly power, and leading the Jewish nation on to victory over its enemies. What connexion has He with suffering?

**214**] (i). Yet Jews do connect suffering with Messiah.

(a). We all know that Messiah ben Joseph will (to quote Prof. Buttenweiser in the *Jewish Encyclopedia*, viii. pp. 511 sq.) "gather the children of Israel around him, march to Jerusalem, and there, after overcoming the hostile powers, re-establish the Temple-worship and set up his own dominion. Thereupon Armilus, according to one group of sources, or Gog and Magog, according to the other, will appear with their hosts before Jerusalem, wage war against Messiah b. Joseph, and slay him. His corpse, according to one group, will lie unburied in the streets of Jerusalem; according to the other, it will be hidden by the angels with the bodies of the Patriarchs, until Messiah b. David comes and resurrects him." Into the origin of this strange notion of a Messiah b. Joseph this is not the place to enter. It may have been connected with the fate of Barcochba in the second century. But observe that Messiah b. Joseph dies.

**215**] (b). It is not so with Messiah b. David. He does not die, but He does suffer. Even Messiah b. David does not attain His heritage without suffering. Let me quote the *Pesiqta Rabbathi* (Lector Friedmann's edition, Vienna, 1880, p. 159*b*): "'Righteous and having salvation' (Zech. ix. 9). This is Messiah, who justifies His punishment for Israel, when they laugh at Him as He sits in prison. Therefore He is called Righteous. But why 'having salvation'? Because He justifies

His punishment for them, and says to them: Are ye not all My sons? But ye shall be saved by the mercy of the Holy One, blessed be He. 'Meek and riding upon an ass.' This is Messiah. Why 'meek'? Because He endured affliction all those years in prison, and the transgressors in Israel laughed at Him ...... Through the merit of Messiah, the Holy One, blessed be He, is a shield over them, and leadeth them by a right way and redeemeth them, for it is said: 'with weeping shall they come,' &c. (Jer. xxxi. 9)." *

It is therefore plain that the connexion of Messiah with suffering is not so contradictory to Jewish teaching as is often supposed.

**216**] (ii). The reason, as may be inferred from the passage from the *Pesiqta Rabbathi*, is that Jews see a close connexion between suffering and merit. A man, they think, can win merit sufficient for his own salvation, and more than sufficient. He can have enough left over to be a benefit to others. Jews therefore are prepared to accept the statement that Messiah by His suffering can acquire enough merit for others. Hence R. Elijah de Vidas (1575 A.D.) is able even to say that Isa. liii. 5 means: "Since the Messiah bears our iniquities which produce the effect of His being bruised, it follows that whoso will not admit that the Messiah thus suffers for our iniquities, must endure and suffer for them himself." †

* צדיק ונושע הוא [זה] משיח [שמצדיק] דינו על ישראל כששחקו עליו כשיושב בבית האסורים. והוא נקרא צדיק. למה נקרא נושע. אלא שמצדיק עליהם את הדין [ואומר] להם כולכם בני הלא אתם. אלא כי תושעו כולכם ברחמיו של הקדוש ברוך הוא. עני ורוכב על חמור זה משיח. ולמה נקרא שמו עני. שנתענה כל אותם השנים בבית האסורים ושחקו עליו פושעי ישראל... בזכות של משיח הקדוש ברוך הוא [מגן עליהם ומוליכם] דרך ישרה וגואל [אותם] שנאמר בבכי יבואו וגו׳.

See also other passages in Dalman, *Der leidende und der sterbende Messias*, 1888, pp. 35—39.

† כמו שהמשיח סובל העונות שלנו עושים לו שיהא מדוכה אם כן מי שירצה שהמשיח לא יהיה מדוכה מעונותינו יסבול וידכה הוא בעצמו.

Pusey, Neubauer and Driver, Isa. liii., *Translations*, p. 386. *Texts*, p. 331. On the mistake of referring this part of Elijah de Vidas' words to the *Tanna d'Bê Elijahu* see Dalman *loc. cit.* p. 70.

**217**] (iii). The doctrine therefore of a Messiah who by His suffering procures the salvation of men is not in itself opposed to Jewish thought. And yet I venture to think that the Jewish form of it is absolutely opposed to true morality and true religion. For the Christian doctrine of a suffering Messiah is the very antithesis to it. The Jewish doctrine is that a man acquires merit by suffering, and that this merit is enough for the whole world, yet nothing can be more opposed to the teaching of the New Testament than this. It is abhorrent to the teaching of the New Testament to think that any man, whoever he is, can ever do more than it is his duty to do, and so can lay up a store of merit available for other people. If some Christians think this possible, it is because they do not weigh the words of their Holy Book, which says, "Even so ye also, when ye shall have done all the things that are commanded you, say, We are unprofitable servants; we have done that which it was our duty to do" (Luke xvii. 10).

**218**] (iv). What then is the Christian Doctrine of a suffering Messiah? Let us put aside all preconceived notions of difficulties, all prejudices either for or against Christianity. Let us ask ourselves whether self-sacrifice is not greater and nobler in proportion to the worth and the position of him who makes it. Let us go on to ask whether the highest conceivable notion of self-sacrifice is not that of the self-sacrifice of God, supposing that such a thing be possible for Him. But that it is possible would appear to be implied in the very fact that His nature is love itself. It would be strange and monstrous indeed if He had given to His creatures the possibility of doing the very noblest thing of which we can conceive, the possibility of self-sacrifice, and were Himself incapable of it. Love must from its very nature, one would suppose, be capable of sacrificing itself for the object upon which it bestows its affection. So we may with certainty affirm that the Eternal, blessed be He, can sacrifice Himself. Of the form and the way in which He would do so, if He were to do so, we, with our ignorance of the Divine nature, could not expect to be able to form any *a priori* opinion. It would be for Him, in His unfathomable wisdom and His ineffable love, to determine that.

But I would ask you to consider this: supposing that He, His very Presence, were to take human nature, and live as man, is it not probable, in the first place, that His life would be such a life as the life of Jesus of Nazareth described for us in the New Testament? Can you form a nobler conception of the life of God upon earth than the life of Jesus? And is it not probable, in the second place, that the Ideal Servant (for we cannot suppose that, if the very Presence of God took human nature, He would take any position of less moral worth than that of an ideal servant, the very culminating point of ethical superiority) would experience something like the treatment which the prophet says the Ideal Servant received? God in human nature would be treated (alas, there is no doubt about it) in much the same way as the Servant was treated in the prophecy of Isa. lii. 13—liii.

We Christians affirm that this was the case. We say that the very Presence of God did take human nature in Jesus of Nazareth, and that He was treated as Isa. liii. describes. The Section in the Book of Isaiah does not suit, as we have seen, the Nation of Israel, and does suit Jesus of Nazareth. If Jesus was indeed God we should expect that He would receive no other treatment than that which He did receive. A suffering Messiah who by His sufferings obtains salvation for men is a strictly moral and ethical conception only if He be Divine, and a Divine Messiah must suffer.

## v. Uncleanness of Heart.

### § 23.

Isa. lxiv. 6 (5). "*For we are all become as one that is unclean, and all our righteousnesses are as a polluted garment: and we all do fade as a leaf; and our iniquities, like the wind, take us away.*"

**219**] A Christian said to R. Isaac of Troki: No one is sinless; even your righteous men (much more your sinners) cannot satisfy God's requirements, as this passage shews; how therefore can you draw near to God, and obtain salvation and release from exile, seeing that you are rejected like an unclean thing?

The Rabbi replied: Yes, your premisses are true, but your conclusion false; our salvation does not depend upon ourselves, but on God's promise. He will save us from this captivity, and forgive us, for His name's sake, not our own deserts. Thus our salvation does not depend, as you suppose, upon our own righteousness.

(1). Pausing here for a moment, we grant freely that the Rabbi has the best of the argument, and confess that the Christian who discussed the matter with him, had, like many another nominal Christian, fallen into legalistic ways of looking at salvation. In fact, here the Jew is the better Christian of the two, for he gives more glory to God, having more faith in His promises.

**220**] (2). But when the Rabbi leaves his general remarks and proceeds to a detailed examination of the passage his exegesis becomes faulty. He says that the verse refers to so-called good deeds done by a man for his own glory. Yet there does not appear to be any hint of this in the passage. His interpretation of the connexion of thought may indeed be right. He finds that it is: Because we are unclean in heart therefore our deeds are imperfect. But according to him the whole passage deals with the ungodly only. To us, at any rate, the confession seems to be of wider reference, and to include all, whether godly or ungodly. If so, although the deduction drawn from it by the person with whom the Rabbi was disputing is false, yet the passage does confirm the interpretation usually current among Christians, that the righteous acts even of the godly are spiritually defective. Jews sometimes believe this in word and in heart, but most Jews, as, alas, most Christians, too often forget it.

### vi. Religion to Permeate all Life.

§ 24.

Jer. iii. 16. "*And it shall come to pass, when ye be multiplied and increased in the land, in those days, saith the* Lord, *they shall say no more, The ark of the covenant of the* Lord; *neither shall it come to mind: neither shall they remember it; neither shall they visit it; neither shall* that *be done any more.*"

**221**] The Christian argues that Jeremiah here informs us that the Law of Moses, which was laid up by the side of the ark, was to be abolished, and not to be mentioned or remembered any more.

The Rabbi replies that this interpretation is untrue for two reasons; first, even Christians acknowledge that they ought to keep the Ten Commandments, which were placed within the ark; and secondly, the true meaning of this and the following verse is that the whole of Jerusalem will be so holy that Gentiles will not come into it, much less think of visiting the Temple and the ark.

**222**] (1). It will be convenient to take the latter argument first. Here again the Rabbi's exegesis is remarkable and indefensible. For *v.* 16*b* is evidently spoken by Jews, not by Gentiles, who do not appear until *v.* 17.* He therefore puts an intolerable strain on the words when he represents them as the utterance of Gentiles, instead of being, as they are plainly, the utterance of Jews. Yet our readers will doubtless notice that whether his exegesis is right or wrong it is irrelevant to the question at issue. For Jeremiah plainly intends his language to mean that not only the Holy of Holies, or the Temple, or the Temple precincts, are holy, but all Jerusalem. Zechariah declares that the very bells of the horses shall have

* The only support that the Rabbi can find for his interpretation lies in the change from the second person to the third. But this is much too common an occurrence in Hebrew to permit any weight to be laid upon it.

inscribed upon them the words found on the High Priest's mitre, "Holy unto the LORD"; and the very "pots in the LORD'S house shall be like the bowls before the altar. Yea, every pot in Jerusalem and in Judah shall be holy unto the LORD of hosts" (xiv. 20, 21). So Jeremiah means that true religion will, one day, permeate the whole of life, and that not the Jews only, but the Gentiles also, will acknowledge this and live accordingly. His statement, that is to say, while deeply interesting and important, hardly touches the question of the permanence, or otherwise, of the Law, although it does not suggest that its observance is not of the primary importance which Jews affirm (see par. 178).

**223**] (2). As for the Rabbi's first point, about the Ten Commandments, we have already shewn in par. 173 that Christians observe them, not because they are part of the Law of Moses, but because they are of permanent validity, whether they are contained in that Law or not. On the general question of the permanence of the Law of Moses it must suffice to refer the reader to what has been said in parr. 166-179.

### vii. A SOJOURNER IN THE LAND.

§ 25.

Jer. xiv. 8. "*O thou hope of Israel, the saviour thereof in the time of trouble, why shouldest thou be as a sojourner in the land, and as a wayfaring man that turneth aside to tarry for a night?*"

**224**] The Rabbi tells us that a Christian scholar with whom he was conversing interpreted these words of the Divine Redeemer who was to appear as a stranger in the land, a prophecy which was fulfilled in Jesus!

I have no word of defence for this interpretation. R. Isaac argues perfectly rightly from this and the next verse that Jeremiah, foreseeing famine, addresses these words to the

LORD, urging that He is no stranger, but the owner of the land, and therefore will surely help. He says also, quite rightly, that the figures used imply that while a mere stranger cannot deliver another, the LORD is no stranger, but One in the midst of us; also that although even a native cannot deliver another if he himself is troubled or oppressed, the LORD is not thus; also that although even a strong man cannot deliver another if the oppressor is too strong, the LORD can never be in such a case. This chapter of the *Chizzuk Emunah* is an excellent example of the Rabbi's power of good and practical exegesis.

**225**] But how did the Christian think of such an interpretation as he puts forward? Perhaps the answer is to be found in the fact that he was a scholar, thus shewing the reality of these conversations adduced by the Rabbi. Certainly he was not a Hebrew, nor, in all probability, a Greek scholar, but if he was accustomed to read Latin commentators he might easily have met with his explanation. For it seems to be due ultimately to the translation in the Vulgate, *Exspectatio*, instead of *Spes*, *Israel*, with Jerome's comment: "We have sinned against Thee, and have done evil before Thee; we wait for Thy coming, Who savest Israel, not by its merit, but by Thy mercy......Our Christian writers think that this is said of the future dispensation of Christ, that He is to be a stranger in the land, and for a little time to use its guest-house, and as a traveller and a strong man, leaving Israel, to go to the multitude of the Gentiles......And Thy name has been invoked upon us, that we should be called Christians, therefore forsake us not, nor forget us, to whom the voices of all the prophets have sung songs of Thy future coming." *

* Tibi peccavimus, et malum coram te fecimus; tuum praestolamur adventum, qui salvas Israel, non suo merito, sed tua clementia...... Nostri de futura Christi dispensatione dici putant, quod futurus sit peregrinus in terra, et parvo tempore terrae usurus hospitio, et quasi vir pertransiens ac robustus, relicto Israel, tendat ad gentium multitudinem;...... Et nomen tuum invocatum est super nos, ut appellemur Christiani, idcirco non derelinquas nos, et ne obliviscaris nostri, quibus de futuro adventu tuo, omnium Prophetarum ora cecinerunt (Vallarsi, IV. 939 sq.). This application of the passage does not appear to have occurred to those writers who used the Septuagint. At least I can find no trace of it in Chrysostom or Theodoret. Neither, I think, does Augustine allude to it.

### viii. THE RETURN TO PALESTINE.

Jer. xvii. 4. "*And I will cause thee to serve thine enemies in the land which thou knowest not: for ye have kindled a fire in mine anger which shall burn for ever*" (§ 26).

**226**] Certain Christian scholars have argued from this verse that it is futile for the Jews to expect deliverance from the present captivity, but the Rabbi, after showing that the phrase "for ever" (עד עולם) is used in more than one sense, reminds his readers that a deliverance is clearly foretold by the Prophets. See, for example, Isa. lxvi. 20; Jer. xxx. 8; Ezek. xxxix. 28, 29. In this we agree with him, so that there is no need to discuss the question further. See parr. 86-89.

Jer. xviii. 7. "*At what instant I shall speak concerning a nation, and concerning a kingdom, to pluck up and to break down and to destroy it*" (§ 27).

**227**] Christians, it is said, argue from this and the following verses that Jews must remember that God's promises are conditional, and that therefore seeing that, in spite of all God's repeated forgiveness of them, they have sinned time after time His promises towards them no longer hold good. The Rabbi replies that of course God's promises are conditional, and that Jews never suppose anything else; but they also remember that if they turn to God in true repentance of heart, they, notwithstanding their many sins, will receive the promises, as many prophecies state. Repentance indeed, he adds, is a great root-principle, a nail on which all hangs. Further, he says, there are also many absolute promises of the return to Palestine, in which no condition is expressly mentioned.

The Rabbi's argument as a whole appears to be perfectly valid, whatever may be thought of some of the details, and therefore there is no occasion to dwell longer upon it.

### ix. Rachel Weeping.

§ 28 and Part II. § 5.

Jer. xxxi. 15. "*Thus saith the Lord: A voice is heard in Ramah, lamentation, and bitter weeping, Rachel weeping for her children; she refuseth to be comforted for her children, because they are not.*"

Matt. ii. 16-18. "*Then Herod, when he saw that he was mocked of the wise men, was exceeding wroth, and sent forth, and slew all the male children that were in Bethlehem, and in all the borders thereof, from two years old and under, according to the time which he had carefully learned of the wise men. Then was fulfilled that which was spoken by Jeremiah the prophet, saying, A voice was heard in Ramah, Weeping and great mourning, Rachel weeping for her children; And she would not be comforted, because they are not.*"

**228**] R. Isaac says that the context of the passage in the book of Jeremiah clearly shows that he did not mean to refer to the massacre of the Innocents by Herod, as Christians say on the strength of the passage in the first Gospel, but spoke of the captivity of the Ten Tribes (Ephraim, and indeed Manasseh, being sprung from Joseph who was the son of Rachel), for the context speaks of their return.

I quite agree with the Rabbi. No one in these days supposes for an instant that Jeremiah referred to the massacre of the Innocents.*

**229**] But to make this an objection to the quotation of the

* Whether Jeremiah refers solely to the Ten Tribes, or includes the Two as well, is quite irrelevant to our subject, as also the question whether he placed Rachel's tomb in the North of Jerusalem (1 Sam. x. 2), or at Bethlehem (Gen. xxxv. 19, 20, xlviii. 7). It has been suggested that the real tomb was at Bethlehem, and that the Benjamites erected a monument in memory of their ancestress upon their own land, on a spot whence the real sepulchre could be seen.

passage by St. Matthew is a mark of ignorance, if the objector be a Gentile, and of a strange forgetfulness, if the objector be a Jew.

It is, for example, amazing to find a recent Jewish writer against Christianity, in an attack which, I fully grant, contains some points worthy of consideration when he is dealing with Christian history, not only saying, "There is here not the slightest scope for the idea that Jeremiah prophesied thereby the slaying of the children at Bethlehem," but also adding, "nor is there any warrant for Matthew's use of the passage for his purpose." For what does the writer mean by "warrant?" He, as a Jew who makes great pretensions to Jewish learning, ought to know that it is impossible to read a page or two of the homiletical Midrashim without meeting quotation after quotation from the Scriptures adduced with just as little basis as regards their literal meaning as this quotation in the First Gospel. Does therefore any educated person, I mean of course educated in Jewish literature, who reads the Midrashim, say: "there is no warrant for the author's use of these passages for his purpose?" If he were to say so every Jewish scholar would reply: "The author adduces the passages, not from ignorance of their literal meaning, much less from any intention to deceive, but because they illustrate his subject, or have some moral teaching bearing upon it, or because they serve one or other of the hundred and one objects with which Jewish writers do quote Scripture." No one in his senses blames the authors of the Midrashim for quoting the Old Testament in Jewish ways.*

No one ought to dream of blaming the author of the First Gospel for doing likewise.† Rather, if he did not sometimes quote the Old Testament in this way, there would be a strong presumption that he was not a Jew by birth and upbringing.

* Mr. W. H. Lowe (whose defection from Hebrew studies one never ceases to regret) gives a striking example in his brilliant *Fragment of the Talmud Babli, Pesachim* (1879, p. 69) from the *Aboth d'Rabbi Nathan* (*ed.* Schechter p. 6): "When Adam ate the forbidden fruit he was cast out, to fulfil (לקיים) Ps. xlix. 12, 'Man abideth not in honour: he is like the beasts that perish.'"

† Especially as Rachel was, as we may say, the patron saint of Bethlehem.

Jews of all people ought to be able to recognize the Jewish mode of thought in the First Gospel, and to understand that when the author was writing a homiletical account of the life of Jesus for his fellow Jewish Christians, he would naturally use the Old Testament in the very way to which he and they had been accustomed.

If R. Isaac, a Karaite, did not remember this, yet Jews of to-day should do so. To object to St. Matthew's quotation from Jer. xxxi. 15 is, I repeat, the mark either of ignorance, pardonable in a Gentile, or of a strange forgetfulness of Jewish methods in quoting Scripture, unpardonable in a Rabbinic Jew. So far from St. Matthew's quotation being evidence against his Gospel, it is evidence in its favour, as the work of a man wholly accustomed to view the Old Testament from a Jewish standpoint. He, a Jew, accepted Jesus as the Messiah on quite other grounds, and, having done so, loved to illustrate his faith by verbal analogies in the Old Testament. He knew that his fellow Jewish believers, taught as they had been by Rabbinic methods, would understand him; he was not concerned with Gentiles, or with the frivolous objections of Sadducees in his own time and of Karaites in the future.

### x. A New Covenant.

§ 29, and Part II. § 97.

Jer. xxxi. 31. "*Behold, the days come, saith the* LORD, *that I will make a new covenant with the house of Israel, and with the house of Judah.*"

**230**] Christians, says R. Isaac, bring forward this verse as a proof-text for their faith, asserting that Jeremiah here prophesies that God will give to the people of Israel a new Law, namely, the Gospel. R. Isaac urges in reply that this is not the case, for a covenant is not the same thing as a

Law. Was not a covenant of peace given to Phinehas (Num. xxv. 12)? Yet no one supposes that he received a new Law. Did not God make a covenant with Jacob, and with Isaac, and with Abraham (Lev. xxvi. 42)? Yet no one thinks that He gave to each a separate Law. No, when God here promises to give a new covenant He means that it shall not be broken, as was the covenant made when Israel came out of Egypt, but shall be permanent, because written on men's hearts. The one Divine Law which they had long possessed shall be on their hearts and nevermore be forgotten.

**231**] (1). The Rabbi is quite right as far as he goes. Jeremiah certainly does not say that there shall be a new Law, and doubtless never imagined such a thing for a moment. Neither does the New Testament anywhere say that a new Law has been given. Christ, as has already been pointed out in par. 182, never professed to give a new Law in the sense that the books of Moses are, or contain, a Law. It is indeed well known that many Christian writers, including some of very early date, have attributed such a new Law to Christ, and have spoken of the "New Law" of Christianity in contrast to the "Old Law" of the Jews, but neither term can be found between the covers of the New Testament. Never, I repeat, in a single passage of the New Testament is the Gospel called a new Law, no, not in Heb. viii. 8, where the passage from Jer. xxxi. is quoted at length. The New Testament writers speak of a "new covenant," as does Jeremiah, and are fully aware that this is not at all the same thing as a "new Law." If Christian writers have used the term a "new Law" as applicable to Christianity, they have done so with a painful lack of precision and with disastrous effects.

For indeed, as already partly indicated by the Rabbi's words, the term "covenant" is used of more things than the inauguration of the Law at Sinai (Ex. xix. 5). It marks God's choice of Phinehas and his line for the priesthood (Num. xxv. 12, 13), and of David and his line for the kingship (2 Sam. xxiii. 5, compare vii. 15, 16, where however the word "covenant" does not actually occur). But its most emphatic and most frequent usage is of the choice of Abraham in the promise to him and his descendants (Gen. xvii. 2-21). In fact it would appear as though all the other "covenants" mentioned, including that of the Law at Sinai, were but means whereby to carry out this covenant with Abraham. Therefore was it that they were repeated, in order that God's promise to him should not fail of accomplishment. Hence if the various covenants mentioned proved to be insufficient for accomplishing the purpose that Abraham and his descendants should be blessed, and also that through them blessing should be brought to the Gentiles (Gen. xxii. 18, see this passage explained in parr. 137-143), it was only to be expected that yet another "covenant" should be given, by which this purpose should be brought about. For Jeremiah does say that God will make a new covenant.

**232**] (2). What he means by this is shown in the verses that immediately follow. He evidently does not suppose any change in the substance of the Law, but only in the manner of being able to observe it: "I will put my Law in their inward parts, and in their heart will I write it." Here we may note the threefold effect of this new covenant. First, instead of the Law being treated as something external, something which stands outside of men, and claims to be fulfilled by them, it will belong to their hearts, being written even there. But when it is there, it will, we may suppose, necessarily work its way thence into every detail of their lives. For what we love, we endeavour to copy. "I will put my Law in their inward parts, and in their heart will I write it;" and if this takes place we "shall be known and read of all men," as though we were the very epistle of God.

Secondly, there shall be a new personal relationship to God, and a knowledge of Him of a far closer kind than ever before: "I will be their God, and they shall be my people: and they shall teach no more every man his neighbour, and every man his brother, saying, Know the LORD: for they shall all know me, from the least of them unto the greatest of them, saith the LORD" (*vv.* 33, 34).

The third effect, or rather the basis upon which this

knowledge rests, is forgiveness: "for I will forgive their iniquity, and their sin will I remember no more" (*v.* 34). Thus it is not by men's actions, *i.e.*, by keeping the Law, that this knowledge of God is obtained, but by forgiveness on God's part of the sins of His people. The new Covenant, through which the Law is written on Israel's heart, begins not with our works but with God's grace, announcing the forgiveness of sins.

Is it not in this that the difference of this New Covenant from the Old really consists, that, unlike that, it starts with forgiveness of sins; that it does not suggest the possibility of sins being forgiven only after a long course of obedience to God's commands, but proclaims that from the first God will remember sins no more, so utterly are they cast behind His back? This appears from the words of Jeremiah to be God's plan of grace. Is it effective? Has it answered its purpose? Let the history of individual persons in the Christian Church supply the answer. For it is of the very essence of St. Paul's experience and teaching, that although he was a sinner he had been saved and forgiven by God, not through works, but of grace. And this have also countless multitudes of Christians found to be true.

**233**] (3). In itself then this statement by Jeremiah has nothing to do with the abrogation of the Law, much less does it affirm that God will issue a new Law. It does say that by this new Covenant the Law shall be far better observed than before.

Let a man accept God's invitation of pardon, exercising personal faith upon Him, especially upon God in His fullest revelation of Himself in Christ (if this glorious message has been brought to him), and he will receive power to keep the Law. Whether he still lays phylacteries, still eats only Kosher food, still observes minute rules about the Sabbath, still, we may even add, circumcises his children—all these things are of secondary importance. They belong, so to speak, to the machinery of acquiring godliness, and (it must be acknowledged) they are forms of machinery which again and again have proved to be hindrances rather than helps. Living union with God, especially living union with God through the knowledge of Christ, makes the Law a delight, and brings the fulfilment of God's demand for holiness infinitely nearer than under the old Covenant of the command, Do this and live.

Thus God's words through Jeremiah do not announce the coming of a new Law, but of a new principle of keeping the Law, according to which God forgives the sinner, writes the Law on his heart, brings him into a new relation to Himself, and makes Himself known to him. It is this which has been prophesied, and this which, as we Christians hold, has been fulfilled through the coming of the Lord Jesus Christ.

## xi. Holy Days.

### § 30.

**234**] R. Isaac tells us that Christians endeavour to prove from Hos. ii. 11 (13) that the observance of holy days is to cease when Messiah comes, and that as He has come it is futile for Jews to keep them now.

I have no desire to contest the Rabbi's argument that this verse has nothing to do with the time of Messiah, but refers to the lonesome days of captivity in Babylon. On the general subject why Christians do not observe Sabbath, but keep Sunday instead, it is sufficient to refer to parr. 166-172.

## xii. The righteous sold.

### § 31.

**235**] Amos ii. 6: "*They have sold the righteous for silver.*" Some Christians assert that this passage refers to Judas, who sold the Lord Jesus for thirty pieces of silver. R. Isaac on the contrary affirms that it refers to the courts of Micah's time, in which judges condemned one who was really in the right because of some small bribe which they received. He also contends in the same section against those who deny the future restoration of the Jews. Both parts of the Rabbi's argument are sound.

### xiii. The Return to Palestine.

§ 32.

**236**] Amos v. 2: "*The virgin of Israel is fallen; she shall no more rise.*" Christians, it is said, urge that this passage shows that Israel shall never arise from captivity, and that the Jews are looking in vain for their redemption from it. The Rabbi shows clearly enough that this interpretation both of this passage and of the fact itself is quite mistaken. I heartily agree with him. On the relation of the Restoration to the time of Messiah see parr. 86-98.

### xiv. Bethlehem, the birthplace of Messiah.

§ 33.

Micah v. 2 (1). "*But thou, Beth-lehem Ephrathah, which art little to be among the thousands of Judah, out of thee shall one come forth unto me that is to be ruler in Israel; whose goings forth are from of old, from everlasting.*"

ואתה בית לחם אפרתה צעיר להיות באלפי יהודה ממך לי יצא להיות מושל בישראל ומוצאתיו מקדם מימי עולם:

**237**] This was one of the very earliest passages in the Old Testament to be quoted in connexion with the Lord Jesus.

For it was adduced by the body of Jewish teachers before whom Herod the Great laid his question where Messiah should be born (Matt. ii. 6). More than thirty years had passed since Herod had murdered nearly all the Sanhedrin (in 37 or 36 B.C.), and those in power now would not be likely to refuse him information of so simple a kind as this, even though they longed for his death, and were only too well acquainted with his dread of a Messiah. Nothing too is more probable than that they would give this answer to Herod's question, for it is entirely in accord with the Rabbinic custom of insisting on the most literal, and most self-evident, meaning of a passage.

**238**] (1). R. Isaac however will have none of it. He affirms that the Prophet refers to Bethlehem, not as the birthplace of Messiah, but as the birthplace of David, the home of the family to which Messiah was to belong.

There is much to be said in favour of the Rabbi's contention. It is quite possible that this, rather than the other, was the meaning of the prophet Micah himself. But every Jew trained in Rabbinic lore will acknowledge that Scripture has a tendency to mean more than it meant even to its human writer, and will confess that the passage would be fulfilled best if the Messiah were not only to be of the stock of David, but also Himself to be born at Bethlehem.

This twofold correspondence took place in the case of the Lord Jesus. He was confessedly of Davidic lineage, for not only was Joseph a descendant of David, but Mary as well (see par. 12). Also He was born at Bethlehem. So far then, He fully satisfies the words of Micah.

**239**] (2). But the Prophet says more. First, that He is to be ruler in Israel (מושל בישראל). We have already seen in parr. 25—30 how hard a saying this is to many Jews. For R. Isaac says that Jesus never did become a ruler, and that, on the contrary, the men of His generation ruled over Him. Yet a little thought would have shown the Rabbi that a ruler is one whom men obey, and that in the whole history of Israel there has never been a person who has had so countless a multitude of subjects, Jews and Gentiles, who have obeyed him, often to the death, as the Lord Jesus. Explain it as we may, this is a simple statement of fact, and if so it cannot be denied that the prophet's words have been wonderfully, if strangely, fulfilled.

**240**] (3). Secondly, Micah says: "whose goings forth are from of old, from everlasting" (ומוצאתיו מקדם מימי עולם). What did Micah mean by this expression so strongly duplicated? Did he mean that the stock from which Messiah was to come had its origin from ancient times, even as far back as the time of David? * If so he must have had a very poor sense of what antiquity is. For not much more than three hundred years had elapsed since the birth of David at Bethlehem. If it is argued that the time counts from David onwards, to the date, perhaps very far distant, of a future Messiah, all that can be said is that this is a most unnatural method of explaining the words, and that they seem to refer plainly to time earlier, not later, than the prophet.

Yes, says someone, they certainly are to be reckoned backwards, not forwards, but they speak of David's ancestry, which went far back, through Boaz to Pharez and Judah, and thence to Jacob, Isaac and Abraham. This explanation is at least better. Yet so also went back the lineage, the known lineage, of many a man in Micah's time. The genealogies in the Books of Chronicles are amply sufficient to prove this. It seems incredible that Micah could use of the Messiah such an expression as "whose goings forth are from of old, from everlasting," if it was intended to describe an antiquity in lineage to which hundreds of others could lay claim.

Another interpretation is that the thought of a Messiah existed in the Divine mind for long ages before the appearance of Messiah. No doubt it so existed. But that does not satisfy the language here. "Goings forth" cannot mean intentions, or plans, or purposes, of going forth. It is an abuse of language to interpret the term thus. It really does look then as though the term were intended to mean that Messiah Himself existed for ages before He appeared.

* Both מקדם (Neh. xii. 46), and ימי עולם (Am. ix. 11), can in themselves refer to David's time. The combination of the two terms is found here only.

**241**] (4). To this the Rabbi replies that, as we Christians affirm that Messiah is God, then if this term "goings forth" refers to His pre-existence, this implies that God has a beginning. Why so? Surely the term "goings forth" does not necessarily involve the conception of beginning. The sun "goes forth" (Gen. xix. 23; השמש יצא) morning by morning, but it does not begin to be each morning. So with Messiah. The term says nothing about the commencement of His existence, but says that He comes forth, and has come forth, "from old, from everlasting." * With this the Christian doctrine of Messiah exactly corresponds. For the Christian doctrine is that there never was a period, time, or moment when He was not God. God the Father never existed without God the Son, any more than God the Son existed without God the Father.

**242**] (5). We need not discuss at length the rest of the Rabbi's arguments. For he is not content with discussing this verse on its own merits. He endeavours to show that the context forbids its application to the Lord Jesus, for the prophet in iv. 11-v. 1 (*Heb.* iv. 11-14) speaks of the coming of Gog and Magog after the return of the Jews to their own land. We have however already examined in par. 45 the relation which these events hold to the coming of Messiah, and must refer our readers to that paragraph. The verses that follow are more important, and R. Isaac devotes much space to an examination of them. They are very difficult, but briefly they tell us that God will give up His people "until the time that she which travaileth hath brought forth" (עד עת יולדה ילדה), and then Messiah shall bring peace, and drive out the foes. Of course the Rabbi interprets the woman as the nation, and the travail-pains as sufferings to be borne before the coming of the Messiah. Even if this be right we may not forget that before the time of the Lord Jesus the nation had had great suffering, in the destruction of Jerusalem by Nebuchadnezzar and the subsequent Captivity, the

* As we have already noted that מקדם and ימי עולם are used of time under earthly conditions, so we may note here that both מקדם (Hab. i. 12) and עולם (Isa. xl. 28, though not, as it seems, ימי עולם) are used of God.

oppression by Artaxerxes Ochus in the fourth century B.C., the persecution and desecration wrought by Antiochus Epiphanes, and the conquest of Jerusalem by Pompey, with the other humiliations inflicted by the Romans.

**243**] Yet the juxtaposition of the travailing woman with the birth of the ideal ruler who has existed "from of old, from everlasting" suggests that the prophecy is rather to be connected with that of the Virgin in Isaiah vii. (see parr. 186-191), and that Micah, like his greater contemporary, adopts as his own the hope (whencesoever derived is of no importance) that the Deliverer will be born of a virgin-mother.

In either case it is plain that on Messiah's coming there are to be full blessings for Messiah's people and land.

**244**] We cannot however imagine that Divine compulsion would be used in order to accomplish this. If then any Jew of to-day were to suppose the possibility of the appearance of the Messiah in the first century of the present era, and to ask himself how He would be treated if, when He appeared, He confined Himself to the noblest and highest of all forms of government, that of moral influence, and his answer were (as we feel sure would be the case) that He would receive treatment similar to that which Jesus did in fact receive, what objection could be made? For God's promises are not absolute but conditional, and based upon moral events, and if the Jews did reject Messiah they had no right to expect the same results to follow as if they had accepted Him. The blessings announced by Micah were necessarily contingent upon the reception of Him through whom the blessings were to come.

## XV. The Latter Glory of this House.

§ 34.

### Haggai ii. 9.

גדול יהיה כבוד הבית הזה האחרון מן־הראשון אמר יהוה צבאות
ובמקום הזה יהיה שלום נאם יהוה צבאות.

**245**] According to R. Isaac and the Christians of his time the right translation of this verse is that of the Authorized Version: "The glory of this latter house shall be greater than of the former, saith the LORD of hosts: and in this place will I give peace, saith the LORD of hosts." The Rabbi tells us that Christians asserted that the second House had greater glory than the first because Jesus was born in its time.

R. Isaac discusses first the meaning of "glory" in this connexion. It may be, he says, the true, *i.e.*, the spiritual, glory, and he notes that during the second temple there was no worship of false gods. Or it may be apparent and inferior glory, *i.e.*, gold and silver (*cf. v.* 8), and he notes that in the time of Herod the Great the second temple received many presents of gold, &c. Or, he says, the greater glory of the latter house may refer to the greater height of the building, or even the length of its existence, when compared with that of Solomon's temple. But as (according to his computation), it lasted only ten years longer, this superiority is hardly worth notice. He decides however that the passage does not really refer to the second temple at all (including Herod's) for in the immediate context God speaks of the shaking of heaven and earth, of the coming of Gog and Magog, of the advent of the true Messiah, prefigured by Zerubbabel, and thus of the building of another temple in His day. Then, adds the Rabbi, when that temple is built, peace will be everywhere, especially in the land of Israel, and then, in that temple, will the five things lacking to the second temple, though found in the first,* be restored, so that it will be greater than the second temple. It will in fact be greater than even the first temple, for the Shekinah, which may be explained as the visible presence of God, will dwell in it not fitfully but continuously.

Lastly, the Rabbi observes that although Jesus was born during the time of the second temple, it was only near the end of its time, and, according to Christians, He brought about its destruction, and could not therefore (for so the Rabbi implies) have brought glory to it. Neither did He bring peace, as He Himself affirms.

Putting the Rabbi's arguments shortly he means to say, first, that the temple of which so much was prophesied is a temple yet in the future; and secondly, that even on the showing of the New Testament the life and teaching of Jesus do not fit in with the supposed reference of this verse to the second temple.

**246**] (1). Leaving for the moment all discussion of the New Testament, we venture to think that few scholars in these days will be found to give their support to the Rabbi's theory that the words in the Book of Haggai refer to a temple in the future. Haggai surely is occupied with the building that was being completed in his own time. He speaks clearly enough of "this house," and this must have been that which was before his eyes. Ah, exclaims the Rabbi, but what of the third verse of this very chapter? Does he not there distinctly use "this house" when he means the first house, *i.e.*, the temple of Solomon? And may he not therefore say "this house" of one which was to come as well as of one which had been? No, surely not. It is one thing to identify a building raised on the same site as its predecessor with that predecessor, and quite another to project oneself in

* R. Isaac gives these as the Ark (and the Mercy-seat and Cherubim), Urim and Thummim, the Holy Spirit, the Fire from heaven, the Anointing oil. But in T. B. *Yoma* 21*b*., the *locus classicus*, the list is: the Ark (and the Mercy-seat and Cherubim), Fire, and the Shekinah, and the Holy Spirit, and Urim and Thummim.

thought beyond the time when the new building shall itself have perished, and still speak of another building (which may or may not be built on the same site) as "this house." R. Isaac's interpretation seems to us, and doubtless to our readers, to be grossly unnatural.

**247**] (2). Here however it seems well to call attention to the fact that probably the Rabbi and the Christians of his time were both wrong in taking the word "latter" (האחרון) as an epithet of "house." In the third verse of this chapter it is quite certainly an epithet of "glory," and this is much the most natural interpretation of it here also. Thus the Revised Version translates: "The latter glory of this house shall be greater than the former." Indeed we have not found any modern scholar of importance who takes it otherwise. If this be the right connexion of "latter" the Prophet is not contrasting one temple with another, but the latter, *i.e.*, the future, glory of the temple which he saw building with the poor and meagre state in which he then saw it. Or perhaps he regards "this house" (see *v.* 3) as one with Solomon's, and says that the latter glory of this one temple, from 520 B.C. onwards, shall be greater than its former glory from the time of Solomon to its capture by Nebuchadnezzar in 586 B.C.

**248**] (3). Wherein then, it will be asked, is this greater glory to consist? Does it lie in the wealth which was indubitably showered down upon it in the time of the Herods? Presumably this was greater than that given to it in Solomon's time, but we cannot affirm this with any certainty. In any case this is not important, for we can hardly suppose (in spite of *v.* 8) that the prophet had in his mind chiefly material wealth. It would be a grievous bathos, after speaking of the shaking of heaven and earth, to add that this building shall have more silver and gold in it than ever was seen there in the time of Solomon. Is he thinking then of spiritual power? This would at least be worthy of the subject, and in some sense must be intended. Yet we may fairly ask whether it was the case that the second temple was the scene of greater spiritual power than the first, or whether in the end of its days the one temple was of greater spiritual power than in the beginning—apart, that is to say, from Christianity? Were, for example, the priests and high-priests of the last seventy years of the second temple superior in spiritual grace and power to Joshua the son of Josedech under whom it was built? Was there during that time, apart from Christianity, a prophet greater than Haggai, and his younger contemporary, Zechariah? We know how history answers these questions. But if we include under the greater glory the work of Christianity, which, as we may say, was begun in the second temple by the presence of Jesus and His disciples, then indeed we can see a reason for the prophet's utterance. For we recall the enormous spiritual force that Christianity has proved itself to be, Jews themselves being witness. Starting from that centre in Jerusalem, there has spread from shore to shore of the whole habitable world a force which has summoned millions of ignorant and idolatrous Gentiles to the worship of the One God, and has succeeded, though the movement is as yet only in its infancy (for what are nineteen hundred years in the purposes of God?), in bringing the laws, the customs, and even the personal habits, of vast multitudes largely under subjection to the law and will of God. Judaism as such has failed to impress the nations of the world; Christianity has succeeded to an extraordinary degree, and the beginnings of it appeared in the second temple. Truly the latter glory of that house was greater than the former.

Yet neither material wealth, nor spiritual power in the ordinary sense of the term, fully satisfies the meaning of "glory." "I will fill this house with glory, saith the LORD of hosts" (*v.* 7), and we cannot but think of some direct manifestation of the LORD Himself. What does He say in Zech. ii. 5 (9 Heb.)? "I will be the glory in the midst of her." This is incomparably more than silver and gold, and more than merely spiritual power. It is the LORD'S own presence, it is the manifestation of Himself. It is the Shekinah in the fullest sense of the word. But what this means we have already seen in parr. 50-54, to which I would refer my readers for a fuller statement of the case. I asked then whether we could imagine a higher and better form by which the Presence of God could manifest Itself than that of clothing Itself with human nature, nature that had never sinned and possessed no trace of sin, and shining through this human nature in a life of holiness, love and righteousness? I suppose that we cannot. If therefore the statements about Jesus in the New Testament are fact and not fable, the presence of Jesus in the temple will have been an important part of the fulfilment of our prophecy.

**249**] (4). The Rabbi however objects that some of the words of our passage, "and in this place will I give peace, saith the LORD of hosts," have not been fulfilled in Jesus, urging that Jesus himself said that He did not come to send peace, but a sword (Matt. x. 34). But why will the Rabbi always limit this word "peace" to its lowest possible meaning? Why suppose that the prophet thought only of the lower, because external, peace? Why should he not at least have included the highest of all kinds of peace, peace with God? If he did in this case, his words are fully in accordance with the teaching of the New Testament, for, according to that, it was at Jerusalem, though not, it is true, in the temple area itself, that the Lord Jesus obtained peace for sinful man, and brought peace, deep and abiding peace, to the hearts of those who venture themselves upon Him. Jesus has brought peace, and if ever His professed followers have not made for peace they have so far been no true followers of Him.

**250**] (5). Yet, after all, I cannot refrain from pointing out that even the New Testament itself suggests that the final and complete fulfilment of our passage lies still in the future. Turn to Heb. xii. 26, 27, where the writer quotes Haggai ii. 6, of the last great testing of all things. This, as need hardly be said, is fully in accordance with Christian teaching. The Shekinah has come already in the person of the Lord Jesus, and will come again in all His perfection of power and beauty on the clouds of heaven, when every eye shall see Him. His people pray: Even so, come Lord Jesus.

---

**251**] *Note.* It is strange that the Rabbi makes no mention of the common Christian translation of ובאו חמדת כל הגוים

(*v.* 7), "and the desire of all nations shall come" (A.V.), and I am not in a position now to explain his omission. Let us hope that he found the Christians of his time sufficiently learned to reject so impossible a rendering. He himself explains חמדת as בחמדת, *i.e.*, "and they shall come with the desirable things of all nations," but perhaps the Revised Version is better, because simpler: "and the desirable things of all nations shall come."

## xvi. "THY KING COMETH UNTO THEE."

### § 35.

Zech. ix. 9. "*Rejoice greatly, O daughter of Zion; shout, O daughter of Jerusalem: behold, thy king cometh unto thee: he is just, and having salvation; lowly, and riding upon an ass, even upon a colt the foal of an ass.*"

גילי מאד בת ציון הריעי בת ירושלם הנה מלכך יבוא לך צדיק ונושע הוא עני ורכב על חמור ועל עיר בן אתנות׃

**252**] R. Isaac argues that this passage refers to the coming of Messiah in the future, when all Israel shall have returned to the Holy Land, and he adds an elaborate exposition of the context to prove his contention. He understands *vv.* 1-8 to say that the Land will be enlarged, for it will be too small for Judah, Israel and the converts; that the Philistines will be subdued, and will no more eat unclean food, but obey the religion of Israel; that Jerusalem and the Temple will also be enlarged, and all nations will be at peace. Then comes *v.* 9, which indicates that these things will take place in the days of Messiah, who is נושע, *i.e.*, saved from Gog and Magog by His righteousness. He will be meek and riding on an ass, both because of His meekness, and to show that Israel will not need horses and chariots. *v.* 10 tells us that Messiah will give peace to the whole world, because He will act as arbiter over it; and *v.* 11, that the congregation of Israel will have been saved by the observance of circumcision in the present exile, and all Judah with Ephraim shall return and defeat Javan (Greece), which is identical with Gog and Magog, to whom Javan is brother (Gen. x. 2).

Now adds the Rabbi, none of these things has taken place, therefore Jesus is not the Messiah; and he then repeats his old argument that Jesus Himself denied that He had come to give peace, or to rule.

**253**] (1). Leaving details for the present let us consider the passage as a whole. In Matt. xxi. 5 (compare John xii. 15), our verse is quoted of the entrance of our Lord into Jerusalem. R. Isaac denies not only that such a reference was intended by the prophet, but also that it is even suitable, because Jesus did not fulfil the statements made in the context. Yet he cannot deny that Jesus was meek, or that He came into Jerusalem riding upon an ass, and that so far at least, the prophecy fits Him. If so (I appeal to every learned Jew to confirm my statement) St. Matthew, as a Jew accustomed to Jewish methods of quotation, may well have quoted the words for that reason and that reason only. See further on this point par. 229.

**254**] (2). Yet it may fairly be argued that the quotation is more than an adaptation of mere words, and that the greatness of Messiah, as described by the prophet in this chapter, is indeed fulfilled in our Lord Jesus. This is especially the case if we allow for the difference of the conception of glory held by the prophet from that which is held by thoughtful Jews of to-day. The prophet speaks of victories great and glorious, performed through Messiah. But, you say, Jesus of Nazareth never performed such earthly victories, never achieved such political success. Yet whose fault was that? Is there not every sign that if the Jews of the first century had as a body accepted the teaching of Jesus of Nazareth, they would never have gone through the terrible experience of seeing their beloved city destroyed and their temple in flames? More than that, is there not every sign that before long the Romans would have been compelled to withdraw from Palestine, and, little by little, Palestine would have resumed the place it held for a short time under King Solomon, and have become the attraction and joy of the whole earth?

Be this as it may, all thoughtful Jews will grant that the prophet and his contemporaries thought more of earthly and political success than we do in this twentieth century. We have larger and truer notions of that in which true greatness consists. As a recent poet says:

> "So in compare of never-ending time
> Less than a moment seem the years of man,
> Yet aught of life outweighs the all of space,
> And aught of love outruns time's endless race."

Is there a Jew living who would care for a Messiah who should astonish the world with victories such as those of Napoleon the Great, and should sweep away his foes and subdue country after country as he did? God forbid, you say, that Messiah should be such! We desire victories indeed, but they must be spiritual; for nations to be trampled down would only be abhorrent to us. Yes, you want them won over to truth, to right, to purity, to love. Would God that we Christians could show you nothing else in Christendom! But in spite of all, alas, that Christendom is, we dare to ask you if the spiritual victories of Jesus of Nazareth do not amaze you; if you are not astounded as you see the barbarians of North, South, East, and West, races which Judaism as such has never touched, submitting to the rule of Jesus? Is not such submission, in so far as it is heart-felt, infinitely superior to all the merely earthly triumphs of the greatest of human conquerors? Lift up then your heads, O ye gates of the house of Israel, and the true Victor, the King of glory, shall come in!

**255**] (3). Lastly, it is necessary to refer briefly to some details mentioned by the Rabbi.

(i). He does well in calling attention to the fact that the Messiah is to be meek, but he does not carry this thought as far as he well might do. Yet he is in fact hardly right in explaining עני 'poor' as though it were ענו 'meek.' For thus he misses something of the true meaning of the prophet. עני suggests that Messiah, when He appears, is not to be among the rich and powerful, in the usual acceptation of the terms, but to be among the poor. The reason why the prophet was led to say this may be that in his time, as often in the world's history, the upper classes showed themselves less disposed to accept the word of God, and to follow His laws, than the poor and needy. The prophet was therefore inclined to identify the poor with the pious. Similar examples of this tendency may perhaps be seen in Hab. iii. 14, Zeph. iii. 12. In any case all our readers will not fail to remember that the Lord Jesus, though of the seed of David, was born into a family which at the time of His coming was poor in this world's goods. עני rather than ענו is but a small matter, yet one not to be overlooked.

**256**] (ii). Messiah enters Jerusalem riding upon an ass. The Rabbi is doubtless in the right when he tacitly accepts R. D. Kimchi's explanation to the effect that His time will be so peaceful that He will not need horses and chariots, the symbols of war. The reign of Messiah is to be marked by peace. This is a point with which we have already dealt several times, as, for example, in par. 249. There is therefore no need to trouble the reader with a repetition of the proofs that the Rabbi's attack completely fails.

**257**] (iii). So also with his argument that our Lord was not a ruler. We have repeatedly pointed out the mistake of the Rabbi about this, especially in parr. 25-30, 72, 239.

**258**] (iv). The Rabbi's explanation of נושע ("having salvation" in the English versions) requires rather more investigation. It is of course truly delightful to find him saying (par. 218): "The Christians have changed the word נושע ('saved') and write instead of it מושיע ('saving') so as to deduce from it an argument in support of their faith."

מלת נושע החליפו הנוצרים וכותבים במקומו מושיע כדי להביא ממנו סיוע לאמונתם.

For he forgets that originally this was not a Christian, but a Jewish, interpretation. It was the Septuagint, the earliest Jewish translation, that read σώζων 'saving,' or 'bringing salvation,' and he can hardly blame Christians for thinking that Jews understood their own Scriptures. Yet, as regards the meaning of the word in itself, there is little doubt but that the Rabbi is right, and that it does not mean 'bringing salvation,' 'saving' others, but rather, 'saved,' 'victorious.' But if Messiah is 'saved,' from what and by what is He saved? From His foes by His righteousness, says R. Isaac, again following Kimchi. Very well; be it so. That exactly fits in with what we know of the Lord Jesus.* For it was by His own righteousness and holiness that victory was secured for Him over the worst foes of all, sin and death. Yet observe that there is nothing about 'righteousness.' It is only deduced from צדיק ('righteous' or 'just') in the context. It is therefore more in accord with the language of the prophet to interpret the word נושע as implying that the LORD God was with Him, and for this reason He was saved and victorious. But notice that this again exactly suits the Lord Jesus, as He is described to us in the New Testament, for God was with Him, and it was by the right hand of God that He was raised from the dead (Acts ii. 33; v. 31). Surely it is worthy of consideration by every thoughtful Jew how closely the words of the prophet do fit in with the circumstances of the life, and death, and resurrection, of Jesus of Nazareth.

* The early Christian Hymn, No. 8 of the *Odes of Solomon*, seems to refer to this passage:—

"And they that are saved in Him that was saved."

## xvii. The Martyr.

### § 36.

Zech. xii. 10. "*And I will pour upon the house of David, and upon the inhabitants of Jerusalem, the spirit of grace and of supplication ; and they shall look unto me* (*or* '*him*') *whom they have pierced: and they shall mourn for him, as one mourneth for his only son, and shall be in bitterness for him, as one that is in bitterness for his firstborn.*"

ושפכתי על בית דויד ועל יושב ירושלם רוח חן ותחנונים והביטו אלי (var. lect. אליו) את אשר דקרו וספדו עליו כמספד על היחיד והמר עליו כהמר על הבכור׃

**259**] Our readers will at once recognize this famous and difficult passage. May He who inspired the prophet be with us as we study it together!

R. Isaac spends much time in proving that the chapter from which the verse is taken refers to events that are not already things of the past, but belong to the future. Personally I accept this, and therefore do not desire to trouble my readers with the longer part of his argument. It seems probable that both the chapter as a whole, and our verse in particular, describe things that are yet to take place. Then the house of David, the inhabitants of Jerusalem, and, as appears from the following verses, all Israel, will mourn much and bitterly.

But for what reason will they mourn? This question brings us at once to a primary question, What is the right text of the verse under consideration? Did the prophet write אלי, "They shall look unto me," or did he write אליו, "they shall look unto him"? Further, in each case, what is the right translation and interpretation of the verse?

**260**] (1). In the editions of the Hebrew Bible in common use to-day we find אלי, without even a sign or note that there is any doubt about it. How then shall we translate the passage? The Jewish Authorities in England, if we may judge by the "Appendix to the Revised Version" issued by them in 1896, tell us to read, "And they (*i.e.*, the house of David and the inhabitants of Jerusalem) shall look up to me because of him whom they (*i.e.*, the nations which come against Jerusalem) have pierced." This startling translation, for it is very startling to any Hebraist who has no controversial axe to grind, follows R. Isaac, who says the verse means that, even if one Israelite is killed by the nations in that great war of the future, the men of Israel will look up to God in prayer. But it is older than R. Isaac, it is the interpretation also of R. David Kimchi. But it is a most remarkable translation. "Because of him whom"! How is it possible to get this out of את אשר? I can understand that the את gives a certain amount of emphasis to אשר, but "because of"! What parallel passage can be adduced in favour of this? Ezek. xxxvi. 27, answers R. Isaac,

ועשיתי את אשר בחקי תלכו.

understanding by this, I presume, "because ye walk in my ordinances." But this again is impossible. Without the את the clause would mean, "And I will cause that ye shall walk in my ordinances," and the את only marks more definitely this consequence as the object of the verb. So in our passage את may mark out definitely the following אשר as an object; it cannot be translated "because of." *

Again, this unlucky rendering, to which the heads of the Jewish community in England have betaken themselves for refuge, is shipwrecked on the verb דקרו. Does the passage read as though there were a sudden change of subject here? Must not, I do not say according to the principles of grammar, but

* It is true that the Septuagint has ἀνθ' ὧν κατωρχήσαντο ("because they have insulted *me*," literally, "because they have danced *in triumph over me*," רקדו) but the Hebrew in front of these translators was certainly corrupt. The Targum too reads ויובעון מן קדמי על די איטלטלו ("and they shall pray before me because they are driven to and fro"), but this is hardly independent of the Septuagint. Further, it is probable that underlying R. Isaac's translation is the rule of the Oral Law that every את in the Bible hints at something additional which is not expressed. But translation depends on grammar, not on what, after all, is an Haggadic subtlety.

according to the natural sequence of thought, they who "pierced" be the same as they who "look up"? That is impossible, Jews cry, we have not pierced Him unto whom we shall look. But this is the very question under discussion. I fear that this translation, both in earlier and in later times, is due to nothing more noble than a desire to meet Christian arguments which have been deduced from this passage.

If then we read אלי it does not seem possible to make any other translation than "they shall look unto me whom they have pierced." If so, how are we to understand the word "pierced"? Shall we say that it is merely figurative of the great pain and anguish caused to God by the sins of His people? This is possible, but nowhere in Scripture is דקר used with this meaning. It always, as it seems, connotes death, even if, as in Lam. iv. 9, this is the result of hunger. Death, literal death, primarily as the result of piercing, is implied in דקר. How then can this term be used of God? Can you wonder that many Christians affirm that the phrase is fully satisfied only by the Christian doctrine that God took human flesh and as man received the spear-thrust in His body? I confess that I myself shrink from this extreme literalism of interpretation. It is easier to suppose that when the prophet writes "They shall look unto me whom they have pierced and mourn for him," &c., he may have had in his mind the vision of a martyr slain by piercing, and have added that God was pierced through that martyr. In other words, the prophet may not have intended here to foreshadow the Incarnation, but to say that a time is coming when the Jewish nation will recognize its sins, and will mourn for the way in which it treated one who was a martyr for God's sake. He means that they pierced and slew that martyr, and that God felt the injury as done to Himself.* It is not necessary to point out how strikingly this is in accordance with the teaching of the New Testament. I dare to go further and say that the verse is in accordance

* This meets the Rabbi's objection that if we translate "me whom they have pierced" we should expect in the following clause "and mourn for me" (עלי instead of עליו).

with the beginning of sorrow felt by many of the Jewish race to-day as they regret the treatment meted out to Jesus of Nazareth.

**261**] (2). We must not however overlook the other reading אליו, "and they shall look unto him whom they have pierced." This is the form in which St. John quotes the passage (xix. 37). A recent Jewish writer, whose zeal against Christianity outruns his Hebrew scholarship, speaks of this quotation as "conveniently transforming the pronoun from the first to the third person, changing thereby entirely the sense as given by the Massoretic text." He seems to think that this is a Christian alteration! But he ought to be aware that it is found in many manuscripts of the Massoretic text, and that it is the true reading of the Talmud. *

There are indeed grave doubts whether it is right, for it is so much the easier reading of the two that it can hardly have been altered save by an anti-Christian bias, which one is very loth to admit, but supposing that it is right, how shall we take it? The word את is still rather curious, and can, as before, only serve to emphasize the following אשר. But אליו undeniably suits the עליו which is found immediately after: "They shall look unto him whom they pierced, and mourn for him."

Yet even here there is a difficulty. How can they "look unto" a person whom they have already slain? I suppose that a Jew can only understand it of a martyr who rises again at the general resurrection, and is then the object of admiration, and of bitter humiliation on the part of those who ill-treated him. Be it so. We must not expect too much from any one prophet. But can you be surprised that St. John saw in the piercing of Jesus on the cross the fulfilment of the statement that a martyr was to be pierced, and says therefore (Rev. i. 7), as he looks forward to the return of the Lord Jesus, "every eye shall see Him, and they which pierced Him"?

**262**] The conclusion, I think, to which we are drawn from

* T. B. *Succa* 52*a* in the Munich MS.:

היינו דכתיב והביטו אליו את אשר דקרו.

a study of this passage is that whether אלי "unto me," or אליו "unto him," be the right text, it does, with any scholarly translation or interpretation, fit in remarkably well with Christian teaching. Perhaps some of us Christians are rather too bold in insisting that it points definitely to the divine nature of the promised Redeemer, but we are not at all too bold, but only making a simple deduction from the plain statement of Scripture, if we see in him for whom the mourning is to be made one whose martyr-death the nation will sincerely mourn. As yet in the history of the Jewish race there has been no martyr who is at all comparable to Jesus of Nazareth. Would God that the nation mourned with deep humiliation of heart for His death. For that mourning and bitter lamentation, deep and bitter as of a father for his only son, yes, for his first-born, shall be synchronous with the great deliverance of the Jewish nation from its last enemies. Victory and humiliation of soul in true repentance will take place together. The Lord hasten that day of promise for the nation of Israel!

## xviii. The shepherd smitten.

### § 37.

Zech. xiii. 7. "*Awake, O sword, against my shepherd, and against the man that is my fellow, saith the* LORD *of hosts: smite the shepherd, and the sheep shall be scattered; and I will turn mine hand upon the little ones.*"

חרב עורי על רעי ועל גבר עמיתי נאם יהוה צבאות הך את הרעה ותפוצין הצאן והשבתי ידי על הצערים:

**263**] (1). R. Isaac's exposition of this passage is singularly quaint. The shepherd, he says, is the Sultan of Turkey, and God calls him "my shepherd" because so many of the Jews, in fact three-quarters of them,—and they are God's sheep—

live under his rule.* God also calls the Sultan my "fellow" or "associate" † because the Sultan reckons himself as God. The prophet here speaks of a time in the future, the time of Gog and Magog, when his power shall be broken. For in Ezek. xxxviii. 6, "the house of Togarmah" is mentioned side by side with Gog and Magog (*v.* 2), and in Hebrew the name for Turkey is Togar (תוגר). Further, "the little ones," upon whom the LORD will also turn His hand in anger, are various kings of the "Edomites," *i.e.*, of the Roman empire, who have some, though fewer, Jews living under them.‡ Lastly, the scattering of the flock refers to the dispersal of the Jews living in different towns of Turkey and elsewhere, when they are gathered to Jerusalem from the four ends of the earth.

It is hardly necessary to waste much time over so fanciful an explanation of the passage. There is not the shadow of a hint that "my shepherd" and "my fellow" refer to a Gentile. The prophet's words much more naturally refer to some one of note in Israel. Equally forced is it to see in "the little ones" kings who are of less rank or importance because they have fewer Jews living under them. It is also strange to explain the scattering as dispersion from temporary homes, when *ex hypothesi* it is in reality the gathering of the Jews to their own home. Lastly, R. Isaac ought to have perceived that the promise of the two following verses, according to which the third part of those that are in the land shall, after great trial, come out as gold refined in a furnace, and call upon God, who will recognize them as His people, can hardly refer to others than men of the house of Israel.

**264**] (2). What then appears to be the true meaning of the passage?

* Rashi, writing some five hundred years earlier than R. Isaac, sees in the first "shepherd" Esau, and in the second the King of Babylon. The Targum understands both of the kings of Babylon. It is probable that "Esau" and "Babylon" alike refer to Rome.

† "My fellow," עמיתי, derived apparently from a root found in Assyrian meaning "united," occurs in the Bible elsewhere only in the book of Leviticus (11 times), where it always means an associate of the person addressed or spoken of, and suggests equality to him.

‡ So also Rashi and Kimchi.

(i). I assume that it is in its right place, although many critics since the time of Ewald are of opinion that it has been transposed by some accident, and should properly follow xi. 17, the prophecy against the foolish shepherd. But some scholars are too ready to move passages if they find their present context difficult, and also see a superficial resemblance somewhere else. Moreover the term "my fellow" (עמיתי) can hardly be used of a false leader.

**265**] (ii). Taking then the passage in the position in which it stands, what can we make of it? It will be observed that xii. 10—xiii. 6 have described the penitence of the nation of Israel, the fountain of cleansing which has been opened for them, the cessation of idol worship and of false prophecy. Immediately thereupon follows the section with which we are concerned, verses 7—9, and we may assume that these verses still refer to Israel, not to Gentiles.

(*a*). Shall we say that they describe the result of the previous section, showing how God deals with the nation when it has repented, and has proved the reality of its repentance by ridding itself of its chief sins? If so we must understand that severe punishment falls on the chief leader of the nation, *i.e.*, the King, or the High Priest, or both, if "my shepherd" and "my fellow" represent different persons. The nation also is dispersed, and passes through a time of terrible trial. In the end however there is hope. However we may regard this interpretation in its details, it is a strange result indeed to follow the heart-moving events described in the previous verses.

(*b*). Again, shall we say that the passage is another aspect of the events described at some length in the preceding section? Parallels may be found for such a method on the part of prophets. But in the case before us, it is well-nigh impossible to trace at all satisfactorily such a resemblance. In fact with the exception of one item there is hardly anything in common between the two passages.

(*c*). But that one item which the two passages have in common is so important that it leads us to what is probably the true solution of our difficulty. The prophet takes it up, and describes both it, and the circumstances closely connected with it, from a different point of view from that taken at first. I refer to the martyr death spoken of in xii. 10. We saw in parr. 260 sq. how, according to that verse, the people were to lament over the martyr whom they slew; here, in our verses 7-9, the prophet regards the deed from God's side, and describes the consequences that it brought upon the nation. The prophet, that is to say, takes up the incident at an earlier period than he did in the section xii. 10 to xiii. 6, and describes that death from God's side and its more immediate results to Israel. He states God's verdict on the deed, the punishment that He inflicts for it, and, ultimately, the hope that still remains for the nation. That pierced martyr against whom the sword awoke was no one less than "my shepherd," saith the LORD of hosts, no other than "my fellow." The shepherd is smitten, those he tended are scattered, and even the little ones connected with him feel the blow. Then comes trouble on the nation of Israel. Two-thirds of it are cut off, and one-third is left for further testing even as by fire. But at last Israel will "call on my name, and I will hear them: I will say, It is my people; and they shall say, The LORD is my God." So interpreted, I venture to think, the position of the prophecy is fully justified.

**266**] (3). If this interpretation be right I need not point out to you how closely it fits in with the facts of history, facts undeniable by any reader. Whatever we may think of Jesus of Nazareth we cannot deny that He perished as a martyr to the cause He advocated, the cause of holiness, the cause of God. But it was almost immediately after His martyr death that the awful troubles of Israel began. Jesus was smitten, His followers were scattered; even the little ones who accepted His teaching felt the blow. But what of the nation? We all know the terrible disasters of the war with Vespasian and Titus, when Jerusalem was taken and the Temple burnt, and the crowning destruction in the time of Hadrian, when Barcochba's and Aqiba's revolt was stamped out in blood and fire. Would it be too much to affirm that in Judæa, in Crete, and elsewhere during the first two centuries of our era, as many as two-thirds of the Jews perished? And what shall be said of the centuries that have elapsed since? Is it not true that the nation has been almost continuously exposed to the fire of persecution, even as God says in this passage: "I will bring the third part through the fire"? These are facts, plain facts of history, and as such are independent both of any interpretation of this prophecy, and of the relative truth of Christianity and Judaism.

**267**] Regarding the subject however in as unprejudiced a manner as it is possible for me to do, I cannot help thinking that when the words "Smite the shepherd," &c., are applied to the Lord Jesus in the Gospel according to St. Matthew xxvi. 31 (see also St. Mark xiv. 27) they are more than a mere application. For it does seem probable (as we saw in par. 262) that the martyr death of xii. 10 is the death of Jesus, and this, as we have now seen, was also the smiting of "the shepherd," whom God calls "my fellow." If this be so, may not you and I hope that as the people of Israel have passed through the fire as silver and as gold, so also they may enjoy the experience stated in the end of this prophecy, that they shall call upon the LORD once more in true repentance, and that He shall hear them, and acknowledge them afresh as His?

### xix. "IN EVERY PLACE INCENSE IS OFFERED."

### § 38.

Mal. i. 11. "*For from the rising of the sun even unto the going down of the same my name is great among the Gentiles; and in every place incense is offered unto my name, and a pure offering: for my name is great among the Gentiles, saith the LORD of hosts.*"

**268**] Christians, says R. Isaac, see in this verse a statement that God accepts their sacrifices and offerings. But, first, there were no Christians in Malachi's days, and, secondly, the prophet desired to recall Israel to more heart-felt worship by stating that the Gentiles in the time when he lived did really intend to worship the true God in their sacrifices, although they associated Him with creatures.

The meaning of the passage is far from certain, but probably R. Isaac is right in referring it to the time then present rather than to the future. But whether the prophet intended actual heathen, as the Rabbi supposes, or proselytes of various degrees, who had heard of the true God and consciously worshipped Him with fervour of heart, it is impossible to say. In either case the verse does not affect the subject of our discussion in these pages, the relative truth of Judaism and Christianity.

## XX. THE COMING OF ELIJAH.

### § 39.

Mal. iv. 5 (*Heb.* iii. 23). "*Behold I will send you Elijah the prophet before the great and terrible day of the* LORD *come.*"

הנה אנכי שלח לכם את אליה הנביא לפני בוא יום יהוה הגדול והנורא׃

**269**] (1). In St. Luke iii. 1, 2, we read, "Now in the fifteenth year of the reign of Tiberius Cæsar, Pontius Pilate being governor of Judæa, and Herod being tetrarch of Galilee,......the word of God came unto John the son of Zacharias in the wilderness." The Evangelist states the date so precisely because he will mark as accurately as possible the year of this strange event, this wonderful renewal of the spirit of prophecy. The word of God had been silent for centuries; now at last He speaks again, and in such and such a year. The cry of the Baptist was heard throughout Judæa and multitudes flocked to him. Was it strange that he who bade the poor and the rich repent, who warned a king of his sin, and suffered martyrdom for his faithfulness, should by his life and words remind the people of the older prophets, especially the earlier among them, and, in particular, of him who was the most striking of them all, Elijah the Tishbite, who turned the hearts of Israel back again to the true God (1 Kings xviii. 37, 39)? Can we wonder that Jesus, seeing how John the Baptist prepared the way for His own preaching, said that John was Elijah, who was to come (Matt. xi. 14, compare xvii. 12, Mark ix. 13)? Of course He did not mean that John was Elijah in person. He meant that he carried out the same preparative work as Elijah, which moreover Malachi in our present passage predicted that Elijah would do. The people were expecting Elijah to come before Messiah came. Jesus says that he had come, in the person of John the Baptist.

**270**] (2). Yet we read in St. John i. 21, that John the Baptist said that he was not Elijah! Of course. What else could he say? He was not Elijah. Ah, says R. Isaac, he prevaricated; he ought to have said, "No, I am not indeed Elijah himself, but nevertheless I claim to represent him, and I am the fulfilment of the prophecy in Malachi." But why should he have said this? Perhaps the thought that he was fulfilling the words of Malachi never occurred to him. Probably, like most Jews of his time, he expected Elijah himself to come later. And certainly, if he had spoken as the Rabbi suggests, the Pharisees would not have accepted his words. The coming of Messiah, according to their expectation, and of His forerunners (for many were looking for Enoch as well as Elijah), was of so utterly different a kind from the coming and work of Jesus that they were not likely to accept a statement by the Baptist that he was the forerunner who represented Elijah. Yet it is plain that if Jesus was the true Messiah the Baptist did a great deal of the preparatory work prophesied of Elijah in our passage. Elijah came, according to the teaching of the Lord Jesus, in the person of John the Baptist.

**271**] (3). It may however be said: Surely Elijah himself

will come? Well, perhaps so. How does that affect our discussion? You answer: "Because if Elijah himself is to come, then Jesus cannot be the true Messiah, because Elijah has not yet come." That is what R. Isaac says. But you see what this argument implies? That Elijah comes before Messiah. I ask the evidence for this, and none is given me except our passage in Malachi, which says nothing of the kind. This says that Elijah comes before the great and dreadful day of the LORD; it does not say "before Messiah come." "Oh," you answer: "that is the same thing." Is it? We have no right to tamper with the Word of God. But you say, "We have always been taught this." I know it, but the repetition of a statement does not necessarily make it true. There is nothing whatever in the words of Malachi to prevent the coming of Messiah taking place long before the coming of the dreadful day of the LORD.

**272**] (4). It will be said that there is a consensus of traditions, to the effect that Elijah will come in person in days yet future. Yes, it is collected in part in Hamburger's *Real-Encyclopädie für Bibel und Talmud*, and much more completely in the *Jewish Encyclopedia*. But all this is not Scripture, and the only passage in the Bible upon which it is based is the very verse in Malachi which we are discussing. Surely a very large pyramid has been built up on a very small apex.*

For, if we endeavour to consider the subject dispassionately and without prejudice, have we any more right to insist on the coming of Elijah himself because of the statement in our passage, than we have to insist on the coming of David himself because of the statements in Ezekiel: "and my servant David shall be king over them...and David my servant shall be their prince for ever" (xxxvii. 24, 25, *cf.* xxxiv. 23, 24)? Yet it has never been seriously supposed that David, the identical David the son of Jesse, will return in his own person to reign in Jerusalem. May not the *Yalqut* on Numbers xxv. 12 (§771) give us a hint when it writes,

* Whatever may be the precise meaning of Ecclus. xlviii. 10, our Jewish friends will not include that verse in the Bible.

"R. Simeon ben Levi said, 'Phinehas is Elijah.' The Holy One, blessed be He, said to him: Thou hast made peace between Israel and Me in this world, even so in the world to come thou art he who shalt make peace between Me and My children, for it is said: Behold I send you Elijah the Prophet, and he shall turn the heart of the fathers to the children."

אמר רבי שמעון בן לוי פנחס הוא אליהו. אמר ליה הקדוש ברוך הוא אתה נתת שלום בין ישראל ובני (lege וביני) בעולם הזה, אף לעתיד לבא אתה הוא שעתיד ליתן שלום ביני לבין בני שנאמר הנה אנכי וגו'.

The *Yalqut* adds a similar passage from the *Pirqe d'R. Eliezer.* Are not these words, I say, a hint that Elijah in our passage in Malachi may be understood not literally but symbolically? If however it be urged that R. Simeon ben Levi's words are only Haggada, I would ask, What else are all the many tales and beliefs about the future coming of Elijah in person? And I would also put this question: Is there any reason against believing that Malachi himself in this passage knew something of Haggada, and, accustomed as he was to speaking in parables, gave his readers credit for insight into his parabolic use of the name Elijah? If this be so, is it unnatural that one endued with so keen an insight into truth as our Lord Jesus, the Prophet of Nazareth, should have perceived his meaning and applied the words rightly to John the Baptist, who did so much of the work foretold of Elijah?

**273**] (5). It is perhaps well that I should here notice two rather curious objections made by our Rabbi.

(i). He affirms that Jesus contradicts Himself, by saying, first, that Elijah shall come, and, secondly, that he has come. The verses to which R. Isaac refers are Matt. xvii. 10-12, (with the parallel Mark ix. 11-13). But R. Isaac misunderstood our Lord's words. Jesus accepts as true the text in Malachi, which evidently He is quoting, and then adds that John the Baptist is the fulfilment of it. He does not say that Elijah will come in the future, as the Rabbi thinks, but assuming the truth of the words of Malachi, gives their true explanation.*

**274**] (ii). The other objection of R. Isaac is still weaker. He says that John the Baptist denied that he was a prophet. He doubtless refers to John i. 21, where the Latin Vulgate, with the inability of the Latin tongue to indicate an article, has *Propheta es tu? Et respondit: Non.* And doubtless those versions which were entirely dependent on the Latin translated the words: "Art thou a prophet? And he answered No." But in the original Greek there is a definite article, and the sentence must be translated: "Art thou the Prophet? And he answered No." John, that is to say, was not asked whether he was *a* prophet, but whether he was *the* prophet, the one whom all were expecting. This, according to the belief current in New Testament times, was the Prophet whose coming Moses had predicted in Deut. xviii. 15. This was Messiah, and John was not He. What other answer than "No" could John have given to such a question?

**275**] (6). Lastly, let me call attention to the need that we all have of taking to heart the preaching of John the Baptist. This is quite independent of whatever we may think of his relation to Elijah. It is the preaching of repentance, it is the message that if we would enter into the kingdom of God we must recognize our sins and leave them. In this, and in this only, have we the true preparation for receiving Messiah, whether we be Christians or Jews. Let us each pray for deep and ever deeper conviction of sin, and a determination, ever growing more and more visible in action, to do what is right in the sight of God. So, and so only, shall we have our eyes opened to see the things of God, and to value His redemption.

* It is true that in Matt. xvii. 11 the future tense is used ("shall restore all things"), but this is part of the quotation, which our Lord applies to John. "All things" appears to be a summary of the final result of the effect of this work, the end of all controversies and disputes.

# CHAPTER V

## A FEW PASSAGES IN THE HOLY WRITINGS

# CHAPTER V.

## A Few Passages in the Holy Writings.

### i. Psalm cx.

§ 40.

"*Now while the Pharisees were gathered together, Jesus asked them a question, saying, What think ye of the Christ? whose son is he? They say unto him,* The son *of David. He saith unto them, How then doth David in the Spirit call him Lord, saying, The* LORD *said unto my Lord, Sit thou on my right hand, Till I put thine enemies underneath thy feet? If David then calleth him Lord, how is he his son?*" Matt. xxii. 41-45. *cf.* Mark xii. 35-37; Luke xx. 41-44.

**276**] This passage from the first Gospel suggests several questions to every thoughtful reader, questions also in some respects different from those which presented themselves to a thinker of the end of the sixteenth century, when R. Isaac of Troki lived. It is proposed therefore to consider the subject more from the point of view of to-day than from that of four hundred years ago.

(1). Was Jesus justified in using the name of David as the author of the Psalm?

(i). Many assert that it was written in the time of the Maccabees, in honour either of Jonathan (161 B.C.), or of Simon (143 B.C.), who secured the independence of the Jews, and drove out the Gentiles from Jerusalem, of whom we read that when "the people saw the faith of Simon, and the glory which he thought to bring unto his nation, they made him their leader and high priest" (1 Macc. xiv. 35). A further argument is adduced that as the initial letters of the clause "Sit thou," and the three following verses, spell the name Simeon (שמען), this is an evident proof of the correctness of the theory. But there is no other example of this form of acrostic in the Bible, common though it was in later times, and if the argument were true, it is hardly likely that all traces of a tradition bearing upon it should have been lost.* Further, it must be remembered that whereas to the King in the Psalm the priesthood is also promised, the Maccabees were priests to begin with, of the family of Levi. Thus they were not even of the family of David, with whom all the hopes of royalty were bound up. Again, the magnificent promises of this Psalm would have a poor fulfilment if they were spoken of those who, after all, were only the vassals of a heathen king (see 1 Macc. xiii. 39). Neither may it be forgotten that the existence of any Maccabean Psalms at all in the Psalter is extremely doubtful, in view of the inclusion of all the Psalms in the Septuagint, for this can hardly be later than the middle of the second century B.C., and may be a century earlier.

**277**] (ii). Many scholars are of opinion that the Psalm was composed during the Kingdom, *i.e.*, before the destruction of Jerusalem by Nebuchadnezzar, but think, both for its language, and for the long experience that would have been required before a writer could write so thoughtfully about the king, that it cannot be placed otherwise than late during that period.† Hence, they say, it was not written by David, but was only attributed to him as found in the collection which bore his name. If so, in reply to the question whether Jesus was justified in using the name of David as its author, we may say that He was not discussing authorship, but was content

* Dr. Driver does not think it worth while to notice this supposed acrostic in his article on the Psalm in the *Expositor* for March, 1910 (VII. 9. 217).

† It may however be pointed out that at no time were the Israelites likely to be ignorant of what a king and a kingdom meant. Their experience in Egypt was continually supplemented by their knowledge of the state of things in neighbouring countries.

to use the common belief of His time. Or it is possible that inasmuch as Jesus, according to Christian teaching, was fully man, the knowledge obtained by Him by virtue of His divinity did not extend to details unimportant for His spiritual work.

**278**] (iii). Yet I cannot forbear asking whether there is anything in the Psalm which is really inconsistent with Davidic authorship? The eighteenth Psalm is attributed to David by all but a few critics. If we do not read Christian teaching into the 110th Psalm, is this on a much higher level than that? And, even if it is, are we not much too completely in the dark as to the extent of the culture of David's time, the education he had received, the theological thought of his surroundings, the influences brought to bear upon him in his wanderings, to be able to affirm that David could not have written it? It may at least be said that the reasons against the Davidic authorship are far from conclusive.

**279**] (2). It is more important to decide whether Jesus was justified in assuming, with the Pharisees to whom He was speaking, that the central figure of the Psalm was Messiah.

(i). R. Isaac of course will have none of it. He interprets the opening words as: "The LORD saith unto my Lord David." He compares the incident at Mahanaim (2 Sam. xviii. 3), and says that God is charging David to sit in God's house, and trust in the power of His right hand (for the "right hand of the LORD doeth valiantly"), even as in Ps. xx. he prays that God will send him help from the sanctuary. As for the priesthood promised, this, says R. Isaac, was fulfilled when he bought the threshing-floor of Araunah, and offered sacrifices there. The Rabbi's explanation is rather poor, for "sitting at the right hand" is in Scripture always a position of honour, not of mere trust and of confidence in power to be exercised.* Besides, David was not really priest, even if he himself did offer as a priest at Araunah's threshing-floor, which is very doubtful. R. Isaac's interpretation does not stand any close examination.

* 1 Kings ii. 19; Ps. xlv. 10; Job xxx. 12.

**280**] (ii). It will indeed seem fairly plain to most people that the Psalm presents features in its description of the King which are too high for David or for any merely earthly monarch of the Davidic line. He is to sit on God's right hand of honour. He is to be a priest after the manner of the old Priest-King Melchizedek. It is then hardly credible that the Pharisees were wrong when they saw in the Psalm a description of Messiah. Modern writers however assume that David at any rate could not have looked forward to the coming of Messiah. Why not? In Gen. iii. 15 (see parr. 131-136), and in Gen. xlix. 10 (see parr. 144-151), the hope of a great Deliverer in the future had been recorded, and, even if the actual writing down of such prophecies should prove to be later than the time of David, there is every probability that he was acquainted with the traditional teaching of his religion, including the hope of a Messiah. If so, he may well have composed the Psalm with direct reference to that Deliverer. With the opinion that David had of that Messiah we are not concerned. He may have regarded Him only as man, for he speaks of Him being refreshed by the water of the *wādy* as He pursues His foes (*v.* 7). But, as we shall see, one of the words he uses implies that he held Him in extreme reverence.

**281**] (3). For let us consider lastly, Why did Jesus ask this question?

Observe that two assumptions lie at the basis of it, besides, of course, the presupposition that the Psalm was inspired by God. One is that the Messiah is the son of David. This was a commonplace in our Lord's time, as it had been for centuries before. The other is that the title "my Lord," with which David addresses Messiah, implies the superiority of Messiah to David, and it is not usual to attribute superiority over oneself to one's own descendant.

Why then did Jesus ask the question? Was it to silence His opponents? Two out of the three questions they had asked Him suggested that it was no sincere love of the truth which prompted their enquiries. Did He wish to silence them once and for all? This may have had something to do with it. But His chief motive, we may say, was to make them think.

To what answer did He desire them to come? Surely that Messiah, as the great Deliverer, even though he were David's son, was nevertheless greater than David. For if this thought did but sink into their minds it would tend to raise the current conceptions about Messiah. David was much more than a man of war; he was also a man of God, a man who in a special degree was near and dear to God. But Messiah was to be greater than David.

The answer would also tend to suggest a higher conception of the nature of Messiah. If so, there would be in this suggestion illimitable possibilities. Messiah then was to be more than man! He was to have perhaps even a divine nature as well as a human! Can we wonder that early believers in Jesus applied the words of the Psalm to Jesus after His resurrection, and saw in that "sitting on the right hand" which was proclaimed of the Messiah a reference to the ascended Jesus?

---

**282**] *Note.* R. Isaac strangely objects to the notion of Jesus sitting at the right hand of God, as though it suggested a local sitting. But he ought to have perceived that the figure, for it is only a figure, of God's right hand belongs to the Psalm, and is not due to Christian teaching. The fact that Jesus, according to Christianity, has ascended in His human nature makes no difference to the use of the figure.

### ii. DANIEL vii. 13 AND ix. 25—27.

**283**] In § 41 R. Isaac discusses Dan. vii. 13, "one like unto a son of man" (כבר אנש), and decides that the writer meant by it not the Messiah, but the people of Israel. On the whole it is probable that the Rabbi is right, and I therefore do not propose considering the passage. See however the second volume.

**284**] In § 42 he fills many pages with an examination of

Dan. ix. 24-27, i.e., the seventy weeks, and the cutting off of the Messiah or the Anointed one. His interpretation is very strange, for he thinks that the Messiah in *v.* 25 is Cyrus, and in *v.* 26 is, of all people, Herod Agrippa ii.! Yet while it is quite certain that the Rabbi's interpretation of the verses is wrong, I cannot find any interpretation that commends itself to me. As therefore these pages are not intended to be a repertory of diverse opinions, but a sincere endeavour to state what is true, it is not necessary to trouble the reader with a discussion of the passage.

# CHAPTER VI

## A FEW ADDITIONAL DIFFICULTIES ADDUCED BY R. ISAAC OF TROKI

# CHAPTER VI.

## A few Additional Difficulties adduced by R. Isaac of Troki.

### i. The Apocrypha.

§ 43.

**285**] Some Christians ask R. Isaac how it is that the Jews do not accept the Apocrypha. In his answer he gives his reasons, which perhaps are rather unduly harsh, but essentially right from the point of view of an English Churchman like myself. For the sixth Article of the English Church says of these books of the Apocrypha: "the Church doth read [them] for example of life and instruction of manners; but yet doth it not apply them to establish any doctrine."

### ii. One Religion.

§ 44.

**286**] With § 44 R. Isaac leaves the consideration of Christian arguments in favour of Christianity, and brings forward his own in favour of Judaism. But of these some have already been adduced by him, especially in §§ 1 and 6 which therefore we need not consider again, while others have to do with the New Testament, and it will be more convenient for us to deal with these in the Second Part of R. Isaac's book. For example, in this section he affirms that in the future there is to be only one religion, the religion of Israel, not that of Christians or of Mohammedans. The reader will find his arguments considered in parr. 31-34.

### iii. Quotations from the Old Testament in the New.

§ 45.

**287**] In this section a string of Old Testament passages quoted in the New is brought forward by the Rabbi to show that the writers of the New Testament were ignorant people who quoted texts without understanding them. It would however be easy to deduce precisely the same argument, and it has been deduced, from the quotations of the Old Testament found in the Talmudic and Rabbinic writings, and the Rabbi ought at least to have perceived that the character of the quotations in the New Testament and those in the Talmud, &c., is so far alike as to testify to the employment of the same methods in making them, i.e., to testify to the thoroughly Jewish character of the New Testament.

But every one of the passages mentioned in this section is brought forward by the Rabbi also in the Second Part of his book, and seeing that, God willing, we shall go carefully through that part in the second volume of this Manual, it is better to postpone any consideration of them in detail until we meet them there.

### iv. The Punishment of Nations which ill-treat the Jews.

§ 46.

**288**] R. Isaac tells us that we see from experience that those nations which have ill-treated the Jews do not escape punishment from God, and he gives examples to prove his statement. Certainly. We Christians do not deny it. From the days of Pharaoh until now persecution of the Jews has injured the persecutors even more than the persecuted. Yet it must not be overlooked that the Judge of the whole world also punishes those who persecute Christians, in particular those Christians who observe most faithfully the teaching of the New Testament.

### v. Was it the will of Jesus to suffer?

§ 47 and Part II. §§ 24–26.

**289**] R. Isaac puts a dilemma: Did the Jews ill-treat Jesus with His will or against it? If you Christians answer "with His will," then those who do the will of God ought to find favour in His eyes, in accordance with Scripture; also Jesus ought not to have been troubled, and to have prayed against the cup of suffering (Matt. xxvi. 39); also, it may be added, His cry on the cross (Matt. xxvii. 46) shows that He was not one with God, for their wills disagreed. If, on the other hand, you Christians answer "He suffered against His will," then how can He be God? And how will He who could not save Himself save His followers? He surely ought to have been greater than Moses, the skin of whose face shone so much that others, even Aaron, were afraid of him. Much more ought men to have been afraid of Jesus.

I have stated the Rabbi's argument at length, because it looks so strong, and yet is so unutterably weak.

The answer to the question is clear; Jesus did suffer willingly. Every Christian will give that answer. But does that, even if Jesus was God, justify the action of those who caused Him suffering? Let me put it another way. If God is willing that suffering shall take place, does that make suffering right? I will answer his dilemma fully when he will answer this, this very old one: Is the sin of any man committed with the will of God or against it? If he answers "with the will of God," then every sinner ought to find favour with God; if he says "against the will of God," then God is not supreme. In other words the dilemma proposed by the Rabbi is precisely the same as that of the existence of evil, and the commission of any act of sin.

Again, R. Isaac's argument is based on a misunderstanding of the Christian doctrine of the Incarnation. He is ignorant that Christians affirm the absolute humanity of Jesus, although He is God. Christians hold that if His Godhead had taken away, or had absorbed, His human will, or even His natural horror of suffering, He would not have been real and complete man. Hence it was necessary that He should have a will which at one and the same time was ready to suffer, if without suffering the purpose of His coming to earth could not be accomplished, and yet dreaded all that this suffering might mean. Thus the Rabbi's questions about Matt. xxvi. 39 and xxvii. 46 are beside the point. Presumably however we shall consider those passages again when we come to them in the Second Part of the Rabbi's book.

Thus, as I have already hinted, the argument of this section appears to be hardly worthy of R. Isaac. He speaks in it either as a mere controversialist who is desirous of entangling his opponent, or else as one who understands neither the meaning of his own words, nor the doctrine of those whom he desires to convince. There must be mysteries in true religion, too deep for the human brain to fathom. It is our wisdom to acknowledge this, and not to allow the fact to turn us away from truth.

### vi. Christians and good works.

§ 48.

**290**] In this section R. Isaac continues to attack Christianity. He tells us that Christians say that Jesus did all His good works for Christians, and justified them from going down to the pit by His life and His sufferings and death. If so, he affirms, there is no need for any Christian to do any good work, and also, even if Christians do all kinds of evil, this will not so hurt them as to bring them down to hell, for Jesus has already redeemed them from it. Then the Rabbi goes on to say that, notwithstanding this, St. Paul writes that the wicked will not inherit the kingdom of heaven (1 Cor. vi. 9), *i.e.*, that the work of Jesus does not profit the wicked. But if this is the case, then, says the Rabbi, since the wicked have no merit of their own, and are not saved by another's merit, and as the righteous have their own merit, and do not need the merit of another (as is clear from the case of the righteous before Jesus came), therefore we must say that Jesus is of no use to any one at all, and those who hope to be saved by the merit of Jesus have a vain hope. If however it be answered that Jesus came to redeem from hell those souls which go there because of the sin of Adam (original sin), I have already proved (says R. Isaac) in § 11, that the souls of the righteous and the prophets do not go to hell, God forbid !, and are not punished at all for the sin of Adam.

Do you not think, my Friends who do me the honour of reading these pages, that our Rabbi might have given the writers of the New Testament credit for some consistency, and that it might have occurred to him that possibly he was misunderstanding them ? The fact is that he sets up a scarecrow which he supposes is Christianity but is not, and then proceeds to knock it down.

**291**] When he says that it makes no difference to a believer whether he commits sin or not, he forgets that, according to the New Testament, it is impossible for a believer to continue in sin. St. Paul in Rom. vi. 1—4 makes this clear. If a man does continue in sin he cannot really be a believer. He may call himself one, but he has no part or lot with Jesus. Thus R. Isaac ought to have understood 1 Cor. vi. 9 aright, *viz.*, that if men, in spite of their professed belief in Jesus, continue to sin wilfully, they *ipso facto* cut themselves off from Him and from the benefit of His death. The fact is that R. Isaac writes as one who is still in the meshes of the crassest form of the Jewish doctrine of merit, as though the performance of good works, as a mere performance, counted for merit. Christianity teaches that real faith in Christ must, without fail, produce union with Christ, and that union with Christ must, equally without fail, produce union in heart with Him, and hatred of sin and love of good.

As to what the Rabbi says about Original Sin, I must refer the reader to parr. 126-130.

### vii. Do Christians believe the New Testament?

§§ 49, 50.

**292**] In § 49 our Rabbi attacks Christians on the ground that although they profess to believe in Jesus they do not believe either His words or the words of His apostles. He gives six examples to prove his statement.

Of these, the first, that Jesus does not call Himself God, but man, has been considered in parr. 113, 114. R. Isaac carefully omits to point out that the Apostles do speak very plainly of Him as God (par. 124). The second example, that Jesus taught the permanence of the Law, has been considered in parr. 173-179. The third, fourth, and fifth (Matt. xix. 16-22, v. 39 with Luke vi. 29, John ii. 4) will be considered in their places in the second Volume. The sixth, forbidden Foods, has been examined already in parr. 152-159.

**293**] You Christians say, writes the Rabbi in the last section of the First Part of his book, that the New Testament is a new Law, given instead of the Law of Moses. If so you ought not to add to it, or take away from it, as is said both in the Law (Deut. iv. 2), and in the end of the New Testament (Rev. xxii. 18, 19). Yet you both add and take away. And the Rabbi gives examples in support of his statement.

First, it may be replied that he has misunderstood the passage in the Revelation. This refers only to the Book of Revelation itself, not to the contents of the New Testament as a whole. Secondly, the Rabbi has again made the very serious mistake of speaking of the New Testament as a new Law. No doubt most Christians whom he met thought that it was, but there is no hint of such a thing in the New Testament itself: see parr. 179, 213. But if it is not a new Law we cannot speak of adding to it or subtracting from it, as the Rabbi does. This is to introduce a wholly fresh idea into the teaching of the New Testament.

**294**] Yet let us suppose that my demurrers do not hold good, and let us see what are the examples adduced by R. Isaac. He says that Christians subtract three commands, *viz.*, to sell their property and give to the poor (Matt. xix. 21, Luke xviii. 22); to turn the other cheek to an opponent, etc., (Matt. v. 39—42, Luke vi. 27—30); and to abstain from forbidden foods. The first two of these will be considered in their proper place in the second Volume, and the third has already been considered in parr. 152—159.

His examples of so-called additions are, first, the doctrine of the Trinity (on this see parr. 105—125), secondly, the appellation of Jesus as God (see par. 123), thirdly, the worship of images. In this last I confess that R. Isaac is right; right also in pointing out that although Christians may argue that images are made by them only for the honour of the saints, male and female, and not for prayer, yet even though this were said with truth of images made in metal, wood and stone, Christians cannot deny that they worship idols of bread, and pray to them, and say of each one of them that it is God. Alas, what can I reply to this most grievous accusation?

Nothing at all, save this, that as a faithful member of the Church of England I can but deplore that sin of idolatry which she in her Articles and Prayer Book distinctly condemns, while she is fully aware that large numbers of professing Christians have fallen into it.

The Rabbi's fourth example is that Jesus never told Christians to hate the Jews and avenge His wrongs upon them, and yet they do so. Alas, yes; this has too often been the case. But the Rabbi should not confuse things that differ. Both Jews and Christians often do things that are contrary to their religion, but no wise man will blame their religion for this. It is plain that it is the duty of every Christian man to show love and kindness to the Jews; if he does not he is so far unlike Him whose disciple he professes to be. For "God is love; and he that abideth in love abideth in God, and God abideth in him" (1 John iv. 16).

---

**295**] We have now come to the end of the First Part of the *Chizzuk Emunah*, and I cannot but thank Almighty God that He has allowed us to travel thus far upon the road. We have, I trust, learned something together. We have endeavoured to see the Lord Jesus as He really was when on earth, in spite of the many veils that human controversies have thrown round Him. We have attempted to get behind mere ecclesiastical Christianity, especially the Christianity of less pure and reformed branches of the Church than the Church of England; we have tried to see the meaning of many passages in the Old Testament, looking at them with eyes dimmed neither by Jewish nor Christian tradition, for we know that it is useless to shut our eyes to truth, and to scholarship based upon truth. Above all, we have endeavoured to learn something fresh about the weakness of our own nature and character, and at the same time something more of the meaning of the Gospel, that it is not a new Law, God forbid, but forgiveness, liberty and strength. Unto which knowledge and life may God, blessed be He, lead us, through His Spirit, for the sake of Jesus Christ, His only Son, our Lord.

# GLOSSARY

# and

# INDICES

# GLOSSARY.*

*Aboth*, "Fathers." A treatise of the Mishna (q.v.), with no Gemara (q.v.) attached to it. To the majority of English readers it is the most interesting of all the treatises, for it contains a large number of important ethical sayings. It may be found with an English translation in Singer's *Authorised Daily Prayer Book*, pp. 184 *sqq.* (price 1/-). The quotations in this *Manual* are generally made from Dr. C. Taylor's *Sayings of the Jewish Fathers*, 2nd edition, 1897.

*Aboth d'Rabbi Nathan.*

An enlargement of the mishna treatise *Aboth*, attributed to R. Nathan, a Tanna (mishna-teacher) of the 4th generation (160—220): but in its present form this treatise is post-Talmudic.

*Al-tiqri*, "Do not read."

A phrase used in the Talmud and elsewhere when a Rabbi desired to give a midrashic (q.v.) explanation of a passage. He said "Do not read" the true text, but read something very like it, such, for example as "r" for "d" (see par. 93).

The object was not, as has been fondly supposed, to throw doubt on the accuracy of the text, but only to deduce a lesson from it.

*Aqiba.*

One of the most famous of the teachers mentioned in the Mishna (q.v.). He was born about 50 A.D. and killed by the Romans as a leader in Barcochba's revolt about 132 A.D. He insisted on the inspiration of every word, and even every letter, of Scripture.

*Baalshem—The*, "The Master of the Name."

The founder of the sect of Chassidim. Born about 1700 in the Bukowina, died 1761 A.D. Apparently a

* This short Glossary, with the accompanying explanations, may be useful to some non-Jewish readers. It is not intended to be of any assistance to Jewish people.

singularly holy man, insisting more on the religious spirit than on the observance of forms of religion. He laid great stress on the Immanence of God.

According to him a really righteous man (*Zaddiq*) stands in a special relation to God. Hence his followers regard him as the great mediator between themselves and God. The same claim (though generally in less measure) is made by and for each leader of a group of Chassidim to-day.

See the *Jewish Encyclopedia* ii. 383—386; and especially Schechter, *Studies in Judaism*, 1896, pp. 1—55.

*Bereshith R (abba).* An exegetical, mostly haggadic (q.v.) midrash (q.v.), on Genesis, mainly dating in its present form from about the sixth century. See Oesterley and Box, *The Religion and Worship of the Synagogue*, 1907, pp. 81 *sq.*

*Bible.*

The Hebrew Bible is arranged under the following heads: I. The Law (*Torah*), *i.e.*, the five books of Moses. II. The Prophets (*Nebiim*): (1) Former, 1 and 2 Samuel, 1 and 2 Kings; (2) Latter, Isaiah, Jeremiah, Ezekiel and the Twelve ("minor") Prophets. III. The Writings (*Kethûbîm*): (1) Psalms, Proverbs, Job; (2) the Five Megilloth or Rolls, viz., Canticles, Ruth, Lamentations, Ecclesiastes, Esther; (3) Daniel, Ezra and Nehemiah, Chronicles. The Jews often refer to the Scriptures as "Law, Prophets and Writings," or as TNK, the initial letters of the Hebrew titles.

*Boethus.*

A Sadducean priest. His son, or perhaps he himself, was made High Priest about 25 or 24 B.C. by Herod the Great. Boethusians became synonymous with Sadducees. See the *Jewish Encyclopedia*, iii. 284 *sq.*

*D'rash*, "explanation," of a passage rather than a book (*midrash*). In contrast to *P'shat* (q.v.) it is an explanation which is either far-fetched or, at the least, does not lie within the ordinary grammatical meaning of the passage.

*Elisha ben Abuyah*, also called *Acher*, "another."

"Our Rabbis have taught, Four men went up into Paradise, and they were these, Ben Azzai, and Ben Zoma,

Acher, and R. Aqiba" (T.B. Chagiga 14*b*). Ben Azzai gazed and died. Ben Zoma gazed and went mad. Acher "cut the plants," *i.e.* (as it seems) divided the Godhead. R. Aqiba alone came out unhurt. It is probable that Acher (Elisha ben Abuyah) adopted some form of Gnosticism. Some scholars are of opinion that his fault was that he disliked Pharisaism and tried to lead Jews to break its precepts. He lived from about 70 to 130 A.D. See Streane's *Translation of Chagigah*, 1891, pp. 83—89; also the *Jewish Encyclopedia*, v. pp. 138 *sq.*

*Gematria*, either "arithmetic," or "letters."

There are no separate numerals in Hebrew, but each letter has a numerical value attached to it in accordance with its position in the alphabet. Hence by adding up the letters of which a word is composed it is possible to say that the whole word equals a certain number. Not only so, but by a process of reasoning which appeals only to those who accept the inspiration of Scripture in every letter, two words which are equal in numerical value may be treated as equal in meaning.

*Gemara*, see Talmud.

*Haggada* (plural *Haggadoth*), "declaration," "narration," "telling."

A term of very wide meaning expressive of all exposition of scripture that does not deal directly with legal decision (*i.e.*, that is not halakic, q.v.). Thus it includes almost, or quite, every other form of Biblical exegesis, and, in particular, illustrative stories. See especially Strack, *Einleitung in den Talmud*, 1908, pp. 5 *sq.*; also Oesterley and Box, *Religion and Worship of the Synagogue*, 1907, p. 75.

*Halaka* (plural *Halakoth*), "walk" "rule," a legal decision determining the walk of life. Contrast "Haggada." It is applied to the legal element of the oral law.

*Karaite*, "Reader." A name given to themselves by the followers of Anan (died between 780 and 800 A.D.), who rejected the oral traditional law taught by the Rabbis, and attempted to derive all customs and doctrine from scripture (*mikqra*) *i.e.*, the Pentateuch. See *Rabbanite*.

*Kōsher*, "correct," "proper."

An epithet describing food ritually correct to be eaten by Jews.

*Law.*

The Hebrew name is Torah, which however does not appear to be used of Law in the abstract, but only of "the Law." This was regarded as (1) Written, contained in the Pentateuch, though occasionally the term is used of other books of Scripture; (2) Oral, a traditional Law taught by God to Moses on Mount Sinai and handed down by him. The Oral Law had no fixed contents, but was continually being enlarged and modified (but only, as was claimed, in accordance with fixed principles guiding its evolution from the first) by successive generations of teachers. The first authoritative code of it was the Mishna (q.v.) of R. Judah ha Nasi. See also *Bible.*

*Maimonides.*

A very famous Jewish writer and codifier of the oral law, born at Cordova 1135, died at Cairo 1204. His principal works are the *Yad-ha-Chazāqa* or Digest of the Oral Law, and the *Môreh-Nebûkim*, a philosophical investigation of many religious subjects.

*Massora*, *māsôreth*, *massoretic*, "tradition," "traditional."

The massoretic text of the Hebrew Bible is the ordinary text, with vowel points. It represents the results of the study of the "Massoretes," the "traditionalists," who lived from the second half of the eighth century to the first half of the tenth century A.D. The most accurate edition of this text is that which is now (1910) being published by the British and Foreign Bible Society, under the editorship of Dr. C. D. Ginsburg.

*Mechilta.*

A homiletical midrash (q.v.) on the book of Exodus (from ch. 12). In its original form belonging to the first part of the 2nd century A.D., in its present form rather later; the most important and valuable of the *midrashim* (q.v.).

*Midrash*, plural *Midrashim*, "explanation," "exposition."

In particular the semi-homiletical explanations of different books of Scripture, *e.g.*, the Midrash on Genesis. They are of very various ages, and generally speaking contain Haggada (q.v.) rather than Halacha (q.v.). See also *D'rash.* For an account of the different Midrashic works see Oesterley and Box, *Religion and Worship of the Synagogue*, 1907, ch. v.

*Mitzvah*, "commandment."
Any action performed out of obedience to the will of God.

*Mishna*, see Talmud.

*Moses de Leon.*
Born at Leon in Spain about 1250, died 1305 A.D. Probably the author of the present form of the *Zohar*, a strange Cabbalistic Midrash, which he pretended was written by R. Simeon ben Jochai, who died at Meron near Safed in Galilee about 161 A.D.

*Onkelos*, see *Targum.*

*Pesiqta Rabbuthi.* A homiletical midrash (q.v.) on the special lessons read in the Synagogue from the Law and the Prophets. It is said to be as old as the second half of the ninth century A.D.

*Pirqe Aboth*, "chapters of Aboth"; see *Aboth.*

*Pirqe d'Rabbi Eliezer* "chapters of R. Eliezer."
A midrashic (q.v.) narrative of the more important events recorded in the Pentateuch, attributed to R. Eliezer ben Hyrcanus, who lived in the end of the first century A.D., but in its present form not earlier than the eighth century.

*P'shat*, "simple."
The explanation of a passage derived solely from a study of grammatical and lexical meaning of the words in their context. Contrast *D'rash.*

*Rabbanite.*
A nickname given by the Karaites (q.v.) about 800 A.D. to their adversaries the orthodox Jews, as "the partisans of authority" (see Grätz, *Geschichte der Juden*, 1871, v. 181.

English translation 1892, iii. 136), "Rabban" ("our teacher") being a title of the president of the Sanhedrin from the time of R. Gamaliel the Elder, teacher of St. Paul.

*Saadiah.*

Head ("*Gaon*") of the Rabbinic academy at Sura in Babylonia. Born 892, died 942 A.D. His book on the Articles of Faith and Doctrines of Dogma ("*sepher Emunoth w'Deoth*") was written in 933.

*Sabbathai Zebi.*

Born at Smyrna 1626, died in Albania 1676. When he was twenty-two years of age he claimed to be the Messiah, at first more or less privately. In 1665 however he claimed the position openly, and multitudes of Jews believed in him, including many prominent Rabbis of the time. But after being imprisoned by the Sultan he became a Moslem in 1666, and persuaded many of his followers to imitate him. See the *Jewish Encyclopedia*, xi. pp. 218—225.

*Shekinah*, "dwelling" (in the abstract sense).

A term used to express the thought of God's dwelling with men, more particularly of His Presence as in some way making Itself visible. See Oesterley and Box, *The Religion and Worship of the Synagogue*, 1907, pp. 191—195; also C. Taylor, *Sayings of the Jewish Fathers*, 1897, pp. 43, *sq*.

*Talmud*, plural *Talmudim*, "study," "teaching."

A summary of the oral traditional law with discussions and illustrative tales. It is in two parts: (1) the Mishna, "repetition," a comparatively short collection made about 190 A.D. by R. Jehuda ha Nasi. It is composed of many treatises known by the names of the principal subject in each. (2) The Gemara, "completion" and "learning," which takes the form of a commentary on the Mishna. Strictly speaking the word "Talmud" is used of the Gemara alone. The Gemara is two-fold: (i.) the Palestinian or Jerusalem Gemara, of the fourth and fifth centuries, containing the opinions of Jewish scholars living in Palestine, cited as T(almud) J(erushalmi). (ii.) the Babylonian Gemara, mostly of the sixth century, containing the opinions of Jewish scholars living in Babylon, cited as T(almud) B(abli). Of these an edition of the Mishna interwoven with the Babylonian Gemara is "the Talmud" *par excellence.* Hence quotations from a Talmudical treatise without either of the prefixes T.B., T.J., refer to the Babylonian Gemara.

*Targum*, plural *Targumim*, "translation."

Aramaic translations of the Hebrew Bible frequently so far from literal as to be rather paraphrases.

I. *On the Pentateuch :* (1) *Targum of Onkelos*, apparently an Aramaic form of "Aquila," of the second century A.D. generally literal. (2) *Targum of Jerusalem I.*, often called by a mistake the Targum of Jonathan. In its present form not older than the second half of the seventh century A.D. Often paraphrastic. (3) *Targum of Jerusalem II.*, or "Fragment Targum," so called because it exists only in many pieces, often quite short. It seems to be of about the same date as the Targ. Jer. I., and is of much the same character.

II. *On the Prophets* (Former and Latter, see *Bible*). *The Targum of Jonathan ben Uzziel*, because attributed to him. He was a pupil of Hillel, at the beginning of the Christian era, but the Targum in its present form is of about the fifth century A.D. It is not so literal as the Targum of Onkelos, especially in the prophecies.

III. *On the Holy Writings* (see Bible). The Targums on these are by many writers, of about the same date as the Targums of Jerusalem; that on Chronicles is later.

On the whole subject see especially Strack, *Einleitung in das alte Testament*, 1906, § 84; also Oesterley and Box, *The Religion and Worship of the Synagogue*, 1907, pp. 44—50.

*T.B.* see Talmud.

*T.J.* see Talmud.

*Torah*, see *Law.*

*Yalqut*, "scrip" (1 Sam. xvii. 40), "collection."

A large collection of materials from various midrashim (q.v.), many of which are no longer extant, covering the whole Hebrew Bible. It is similar in character to the patristic *catenae*. The Yalqut *par excellence* bears the name of Simeon. It is not earlier than the middle ages. Who the Simeon was is unknown.

*Yiddish*, Jüdisch, "Jewish."

A language of which the basis is mediæval High German, into which have been wrought many Hebrew words and phrases, and, in addition, not a little of the language of the country in which any Jew who uses it happens to live. Its German basis forms the real distinction from the *Ladino*, or Jewish-Spanish, of Levantine Jews, which is a fairly pure mediæval Spanish, with the addition of a certain amount of Hebrew. Both forms of "Jargon" are of extreme interest philologically. The dialects of Yiddish are innumerable, their differences depending on the amount of the third ingredient, non-German and non-Hebrew words. Hence if in a company of Yiddish-speaking Jews from various parts of the world the question "What is true Yiddish?" is asked, a satisfactory answer is seldom received. Each person naturally supposes that his own form of it is the best. Mr. Leo Wiener, the chief authority on the vast Yiddish literature, says in the *Jewish Encyclopedia* (vii. 305), that the dialects "may be conveniently grouped in three divisions: (1) the southern, spoken in the south of Russia, in parts of Galicia, and in Roumania, and corresponding more closely to a variety of Bavarian; (2) the Polish, the dialect of Poland and parts of Lithuania and Galicia; and (3) the Lithuanian, the dialect spoken in the greater part of Lithuania, and bearing strong resemblances to the dialects of Henneberg and of parts of Saxony." There is no good dictionary of Yiddish into English, Harkavy's (New York, 1901, 1905) containing little more than the debased modern German in which many Jewish newspapers are written. The Hebrew character is always employed for Yiddish.

# INDICES

*The numbers refer to the paragraphs, not the pages.*

---

## i. GENERAL

## ii. BIBLICAL AND POST-BIBLICAL PASSAGES

*Large type indicates that the passage is examined at length.*

*The Old Testament books are in the Hebrew order.*

---

---

# A MANUAL

OF

# CHRISTIAN EVIDENCES

FOR

# JEWISH PEOPLE

BY

A. LUKYN WILLIAMS, D.D.

*Vicar of Guilden Morden and Hon. Canon of Ely Cathedral, formerly Tyrwhitt Hebrew Scholar in the University of Cambridge*

VOLUME 2 OF 2

With Glossary and Indices to the whole Work

עשה שלום במרומיו הוא יעשה שלום

עלינו

ועל כל־ישראל

ואמרו אמן :

# CONTENTS

## PREFACE

THE primary object of the following pages is to make Christianity better understood of Jews. For nothing is more astounding to Christian people than the strange notions about it which Jews still hold. The author, indeed, cannot hope to be always right in his own statements about Judaism, though he is much encouraged by the fact that none of the Jewish reviews of the first volume * pointed out any errors in this respect,† but Jewish writers go wrong not so much in details as in their general idea of what Christianity is, and especially of what it holds with regard to Christ Himself. Further, they often assume that Christianity is identical with Roman Catholicism. This is not unnatural on the part of non-Christians, but it is not true. In any case, not Roman Catholicism but the New Testament alone is the standard adopted in this work. No doubt, however, as the author belongs to the Anglican branch of the Catholic Church, he is inclined to regard the New Testament from the standpoint of the Book of Common Prayer and the Thirty-nine Articles.

The Jewish writer of a review of the first volume complained that the book was a *petitio principii*, on the ground that the truth of the Christian religion was assumed, and therefore it had no force for a Jew. Naturally, a Christian must assume the truth of Christianity, and he has only to consider how best he may expound it and defend it. In the

* *A Manual of Christian Evidences for Jewish People.* Vol. i. Cambridge. W. Heffer & Sons. 1911.

† Naturally they disagreed both with the work as a whole, and with some of its interpretations of the Old Testament in detail.

present case the form adopted is due to the fact that there has not been in English any systematic reply to the arguments of R. Isaac of Troki, and that these arguments are used to-day, with hardly any change, by almost every Jew who writes about Christianity. R. Isaac's work is in two parts, the First on the Old Testament, which has been considered in the first volume, the Second on the New Testament, which is the subject of this. He found it impossible to keep the two subjects quite distinct, but a mere repetition of arguments has been avoided here.

It was originally proposed to produce a third volume dealing with other and newer arguments put forth by Jews, but if that volume is ever written it will be on such very different lines from these that it will require a new name, and be an independent work. It needs to be done by some one, and the present writer cannot but hope that these two volumes may in some measure have prepared the ground for it.

For the attacks of Judaism upon Christianity are certain to become stronger as Jews acquire more independence and power, and Christian people will be obliged to arouse themselves out of their lethargy if they are not to lose the day. It is the duty of us Christians to study Judaism, and, with increasing knowledge of it, to present to Jews our blessed Lord Jesus as the true Messiah of Jews and Gentiles alike.

There is another matter which may not be passed over. The writer has been blamed by some for dealing too tenderly with his opponents, and especially for acknowledging that they are sometimes in the right. Yet absolute frankness is in the end by far the best policy, and the wrath of man has never yet forwarded the righteousness of God. The writer also has but little sympathy with those godly and earnest Christians who are unable to see the spiritual side of the religion of modern Jews. For, after all, it, and nothing less, has been the salt which has preserved the Jewish nation until now, in spite of the officialism that has only too often hampered its development.

Lastly, it is a privilege to be allowed to write at a time

when the first stage in the fulfilment of God's many promises to the Jews is already accomplished, in the deliverance of the Holy Land from its oppressors. May that Land soon become the home of a Nation of Jews who little by little learn to recognize the Glory of their greatest Son, acknowledging Him as King and LORD.

A. L. W.

GUILDEN MORDEN,
*The Festival of the Conversion of St. Paul, 1919.*

# A MANUAL OF CHRISTIAN EVIDENCES FOR JEWISH PEOPLE

## THE PREAMBLE (הצעה) TO PART II.

**296**] In Part II. R. Isaac leaves the Old Testament as such, and turns to examine the New Testament itself. With the change of subject he makes also some change in method. For he deals much more concisely with each point under discussion. Hence, although the Second Part contains 100 sections as against 50 in the First Part, it fills in Deutsch's edition only 72 pages as against 282.

After stating that his text-book for the New Testament has been the latest translation made by Simon Budny in 1572 A.D. (into Polish), the Rabbi writes a brief Introduction to this Second Part, the object of which is to represent the New Testament as completely untrustworthy. He begins by saying that although Christians affirm that the Gospel is a new Law, the Gospel itself never says that Jesus gave a new Law, but, on the contrary, that He affirmed the permanence of the Law of Moses.

We have already considered this statement in our examination of Part I. §§ 19, 20, 29, parr. 179–181; 230–233.

**297**] The Rabbi then makes the amazing assertion that it is well known that the New Testament was not written till the time of Constantine, three hundred years after the death of Jesus. He refers to Part I. § 2, but he does not actually say so there, nor is it a necessary deduction from what he does say.*

But it is not worth while delaying the reader with a refutation of so absurd a statement.†

* His words are: "Constantine was the first Roman Emperor to accept the religion of Jesus," adding וחקק תורת הנוצרים, which Deutsch, apparently rightly, translates by "und als Staatsreligion einführte," *i.e.* "made it the religion of the State." R. Isaac, as it seems, now interprets his own words to mean, "*wrote* the law of the Christians."

† In virtue, however, of the fact that the statement is repeated in some quite recent Jewish books, it may be well to point out: (1) Though R. Isaac says the

He goes on to say that if the New Testament was written long after Jesus' death, He evidently could not have given the new Law. But no Christian has ever supposed that Jesus wrote the New Testament. We say only that it contains a true record of His life, His teaching, His death, and His resurrection. But, replies the Rabbi, Jerome in his Preface to the books of the New Testament says that Mark and Luke wrote things they had heard from others, meaning that they wrote long after the death of Jesus, for they were not born during His lifetime. How strange it is that so learned a man as R. Isaac could have made so childish a remark! * Jerome was but following the statements of the New Testament itself in pointing out that neither Mark nor Luke was one of the Twelve Apostles (though plainly enough they were both born during our Lord's life on earth), and that therefore they had not themselves seen and heard what they recorded. But the Rabbi might have known also that Jerome in the same place speaks of Mark as the interpreter of Peter himself, and that he wrote down what Peter preached. Further, no one doubts that St. Peter had seen and heard everything, so that if St. Mark wrote down his words there is not much room left

New Testament was not written till three hundred years after the time of Jesus, translations of it were made in Latin and Syriac at least as soon as a hundred and twenty years after His death; (2) Allusions to it are found in writings composed less than ninety years after His death (Ignatius's Letters, the Epistle of Polycarp, the Epistle of Barnabas); (3) St. Paul died less than forty years after the death of Jesus, and there are very few scholars of our time who deny that he wrote most of the Epistles attributed to him; (4) The earliest of these (1 Thessalonians) was written in 50 or 51 A.D., *i.e.* not more than twenty-one years after the death of Jesus, and presupposes throughout the chief events recorded in the Gospels; (5) Harnack, who certainly holds no brief for orthodox Christianity, dates the Gospel according to St. Mark at least as early as 50–60 A.D.

* Had the Rabbi turned to the actual words of Jerome he would have seen his mistake: "Secundus Marcus, interpres Apostoli Petri, et Alexandrinae Ecclesiae primus Episcopus, qui Dominum quidem Salvatorem ipse non vidit, sed ea quae magistrum audierat praedicantem, juxta fidem magis gestorum narravit, quam ordinem. Tertius Lucas Medicus, natione Syrus Antiochensis (cujus laus in Evangelio) qui et ipse discipulus Apostoli Pauli, in Achajae, Boeotiaeque partibus volumen condidit, quaedam altius repetens, et ut ipse in Prooemio confitetur, audita magis, quam visa describens" (*Vallarsi*, vii. 4).

for inaccuracy! R. Isaac's appeal to Jerome weakens, instead of strengthens, his argument.

**298**] Yet, says R. Isaac, the Gospels contradict each other! But they all agree about the important facts. What more would he have? Had their agreement extended to every little detail of action and word he would have been the first to cry: "This is not natural; there must have been collusion; there never were in all the ages of the world three or four witnesses (however truthful) who agreed in everything, unless they had arranged together beforehand what exactly to say." No, the very disagreement about small points, and unimportant words, shows the independence, and the general trustworthiness, of the writers. Cf. par. 368.

**299**] Lastly, R. Isaac calls attention to the disagreement between the words of quotations from the Old Testament and the words in the Old Testament itself; and he adds that often not only the words of such passages are changed, but also their meaning. With this objection of R. Isaac's we have already dealt briefly in parr. 137–142 and elsewhere, to which we would refer our readers. Here it must suffice to say bluntly that the divergence of the quotations in the New Testament, whether in words, or in meaning, or in both, is no greater than that of the quotations found in the Talmud and the Rabbinic writings. The writers of the New Testament were Jews (except presumably St. Luke, who wrote the Third Gospel and the Acts), and they quoted and explained the Old Testament after a Jewish fashion. We could not expect them to do anything else. R. Isaac was a Karaite, so perhaps did not himself indulge in such Midrashic methods. But the Karaites arose long after the time of the writers of the New Testament, who naturally pursued the methods of their contemporaries and fellow-Jews.

## The Genealogies of the Lord Jesus.

§ 1.

300] These have been fully discussed in parr. 8–13. See also *infra*, § 35, parr. 408, *sq*.

## The Virgin.

§ 2.

Matt. i. 22, 23, and Isa. vii. 14.

301] This also has been considered in parr. 186–191.

## The Perpetual Virginity of Mary.

§ 3.

302] R. Isaac says that this doctrine is contradicted by Matt. i. 25. Even if this be so, it is not of great importance, for the doctrine is at best only a pious opinion, not contained in the Creed, nor belonging to the foundation of faith. R. Isaac, no doubt, thought that it was, for round him lived many Romanists. Here he says that Mary's other sons were James, Joses, Simon and Judas (cf. § 17). Perhaps so, but on the whole the older tradition, which "seems especially to represent the Palestinian view," is more probable, that these were the half brothers of our Lord, sons of Joseph by a former wife.*

* See the classical discussion on this subject in Bishop Lightfoot's *Galatians*.

**303**] R. Isaac also is surprised that Joseph did not "call His name Immanuel," after the prophecy. Had he done so, however, the Rabbi would certainly have suspected fraudulent agreement with it. According to Christian teaching the title, "God with us," was completely fulfilled when the Divine Person took human nature. See par. 191.

## Christ and Egypt.

### § 4. Compare Part I. § 45.

Hos. xi. 1, and Matt. ii. 15. "*Out of Egypt did I call my son.*"

**304**] R. Isaac says that these words quoted by St. Matthew from the book of the Prophet Hosea do not in reality refer to Jesus at all, but to the nation of Israel. For the whole sentence is, "When Israel was a child, then I loved him, and called my son out of Egypt." So also God speaks to Moses: "Thou shalt say unto Pharaoh, Thus saith the LORD, Israel is my son, my firstborn: and I have said unto thee, Let my son go, that he may serve me" (Ex. iv. 22, 23).

Now it may be granted at once that no Christian scholar of to-day supposes that Hosea consciously referred to Christ. "Son" is evidently the nation of Israel. So far R. Isaac is right. But I ask: Did St. Matthew think that Hosea referred consciously to Christ? I see no sign that St. Matthew did. Why then did he quote the passage, with the prefatory words, "that it might be fulfilled which was spoken by the Lord through the prophet"? The answer to this is of deep importance for understanding not only this passage but also many other passages in the New Testament.

**305**] St. Matthew did not want to *prove* anything, as, for example, that Jesus of Nazareth was the Messiah because He went down to Egypt as Hosea said He would, but he desired to *illustrate* the history of Jesus from the history of the Jews. Jesus the Messiah, writes St. Matthew, went down into Egypt. "Down into Egypt," we can imagine a Jew crying, "that seems strange for Messiah." Not at all, answers St. Matthew, even Israel went down there in the childhood of the nation, as Hosea says. And further, the suggestion lies close at hand that as Egypt was connected with the beginning of a new era for the people so also was a new era connected with the visit of Jesus. I grant that St. Matthew loves to draw parallels between the history of Messiah and that of Israel, and even to find it fitting that He who was the noblest flower of the stock of Israel should correspond perfectly to Israel, but what of that? Did not the Rabbis themselves love to draw parallels between Israel and its parent stock of Abraham? * If one Jew does this, may not another Jew? Wherein is the harm? Save perhaps that no liberty of thought, no brilliancy of illustration is to be allowed to a Jew who is also a believer in Jesus! No, in his case everything must be taken as literally as possible, lest after all it be seen too convincingly that the writers of the New Testament were thorough Jews, none the less so for their faith in Jesus, and thus some of the old controversial weapons employed by Jews for centuries should be found worthless!

**306**] Or is the fault that Messiah is termed God's Son? Hardly. No learned Jew can find fault with that. The Nation of Israel is called God's son in Ex. iv. 22, 23; the King of Israel is called God's son in Ps. ii. 7; and in the Talmud this second Psalm is applied to Messiah.† See Rashi on T. B. *Sukkah*, 52*a*, "To-day have I begotten Thee: To-day I will reveal to creation that Thou art My Son"

(היום ילדתיך: היום אגלה לבריות שבני אתה).

* See the *Breshith R.* on Gen. xii. 20, § 40 end, where it is said, "Everything that is written of Abraham is written of his children," in proof of which statement eleven examples are given, amongst them, "Abram went down into Egypt to sojourn there" (Gen. xii. 10), and "our fathers went down into Egypt" (Num. xx. 15).

את מוצא כל מה שכתוב באברהם כתוב בבניו וגו.

† On the second Psalm, see parr. 480-493.

No, it is not the word "Son," when used of Messiah, to which Jews can object; it is the full meaning of the word which is given to it by Christians. But it is unjustifiable to turn round and blame a Christian man, such as St. Matthew was, for applying the term "Son" to Messiah, without at the same time defining the point to which objection is taken. I repeat once more that St. Matthew's object was not to furnish a proof for the divinity of Messiah, who, as he believed, was Jesus of Nazareth, but only to illustrate His history, and to enlarge on the treatment He received. "The King of the Jews, like the Jewish nation itself, left Palestine and took refuge in Egypt, and then returned to Palestine again" (Plummer on Matt. ii. 14). Hos. xi. 1 is not a proof-text in the ordinary sense of the word, and cannot be used for one. But St. Matthew was fully justified in quoting it.

### Rachel Weeping.

### § 5.

**307**] Matt. ii. 16–18. See the discussion of the quotation from Jer. xxxi. 15 in Part I. § 28, parr. 228 *sq.* Observe also that in Jeremiah happiness and blessing follow lamentation. So in the mind of the Evangelist the massacre connected with the infancy of Christ was a prelude to His appearance as the Deliverer.

### Nazareth.

### § 6.

Matt. ii. 22, *sq.* "*And being warned* of God *in a dream, he* [i.e. *Joseph*] *withdrew into the parts of Galilee, and came and dwelt in a city called Nazareth: that it might be fulfilled which was spoken by the prophets, that he* [i.e. *Jesus*] *should be called a Nazarene.*"

**308**] Upon this passage R. Isaac remarks: "With regard to this Matthew had a false dream, for this saying is nowhere to be found among the sayings of the prophets."

The difficulty of the passage is well known, for it is a fact that the saying, "He shall be called a Nazarene," is not to be found in the Old Testament. So far the Rabbi is right. Was then St. Matthew wrong? That is another question altogether. My readers, I trust, will have learned by this time to look somewhat below the surface when they meet with a quotation, or what looks like a quotation, in the New Testament, just as they are accustomed to look below the surface with almost every quotation of the Old Testament in the Talmudic writings. For all Talmudic scholars know that quotations from the Bible have more than meets the eye at the first glance.

**309**] Yes, the passage is no quotation in the strict sense of the word. But we must not forget that Messiah is called a *Nezer* (נצר) in Isa. xi. 1 ("And there shall come forth a shoot out of the stock of Jesse, and a *branch* out of his roots shall bear fruit"), as the Targum itself testifies, when it translates נצר by Messiah (ויפוק מלכא מבנוהי דישי ומשיחא מבני בנוהי יתרבי:).

Every learned Jew knows that it was quite in accordance with Jewish custom to make such a play on words as is implied in our passage in the First Gospel. Jesus lived at Nazareth, for the Prophets said He was to be a *Nezer*. Of course in these days no Christian would use this as "a proof-text," a text, namely, to prove to an opponent that the Old Testament said that the Messiah was to live at Nazareth. But St. Matthew never intended his words to have this meaning, or to be so used. He was writing for Jewish Christians like himself, themselves called Nazarenes, and he was pleased to discover in the Old Testament by Jewish methods an allusion to *Nezer* as a name of Messiah. It is worth noticing that in much the same way the legendary list of five of our Lord's disciples, recorded in T. B. *Sanhedrin*, 43*a*, gives the names of one of them as Nezer, and adduces Isa. xi. 1 in an argument on his behalf.*

**310**] We thus see that the "quotation" in Matt. ii. 22, *sq.*, is fully in accordance with Jewish modes of illustrating facts and doctrines from passages in the Old Testament, although these had nothing to do with the case in point according to their proper and literal meaning. As we have seen repeatedly, the writer of the First Gospel believed in the Messiahship of Jesus on quite independent grounds, and for the edification of himself and his fellow-believers illustrated his belief from the Old Testament by methods which large numbers of Jews of his day adopted. Can any thoughtful Jew blame him for this ? †

## THE TEMPTATION OF OUR LORD JESUS CHRIST.

## § 7.

Matt. iv. 1–11 ; Mark i. 12, 13 ; Luke iv. 1–13.

**311**] R. Isaac asserts that the story of the Temptation shows that Jesus could not have been God, for Satan would be afraid to tempt God, and also God could not be tempted,

* The passage, with the best form of text, may be conveniently studied in Strack's *Jesus, die Häretiker und die Christen*, 1910, § 13.

ת״ר חמשה תלמידים היו לו לישו מתאי נקאי נצר ובוני ותודה · · · אתיוה לנצר אמר נצר יהרג דכתיב ונצר משרשיו יפרה.

"Our Rabbis have taught us : Jesus had five disciples, Mattai, Naqqai, Netzer, and Buni, and Toda. . . . They brought Netzer. He said to them : Shall Netzer be slain ? It is written, 'and a Netzer out of his roots shall bear fruit.'"

† It should also be borne in mind that the title צמח ("Branch"), which is used of Messiah in Jer. xxiii. 5, and recognized by the Jews as a Messianic term, may have had something to do with the mention of נצר, a word of similar import. Perhaps St. Matthew's reference to "the prophets" (in the plural) is in favour of this.

nor led about against His will. The whole story, he adds, is plainly the nonsensical product of ignorant men.

Let us see whether this harsh verdict is justified. After all, these ignorant men have moved the world! Perhaps there is more even in this narrative than is visible to so sharp-sighted a critic as R. Isaac.

If Jesus was God, he says, Satan would have been afraid to tempt Him. But why assume that Satan knew He was God? Have we any reason to suppose that Satan is omniscient? It is at least within the bounds of possibility that this was hidden from him. Or again, and this is much more probable, Satan may have known Jesus better than R. Isaac knew Him, and may have understood that even though Jesus was God, yet inasmuch as He was also man He could be tempted as man. For it is in this very point that, as we have seen again and again, R. Isaac misunderstands the whole doctrine of Christianity. This rests on the foundation-belief that Jesus was as perfectly man as He was perfectly God, not "half-man and half-God," but wholly God and wholly man. If so, it stands to reason that as man He could be subject to temptation, or, so far, He would be exempt from the common lot and experience of man. If the first Adam was tempted, the Second must be tempted also.

**312**] If then Jesus, as the New Testament teaches us, was entirely man, as well as God, it was necessary for Him to undergo temptation. Suppose, therefore, that the story of the Temptation were false, it might well be no mere nonsense due to the vapourings of a frivolous mind, as the Rabbi thinks, but might still contain deep spiritual truths. On the other hand, if the story be true, as we believe (for it is all of a piece with the doctrine of the Incarnation), it is of the very greatest value. We learn from it, for example, that temptation is necessary for all, that it is part of the process by which spiritual advance is made. Also we see that sin is no necessary part of human life. For a sinless Being, though man, can resist temptation. We may gather also that the more completely a person resists temptation the more deeply he feels the attack. He who yields to temptation can never have gauged its full force; it must always have contained a further degree of strength which the Arch-tempter did not find necessary to bring to bear upon him. But He who fights so successfully that He endures the whole extent of the temptation, and comes off conqueror, knows how sore and bitter a thing temptation can really be. Hence He is able to sympathize to the uttermost with all who are tempted, however fierce the temptation to which they are exposed.

**313**] Observe, secondly, from the history of the Temptation, that even a sinless human Being must use the right means if He is to overcome. It was by no accident, but by the very necessity of the case, that the Lord Jesus quoted Scripture as His weapon against Satan. Neither, may we add, was it by accident, but in accordance with psychological probability, that the passages He cited were, as it seems, verses that He had learned as a child. It is in times of stress and danger that our earliest lessons produce their full effect upon us.*

**314**] Thus the Temptation is all of a piece with the perfect humanity of the Lord Jesus Christ, according to the description of Him in the New Testament. If it be granted that Jesus was fully man as well as fully God, then some such temptation as that related in the Gospels was to be expected, especially if the narrative of His Baptism be accepted as historical. Grant that Jesus was baptized, then we must allow also that a temptation of special strength was likely to follow it. Consider the circumstances. Jesus, brought up as a carpenter at Nazareth, had dedicated Himself to His work. He had been baptized, and, we are told, had heard a voice of encouragement, and had received an outpouring of the Holy Ghost. He had then been led up by the Spirit into solitude.

**315**] When we endeavour to understand ever so slightly the mind of Jesus at this time, what can we discover? It may be presumed that He had been brought up in the common opinion of His contemporaries, that Messiah was to be a great king, leading the Jews to victorious war against

* Our Lord's three quotations are from Deut. viii. 3; vi. 16, 13. Every child learned portions of Deuteronomy (vi. 4-9; xi. 13-21), as included in the Shma', and it is probable that neighbouring portions were often added.

Gentile nations, whom He was to subdue and bring under the yoke of the kingdom of God by their submission to Judaism. Seeing then that He was man, with absolutely human thoughts and feelings, and limited by the conditions of His Incarnation to human methods of plan and action, surely it is probable, not to say certain, that after His formal consecration to His work He should consider the best method of accomplishing it. Perhaps one object of the descent of the Holy Spirit was to make things more clear to His human understanding. If so, what wonder that His time of meditation in the wilderness should also be a time of conflict? What wonder that the arch-fiend should use whatever powers over nature he possessed (and of the extent of these powers we are supremely ignorant) to suggest to Him (for there is no hint that such a doubt originated with Jesus), and to convince Him, that spiritual means alone would be insufficient to accomplish His purpose? Jesus was starving! Why not, since all power was at His disposal, change the breadlike stones into actual food? Convinced, however, that human life does not depend ultimately on material food, Jesus will wait, and trust His Father. He will work miracles later, but He will work none for Himself. Satan sees that Jesus can trust! He suggests to Him, therefore, that He should trust God's protection utterly, even to the specific word of promise in the Psalms, that God's angels should keep Him against dashing His feet against a stone. "See," he says, "Thou art standing on the Temple's pinnacle above the Temple area, or rather [if the interpretation be right] on the very edge of the precipitous ravine on the eastern side of the Temple wall, show then Thy trust!" But Jesus can distinguish between trust and presumption. Where God calls He will follow, and will be safe; otherwise He has no warrant to expect protection. Man may not thrust himself out into needless dangers.*

* Edersheim writes: "Jesus stands on the watch-post which the white-robed priest has just quitted. Fast the rosy morning-light, deepening into crimson, and edged with gold, is spreading over the land. In the Priests' Court below Him the morning-sacrifice has been offered. The massive Temple-gates are slowly opening, and the blast of the priests' silver trumpets is summoning Israel to

**316**] Both these, however, were but lesser forms of temptation. With men of power beyond their fellows Satan employs a form much more subtle and enticing. Jesus was Messiah! Let Him then use the means. All the powers and opportunities of this world should be placed at His disposal, if He would but acknowledge Satan in some degree as the rightful master of the world, using (as the phrase seems to mean) methods generally in vogue, which, by reason of the fact that they were not based on trust in God, were ultimately due to evil influence. But Jesus answers: "Get thee hence, Satan; for it is written, Thou shalt worship the Lord thy God, and Him only shalt thou serve." The reply is final. For it cuts up by the roots all suggestion that He will win His victories, and accomplish His work, by worldly means. It is God, God alone, whom He will obey and follow, God alone to whom He will look for the gift of a world. The result is that He is able to say in the closing verses of the First Gospel, "all authority hath been given unto me in heaven and on earth" (Matt. xxviii. 18).

**317**] Thus the narrative of the Temptation is no idle tale, but fits in admirably with the rest of the message of the New Testament. For the central lesson of the narrative is that the work of Messiah is to be spiritual, and the means He uses are to be spiritual also. Material and external victories are not necessarily the road to spiritual conquest. His method is to start from within and to work outwards, to purify the heart, knowing that by so doing the life will gradually correspond. Herein indeed lies for all time the great contrast between the religion of the world and that of the Lord Jesus. True success

begin a new day by appearing before their Lord. Now then let Him descend, Heaven-borne, into the midst of priests and people. What shouts of acclamation would greet His appearance! What homage of worship would be His! The goal can at once be reached, and that at the head of believing Israel" (*Life and Times of Jesus the Messiah*, 1887, i. 304). The brilliancy of the word-painting almost blinds us to the fact of the absence of the smallest hint of the presence of the priests and people. This interpretation also implies that Jesus was already visible where He stood on the pinnacle, in itself a matter that would demand grave inquiry. It is interesting to notice that in T. J. *Peah*, viii. 9 [8] (21*b*) the devil quotes Scripture, and is answered by another text.

(He will teach us), true victory, lies not in the Law, but in the Promise; not in Works, but in Grace; not in the Flesh, but in the Spirit.

### The Light in Galilee.

§ 8.

Matt. iv. 13–16. "*And leaving Nazareth, he came and dwelt in Capernaum, which is by the sea, and in the borders of Zebulun and Naphtali: that it might be fulfilled which was spoken by Isaiah the prophet, saying, The land of Zebulun and the land of Naphtali, Toward the sea, beyond Jordan, Galilee of the Gentiles, The people which sat in darkness saw a great light, and to them which sat in the region and shadow of death, to them did light spring up.*"

Isa. ix. 1, 2 (viii. 23; ix. 1, Heb.). "*In the former time he brought into contempt the land of Zebulun and the land of Naphtali, but in the latter time hath he made it glorious, by the way of the sea, beyond Jordan, Galilee of the nations. The people that walked in darkness have seen a great light. They that dwelt in the land of the shadow of death, upon them hath the light shined.*"

כעת הראשין הקל ארצה זבלון וארצה נפתלי והאחרון הכביד דרך הים עבר הירדן גליל הגוים: העם ההלכים בחשך ראו אור גדול ישבי בארץ צלמת אור נגה עליהם:

318] R. Isaac complains that the Evangelist purposely misinterpreted the quotation from Isaiah by omitting all reference to the context, and he proceeds to give his own explanation of it. This is to the effect that the prophet referred, first, to the comparatively light affliction of the country under Tiglath-Pileser, and then to the much more heavy affliction of it under Sennacherib. For this reason too the prophet mentions both the Mediterranean Sea and the Jordan, that he may include the borders of the Holy Land, west and east. The Gentiles then are those strangers who lived in the midst of Israel, as well as the Philistines on its borders. The Light refers to God's deliverance of Israel by the destruction of Sennacherib. Israel then was raised on high among the nations by this deliverance wrought on her behalf, and its joy was increased in its thanksgiving in the Temple, while the joy of the enemy was not increased. The following verses then refer to the destruction of the enemy by the angel of God, and the prophecy is connected with the son who was born to Ahaz, namely Hezekiah, who was more than nine years old when the prophecy was given.

**319**] The Rabbi's explanation, however, is rather grossly inaccurate. In the first place, he can hardly be right in his interpretation of הקל and הכביד, although it is that of the English Authorized Version ("he lightly afflicted," "did more grievously afflict"), for surely the emphasis of the passage is laid upon the greatness of the light and the glory that is to come. The translation adopted by the English Revised Version, and by most scholars of our time, is far more probable, viz. "he brought into contempt," "hath he made it glorious."

In the second place, it is hardly possible to drag in the conquests of Sennacherib and the deliverance of Judah (not Israel, for by that time the Northern Kingdom had fallen) as early as these verses. They clearly refer to the North, and to the North alone. The prophet, that is to say, desires to comfort Northern Israel for its losses, and foretells the glorious Light that shall one day shine upon it.* No one who acknowledges the greatness of Jesus of Nazareth can fail to find

* We assume that Isa. xi. 1*b* (viii. 23*b*, Heb.) is genuine. Of course, if it is an addition by a later editor, ix. 2 (ix. 1, Heb.) and succeeding verses have no connexion with Galilee, then it was only the editor who contrasted the contempt for Galilee with its future glory, not Isaiah himself. But we have to deal with the text as we find it.

in the language of this passage of the Book of Isaiah a fitting illustration (to say the very least) of His work.*

**320**] Having shown that it is quite allowable to see in the words of the Prophet an indication of the great light that shone on Galilee in the person of the Lord Jesus, we turn to consider very briefly the form in which the Evangelist presents them. In the first place, he omits all direct mention of the contrast of the contempt and the glory. Therefore after mentioning Zebulun, Naphtali and Galilee, etc., he at once declares that on this people which had been in darkness there arose a great light. He assumes it as well known that Galilee had been in darkness. To this statement, at least, no Talmudically trained Jew is likely to object. For the Talmud has many well-known passages affirming the ignorance of the Galileans in legal matters, which was due largely to their inaccuracy of pronunciation.†

**321**] Secondly, the Evangelist seems to put Capernaum on the borders of Zebulun and Naphtali, whereas it appears to have been wholly within the boundaries of the latter. In fact, however, the word translated "borders" never means in Matt. the lines dividing the two countries, but their districts (see ii. 16; viii. 34, etc.). St. Matthew regards the lands of Zebulun and Naphtali as one: so also those of Tyre and Sidon (xv. 21). In any case, Zebulun was not far off, and

* Mr. C. G. Montefiore in his Commentary on the passage in St. Matthew writes: "The obscure passage from Isaiah, here quoted with various modifications from the original Hebrew text, is, however, a Messianic prophecy" (*The Synoptic Gospels*, 1909, p. 471).

B. H. Gebhardt quotes the following passage from the *Zohar* on the authority of the *Yalqut Chadash*, p. 142, c. 4: "Messiah will be revealed first of all in Galilee, for there the Captivity began."

משיח יתגלה בתחלה בגליל כי שם התחיל הגלות

(*Centum loca Novi Testamenti*, 1699, p. 25).

But I have not been able to verify the quotation, and it sounds suspiciously like a tradition manipulated in the interests of Christian readers. In any case the saying states succinctly one reason that doubtless led the author of the First Gospel to make his quotation.

† See such passages in Neubauer, *La Géographie du Talmud*, 1868, pp. 183 *sqq*., or Buxtorf, *Lexicon*, 1640, pp. 434 *sqq*.

numbers of those who frequented Capernaum must have come thence. It may be pointed out that some mention of Zebulun in this connexion was almost imperatively necessary, because Nazareth was in Zebulun, and, though the Light shone at its brightest in Naphtali, it was in Zebulun that it actually arose.*

**322**] Lastly, it may be observed that St. Matthew, who had noticed the coming of distant heathen to worship Messiah (ii. 1–12), though He was persecuted by the then ruler of the nation, found it very significant that His public activity should begin at a distance from the home of the hierarchy, and in a district which had been the first to suffer from heathen attacks in the past, and possessed at the present moment a population in which there was a great mixture of the heathen element. The Evangelist's quotation of the passage was fully justified.

## Catching Men Alive.

### § 9.

Matt. iv. 18, 19. "*And walking by the sea of Galilee, he saw two brethren, Simon who is called Peter, and Andrew his brother, casting a net into the sea; for they were fishers. And he said unto them, Come ye after me: and I will make you fishers of men.*"

Luke v. 10. "*And Jesus said unto Simon, Fear not, from henceforth thou shalt catch men.*"

**323**] R. Isaac bids his readers notice that here by chance Jesus spake the truth, for His aim is to catch men as people catch fish, and just as fish gathered in a net die at once, so

* See Zahn *in loco*. "By the way of the sea" probably means the country lying towards the Mediterranean, *i.e.* Western Galilee. Then "beyond Jordan" marks the portion adjacent on the east, and "Galilee of the nations" in particular the northern district.

men who are caught in the Christians' net cannot have any spiritual life hereafter.

On such a subject as this the Rabbi's jokes are unseemly, and not worthy the attention of serious thinkers. For every educated man is aware that there are few metaphors which cannot be pressed to mean something absurd, and contradictory to the general sense of the passage in which they are found. In case, however, any one be found inclined to take his remarks seriously, it may be well to point out that the word translated "catch" in St. Luke is a technical word meaning to take alive, and does not contain the least hint of death as the result, but rather the reverse. The thought of Jesus' words is that of saving from the ocean of sin, and bringing into life eternal. There is, it may be added, no suggestion of the death to sin through which every true believer passes, or of the suffering endured by many Christians in the cause of Christ, suffering sometimes even to death, in the case of converts from heathenism, Mohammedanism, and even Judaism.

### The Permanence of the Law.

§ 10.

Matt. v. 17–19; Luke xvi. 17.

**324**] R. Isaac has already discussed this subject at greater length in Part I. § 19. See parr. 173–179, also *The Hebrew-Christian Messiah*, Lect. V.

### "Love Your Enemies."

Matt. v. 44.

§ 11.*

**325**] A fierce battle has been waged round these words; on the part of Christians to prove that the Jews knew nothing

* Parr. 325–332 are taken almost verbatim from *The Hebrew-Christian Messiah*, pp. 167–176.

of the precept, "Love your enemies"; on the part of Jews to show that it contains nothing new, for Jews have always taught it, and practised it much better than Christians.

It may, however, be questioned whether either party in the strife has taken the trouble to recognize certain facts, and it may, therefore, be worth while to attempt to state the more important of these.*

**326**] The first is that at the time when Christ quoted the precept: "Thou shalt love thy neighbour, and hate thine enemy," it did truly represent the common teaching and practice of men in general. No one will deny this in the case of the non-Jewish nations;† and, unless their statements about the Jews are wholly untrustworthy, the impression produced by Jews upon non-Jews was in accordance with it. Jews did appear to Gentiles to be kind to members of their own race, but to them only.‡ Further, we all know that in the early days of the Hebrew nation, when public justice was weak, much was left to the action of the individual, and he who was wronged satisfied justice by personal retaliation on his enemy, his private enemy, though not one of the enemies of his nation, nor necessarily an enemy of his God.§ It is true that in the

* Observe that when our Lord quotes the words, "Thou shalt love thy neighbour, and hate thine enemy," He does not say by whom this saying was uttered. He does not even add, as He does in *vv.* 21 and 33, that it was said "to them of old time." This is important, for, if we assume with many Jewish writers, that He was speaking directly of the contents of the Law of Moses, we are going further than the language warrants. It is more probable that He had in His mind the popular teaching of His time, which, however, as we fully grant, made the claim to have been handed down from of old.

† Among them "preparing for enemies things of enmity" (ἐχθροῖς ἐχθρὰ πορσύνων, Æsch. *Agam.* 1374) was both the normal state of a man and also his duty; as Euripides says: πρὸς σοῦ μὲν, ὦ παῖ, τοῖς φίλοις εἶναι φίλον, τά τ' ἐχθρὰ μισεῖν, "Be it thine, my son, to be friendly to thy friends, and to hate thine enemies" (*Herc. Fur.* 585, quoted by Wetstein).

‡ As Tacitus says: "With each other resolute trust, ever-ready pity: but towards all others enmity and hatred" ("apud ipsos fides obstinata, misericordia in promptu, sed adversus omnes alios hostile odium," *Hist.* v. 5). Consider also Ecclus. xii. 4.

§ For the Curse on apostates and Hebrew-Christians in the early forms of the Eighteen Benedictions see *The Hebrew-Christian Messiah*, pp. 162-165. Compare time of Christ public justice was better administered than of old, but it was very far from perfect, and there is no reason to think that the common doctrine and practice of Jews towards other Jews was greatly altered. "Thou shalt love thy neighbour, and hate thine enemy," did represent the popular teaching and practice of the day.

**327**] The second fact is that in the atmosphere in which the Lord Jesus was brought up there were currents breathing the warm air of love towards all men. It cannot be denied by fair-minded scholars that this precept of "Love your enemies" is found essentially, both as theory and as practice, in the Old Testament, as well as in other Jewish teaching earlier than the time of Christ. Read Exod. xxiii. 4, 5: "If thou meet thine enemy's ox, or his ass going astray, thou shalt surely bring it back to him again. If thou see the ass of him that hateth thee lying under his burden, and wouldest forbear to help him, thou shalt help with him." Read Lev. xix. 17, 18: "Thou shalt not hate thy brother in thine heart: thou shalt surely rebuke thy neighbour, and not bear sin because of him. Thou shalt not take vengeance, nor bear any grudge against the children of thy people, but thou shalt love thy neighbour as thyself: I am the LORD." True, that in this last passage the reference is exclusively to fellow-Hebrews, "the children of thy people," and therefore we may *not* find in it a direction to treat all men kindly, in spite of their enmity, and regardless of whatsoever nationality they may possess, but for the moment we are not considering this. The point is that the Jew is directed by the Law to show love towards his personal enemy. So again the words of Job tell us that anything like joy at disaster to such an enemy is contrary to the mind of God, for we find Him saying: "If I rejoiced at the destruction of him that hated me, or lifted up myself when evil found him"

also T. B. *Taanith*, 7*b*. "Rabba bar Huna said: 'In the case of any man who is arrogant, it is permissible to call him "wicked," for it is said, "The wicked man hath hardened his face"' (Prov. xxi. 29). R. Nachman bar Isaac said: 'It is permissible to hate him, for it is said, "The hardness of his face is changed" (Eccles. viii. 1); read not, "is changed" (יְשֻׁנֶּא), but "one shall hate"' " (יִשָּׂנֵא); *i.e.* one shall hate the hardness of his face.

(Job xxxi. 29). That this kind of instruction did not remain only a matter of theory, but was carried out into practice by the best men, is seen by the behaviour of David to Saul twice over (1 Sam. xxiv. and xxvi.). A later passage of Scripture teaches us the same duty, though it appends two reasons which hardly belong to the highest strata of ideal ethics: "If thine enemy be hungry, give him bread to eat; and if he be thirsty, give him water to drink: for thou shalt heap coals of fire upon his head, and the LORD shall reward thee" (Prov. xxv. 21, 22). And we may perhaps adopt the more charitable explanation of Prov. xxiv. 17: "Rejoice not when thine enemy falleth, and let not thine heart be glad when he is overthrown: lest the LORD see it, and it displease him, and he turn away his wrath from him,"* that this means "from him to thee," because of thy selfish joy in his shame.†

**328**] Similar teaching may be found in post-Biblical Jewish books which were written either before the time of Christ, or approximately at the same time. In Ecclus. xxviii. 2 we read: "Forgive thy neighbour the hurt that he hath done *thee;* and then thy sins shall be pardoned when thou prayest." Still plainer examples are to be seen in the Testaments of the Twelve Patriarchs. Issachar vii. 6: "I loved the Lord; likewise also every man with all my heart." Zebulun viii.: "Have, therefore, yourselves also, my children, compassion towards every man with mercy, that the Lord also may have mercy upon you. . . . For in the degree in which a man hath compassion upon his neighbours, in the same degree hath the Lord also upon him. . . . Do not set down in account (*i.e.* as a ledger account), each one of you, evil against his brother." Dan. v. 3: "Love the Lord through all your life, and one

* It is, by the by, worthy of notice that in the best texts of Aboth iv. 19 (26), R. Samuel the Little, or the Younger, makes this passage his own, without the addition of the last two clauses. It may be that by this time (about 125 A.D.) higher motives were generally accepted. But this did not prevent him from composing the curse on the heretics in the Eighteen Benedictions.

† See Dr. I. Abrahams, *Studies in Pharisaism and the Gospels*, 1917, p. 152.

another with a true heart." Gad. vi. 1, 3: "And now, my children, I exhort you, love ye each one his brother, and put away hatred from your hearts, and love one another in deed, and in word, and in the inclination of the soul. . . . Love ye one another, therefore, from the heart; and if a man speak against thee, cast forth the poison of hate and speak peaceably to him, and in thy soul hold not guile; and if he confess and repent, forgive him"; vii. 7: "Put away, therefore, jealousy from your souls, and love one another with uprightness of heart." Joseph xvii. 2: "Do ye also love one another, and with long-suffering hide ye one another's faults"; xviii. 2: "And if any one seeketh to do evil unto you, do well unto him, and pray for him, and ye shall be redeemed of the Lord from all evil."

**329**] Still more striking is the saying in the *Book of the Secrets of Enoch*, l. 3, 4, which is thought to be not later than 50 A.D.: "Every wound, and every affliction, and every evil word and attack, endure for the sake of the Lord. And when you might have vengeance do not repay, either your neighbour or your enemy. For God will repay as your avenger in the day of the great judgment. Let it not be for you to take vengeance." So again Philo writes (on Exod. xxiii. 4; *de Humanitate*, § 15, Young's translation iii. 439): "If you see the beast of one who is thy enemy wandering about, leave the excitements to quarrelling to more perverse dispositions, and lead the animal back and restore him to his owner; for so you will not be benefiting him more than yourself: since he will by this means save only an irrational beast which is perhaps of no value, but you will get the greatest and most valuable of all things in nature, namely, excellence. And there will follow of necessity, as sure as shadow follows a body, the dissolution of your enmity." We know very little of Hillel, but the following sentence may, no doubt, rightly be attributed to him: "Be of the disciples of Aaron; loving peace, and pursuing peace; loving mankind, and bringing them nigh to the Torah" (Aboth i. 12 (13)). So also his charge, good enough as far as it goes, "What is hateful to thyself do not to thy fellow: this is the whole Torah, and the rest is commentary" (T.B. *Sabb.* 31*a*), following in the wake of Tobit iv. 15, "What thou thyself hatest, do to no man."

**330**] Can, however, this be said of the Talmud and later Jewish writings, which claim to have absorbed the essence of pre-Christian Judaism? Can such a spirit of love be attributed to them? On the whole, yes. I am indeed well aware that passages are often quoted from the Talmud, as well as from Maimonides and other writers, to the effect that Gentiles are to be treated unscrupulously, and the commonest actions of ordinary humanity are not to be shown them. But in some of the cases cited the rules were due to fear of complicating matters with the Gentile authorities, who were ever on the look-out for opportunities of accusing the Jews of proselytizing, and in others they represented only the opinions of individual teachers.*

Something, no doubt, must also be attributed to the arrogance of certain Rabbis, especially in their relation to those co-religionists who expressed opinions contrary to their own. No sensible man to-day, it is true, whether Jew or Christian, will claim that the Talmud is a miracle of kindliness, but much less will he affirm that it is the concentration of brutality and ignorance. The prayer at the Daily Morning Service has not been in vain: "Oh my God! guard my tongue from evil and my lips from speaking guile; and to such as curse me let my soul be dumb, yea, let my soul be unto all as the dust" (Singer, p. 54).

It may then be fully granted that the saying, "Love your enemies," or its equivalent, was both known to Jews and practised by them before it was spoken by the Lord Jesus, and that, in some degree, it has always been a part of Jewish ethics from the very first.

**331**] If so, how is it that our Lord can say in so many words: "Ye have heard that it was said, Thou shalt love thy neighbour, and hate thine enemy: but I say unto you, Love your enemies"? Yet why should He not? For though love

* See also the catena on the subject in the *Jewish Encyclopedia*, *s.v.* Gentile, v. pp. 617 *sqq.* On the Golden Rule see C. Taylor, *Pirqe Aboth*, 1897, p. 142.

to enemies was taught in the Law (and He does not say the contrary), and though it was taught by individual Jewish leaders before our Lord's time, or independently of Him about the same time, there is no reason to think that it was ever the popular theory or practice. So far from this, it may be pointed out that the precept "Love your enemies" is not the popular theory or practice even now, either among Jews or Christians. The religion of an ordinary man down to this twentieth century has always permitted hatred of a private enemy.

Popular religion has ever said, "Love thy friend and hate thine enemy." There is still need for Christ to add: "But I say unto you, Love your enemies." * If, however, Christ were to come to us Christians and utter these words now there would be this difference from His language to the Jews of old. He would add: Remember what you have heard from your earliest youth; you have been brought up as Christians, and the essence of Christianity is the news of God's love to men, the very worst of men. You as Christians, and because you are Christians, must endeavour to imitate God. More than this. You as Christians profess to have accepted as your own the wonderful love which God has shown you; surely then you feel your own hearts moved with love to others? Afterwards perhaps He would quote statements of the New Testament to the effect that love is in reality the greatest of all principles (1 Cor. xiii.); that it sums up the whole Law (Gal. v. 14); and that every one that loveth is begotten of God, and knoweth God, while he that loveth not, knoweth not God, for God is love (1 John iv. 7, 8).

* "Der berühmte christliche Maler Anselm Feuerbach mahnt, nach folgendem Grundsatz zu handeln: 'Wenn dich einer auf die rechte Backe schlägt, so gib ihm dafür zwei auf die linke'" (*Ein Vermächtnis*, 11–14 Auflage, Berlin, 1911, p. 258, quoted by J. Scheftelowitz in the *Monatschrift für Geschichte und Wissenschaft des Judentums*, 1912, p. 369). "He is a fool," said Frederick the Great, "and that nation is a fool, who, having the power to strike his enemy unawares, does not strike and strike his deadliest" (J. A. Cramb, *Germany and England*, 1914, pp. 42 *sq.*). Mr. G. Friedlander, by the by, rightly calls attention to the fact that the phrase, "But I say unto you," is found at least once in Philo, *Quod det. pot.* § 43, Cohn's edition, § 158 (*Hellenism and Christianity*, 1912, p. 122).

332] We grant, of course, that in Judaism, past and present, love to others is a duty; but in Christianity it is the very central duty of all. We affirm that while the golden thread of love as a moral obligation is visible here and there in the Old Testament and in Jewish books, it enters into the very web and woof of Christ's teaching and of Christianity. The prayer: "Father, forgive them, for they know not what they do," * may not be part of the original form of the Third Gospel, but at least it represents the feeling of the early Christian Church, a feeling due to Christ's teaching. His whole existence here on earth, and His endurance of the Cross, were, according to the New Testament (and it is the Jesus of the New Testament whom alone we know), the outcome of love for us sinful men, Jews and Gentiles alike. There is no such transcendent emphasis on love in any other religion. Christianity alone is the religion of love, based on love and carried out by love. But it is not a religion which can be learned by rote; it is not a religion simply of the head. Only so far as it becomes part and parcel of our very life does it become real. Hence, unless an individual Christian appropriates to himself the love of God in Christ, he has not learned in truth what Christianity means, and he may very easily come terribly short in love to others, and treat them with shocking cruelty. Still, in spite of all the failings of its followers, Christianity has been, and still is, the one active religion of love in the world, the one religion that urges its professors to do all, and suffer all, from love to God and man. Jews have never shown a tithe of the activity of love to men which Christians have shown. What is the cause? Love is not the centre of Judaism; it is the centre of Christianity. To quote a well-known commentary on the Epistle to the Romans: "In Christianity this principle, which had been only partially understood and imperfectly taught, which was known only in isolated examples, yet testified to a universal instinct, was finally put forth as the paramount principle of moral conduct, uniting our moral instincts with our highest religious

* Luke xxiii. 34.

principles. A new virtue, or rather one hitherto imperfectly understood, had become recognized as the root of all virtues, and a new name was demanded for what was practically a new idea." * Christ desired to enforce the law of love towards all, whatever might be the relation in which any of His followers stood to others, and whatever the treatment they received. The popular religion was: "Thou shalt love thy neighbour and hate thine enemy." The Messiah added: "But I say unto you, Love your enemies." †

## The Son of man.

### § 12.

Matt. viii. 20. "*And Jesus saith unto him, The foxes have holes and the birds of the air* have *nests, but the Son of man hath not where to lay his head*" (parallel passage, Luke ix. 58).

**333**] Three objections are raised by R. Isaac with regard to these words. First, if Jesus was God, why did he call himself the Son of man? Secondly, seeing that he does call

* Sanday-Headlam, *Romans*, 1896, p. 376.

† It will be apparent that our Lord's words are interpreted above as referring primarily to the current and popular conception that hatred of an enemy is allowable, or even praiseworthy, whether he be national or personal. But two other explanations may be mentioned. One, earnestly advocated by the present learned Dean of Lichfield, Dr. Savage, is that our Lord was defending the best Jewish teaching and practice of the time, as regards duty to a foreign nation, and was opposing all hatred of Gentiles, especially of the Roman conquerors (*The Gospel of the Kingdom*, 1910, pp. 126–134. *Cf.* also Malwyn Hughes, *The Ethics of Jewish Apocryphal Literature*, 1909, p. 121). But there is nothing to limit the reference of the words to this. The second explanation is that our Lord was speaking against the bitterness of one Jewish sect towards another, as, for example, of the Pharisees towards the Sadducees; or of factions among the Pharisees themselves, as, for example, of the followers of Hillel towards those of Shammai, or again of both Pharisees and Sadducees towards less orthodox sects, as, for instance, the Essenes. But again this interpretation limits the meaning of Christ's words. In reality, He desired to enforce the law of love towards all, whatever might be the relation in which any of His followers stood to others, and whatever the treatment they received.

himself Son of man, it is not fitting that men should trust in him; for Ps. cxlvi. 3 says, "Put not your trust in princes, nor in a son of man." * We read also in Jer. xvii. 5, "Thus saith the LORD: cursed is the man that trusteth in man, and maketh flesh his arm, and whose heart departeth from the LORD." Thirdly, if Jesus was God, how could he say that he had not where to lay his head, for the whole world is his? "The earth is the LORD'S, and the fulness thereof" (Ps. xxiv. 1).

**334**] As to the second of these objections we may point out that it is valid only if Jesus is no more than a son of man, and that, if, on the contrary, there is something about Him which removes Him from the category of ordinary men, this objection fails. As to the third objection, we answer that it is of no weight at all. If it is anything more than a verbal quibble, it is due to a misunderstanding of the Christian doctrine of the Incarnation. After all, we must suppose that Jesus did not intend to talk nonsense, and also that the Evangelist who recorded His saying saw some meaning in it. It is quite self-evident that the whole world belongs to God. If, therefore, Jesus was God, and knew Himself to be God, it is plain that He was speaking of something which was not affected by His Godhead. He who spoke was certainly also man, and His hearers, whatever they thought about His Godhead, would understand that He was referring to His state as man. But it is a fact that as man He owned no spot on earth which He could call His own.

**335**] The first of the Rabbi's questions is of more importance, and demands fuller consideration. Yet observe his carelessness, due, no doubt, to his ignorance of the Greek language, and his trust in Latin, or more probably Polish, neither of which languages has an article (cf. par. 274). For he writes, "If Jesus was God, as they say, why did he call himself son of man?"

ואם היה הוא אלקים כדבריהם למה היה קורא את עצמו בן אדם.

For we may fairly answer that Jesus never calls Himself

* *ben-'adam.*

"son of man."* The Greek phrase at least is always "the Son of man" (*ὁ υἱὸς τοῦ ἀνθρώπου*), and if He originally spoke Hebrew the original of this cannot have been בן אדם but בן האדם. It may, indeed, be granted that if the Greek is the translation not of Hebrew but of Aramaic, the meaning of the latter (בר אנשא) is not quite so certain. But as אנשא alone means a human being, we must assume that the בר has some force. In any case, as Dalman,† the greatest living authority on the Palestinian Aramaic of the first century, points out, "בר אנשא like בן האדם is quite unheard of in the older Jewish Aramaic literature. 'The human being' is there called merely אנשא." We can at most, he implies, only think it probable that בר אנשא was used in the time of the Lord Jesus. He goes on to say that בר אנשא "must not be rendered simply by 'the human being' (der Mensch), but only by 'the son of man' (der Menschensohn), if the essential character of the expression is not to be entirely obliterated." Further, he says, it is not to be translated by "the son of the man," which would be expressed in Aramaic by ברה דאנשא (literally "his son, that of the man"). It is evident that this last expression in Aramaic, like *ὁ υἱὸς τοῦ ἀνθρώπου*, might lead to the false suggestion that the Person so entitled was the son of some man in particular, and was, therefore, nothing more than an ordinary human being. Hence neither in Aramaic nor in Greek would it commend itself for general use by Christians as a title of the Lord Jesus. He Himself indeed, speaking in Jewish surroundings, might use it of Himself, but His followers would shrink from using it of Him, because it could be so very easily misunderstood.

**336**] It would take us very far afield to discuss at any length the reasons why the Lord Jesus gave Himself this title.‡ Probably He took it from Ezekiel (*e.g.* ii. 1). For, as

* Except in John v. 27, where *υἱὸς ἀνθρώπου* is not a title, as is *ὁ υἱὸς τοῦ ἀνθρώπου*.

† *Die Worte Jesu*, 1898, pp. 195 *sq.*; E.T., *The Words of Jesus*, pp. 238 *sq.*

‡ Perhaps I may be allowed to refer to *The Hebrew-Christian Messiah*, Lect. VIII., where I have entered fully into the subject, including the relation of the term to the use of a similar phrase in the Book of Enoch and elsewhere.

Kimchi points out in his commentary on that passage, the address "Son of man" is associated there not only with the idea of weakness common to humanity, but also with that of power. For immediately after the Prophet had seen above the firmament "the likeness of a throne . . . and upon the likeness of the throne . . . a likeness as the appearance of a man upon it above," and he had said, "This was the appearance of the glory of the LORD," then we read, "And he said unto me, Son of man." He who was the Charioteer of that great chariot had the appearance of a man, yet addressed the Prophet by the title of Son of man, recalling at once weakness with suffering, and yet power with glory. Man belongs not to earth alone, but to heaven also; glory is his prerogative as well as weakness and suffering. So Jesus claims the title for Himself, and uses it when He is speaking of His sufferings (*e.g.* in this passage, Matt. viii. 20), and of His present power (*e.g.* Matt. ix. 6), and also of His future glory (*e.g.* Matt. xxvi. 64), in the last passage appropriating to Himself the language of Dan. vii. 13.

**337**] We can thus see that on the lips of Jesus the phrase meant very much more than a statement that He was a mere man. It meant that He was man indeed, man to suffer, but man also related to God, and man about to be glorified on high. It is evident then that this is quite consistent with the Christian doctrine about Him, that although He was God He was also fully and truly man. To say that because He was man therefore He could not be God is a mere assertion without proof. And, we may add, it contradicts Ezekiel's vision of God as man. But perhaps that is why Jewish teachers have always felt shy of studying "The Chariot." Cf. also parr. 561–563.

### MESSIAH AND PEACE.

§ 13.

Matt. x. 34, 35. "*Think not that I came to send peace on the earth: I came not to send peace, but a sword. For I came to set a man at variance against his father, and the daughter against her mother, and the daughter in law against her mother in law.*" Cf. Luke xii. 51.

**338**] R. Isaac here repeats the arguments that he used as far back as the first section of the First Part of his book, and also says that to separate a son from a father is contrary to the work of Messiah, for in the last verse of Malachi we read that Elijah will come to turn the hearts of the children to their fathers. Hence, argues the Rabbi, Jesus cannot be the Messiah.

Our readers, however, will hardly expect us to imitate R. Isaac in this repetition. We therefore refer them to the reply made in parr. 14–20. As for the Coming of Elijah, we may refer to what has been said in parr. 269–275.

### THE SENDER AND THE SENT.

§ 14.

Matt. x. 40. "*He that receiveth you receiveth me, and he that receiveth me receiveth him that sent me.*" Cf. Luke x. 16.

**339**] It should be observed that there is some doubt about the actual words employed by R. Isaac in his remarks upon this passage, but, as usual, we follow the text preferred by his editor, D. Deutsch. The Rabbi tells us that from this passage Christians deduce their belief that Jesus is one with Him who sent Him. If so, he goes on to say, we must also believe that the Twelve are one with Him, *i.e.* that not only the Three are One but the Fifteen are One. He refers also to John x. 38.

**340**] No doubt, since the Rabbi says so, there were some persons who deduced the proof of the Trinity from this verse (though it is a little hard to believe it), and so far the Rabbi was right to mention the argument and to ridicule it. But one would have supposed that most readers, whether Jews or Christians, would have perceived the meaning intended by the Lord Jesus: he who receives you receives My message, and thus receives Me, and he who receives Me receives the message with which I was entrusted, and so receives Him who sent Me with it. The words of Jesus are in fact nothing more than a somewhat elaborate form of the Jewish saying recorded in the Mishna, *Berakoth* v. 5.

שלוחו של אדם כמותו.

"A man's messenger is as himself." Compare also the words of Rashi on Exod. xxxiii. 7.

למבקש פני זקן כמקבל פני שכינה.

"He who seeks the face of an elder is as if he receives the face of the Shekinah." * Consider also what the Lord Jesus says upon another occasion: "And the King shall answer and say unto them, Verily I say unto you, Inasmuch as ye did it unto one of these my brethren, *even* these least, ye did it unto me" (Matt. xxv. 40). In the same way He speaks to the zealous Pharisee on the road to Damascus: "Saul, Saul, why persecutest thou me?" (Acts ix. 4). Let it, however, be fully granted to the Rabbi that the Lord Jesus had in His mind

* From Tanchuma on Exodus (ed., Buber, p. 115), which, however, qualifies the elder as "full of the law" (מלא תורה). The whole page deserves study. Cf. Bechai on Exod. xxiii. 21 (Amsterdam, 1736, p. 113[c] bottom), "Every one who rebels against him (the Angel) rebels against my proper Name which is in him."

(כל הממר בו ממר בשמי המיוחד שבקרבו).

See also T. B. Sanhedrin, 38[b].

D

something stronger than the Jewish unity of representation which is expressed in the two Jewish sayings quoted above. For though it were sheer folly to suppose that Jesus were numerically one with His people, there is a sense, a spiritual sense no doubt, but none the less real on that account, in which He is joined to His people. Yes, the union of Christ with those who believe on Him, not with the mere recognition of the brain, but with the full acceptance of the heart, is so close that it can be compared to nothing less than the union of members of a body with their Head. On this see Eph. iv. 15, 16.

As regards the Rabbi's absurd mathematical argument against the Trinity in Unity, it is sufficient to refer our readers to par. 110.

## UNTIL JOHN.

### § 15.

Matt. xi. 13, 14. "*For all the prophets and the law prophesied until John. And if ye are willing to receive* it, *this is Elijah, which is to come.*"

Luke xvi. 16. "*The law and the prophets were until John.*"

**341**] In this section R. Isaac makes three remarks: first, the statement that the Law and the Prophets were to cease when John the Baptist came is contrary to the words of Jesus Himself in Matt. v. 17: "Think not that I came to destroy the law or the prophets," as has been shown in Part I. § 19. Secondly, the prophets plainly did not come to an end in the time of John, for there are still a great many prophecies which have not been fulfilled (see Part I. §§ 6–8). Thirdly, although Jesus says that John was Elijah, this is contradicted by the statement of John himself that he was not a prophet (see Part I. § 39).

**342**] With the second of these points we have already dealt at sufficient length in parr. 25–71 and 94–104, and with the third in par. 274. Also we have considered the first point in par. 174, so far as regards Matt. v. 17 alone. It seems, however, desirable to study the two passages, Matt. xi. 11–14 and Luke xvi. 15–17, somewhat more, in order that by doing so the objections raised by R. Isaac may be more completely answered.

**343**] Consider first Matt. xi. 11–14. "Verily I say unto you, Among them that are born of women there hath not arisen a greater than John the Baptist: yet he that is but little in the kingdom of heaven is greater than he. And from the days of John the Baptist until now the kingdom of heaven suffereth violence, and men of violence take it by force. For all the prophets and the law prophesied until John. And if ye are willing to receive *it*, this is Elijah, which is to come." These are confessedly difficult verses, but the connexion of them appears to be this: John is the greatest of the prophets, yet the least in the kingdom of heaven; the weakest and most insignificant of those who believe in Me, has greater privileges than he. For a great change has taken place. True religion is no longer a matter of birth and early training. It is obtained by personal grasp of faith. Only men of real determination seize the kingdom for themselves. For now has come that consummation to which the prophets, and even also the Law itself, looked forward, so that their work is done. If we may explain the meaning in another way, we may say that as the moon and the stars are not abolished by the advent of the dawn, yet do become insignificant in the rays of the sun, so it is with the prophets and the Law now that the Light of the world has appeared. And the herald of the dawn was John, foretold under the name of Elijah.

**344**] Let us now consider the second passage, Luke xvi. 15–17. "And he said unto them, Ye [Pharisees] are they that justify yourselves in the sight of men; but God knoweth your hearts: for that which is exalted among men is an abomination in the sight of God. The law and the prophets were until John: from that time the gospel of the kingdom of God is preached, and every man entereth violently into it. And it is easier for heaven and earth to pass away, than for one tittle of the law to fall." The connexion of thought appears to be this: You Pharisees think yourselves so good! You trust to the way in which you have fulfilled the Law! But a great change has come. The time-limit for the Law and the Prophets has expired. Every one, even though he knows himself to be a sinner who has not kept the Law, is pressing into the Kingdom of Heaven, the good news of which I am proclaiming. Does the Law then cease, so that godliness is of no account? Far from it, as you will discover to your cost. The teaching of the Law stands firm, firmer than the earth or the very sky itself, condemning every shade of unholiness, stands as the aim set before men which they should endeavour to attain.

**345**] Is it not remarkable how closely connected in the thought of this passage is Christ's statement of the permanence of the Law with His other statement that it lasted only until John? None but a very superficial reader could suppose the two statements to be contrary to each other. But if they are not contrary when in immediate connexion, as in this passage of the Third Gospel, neither are they when they are separated by six chapters in the First. There is, then, no real contradiction between Matt. xi. 13 and v. 17.

On the permanence of the Law, see parr. 173–179.

### "A Word against the Son of man."

### § 16.

Matt. xii. 32. "*And whosoever shall speak a word against the Son of man, it shall be forgiven him; but whosoever shall speak againstt he Holy Spirit, it shall not be forgiven him, neither in this world nor in that which is to come.*" See also Luke xii. 10.

**346**] Our Rabbi argues that these words show that Jesus is only human and not divine; also they show that the Son and the Holy Spirit are not one; and that therefore the Three are not one. It is sufficient to refer our readers to what has been said on the real meaning of the term "Son of man," as applied to Himself by the Lord Jesus, in parr. 333-337, where we considered § 12. On the passage in relation to the doctrine of the Trinity in Unity, see par. 113. See also *The Hebrew-Christian Messiah*, pp. 295 *sq.*

## THE WORDS OF THE MEN OF NAZARETH.

### § 17.

Matt. xiii. 55. "*Is not this the carpenter's son? is not his mother called Mary? and his brethren, James, and Joseph, and Simon, and Judas? And his sisters, are they not all with us?*" See also Mark vi. 3, where, however, Jesus is not called the carpenter's son, but the carpenter.

**347**] R. Isaac argues that these passages show the falsity of the Christian doctrine that Joseph did not know Mary either before the birth of Jesus or afterwards.

With regard to the first part of the Rabbi's assertion, we may point out that nothing is proved against the Christian doctrine of birth of the Lord Jesus from a pure virgin by the popular language of the men of Nazareth. They certainly were not aware of the relation in which Joseph and Mary stood to each other before the Nativity. On the subject of the Virgin-Birth in general, see par. 13; also *The Hebrew-Christian Messiah*, pp. 24-26.

As to the second part of the Rabbi's assertion, we may say

that the Perpetual Virginity of the Virgin Mary is not a doctrine contained in the New Testament. For several centuries it was no more than a pious opinion among Christian people. As, therefore, it is not a Christian doctrine in the strict sense we are not concerned to defend it. See further, par. 302.

### The Dietary Laws.

### § 18.

Matt. xv. 1–20, especially *v.* 11. "*Not that which entereth into the mouth defileth the man; but that which proceedeth out of the mouth, this defileth the man.*" See also Mark vii. 1–23; Luke xi. 37–41.

**348**] All the arguments which R. Isaac adduces here have been considered in parr. 152–159, to which, therefore, we refer the reader.

The question, however, has lately been raised among scholars whether the Gospels state the case accurately, when they imply that the careful attention to the Dietary Laws was observed by all Jews in the time of the Lord Jesus, or whether, as is affirmed, many of the rules referred only to priests in their attendance in the Temple. The question is interesting, and still under discussion. But perhaps it is not very practical. For, after all, the Gospels, which were written more than a hundred years before the Mishna, are quite as good evidence as it for the habits and customs of the Jews in the first half of the first century of our era; and, secondly, it is certain that the general precepts connected with the Dietary Laws were observed as early as then, even if all the minutiæ of the Rabbinic rules had not been worked out, or applied to the community generally. See also parr. 418 *sq.*, 478.*

* Cf. Mr. G. Margoliouth, *Expository Times*, April, 1911 (vol. xxii. pp. 261–263).

"WHY CALLEST THOU ME GOOD?"

§ 19.

Mark x. 18–21. "*Jesus said unto him, Why callest thou me good? none is good save one,* even *God. Thou knowest the commandments. . . . And Jesus looking upon him loved him, and said unto him, One thing thou lackest: go, sell whatsoever thou hast, and give to the poor, and thou shalt have treasure in heaven: and come, follow me.*" See also Matt. xix. 16–22; Luke xviii. 18–23.

**349**] It should be observed that we are not absolutely certain of the exact words used by the Lord Jesus in His reply to this rich young ruler. For although the three Evangelists agree in their record of the incident as a whole, they differ in details, as all true witnesses always do (see par. 298).

The opinion of most scholars is that St. Mark represents the first and most important saying of the Lord Jesus more accurately than St. Matthew, and therefore we have quoted his language.* We do this the more willingly in that it agrees essentially with the common text of St. Matthew, which, of course, is the one quoted by R. Isaac. We give, that is, the saying in almost exactly the same form as that in which it appears in the *Chizzuk Emunah.*

**350**] (1) The first argument of R. Isaac is that the words of Jesus, "Why callest thou me good? none is good save one, *even* God," prove that He was not God. Other Jewish writers argue also from these words that He knew Himself not to be sinless. It will be well to consider the two arguments together. The fact is that all Jews assume both that He was not divine, and also that He was like other men, not free from sin, and they read His words to the young ruler

* St. Luke gives the first part of our Lord's words in precisely the same form.

under these assumptions. Whether, however, it is scholarly, or strictly in accordance with a scientific spirit of inquiry, to allow assumptions to determine the meaning that is to be given to a saying, may be more than doubted. For Jesus does not say, in so many words, I am not good, neither does He expressly say, I am not God, and it is only right that we should be very careful how we go beyond the letter of what He actually does say. Further, it is but right to ask what meaning the writer of the Gospel gave to the words, and, at the same time, to remember that the later we suppose the Gospel to have been written, the more difficult is it to believe that the writer understood the words to be a denial of the sinlessness and the divinity of Jesus. Bearing in mind the clear-cut statements of the belief in the divinity of Jesus contained in the Epistles of St. Paul, it is impossible to suppose that the writers of the Second and Third Gospels did not acknowledge both His sinlessness and His divinity. The writers, then, of these two Gospels certainly did not see in these words of Jesus a statement that He was not sinless, and that He was not God.

**351**] What, then, does He mean, when, to the rich young man who asked, "Good Master, what shall I do that I may inherit eternal life ? " He replies : " Why callest thou me good ? none is good save one, *even* God" ? May He not mean this ? Do not come to Me as to a teacher on whose authority you wish to lean, however good you may think Me to be ; look up to God. It was not an occasion on which Jesus could, with any respect either for Himself or for His inquirer, reply, " I am God, therefore worship Me." To have done so would have been to have made Himself, if we may say it with reverence, a mere fetish, and it would certainly have been completely contrary to the whole method of His teaching, which was to bring out character, and lead on inquirers, from what they already possessed, to further truth, in a natural and orderly way. You come to Me, the reply may mean, as a teacher from whom you would take orders ; nay, look to God alone. In other words, His reply cuts at the very root of much of the Jewish teaching of the time, subservience to mere authority. Human teachers, human institutions, however good they are, must not usurp the place of God. This young ruler, who assuredly has no real knowledge of the divine nature of Him whom he is addressing (and Jesus cannot at this stage enlighten him on this point without doing him more harm than good), is bid seek God rather than man. Alas, for the ever-recurrent need of the Lord's warning! Judaism has suffered, and is suffering, from insisting on tradition, instead of bidding men see that they come into touch with the living God. Christianity also has far from escaped the danger. Many and many a so-called Christian leans upon the teaching of the Church instead of leaning directly upon God. If this interpretation of the Lord's saying be right, it is obvious that the Rabbi's argument is unsound.*

**352**] (2) R. Isaac argues next that the direction by Jesus to keep the commandments proves that it is impossible for a man to be saved without observing the commands contained in the Law of Moses. Yet what else could Jesus say to a Jew who came to Him thinking himself good? There was as yet no higher test of righteousness than the Law of Moses. Besides, the Rabbi's objection is in all probability due largely to his misconception of what faith in Christ involves. In Part I. § 48, he stated that Christians thought that if a man believed on Christ there was no need for him to practise good works. We showed the error of this supposition in parr. 290 *sq.*

**353**] (3) "Go, sell whatsoever thou hast, and give to the poor." This, affirms R. Isaac, contradicts the very foundation of the Christian religion (זה הדבר סותר יסוד דתם). For Christians, he says, assert that just because the Law of Moses was too heavy in its demands, the lighter law of Jesus was given, and here Jesus decrees that this young ruler should give all his inheritance to the poor! The Law of Moses, on

* We may, perhaps, compare with our Lord's reply to the young ruler the way in which He dealt with another inquirer. Nicodemus was inclined to patronize Jesus, but he is told that he must experience a complete change of heart and life before he can even understand the things of God. In each case Jesus bids the inquirer go much deeper, further down into realities, than he was prepared to go at first (John iii. 3, 5).

the contrary, ordered that a man should give to the poor only one-tenth of the increase of his inheritance, and that the rest of the increase, as well as the inheritance itself, should remain his own. Therefore it is plain, says the Rabbi, that the Law of Moses is not as heavy as Christians assert, but it is for the advantage of our bodies and souls, as has been explained in Part I. § 19. The Rabbi also refers to Luke vi. 27, which will be considered later, parr. 415-417.

**354**] (i.) To this we reply, first, What right has R. Isaac to assume that when the Lord Jesus speaks thus to one man, He is giving a command binding upon all? When a physician bids his patient take a certain medicine, it is more than rash to assume that he is at the same time ordering all his patients to take it, or that he even wishes them to do so. That the early Christians, those of the time before the Gospels were written, did not so understand the words is clear from the fact that although St. Paul again and again speaks of collecting gifts of money, there is not a word in all his writings which leads us to suppose that he expected every believer to part with all he possessed. Plainly, however, to the young ruler it was a decisive test of the reality of his faith on God, for, alas, he went away grieved. He put the things of the world before the service of God.

**355**] (ii.) Yet when the Rabbi speaks of the Law being easier than Christianity he has some right on his side. For the Law is full of clear and definite commands, and these are entirely absent from Christianity. But it is always easier to understand, and therefore, if one chooses, to obey, definite commands, than to learn the will of God generally. When Christ does give definite commands, they are either given with the aim of bringing out the ideal of religious life, and are therefore generally stated in a paradoxical form, or they are intended to refer only to an individual case, as with the young ruler. For indeed, in the truest sense of the words, Christianity is harder, far harder, than Judaism. How this is we have explained in some measure in par. 179.* Suffice it

* See also *The Hebrew-Christian Messiah*, pp. 233-236, and the references there.

here to say that Christianity is harder inasmuch as it is a fuller revelation of God and His will than Judaism is. Yet, on the other hand, it is, blessed be God, incomparably lighter, inasmuch as it proclaims in Christ the freeness of pardon, and the promise of grace. In Christ there is not only forgiveness and acceptance, but also power. See further, parr. 179, 415-417.

### "Not Mine to give."

§ 20.

Matt. xx. 23. "*To sit on my right hand, and on* my *left hand, is not mine to give, but* it is for them *for whom it hath been prepared of my Father.*" See also Mark x. 40.

**356**] R. Isaac deduces from these words of the Lord Jesus that as it was not in His power to do what He liked, therefore the Father and the Son are not one. They, therefore, who trust in Jesus will be ashamed.

This, however, is only one more instance of the way in which our Rabbi has misunderstood the Christian doctrine of the Incarnation. For it is plain to any thoughtful Christian that He answered in the character in which He was addressed. The two disciples, and their mother, did not make their request to Jesus as God, but as Messiah, the leader of Israel, and Jesus answered in the same capacity. You address Me as man, He might have replied, and as man I am unable to do this for you. It rests with My Father in heaven, and with Him alone. In other words, the question of the Divinity of Jesus is not raised. We should add that an attempt has been made by well-meaning Christian expositors to translate our Lord's words: "To sit on My right hand . . . is not Mine to give except to them for whom," etc. But it is barely possible to translate the Greek in this way.

### THE SON OF MAN AS MINISTER.

§ 21.

Matt. xx. 28. "*The Son of man came not to be ministered unto, but to minister, and to give his life a ransom for many.*" See also Mark x. 45.

**357**] The objection raised here is that Jesus shows in two ways that he is not God: first, because he calls himself the Son of man; secondly, because he ministers, and is not ministered unto. Further, he thus declares that he is not Messiah, for of King Messiah it is said: "His dominion shall be from sea to sea, and from the River to the ends of the earth" (Zech. ix. 10); "Yea, all kings shall fall down before him: all nations shall serve him" (Ps. lxxii. 11); "And all dominions shall serve and obey him" (Dan. vii. 27).

Mark this last verse. After all, R. Isaac does think that Dan. vii. refers to the Messiah! See par. 283.

**358**] With regard to the employment of the term Son of man, and its relation to the opinion that Jesus was not divine, see parr. 333–337. With regard to Messiah not serving, it may be replied, as has been replied by Christian writers, that the Servant of God may be expected to serve, and that the Shepherd may be expected to tend the sheep. But that service, and even suffering, in the service is compatible with the Messiah, and even the divine Messiah, is shown at perhaps sufficient length in parr. 213–218. Mr. C. G. Montefiore, on Mark x. 45, says rightly, "The ethical conception of greatness realized in lowly service may surely and safely be ascribed to Jesus."

ZACHARIAH SON OF BARACHIAH.

§ 22.

Matt. xxiii. 35. "*That upon you may come all the righteous blood shed on the earth, from the blood of Abel the righteous unto the blood of Zachariah son of Barachiah, whom ye slew between the sanctuary and the altar.*"

Luke xi. 51. "*From the blood of Abel unto the blood of Zachariah, who perished between the altar and the sanctuary.*"

**359**] We cannot be surprised that R. Isaac lays hold of the expression, "Zachariah son of Barachiah," found in the First Gospel, and brands it as an evident mistake (טעות מפורסם). For that it constitutes a real difficulty no Christian will deny. Taking it, however, at its worst, we must beware of attributing to it a greater importance than it possesses. For we must remember that no thoughtful Christian regards the New Testament in the way that the orthodox Mahommedan regards the Qoran. This, it is asserted, is miraculously perfect in every word and letter. Christians do not say this of the New Testament, and never have said so by the mouth of their theologians. If, therefore, it be proved that there is an error in the New Testament as such, it goes little further in their mind towards sullying the fairness of the whole than a drop of ink towards sullying the ocean.

**360**] The difficulty is as follows. The phrase, "Zachariah son of Barachiah," suggests the writer of the prophecy contained in the Book of the Twelve, or, as we say, the Minor Prophets, whose full name is "Zechariah the son of Berechiah, the son of Iddo" (Zech. i. 1). But no hint is given in Scripture that he died in any such cruel way as is here stated. Another Zechariah, however, did so die, Zechariah the son of Jehoiada the priest, who "stood above the people, and said unto them, Thus saith God, Why transgress ye the commandments of the LORD, that ye cannot prosper? Because ye have forsaken the LORD, he hath also forsaken you. And they conspired against him, and stoned him with stones at the commandment of the king in the court of the house of the LORD" (2 Chron. xxiv. 20, 21).

**361**] It does look, then, as though the phrase in the First Gospel was due to an error, the confusion of Zechariah the son of Berechiah, the writer of the canonical book, with Zechariah the son of Jehoiada. If so it is worth noting that even this error is in accordance with the thoroughly Jewish character of the writer of the First Gospel, for precisely the same mistake is made by the writer of the Targum on Lamentations ii. 20: "As ye slew Zechariah the son of Iddo, the high priest, and a faithful prophet, in the sanctuary of the LORD on the Day of Atonement." * Here, it will be observed, the name of the Minor Prophet, Zechariah son of Berechiah, son of Iddo, is given in error for that of Zechariah the son of Jehoiada. The Christian Jew and the Rabbinic Jew make the same mistake.

**362**] Curiously enough another cause may have had part in the confusion. Josephus tells us in his *War*, IV. v. 4 (§§ 334-344) that, during the siege of Jerusalem by Titus, as the zealots "intended to have Zacharias, the son of Baruch,† one of the most eminent of the citizens, slain, for what provoked them against him was that hatred of wickedness and love of liberty which were so eminent in him: he was also a rich man, so that by taking him off, they did not only hope to seize his effects, but also to get rid of a man that had great power to destroy them. . . . Zacharias was accused of a design to betray their polity to the Romans, and of having traitorously sent to Vespasian for that purpose. Now there appeared no proof or sign of what he was accused. . . . Now the seventy judges brought in their verdict, that the person accused was not guilty, as choosing rather to die themselves with him, than to have his death laid at their doors; hereupon there arose a

* כמה דקטלתון ית זכריה בר עדו כהנא רבא ונביא מהימן בבית מוקדשא דיי ביומא דכפוריא על דאוכח יתהון וגו׳.

† In the best text of the Greek, however, we find Zecharias son of Baris (Βάρεις, Niese).

great clamour of the Zealots upon his acquittal . . . so two of the boldest of them fell upon Zacharias in the middle of the temple, and slew him." * This murder took place in 67 or 68 A.D., and it is possible that the writer of the First Gospel may have himself written "Zachariah son of Barachiah," to suggest to the thoughtful Jewish reader that even to the latest times, immediately before he wrote, the Jews continued to slay persons who had a "hatred of wickedness." If so, his addition to the words of the Lord Jesus would come very near to that spirit of Haggada to which we have already had occasion to refer.

**363**] Yet it must be remembered that it is not absolutely certain that the words "son of Berachiah" belong to the original form of the First Gospel. They are absent from the great Sinaitic manuscript, and from at least two others which are late. It may be granted, however, that this evidence is insufficient to outweigh the probability that the author of the First Gospel did himself write the phrase.

**364**] Whether the Lord Jesus used it is another question altogether. It does not occur in the Third Gospel, and, following the rule that the shorter reading is to be preferred to the longer, it is probable that He said only what St. Luke records: "From the blood of Abel unto the blood of Zachariah, who perished between the altar and the sanctuary."

**365**] Assuming, then, that the Lord Jesus did intend to refer to the murder of Zechariah the son of Jehoiada, why should this be deemed of such importance? Now this is not a question which concerns the Gospels only. For in the Talmud we find that it took quite a special place, just as it does in the Gospels, among the awful sins of the nation which called down the wrath of God. See in particular the Jerusalem Talmud, *Taanith*, IV., near the end (69 a, b), where R. Jochanan says that 80,000 priests were killed by Nebuzaradan because of the blood of Zechariah; and more fully in the Babylonian Talmud, *Sanhedrin*, 96, b. Yet wherein lay the importance of this particular murder, that such emphasis

* Whiston-Margoliouth's translation.

should be laid upon it? The name of Abel suggests the reason. The murder of Abel comes in the first book of the Hebrew Bible, and the murder of Zechariah comes in Chronicles, the last book. The whole sentence, then, is as much as to say: from the very first to the very last pages of the Bible you oppose and kill those who would tell you faithfully of your sins against God, and warn you of approaching punishment. Would that the solemn words of the Lord Jesus had not passed unheeded! *

### The Anointing of Jesus' Feet.

§ 23.

Matt. xxvi. 6, 7. "*Now when Jesus was in Bethany, in the house of Simon the leper, there came unto him a woman having an alabaster cruse of exceeding precious ointment, and she poured it upon his head, as he sat at meat.*"

Mark xiv. 3. "*And while he was in Bethany, in the house of Simon the leper, as he sat at meat, there came a woman having an alabaster cruse of ointment of spikenard very costly;* and *she brake the cruse, and poured it over his head.*"

Luke vii. 37, 38. "*And behold, a woman which was in the city, a sinner; and when she knew that he was sitting at meat in the Pharisee's house, she brought an alabaster cruse of ointment, and standing behind at his feet, weeping, she began to wet his feet with her tears, and wiped them with the hair of*

* It has been suggested that one reason why the Lord Jesus referred to the death of Zechariah the son of Berechiah was that his tomb (of Herodian date) had just been built in the Valley of the Kedron. If so, He may well have referred to him also as the latest example of hypocritical eulogy (see W. Becker, *Anmerkungen zu ausgewählten Stellen des Alten Testaments*, 1904, p. 36).

*her head, and kissed his feet, and anointed them with the ointment.*" Compare verse 46, where Jesus says to Simon his host, "*My head with oil thou didst not anoint: but she hath anointed my feet with ointment.*"

John xii. 3. "*Mary therefore took a pound of ointment of spikenard, very precious, and anointed the feet of Jesus, and wiped his feet with her hair.*"

**366**] On these passages R. Isaac remarks: "See, attentive reader, how the writers of the Gospel in relating a single incident do not agree with each other in their language. Hence we see that a lie is in their mouth."

**367**] (1) Observe the assumption of our Rabbi that the incident recorded in all four Gospels is one and the same. Perhaps he is right, but it is very far from certain. No doubt the incidents related in Matthew and Mark are the same, and probably also that found in John. But the position of it is so different in Luke, nearly at the beginning of Jesus' ministry instead of at the very end, and (of much more importance) the character of the woman in Luke is so alien from that of Mary the sister of Martha, described in Luke x. 38–42, and in John xi. 1–44, that it is hard to suppose that he is relating the same event.

**368**] (2) Yet, granting that it is the same, what follows? It is a well-known principle of evidence in courts of law that if witnesses agree in words, then they have made up their evidence, and, further, that their agreement in the greater facts of the case, together with disagreement in details, is the best possible proof of the truth of the incident to which they bear witness. Why are we to change our procedure when we examine the evidence of witnesses in regard to an incident in the life of Jesus? What does Lessing say, a writer whom every Jew respects? "Suppose that Livy and Polybius and Tacitus describe the same event, engagement, or siege with such differing circumstances that the details as given by one writer seem to contradict entirely those narrated by another, has there ever been any doubt about the event itself on which they all agree?"* In a word, variety of detail confirms, not weakens, the general truth of a narrative (see par. 298).

### CHRIST'S WILL TO SUFFER.

§ 24.

Matt. xxvi. 39. "*And he went forward a little, and fell on his face, and prayed, saying, O my Father, if it be possible, let this cup pass away from me: nevertheless, not as I will, but as thou wilt.*" See also Mark xiv. 35 *sq.* and Luke xxii. 41 *sq.*

**369**] This passage has already been considered in par. 289, but here R. Isaac asks an additional question, Why was Jesus troubled if it was His will to suffer? What? Did the Rabbi never make up his mind to perform a difficult task, and yet shrink from it, even pray God that he might not have to carry out his purpose? I have no doubt that as a God-fearing Jew he did. And should not Jesus (man in the truest and fullest sense, though also God) shrink from what was ten thousand times worse for Him than for men generally, death, with the hiding of that Face for a moment, in the light of which He had up to that time continuously walked? See also parr. 376–378.

### THE THIRTY PIECES OF SILVER.

§ 25.

Matt. xxvii. 9, 10. "*Then was fulfilled that which was spoken by Jeremiah the prophet, saying, And they took the*

* Lessing's *Duplik;* quoted by Prof. König in the *Expositor*, VIII. iv. p. 313 (April, 1911).

*thirty pieces of silver, the price of him that was priced, whom* certain *of the children of Israel did price ; and they gave them for the potter's field, as the Lord appointed me.*"

Zech. xi. 12, 13. "*So they weighed for my hire thirty* pieces *of silver. And the* L*ORD said unto me, Cast it unto the potter* [or, *into the treasury*], *the goodly price that I was prised at of them. And I took the thirty* pieces *of silver, and cast them unto the potter* [or, *into the treasury*], *in the house of the* L*ORD.*"

**370**] The passage is very difficult, both in the Old Testament and in the New. Let us first examine the passage as it stands in the Book of Zechariah.

R. Isaac gives us a long explanation of Zech. xi. 7–17, but, as it is of a kind which no living scholar to-day would accept, it is hardly necessary to attempt to reproduce it. The salient points of it are that the chapter refers to time that was still future when the prophet wrote, the intention of the prophet being to show how the children of Judah will be guided by God all the days of the Second Temple until its destruction. The three shepherds slain (*v.* 8) are Haggai, Zechariah, and Malachi, all of whom died in one month, and with whose death prophecy came to an end in Israel. They were cut off because Israel refused to receive reproof, God's soul being weary of the people of Israel. The thirty shekels are the thirty righteous men who kept God's commandments in the generation after the death of Zerubbabel and Nehemiah. The potter should be read as the treasurer. The foolish and worthless shepherds are the members of the House of Herod, who were the cause of the destruction of the kingdom.

It will be observed that R. Isaac, with some Jewish and most Christian commentators, is of opinion that the prophet is directly foretelling events then lying in the future. But while Christians, generally speaking, say that he is predicting events connected with the death of the Lord Jesus, R. Isaac says that the events in part immediately precede the death of Zechariah, and in part happen some hundreds of years later.

**371**] To our own mind both one and the other of these

systems of interpretation are mistaken. We understand *vv.* 1–14 (it is hardly necessary to go further) as follows: *Vv.* 1–3. The land is desolate. *Vv.* 4–6. The cause of its desolation is stated generally; the rulers, and the king, treat the nation as their own, crushing them to pieces, and so in turn shall they themselves be treated, and not be delivered out of the hand of the enemy. *Vv.* 7–11. The cause is described more particularly, but in words the exact meaning of which is sometimes doubtful. This is due in part to the presence of many allusions, which probably were intelligible enough at the time, but of which the meaning is now lost, and in part to the way in which the prophet employs the first person singular. Sometimes he speaks as the shepherd appointed by God, at others he identifies himself with God, using the first person of actions which God alone can perform. "So I fed the flock that was appointed for slaughter" (*v.* 7). He then took two staves, one called Beauty, signifying the Delight that God's people are to Him, and one called Bands or Brotherhood (*v.* 14), signifying the union God's people ought to have with one another.* Thus were the sheep tended. But sin entered; for God cut off three shepherds (doubtless three kings, but who, we know not†) in one month, "and my soul lost patience with them [that is, with the people], and their soul also loathed me." Henceforth they were to be left to themselves, God would shepherd them no more, and the covenant staff of Beauty was solemnly broken. Then come the verses in which we are more immediately interested, *vv.* 12, 13. Here God is insulted in the person of His prophet. The latter has performed his office as shepherd, and now asks for his payment for his duties. Observe the result. They (the representatives of the nation) do not like to give nothing; they are too selfish and

* Perhaps "Beauty" means the Priesthood with the temple and its services, and Bands, the House of David.

† The latest commentator, Prof. W. Emery Barnes, says: "The three last kings, Jehoiakim, Coniah, and Zedekiah, were cut off in a short space (about eleven years), as it were 'one month'" (*Cambridge Bible for Schools*, 1917, pp. 83, 86).

worldly to give much. They therefore weigh out to him thirty shekels, which was in fact the sum paid for a slave killed by accident (Exod. xxi. 32). God's representative, therefore God Himself, is valued at no more than the very lowest of the people! A baser insult could hardly be imagined; it shows that the nation, in spite of all its talk and profession, cares nothing for God. We cannot wonder that the prophet is bid throw the money away. Whither? Probably "into the treasury." Standing, as he seems to have been, in the Temple court, he throws it down towards the treasury. Then (*v.* 14) he breaks also the second staff called Bands, because there is no brotherhood any more between the different parts of the nation. The nation's ill-treatment of God in the person of His prophet brings destruction.

**372**] If this, as seems probable, is the general meaning of the passage, is it very unreasonable of the author of the First Gospel to quote it in reference to the Lord Jesus? To him the treatment received by Jesus was a shocking example of ingratitude, and, so far, it was certainly a fulfilment of the principle underlying the prophecy. We may go further and say that it would be very hard indeed to find in all history an incident that fulfils it so completely.

**373**] It is necessary, however, for fear of being misunderstood, to point out clearly that the quotation of this prophecy is not intended to be of the nature of a mathematical proof. Probably the Evangelist never so intended it; certainly no thoughtful Christian of to-day could so employ it. We Christians do not ask any Jew to believe on the Lord Jesus because this passage directly refers to Him. What we do say is that when a person has accepted Jesus on quite other grounds, he sees that the treatment of his Master when He was on earth fulfilled in a very remarkable degree the principle of this passage. The Evangelist is fully justified in his use of the passage generally.

**374**] With regard to the details of the manner and form of the "quotation" the case is different. R. Isaac indeed does not mention what is to most persons the chief difficulty, the fact that the Evangelist quotes the words as spoken by

Jeremiah. For with our present information we must accept this as the right reading of the Greek text. There are many theories to account for the word "Jeremiah," none of them satisfactory. One is that it was due to a lapse of memory, a very crude, not to say childish, solution. Another is that the Evangelist used a summary of sayings taken from the Old Testament, in which a passage from Jeremiah was the first in a series which included these words from Zechariah. Another, that because in the Babylonian Talmud and some manuscripts of the Bible the Book of Jeremiah is found at the head of all the Latter Prophets (see Ginsburg, *Introduction to the Massoretico-critical edition of the Hebrew Bible*, 1897, p. 5), it may have given its name to all. Another, that some of the terms in the form employed by St. Matthew do actually occur in Jeremiah, and therefore he quotes all as belonging to that prophet. But there is no absolutely certain reply to the difficulty. Yet it should not be forgotten that, according to modern scholarship, the Evangelist is at least right in attributing the words to some one else than Zechariah, for the author of Zech. xi., whoever he is, certainly cannot be he.* The contrast between Zech. i.–viii. and the remaining chapters is too great for the whole book to have been written by Zechariah, the grandson of Iddo, who returned from Babylon. Whether the eleventh chapter was written later than the Return, as some scholars think, or earlier, as others maintain, is a very interesting question, but one which does not really affect our present discussion.

**375**] So also with the form of the quotation. R. Isaac blames the author of the Gospel because it is not verbally exact. As if quotations in the Talmud and the Midrashim were always verbally exact, and not sometimes compounded of phrases from various parts of Scripture! But indeed I frankly confess that we do not at present possess sufficient means whereby to solve all the difficulties of St. Matthew's language here. We are not in a position to explain in detail

* Prof. W. Emery Barnes (see par. 371), however, thinks that the two writers are separated only "by perhaps half a generation" (p. xx).

his choice of words. He is fully justified in his quotation as a whole, but we cannot say more.

FORSAKEN.

§ 26.

Matt. xxvii. 46. "*My God, my God, why hast thou forsaken me?*" So also Mark xv. 34.

**376**] The argument of R. Isaac is that by these words the Lord Jesus showed He was not God, but only a man like other men, who call upon God in the time of their distress.

But what would the Rabbi have? Would he wish Him not to call upon God? For the objection shows a complete failure to grasp what the Christian doctrine of the nature of Jesus Christ really is. Jesus, we Christians affirm, was man as well as God. If so, was He not to have human suffering? And, if He suffered, was He not to pray for help from His Father in heaven, as men do? Not so, argues the Rabbi. If He was God, then He must have no experience of human trial and suffering, in other words, He must have no experience of human life, and, above all, no experience of human life on its spiritual side. But this can only mean that, according to the Rabbi, He was man only in appearance, not in fact. This, however, is not Christianity, not the Christian doctrine of Christ at all. If this indeed were the Christian faith, the Rabbi might well argue that those passages of Scripture which speak of the sufferings, and the prayers, of the Lord Jesus proved the inaccuracy of the belief that He was divine. As the case stands, the Rabbi has but set up a scarecrow which he labels Christianity, and then proceeds to demolish. May all the readers of these pages be saved from such misunderstanding of the facts, with correspondingly false conclusions.

**377**] There is, however, a real difficulty underlying the Rabbi's objection. Many Christian people do not understand the use of these words by our Lord. They ask: How is it that Jesus, who had always lived in the full light of His Father's countenance, should, in this very moment of His sorest need, have had that countenance hidden from Him?

Yet, if Jesus came, as He said He came, to save the lost (Luke xix. 10), and to offer a ransom for many (Matt. xx. 28), is it unreasonable to suppose that the supreme point of such a sacrifice would take place at His death? Should not we expect to find, on the contrary, that at His dying He reached the lowest depth in self-sacrifice? If a sacrifice for sin were required would not this imply some contact with sin? And, if so, would not this necessarily involve an experience far more terrible than can be conceived by us, who are accustomed to the presence of sin from our childhood? Would it not be agony to a perfectly holy person to lose the sense of communion with His Father in heaven? Would it not also be probable that some such cry as that recorded in the First and the Second Gospels, expressive of His awful sense of desolation, would be wrung from Him? We Christians see in these words the very bitterness of death, of which no true believer in Christ shall have experience (John viii. 51).

**378**] Lastly, it is important to remember that this is not the last recorded cry of the Lord Jesus. For lower down in this same chapter of the First Gospel (*v.* 50) we read: "And Jesus cried again with a loud voice, and yielded up His spirit." See also Mark xv. 37. What He said at this last cry we may learn from the other two Gospels. St. Luke's words are: "And when Jesus had cried with a loud voice, he said, Father, into thy hands I commend my spirit: and having said this, he gave up the ghost" (xxiii. 46). St. John writes: "When Jesus therefore had received the vinegar, he said, It is finished: and he bowed his head, and gave up his spirit" (xix. 30). In either case, that is to say, He uttered words of solemn acquiescence and thankful confidence. The victory over death had already begun (cf. par. 369).

### The Victorious Christ.

§ 27.

Matt. xxviii. 18. "*And Jesus came to them and spake unto them, saying, All authority hath been given unto me in heaven and on earth.*"

**379**] (1) The words show, according to R. Isaac, that Jesus was not God, because he received his power from another, while the Creator gives power, but receives it from none.

We answer that once more R. Isaac's argument does not touch the Christian position in the least. We affirm emphatically that Jesus was Man, and that as man He received this power from on high. If, on the other hand, it be asked, Why did not Jesus take such power as God? Why was He given it as man? we reply that for Him to have taken it as God would be contrary to the whole idea and doctrine of the Incarnation. If Jesus were, during His time on earth, to use His divine power as such, He would so far be acting contrary to the spirit in which He became incarnate; He would cease to be living in all respects as man.* It was just because He humbled Himself, and became obedient to His Father in heaven, even as far as death, yea, the death of the cross, that God, on His part, highly exalted Him, and gave unto Him the name which is above every name, that in the name of Jesus every knee should bow, of things in heaven and things on earth, and things under the earth, and that every tongue should confess that Jesus Christ is Lord, to the glory of God the Father (Phil. ii. 8–11). For the gift which Jesus here says He had received was stupendous. Before, He had received power for special acts (see xi. 27); but now

* This applies to our Lord's miracles also. See *The Hebrew-Christian Messiah*, pp. 111, 123, 338, 340.

it is the full possession of might and authority. The conqueror of death has received His reward, nothing less than the government of the whole universe, earth and heaven. It is the beginning of the state described in Eph. i. 19–22: "That working of the strength of his [*i.e.* God's] might which he wrought in Christ, when he raised him from the dead, and made him to sit at his right hand in the heavenly *places*, far above all rule, and authority, and power, and dominion, and every name that is named, not only in this world, but also in that which is to come: and he put all things under his feet."

**380**] (2) R. Isaac, however, urges that if Christians say that it is the Father of the Lord Jesus who gives him this authority, and no other than He, this shows that, after all, the Father and the Son are two, not one, for there is a Giver and a Receiver. Christians, however, say that the Father and the Son are one.

The difficulty felt by the Rabbi is more reasonable this time, but he is led away by words. For in fact he makes a much more complete division between the two Persons of the Trinity in Christian doctrine than the Christian doctrine itself makes. He thinks that the word "Person" when used of distinctions in the Godhead has precisely the same sense as when it is used of men. Christians do not believe this. One of the first of living theologians, Professor Sanday, of Oxford, writes as follows: "'Person,' in Trinitarian usage, is a mode of being which serves as a ground or basis (a *real* ground or basis) of special function, but just stops short of separate individuality. It implies distinction without division" (*Personality in Christ and in Ourselves* (Oxford, 1911, p. 19)). The definition, no doubt, is hard, and, strictly speaking, beyond our human comprehension, but the Jewish controversialist may not, for that reason, attack Christian teaching, for what, in reality, it does not teach.

## David and the Shewbread.

§ 28.

Mark ii. 24–26. "*And the Pharisees said unto him, Behold, why do they on the sabbath day that which is not lawful? And he said unto them, Did ye never read what David did, when he had need, and was an hungred, he, and they that were with him? How he entered into the house of God when Abiathar was high priest, and did eat the shewbread, which it is not lawful to eat save for the priests, and gave also to them that were with him?*" See also Matt. xii. 2–4; Luke vi. 2–4.

**381**] This passage presents several points of interest, of which the best known is the difficulty about Abiathar. For we should have expected to find the name of Ahimelech instead. It was Ahimelech who was Priest when David came to Nob, not his son Abiathar (1 Sam. xxi. 2, compare xxii. 20). R. Isaac and many Jews make merry over this discrepancy. But they forget that they ought to find fault with the Old Testament as much as with the New. For in both there is the same confusion of names. While in 1 Sam. xxi. 2–10 (I take the Hebrew numeration of the verses), and xxii. 9, 11, 14, 16, the Priest (*i.e.* the High Priest, no doubt) is called Ahimelech, and in xxii. 20 Abiathar, his son, succeeds him, yet in 2 Sam. viii. 17; 1 Chron. xviii. 16, xxiv. 6, Abiathar is spoken of by the name of "Abimelech (or 'Ahimelech'), son of Abiathar." Thus in one set of passages in the Old Testament (naturally I am referring to the Massoretic text, and not to emendations of it found in critical commentaries) the Priest at the time when David went to Nob is called Ahimelech and his son Abiathar, in another set the Priest's name is Abiathar, and his son is called Ahimelech. It is therefore thoroughly inconsistent for a Jew to find fault with the New Testament for saying that the Priest's name when David came to Nob was Abiathar, when the Old Testament says as much in certain passages. The fact is that it has not pleased the LORD that the records of either the Old Testament or the New should be absolutely free from human errors. We might have supposed that they would be, but they are not.*

382] Another point raised by R. Isaac is that the New Testament says that David gave also to them that were with him, whereas David came alone (1 Sam. xxi. 2). For, says the Rabbi, although David told the Priest that he had bid the young men wait at a short distance, this was only to put him off the scent, just as in 1 Sam. xxvii. 10, he tells Achish he had raided the South of Judah, when in reality he had smitten the Arabian tribes who dwelt in the district towards Egypt. R. Isaac's explanation is possible, no doubt, but it seems rather gratuitous to make out that David told a lie unless we have direct confirmation that he did. Most Jewish commentators upon the narrative describing the events at Nob assume that he spoke the truth.†

383] We are surprised that R. Isaac makes no attempt to consider the meaning of our Lord's answer, and to see the relation in which the passage adduced from the Old Testament stands to the objection urged by the Pharisees. Dr. Emil G. Hirsch (*Jewish Encyclopedia*, x. 597) is more thoughtful. He writes: "The disciples plucked and rubbed the ears of corn and thus violated a rabbinical sabbath ordinance (Maimonides, *Yad*, *Sabb.* viii. 3; Talm. Jer. *Sabb.* 10*a*, *Sabb.* x. 7). But the defence of Jesus assumes that the disciples were in danger of dying of starvation; he charges his critics with having neglected charity. This must imply that they had not provided the sabbath meals for the poor (*Peah*, viii. 7). Thus he answers their charge with another. For the act of the disciples there was some excuse; for their neglect to provide the sabbath meals there was none."

Dr. Hirsch's argument is ingenious, but very far-fetched.

* It is unnecessary to do more than mention such explanations as (*a*) there were two Priests at Nob, Ahimelech and Abiathar, of whom Abiathar was the more important; (*b*) Ahimelech was old, and Abiathar was High Priest *de facto*, though not *de jure*.

† *E.g.* Rashi, D. Kimchi, Levi ben Gerson.

For nothing in the narrative suggests that the disciples were in danger of starvation. Neither can we assume, without more proof than Dr. Hirsch adduces, that the sabbath meals for the poor were customary at so early a date.

It is more probable that our Lord's answer was intended, as usual with Him, to confute the principle underlying the objection adduced by the Pharisees, rather than to blame them for some specific neglect. The Pharisees permitted work on the sabbath only if life were in danger (Mishna, *Sabb.* xviii. 3). Our Lord shows them that they cannot defend such a limitation by Scripture. For Scripture itself gives an example of a saint of God, no less a person than David himself, with the full consent of the High Priest of the time, profaning holy things. The shewbread, by the direct order of the Law itself (Lev. xxiv. 9) was reserved, because of its special holiness, for the priests alone. Yet David and his followers ate of it, although they were scarcely in danger of starvation. It was a great convenience to them, hardly more. The Pharisaic principle of danger of death did not apply in their case. The holiness of material or time ought not to be so rigidly restricted as the Jewish teachers supposed.

**384**] It should also be noticed that in St. Matthew's account of the discussion a second example is quoted, even more direct. The sabbath indeed is holy, yet not only are sacrifices to be performed on it (Num. xxviii. 9, 10), but also the shewbread is to be prepared. So 1 Chron. ix. 32: "And some of their brethren, of the sons of the Kohathites, were over the shewbread, to prepare it every sabbath." Jesus asks therefore: "Have ye not read in the law how that on the sabbath day the priests in the temple profane the sabbath, and are guiltless?" This, at any rate, was no matter of life or death. The sanctity of the sabbath was not, as the Pharisees supposed, intended to exclude actions that conduced to the better carrying out of the Divine will. Rules and regulations may easily be made a bondage contrary to the purpose of the Divine Lawgiver. The Pharisees interpreted the law about the sabbath by virtually turning it into a series of negative commands, "Thou shalt not do this, and shalt not do that." But the Old Testament itself teaches that all such negative commands fail to reach the purpose of the Law. God wishes His people to enjoy fuller liberty than that conceded by Rabbinic rules.

### His Mother and His Brethren.

§ 29.

Mark iii. 31–35. "*And there come his mother and his brethren; and, standing without, they sent unto him, calling him. And a multitude was sitting about him; and they say unto him, Behold, thy mother and thy brethren without seek for thee. And he answereth them, and saith, Who is my mother and my brethren? And looking round on them which sat round about him, he saith, Behold, my mother and my brethren! For whosoever shall do the will of God, the same is my brother, and sister, and mother.*" See also Matt. xii. 46–50; Luke viii. 19–21.

**385**] On this passage R. Isaac remarks that when the mother and brethren of Jesus saw that he was deceiving the simple among the people and leading them astray, they did not wish to enter into the house where he was, but sent to call him outside, so that they might keep him back from that work. He, however, did not listen to their voice, and was not willing to go out to them, even as they would not listen to him. The proof that their action was taken in unbelief is to be seen in John vii. 5: "For even his brethren did not believe on him."

**386**] The Rabbi says, it will be observed, that the reason why the mother and the brethren of the Lord Jesus did not enter the house was that they considered Him to be a deceiver. This, however, as Gusset remarks in his reply to our author, is only an impudent suggestion. Judging by the narrative of both St. Mark and St. Matthew it is at least quite as likely that they could not approach the door of the house because of the crowds that surrounded it,* and, in fact, this is expressly told us by St. Luke: "They could not come at him for the crowd" (viii. 19). It was a very different thing for a message to be passed in. Besides, even if it were just possible for them to squeeze their way up to Him, they would hardly care to reason with Him in the presence of others. Family arguments are best conducted in private. This portion of the Rabbi's remarks may be dismissed.

**387**] The important part, however, of what he says in his suggestion that the unbelief of His mother and brethren would be impossible if He had been really divine; if His own mother and brethren did not believe on Jesus no one else ought to do so; they could not be mistaken.

Consider, first, the case of His Brethren. Is their unbelief unnatural, even if Jesus were all that Christians believe Him to be? "A prophet is not without honour, save in his own country, and among his own kin, and in his own house" (Mark vi. 4), and we should have supposed that it was especially difficult for His brothers to perceive that He with whom they had lived and worked and played was, after all, superior to themselves. They did, however, believe on Him after His resurrection (see 1 Cor. xv. 7, and Acts i. 14), but at this stage in Christ's history they did not. On the contrary, with the same readiness to rush to conclusions that has marked the worldly in all ages (see Festus' words to St. Paul, Acts xxvi. 24), they said He was beside Himself (Mark iii. 21), a phrase which may mean only that He was over-excited, or else that He was mad. But no thoughtful person to-day, believer or unbeliever, regards Jesus in this light.

**388**] Consider next the case of His Mother. There would, as may be granted, be a real difficulty if she did not believe that He was the Messiah, when she remembered the circumstances of His birth. Yet it is not said, either here or in any other passage of Scripture, that she did not believe on Him.

* In Mark iii. 20 we are told that the throng was so great that He and His disciples "could not so much as eat bread."

Surely her anxiety for Him was very natural. She showed lack of trust, it is true, but a mother's heart will ever yearn over the safety of her child. Neither can any reason be alleged why the fact that she knew He was the Messiah should weaken her anxiety. It might well increase it, as she came to perceive more clearly whither He was being led, and to what contumely and suffering He would be exposed. St. Peter, it must be remembered, acknowledged Him to be the Messiah, and almost immediately after doing so, tried to persuade Him that He would not be called upon to endure suffering and death (Matt. xvi. 16, 22).

**389**] Before leaving this passage it may be well to observe, first, that the Lord Jesus had intimate knowledge of the purport of the conversation which His mother and brethren desired to hold with Him, although it did not actually take place. Perhaps He had had previous experience of their arguments, or perhaps His knowledge was due to His unique power of knowing what was in man (John ii. 25).

Secondly, notice the beauty of His words, free from all trace of impatience or irritation at the interruption: "Looking round on them which sat round about him, he saith, Behold, my mother and my brethren! For whosoever shall do the will of God, the same is my brother, and sister, and mother." He invites all, and promises them the warmest reception into His most intimate affection.

**390**] Lastly, if we are at all surprised that the Lord Jesus did not at once leave the crowd and go to His mother and brethren, it must be remembered that in a life of complete devotion to God's cause there are times when one's own nearest and dearest must take only a secondary place. Martyrdoms, of Jews and Christians alike, testify to this. "Who said of his father, and of his mother, I have not seen him; neither did he acknowledge his brethren" (Deut. xxxiii. 9), are not words easily forgotten. If the Lord Jesus acted upon them, when occasion rose, who dare blame Him? Certainly no pious Jew. That however this zeal in the cause of God is fully consistent with the utmost tenderness and love may be seen from the thoughtful care of the Lord Jesus for

His mother, as He hung upon the cross: "When Jesus therefore saw his mother, and the disciple standing by, whom he loved, he saith unto his mother, Woman, behold thy son! Then saith he to the disciple, Behold thy mother! And from that hour the disciple took her unto his own home" (John xix. 26, 27).

## THE FIG-TREE CURSED.

§ 30.

Mark xi. 12–14. "*And on the morrow, when they were come out from Bethany, he hungered. And seeing a fig tree afar off having leaves, he came, if haply he might find anything thereon: and when he came to it, he found nothing but leaves; for it was not the season of figs. And he answered and said unto it, No man eat fruit from thee henceforward for ever.*" See also *vv.* 20–24, and Matt. xxi. 18–22.

**391**] R. Isaac makes some very strong remarks upon this miracle, most of which there is no need to reproduce here. His arguments are three: first, that if Jesus had been God, or even had had the Spirit of God resting upon Him, He would have known that there were no figs on this tree before He came near it. In any case He had no right to blame the fig-tree. Secondly, He had better have decreed that the tree should be changed into figs for His own advantage, and for the satisfying of His hunger, if He had the power to change Nature as He liked, as His followers believe. Thirdly, a Christian argued that the narrative was not to be understood literally, but as a parable. Israel is compared to a fig-tree, and when Christ came He found no wise men in the Nation, which, alas! did not receive Him, and was punished accordingly.* The Rabbi replies that his argument was against the

* See also Jerome, in his Commentary on Matt. xxi. 18 *sq.* (Vallarsi, vii. 167).

F

words of the prophets, who said that in the days of Messiah knowledge should abound.

**392**] To take the last point first. When R. Isaac maintains that knowledge was to abound in the days of Messiah, and that therefore He could not have found ignorance in Israel, he confounds facts with results. Knowledge was to be the result of the coming of Messiah; it was not necessarily great before His appearance. He would bring it about; He would not certainly find it already existing.

R. Isaac, however, is doubtless right when he objects to his opponents' argument that the narrative as a whole is allegorical and has no basis of fact. Whether or not it has a parabolic lesson as well as moral and spiritual lessons, we will consider later on. But in itself we must, with the Rabbi, treat it as historical, and learn its lessons first on that supposition.

**393**] The incident has produced many misinterpretations, but in reality presents no great difficulties. One theory may be put on one side at once. It is said that on the fig-trees in Palestine may sometimes be found in the spring, even as late as immediately before Passover (say, in the end of March or the beginning of April), winter figs, which, being the latest, or third, harvest of the fig-tree, have survived throughout the winter. It is not very probable that such figs would have been left unpicked on a tree so near the city as this tree was, but in fact the narrative is wholly opposed to this theory. For it does not explain how it was that the presence of leaves induced our Lord to expect to find figs upon the tree.

**394**] No, we must take the narrative as it stands, and it will explain itself. He saw from afar the fig-tree in full leaves, and therefore He hoped to find some of the early little figs known as *taksh* growing upon it. The point is that other fig-trees were not in full leaf, this one was; therefore it might have such figs also, although the time for ordinary edible figs (*dafur*), about June, was not yet. But neither was it the time for most fig-trees to be in full leaf. Early leaves implied early figs. But on this pretentious and precocious tree there were leaves only and no figs. Jesus had a right to expect that a tree which had such good leaves would have some figs.

But it had none. Hence He was justified in being disappointed with it.*

**395**] R. Isaac, to be sure, says that if Jesus was God He would have known there were no figs upon even this fig-tree. The Rabbi once more misunderstands the Christian doctrine of the Godhead and manhood of Jesus. For according to this He put aside His attributes as God when He was living the life of man. It was not in accordance with His method of living out the human life as it ought to be lived, for Him to exercise His power as God, even in foreknowledge.

**396**] Similarly, R. Isaac's objection that Jesus, if He was divine, ought to have changed the fig-tree into figs, shows a curious ignorance of the conditions by which Christ fulfilled His work. This was the very thing which the devil challenged Him to do at the temptation, to change stones into bread for His own benefit, and He would have none of it. No, you will find no selfishness of any kind in the actions of Jesus of Nazareth.

**397**] Yet, granting that Jesus felt disappointed with the fig-tree, why did He curse it, and make it wither away? In part to show His power. It was very salutary for His disciples, and through them for others, to learn the power of the Christ. The Master is no weak person upon whom one can play with impunity tricks of shallow pretentiousness. He is the Lord, to whom even in His human capacity is given awful power. If we have leaves we ought also to have fruit, or we shall bear the punishment of our empty show.

Further, this exercise of power was, as the Lord Himself says, to encourage His followers in prayer. The forces which He used were at their disposal also. If their faith was real they should say to this mountain: "Be thou taken up and cast into the sea," and it would obey them (Mark xi. 23) Probably no one is foolish enough to ask how it is that believers in Christ do not throw mountains about in this way, for the reply is evident, that to do so without sufficient reason would not be an act of faith at all, and that we can hardly

* See especially Dr. Masterman's article on *Fig* in Hastings' One Volume Dictionary.

conceive any reason sufficient to justify such an act. Again, every thoughtful person would say that those Orientals, at least, to whom our Lord was speaking in the first instance, would perceive that He was using a hyperbolical expression, which few people then would fail to understand. Difficulties as great in the moral world as mountains are in the physical have been overcome again and again by the power of a Christian's faith.

Some persons, however, may be inclined to think, rather strangely it must be confessed, that Christ had no moral right to destroy a tree, which in its ignorance had done no harm But this is folly. For every day we destroy plants and trees to satisfy our bodily desires, or minister to the physical well-being of ourselves or others. Much more are we, or the Lord Jesus, justified in doing so for the sake of moral and ethical well-being. If the destruction of the fig-tree tended to the spiritual advantage of the disciples and other believers, the Lord cannot be blamed for destroying it.

**398**] Yet, when all is said, it remains probable that behind the action, with its immediate moral and spiritual lessons, there was a parabolic meaning also. R. Jose the son of the Damascene woman, about the middle of the second century, compares the Holy Land to a fig-tree,* and it is not at all impossible that, if not to our Lord, at least to those who recorded the act, it suggested the state of the Nation of Israel in the early part of the first century, and its fall in the latter part. For, disguise it as we may, there is much similarity between the fig-tree and the Nation. The Nation was pretentious; it had a show of personal righteousness far exceeding that of the other nations of the world; for it had had privileges of position and of religious culture; yet when the Lord came to it He was rejected; it gave Him no fruit wherewith to satisfy His hunger for the righteousness that He ought to have found in it. A short time passed, and Jerusalem was destroyed, and the Nation scattered. There is no occasion to go into details; parables will never bear too close an examination. It is

* *Siphre*, Deut., § 1 near end, ed. Friedmann 65*a*; see Klausner, *Die Messianische Vorstellungen des jüdischen Volkes im Zeitalter der Tannaiten*, 1904, p. 107.

enough that the general outline fits the circumstances. Thank God that the fig-tree is unlike the Jewish nation in this particular, that the latter shall one day recover its vigour, and, recognizing its Lord, yield to Him its fruit. The LORD hasten it in His time!

## KNOWLEDGE OF THE DAY OF THE LORD.

### § 31.

Mark xiii. 32. "*But of that day or that hour knoweth no one, not even the angels in heaven, neither the Son, but the Father.*" See also Matt. xxiv. 36.

**399**] R. Isaac urges that this passage shows that the Son is not God, seeing that He does not know the things of the future. We have already considered the Rabbi's objections in par. 114, but we may make a few additional remarks.

It would be well if the Rabbi had seriously considered the place which is here attributed to the Son. The order, it will be observed, is man, angels, the Son, the Father. Who or what, then, is the Son who is set above the angels? Scripture, in the Old Testament and the New alike, knows of no being who is above them save God Himself. When, therefore, Jesus sets the Son above them, as He does in this verse, He is claiming for the Son equality with God. Let our Jewish readers take this to heart, and endeavour to answer the question why He does so.

**400**] They will reply, however, whether they face the difficulties of that question or not, that Jesus of Nazareth attributes to the Son ignorance of the great event of the future, the Day of the LORD, and will repeat R. Isaac's argument. Yet no thoughtful Christian can be surprised that such ignorance is attributed to the Son. It is only in accordance with the Christian doctrine of the Incarnation. For according to this we have no right to expect that the incarnate Son of God should know everything with such knowledge as can be expressed in human words. Probably indeed His knowledge as God was altogether in abeyance, this being one of the things which He put off from Him when He became man (see par. 590). But in any case there must have been many things known to the Son as God which it would be impossible for Him to receive into His intellect as Man, unless we make the human nature of the Lord Jesus an altogether monstrous and unhuman thing. It is true that we cannot well blame R. Isaac himself for not perceiving this somewhat evident truth, for in his days it had not been properly perceived by Christians. But every Jew of to-day ought to be free from the temptation to be surprised when Christians speak, or the New Testament itself speaks, of the Lord's ignorance. We must, if we are students of the Bible in either of its parts, be very jealous for the truth of the human nature of the Lord Jesus, and not minimize the reality of that nature in honour of the divine. It is plain that the knowledge of the time when the Day of the LORD will come has no practical connexion with holiness, either for the Lord Jesus or for ourselves, or again either for His or for our ministry on earth. In fact, to require that He should know it would be much on a par with the demand made to Him that He should show a portent out of heaven (Matt. xvi. 1). The knowledge would be as unnatural as the action. Both would be altogether contrary to the limitations of human nature, as well as to the methods of work by which from the very first the Messiah determined to accomplish His task of bringing salvation to the world (Matt. iv. 1–11).

### THE MESSAGE OF THE ANGEL GABRIEL TO THE VIRGIN MARY.

### § 32.

Luke i. 30–33. "*And the angel said unto her, Fear not, Mary: for thou hast found favour with God. And behold, thou shalt conceive in thy womb, and bring forth a son, and shalt call his name JESUS. He shall be great, and shall be called the Son of the Most High: and the Lord God shall give unto him the throne of his father David: and he shall reign over the house of Jacob for ever; and of his kingdom there shall be no end."*

**401**] These words are said to be contrary to other passages in the Gospels, and therefore, as two contraries cannot both be right, if the other passages are true this is false. Our Rabbi has plainly been to school and learned his Euclid, or whatever was the equivalent for a book of logic suitable for boys in his day. His proposition is self-evident. Things that are really contrary to each other do not agree, and cannot both be right. Unfortunately he does not prove that this contrariety exists in the cases under discussion, so that his deduction falls to the ground.

1. Had Mary, it is affirmed, received the assurance of the angel she would have told His brethren, and she and they would have taken the lead in acknowledging Him, and His brethren would not have disbelieved in Him for a time. We have already considered this argument to some extent in par. 387, and need hardly repeat what was said so recently. It may, however, be pointed out that there were good reasons why Mary should not mention the Virgin Birth at first, even to the Brethren. For they could hardly have kept the information to themselves, and if it had become widely known most people would not have believed it, and it would only have been an additional stumbling-block in the way of true belief in the Lord Jesus. For, we must repeat it again and again, in spite of the danger of becoming wearisome to our readers, Jesus of Nazareth never invited belief in Himself on the ground that He was God, and performed miracles as God. His own miraculous birth is the very last thing to which we can imagine Him appealing as evidence for the truth of what He taught, and of His claim to be the Messiah.

**402**] 2. R. Isaac here repeats his foolish objection that the angel ought to have said that the name of Messiah was to be Immanuel, not Jesus, in accordance with the words of Isa. vii. 14. We have already dealt with this in par. 191.

**403**] 3. As for the supposed difficulty that Jesus was never king, sitting on the throne of David, see the discussion in parr. 25–30, 79, 198.

4. His descent from David is considered in parr. 8–13.

**404**] 5. The angel says that there will be no end to His kingdom, and yet St. Paul says in 1 Cor. xv. 24–29 that Jesus will give back the kingdom to God. This is another ridiculous objection. For every thinking man knows that terms which are used with reference to things of time may not be transferred to things of eternity. Thus it is self-evident, one would have supposed, that the words of the angel refer to this world, and St. Paul's language to the next.

Observe, however, as Mr. J. Z. Lichtenstein has pointed out,* that the belief that Messiah will, at the end, when His work is finally accomplished, hand over His kingdom to the Father, is quite in accordance with Jewish belief. For in the *Pirqe d'Rabbi Eliezer*, § 11, ten kings of the world are enumerated, viz. God, Nimrod, Joseph, Solomon, Ahab, Nebuchadnezzar, Cyrus, Alexander of Macedon, and the ninth, the Messiah. But as for the tenth: "He who was the first king will be the last king, as it is said: Thus saith the Lord, the King, . . . I am the first, and I am the last; and beside Me there is no God" (Isa. xliv. 6).† The Rabbinic doctrine that Messiah will give back the kingdom to God is therefore accepted by St. Paul, who does but explain its meaning.

**405**] 6. But if so, argues the Rabbi, the Son and the Father are not one! This, however, is to reopen the whole question of the Three in One. We have already considered this at length in parr. 105–125, and do not think it necessary to repeat here what has been said already. But our Rabbi completely misunderstands the Christian doctrine of the Blessed Trinity.

* חזוק אמונת אמת, *in loco*.

† The translation is that of Mr. G. Friedlander, 1916.

## The Feast of the Conception of the Blessed Virgin Mary, December 8.

### § 33.

Luke ii. 6, 7. "*And it came to pass, that while they were there* [at Bethlehem], *the days were fulfilled that she should be delivered. And she brought forth her firstborn son.*"

**406**] At this point our Rabbi makes a ridiculous mistake, saying that according to the Christians Mary conceived on December 8, and brought forth her Son on December 25, Christmas Day. Of course December 8 is the feast of the conception of Mary by her mother, as he confesses certain Christians told him. He forgets the other Christian Feast of the Annunciation on March 25. His mistake was doubtless due, as Gusset points out, to his ignorance of Latin, and his consequent assumption that the Latin *conceptio* answered exactly to the Hebrew הריון. For while the Latin *Dies conceptionis Mariæ* can only mean the day when Mary was conceived, he translated it by יום הריונה של מרים, which can only mean the day when Mary herself conceived. There is, however, this excuse for the Rabbi, that he may have heard something of the extravagant way in which the Roman Church employs on December 8 the words addressed to Mary by the angel at the Annunciation.

## The Virgin Birth.

### § 34.

**407**] R. Isaac here quotes several passages from the Third and Fourth Gospels in support of his contention that Joseph was the father of the Lord Jesus, but does not add anything fresh to what he has already said. It therefore seems unnecessary to do more than refer the reader to the arguments adduced in parr. 8–13, 388, 401 *sq.* See also the two paragraphs following.

### The Genealogies once more.

§ 35.

Luke iii. 23–38. "*Jesus . . . being the son (as was supposed) of Joseph, the* son *of Heli . . . Seth, the* son *of Adam, the* son *of God.*"

**408**] Our Rabbi brings forward once more the difficulty of the differences between the genealogy contained in Matthew and that contained in Luke, asking in particular which Joseph was the husband of Mary, for St. Matthew says that "Matthan begat Jacob, and Jacob begat Joseph," while St. Luke says, "Joseph, the son of Heli, the son of Matthat." He afterwards asserts that Jesus was called "Son of God" because He was descended from "Adam, the son of God."

I do not propose repeating the argument adduced in the first volume, parr. 8–13. It was shown there that both genealogies are those of Joseph, and that while St. Luke traces the natural descent of Joseph, St. Matthew traces his heirship. Also it was shown that Mary herself was in all probability descended directly from David, the evidence for this lying not in the genealogy of St. Luke, as has fondly been thought, but in the statements of other parts of Scripture, and in the early belief of the Christian Church.

**409**] With regard to the Rabbi's last point, a few words will suffice. He carefully omits the words, "as was supposed," for they would have shown plainly enough that St. Luke knew well that Jesus was not the actual son of Joseph, as R. Isaac implies. Why, however, St. Luke carries his genealogy as far back as Adam is not certain. According to the Rabbi it is in order that he may show that Jesus was called the Son of God because He was descended from Adam! This in reality means that Jesus was like other men, which stands in such flagrant contradiction to St. Luke's own record of the angel's words in i. 35 ("The Holy Ghost shall come upon thee, and the power of the Most High shall overshadow thee: wherefore also that which is to be born shall be called holy, the Son of God"), that this explanation is quite untenable.

It is more likely, as has been suggested (see J. Lichtenstein's Hebrew commentary *in loco*), that St. Luke is giving a hint that as Adam was son of God in a special sense, so also was Jesus born of Him in a unique way (cf. Rom. v. 14), the reference being in that case, as it appears, not to His eternal sonship, but to His Virgin Birth. Other scholars, however, are content to see in St. Luke's words only a desire to draw the attention of Gentile readers, who were not well acquainted with the Old Testament, to the fact that the human race had a divine origin. This would be a means of reminding them of their rightful position, and of summoning them to use their privileges. On the whole the former interpretation is the more probable.

## The Proclamation at Nazareth.

### § 36.

Luke iv. 17–21. "*And there was delivered unto him the book of the prophet Isaiah. And he opened the book, and found the place where it was written, The Spirit of the Lord is upon me, because he anointed me to preach good tidings to the poor: he hath sent me to proclaim release to the captives, and recovering of sight to the blind, to set at liberty them that are bruised, to proclaim the acceptable year of the Lord. And he closed the book, and gave it back to the attendant, and sat down: and the eyes of all in the synagogue were fastened on him. And he began to say unto them, To-day hath this scripture been fulfilled in your ears.*"

**410**] The inauguration of the new reign! A king has come! One whose kingdom possesses those qualities and characteristics which poets and prophets of all time have foretold of the great King, and courtiers of earthly monarchs have ever loved to portray, as marking the reign of their own sovereign. "Him whom his sins had delivered up to death, my Lord the King has let go live. Those who many years sat prisoners, hast thou set free! Those who many days were ill, hast thou restored to health! The hungry are satisfied, the emaciated are become fat, the naked are clad with garments!" So writes a courtier to his master Assurbanipal, king of Assyria.* And so, as Kimchi says in his *Lexicon*, *s.v.* משח † and as Saadiah says in his *Emunoth w'Deoth*,‡ the Prophet in Isa. lxi. 1, 2 puts into the mouth of Messiah a description of the glories of his reign: "The spirit of the Lord GOD is upon me; because the LORD hath anointed me to preach good tidings unto the meek; He hath sent me to bind up the brokenhearted, to proclaim liberty to the captives, and the opening of the prison to them that are bound; to proclaim the acceptable year of the LORD." What wonder if the Lord Jesus, conscious of the changes that His coming would call forth; remembering the comfort that the good news would bring to those in sorrow of heart; the work that His servants would do in alleviating the misery of prisoners (yes, and in

* See Gressmann, *Der Ursprung der Israelitisch-jüdischen Eschatologie*, 1905, pp. 260 *sq*.

† יען משח י״י אתי דברי הנביא כנגד המשיח שהמשיח יאמר כן יען משח י״י אתי וגו׳.

At the end of the present text of the article is found:

הם דברי הנביא על עצמו.

But these words are evidently a gloss by some copyist, taken from the commentary on Isaiah.

‡ Chapter viii., § 9. Fürst's German translation, p. 439.

literally setting free from prison many a man and woman, who in earlier times would have been kept there); foreseeing also the impetus that His coming was to give to the medical art, and the consequent release of many a blind man from the darkness in which he lived for years; remembering also the liberty of soul to be enjoyed by the sinner, when he experiences in his own heart the knowledge of the redemption procured for Him by the Messiah—I ask again, can we wonder that the Lord Jesus made this proclamation of the character of His reign, when He first stood up to preach in the synagogue at Nazareth? Regard the Lord Jesus as we may, it cannot be denied by any thoughtful person, be he Gentile or Jew, that His coming was the beginning of a new era of spiritual power, of mental activity, of the ever-increasing conquest of social enormities and physical ills. The claim in the synagogue at Nazareth that a new kingdom had begun, established on the lines foretold by the prophet, has been fully justified at the bar of history.

**411**] R. Isaac, however, raises a twofold objection to the quotation of the passage from Isaiah made in the Gospel. He says that it is inaccurate, both in its language and in its general tenour.

Probably it has often occurred to the readers of the *Chizzuk Emunah* that its arguments are intended for use among Gentiles, and not for home consumption among the Jews. Its author may well have expected a Gentile reader to be impressed, for example, by the argument that a quotation found in the New Testament is inaccurate, and that therefore the writing in which it occurs is to be rejected as untrustworthy. But he must have known better than to suppose that any Jew worthy of the name, with at least some knowledge of Jewish literature, would be caught by it. For every Jew who has read even a few pages of Talmud or Midrash knows perfectly well that quotations in those writings from the Hebrew Bible are almost as often inaccurate as accurate. But he does not, for that reason, turn round and refuse to have any more to do with books and writers which can make such mistakes. On the contrary, he is well acquainted with the fact that the more accurately persons know their Bible, and the more directly they have in their minds, when they are writing or arguing, persons who know the Scriptures as well as they do themselves, the more easily they omit words, or add clauses from other contexts, if, by doing so, they can either make their argument more concise, or can express it more clearly. With Jewish writers mere verbal accuracy in a quotation is almost of no importance at all. When a Jew, in arguing with a Gentile, pretends that it is, he is presuming on the Gentile's ignorance of things Jewish.

**412**] Into the reasons for the inaccuracies in this quotation it is hardly necessary to enter. J. Z. Lichtenstein,* on the basis of Azariah dei Rossi's *Meor 'Enayim,* c. ix., argues that as the quotation agrees verbally neither with the Hebrew nor with the Septuagint, it was probably taken from an Aramaic translation, a Targum, which was used in the synagogue at Nazareth instead of the Hebrew text. But it can hardly be true, as this theory presupposes that in the time of our Lord Hebrew rolls existed only at Jerusalem or in the houses of wealthy men, and that the synagogue of even a small town, such as Nazareth, did not possess one. It is indeed probable that there was an Aramaic version of the Scriptures in use in Palestine at that date, but we have at present no direct evidence of its existence, and therefore cannot fall back upon this suggestion. It seems more likely that the narrator has combined in his account the words of our Lord's explanation with those of the passage of Holy Writ which He had just read.

**413**] It is more serious that the Rabbi complains that the Evangelist misrepresents the tenour of the Prophet's language. He asserts that the prophet not only speaks the words in his own person, but also intends them to afford comfort to those who were to be long years in Exile, so that they should not forsake the Law of God. Had the Evangelist, he says, only quoted the verses further on in the chapter, and as well as those which preceded it, it would have been clear that there was no reference to Jesus at all; Isaiah was thinking of the

* In his reply to R. Isaac, *Chizzuk Emunath Emeth,* 1879.

Jews in Exile, not of any deliverance brought about by the Messiah. So at least seems to be the meaning of the Rabbi's remarks.

**414**] I grant quite frankly that the Prophet's words were intended to comfort the exiles in Babylon. But, as Kimchi and Saadiah saw, the language is too great to fit the prophet himself, similar words had already been placed in the mouth of the Servant of the LORD (xlii. 1, xlviii. 16, compare xlix. 1 *sqq.*, l. 4 *sqq.*), and the blessings described had been already attributed to the "shoot out of the stock of Jesse" in xi. 1–9. And, in any case, even if it could be shown that the words were to be referred to the Prophet himself, the events are far greater than can be satisfied by the blessing received in the return from the Exile. They refer much more naturally to the great Redemption to which the Prophet and the Exiles alike looked forward, the coming of the King whom all Israel was expecting. If so, Jesus (who believed Himself to be that King), and the Evangelist (who fully accepted Him as such), cannot be blamed for quoting them. The words accurately describe the work of Jesus, as it has become known in history, and as it promises to show itself in ever-increasing measure. Would that all the professed followers of Jesus were doing their part to bring home to all men the reality of His rule, by the submission of their own lives and characters to Him!

## TURNING THE OTHER CHEEK.

## § 37.

Luke vi. 27–29. "*Love your enemies, do good to them that hate you, bless them that curse you, pray for them that despitefully use you. To him that smiteth thee on the* one *cheek offer also the other; and from him that taketh away thy cloke withhold not thy coat also.*"

Compare Matt. v. 39: "*But I say unto you, Resist not him that is evil: but whosoever smiteth thee on thy right cheek, turn to him the other also.*" See parr. 325–332.

**415**] Nothing seems more astonishing to an Englishman who is discussing the New Testament with a Jew than the forgetfulness of the latter that the New Testament was written at first by Eastern teachers for Eastern people, and that therefore many of its sayings were never intended to be understood literally. Yet it is seldom that a Jew makes a similar mistake with regard to the writings which he himself accepts and honours. How ridiculous, for example, it would be, if, after reading in T.B. *Baba Qama*, 92*b*:

חברך קרייך חמרא אוכפא לגביך מוש.

("If thy companion calls thee an ass make thy back feel the saddle"), he were, when called an ass, to go off straightway to the stable, and, fetching out the saddle, solemnly proceed to fasten it on himself, because, as he asserts, he desires to carry out the precepts of his teachers! How completely he would be misunderstanding, not only their words, but even the very spirit of their charge!

So also is it with these passages of the New Testament. When R. Isaac solemnly remarks that he has not seen any Christian turn his cheek to be smitten the second time, he forgets that in all probability Christ never supposed any of His hearers would be so stupid, so slow at the "uptake," as our Scottish friends would say, as not to understand that He was using a figure of speech. "Of two evils choose the less." It is better to suffer more injury than to lose one's temper; it is better (do not the Jews themselves somewhere say so?) to be among the number of the afflicted than to be among those that afflict; it is better to be of those that are persecuted than of those that persecute.

Christ Himself shows us that He did not intend His words to be understood absolutely but relatively, for when He was struck by an officer in front of the High Priest, He did not, in the senseless literal fashion that R. Isaac would have us interpret His saying, turn His face round on the other side to receive another blow, but quietly, and without any feeling of irritation or vexation whatever, asked for legal treatment and proper behaviour: "If I have spoken evil bear witness of the evil: but if well, why smitest thou me?" (John xviii. 23).

**416**] R. Isaac thinks that he scores another point against us Christians when he says that St. Paul objected to being smitten on the mouth, and cursed the High Priest who ordered this blow to be given him. But he forgets that no Christian claims perfection for St. Paul, and also that St. Paul apologized for speaking thus of the High Priest, and frankly confessed his ignorance that his judge held that high position: "I wist not, brethren, that he was high priest: for it is written, Thou shalt not speak evil of a ruler of thy people" (Acts xxiii. 5). In fact, he carried out the spirit of the Lord's command, at least as soon as he was informed of the status of his judge. Christ's words plainly meant that His followers were not to pay back evil with evil. For, as Mr. C. G. Montefiore says: "Not to answer rudeness by rudeness, to suppress a retort, to forgive an injury—what are all these things and dozens like them but not resisting evil?" *

**417**] Enough has been said to show that when R. Isaac goes on to argue that the passage shows the extreme difficulty of keeping the Christian religion, he is lying under a misapprehension of its true meaning, for it regards the heart, not the merely external action. But we have already considered the relative difficulty of Judaism and Christianity in parr. 179, 352–355, and it is not necessary to repeat what has there been said. To put the matter in a nutshell, compared with Judaism, Christianity is far easier for the repentant sinner, and far harder for the conscientious believer.

* *The Synoptic Gospels*, 1909, ii. 514.

## Washing Hands.

§ 38.

Luke xi. 37–41. "*A Pharisee asketh him to dine with him: and he went in, and sat down to meat. And when the Pharisee saw it, he marvelled that he had not first washed before dinner. And the Lord said unto him, Now do ye Pharisees cleanse the outside of the cup and of the platter; but your inward part is full of extortion and wickedness. Ye foolish ones, did not he that made the outside make the inside also? Howbeit give for alms those things which are within; and behold, all things are clean unto you.*" Compare Matt. xv. 1–11.

**418**] Our Rabbi is surprised that in spite of these words Christians do wash their hands before meals. Certainly. Why not? Would he have us go dirty? Christ did not tell us not to wash our hands. What He said was that it was not necessary to wash them. And we have obeyed Him. No Christian makes a conscience of eating with washed hands; washing is not to him a religious action, as it was to the Pharisees, for fear that otherwise they might by some possibility partake of something ceremonially unclean.

**419**] R. Isaac also says that he can see no sense in the answer given to the Pharisee. If so, it is because he has not considered the connexion of thought. The Pharisee blamed our Lord for eating with unwashen hands. Christ speaks in reply of ritual washing generally, and points out that there is always a danger of caring about the ritual, and neglecting that which the ritual represents. The cleansing of the heart is more important than the cleansing of the hands; it is better to give the contents of the dishes in alms to the poor than to be so very particular about the polishing of the outside! What fault can the most orthodox Jew find with such teaching?

See also parr. 152–159, 348, 478.

### The Parable of the Rich Man and Lazarus.

§ 39.

Luke xvi. 19–31.

**420**] R. Isaac here repeats his false impression of Christian doctrine about the Fall and its effects, which we have already considered in parr. 126–130.

### Christ prays His Father to forgive His Enemies.

§ 40.

Luke xxiii. 34. "*Father, forgive them, for they know not what they do.*"

**421**] Here we have another of those delightful dilemmas on the horns of which R. Isaac tries to impale us Christians. He tells us we say that God afflicted the Jews because of their ill-treatment of Jesus; if so, then God did not hear the prayer of Jesus; on the other hand, if He did hear the prayer of Jesus, then the Jews were not punished because of their treatment of Him.

At any rate every Jew must confess that Jesus here gives a practical exemplification of His own charge in vi. 28: "Bless them that curse you, pray for them that despitefully use you," and that "at the supreme and most difficult moment" (C. G. Montefiore).*

**422**] Yet was His prayer not heard, even though the Jews were punished for their treatment of Him? If He was all He claimed to be, the supreme revelation to them of the will of God, would it not have been much worse punishment if they had either been destroyed utterly, or left alone to go

* *The Synoptic Gospels*, 1909, ii. 1079.

on as before? Is not chastisement one of the surest signs of love, though not, of course, of satisfaction with the person loved? As Moses interceded so also did Jesus intercede; the preservation of the Jews until this very day is the surest proof that His prayer was heard.

It may, however, be questioned whether it is right to limit this prayer to the Jews. Many have thought that He had in mind the Roman soldiers who were the instruments in putting Him to death. I do not know. I am glad that I am not called upon to decide. But two things are clear; first, that neither the Roman soldiers nor the Jews were conscious of the enormity of the sin they were committing; and secondly, that both Gentiles and Jews have reaped the benefit of that prayer. It breathes the very spirit of the Lord Jesus Christ. For He came not to judge the world, but that the world might be saved through Him (John iii. 17). We none of us know the depth and awfulness of any sin we commit. It is God's crowning mercy that forgiveness has been won for us by Christ, that God's pardon for our sins may be obtained on our petition.

### John the Baptist denies that he was either Elijah or the Prophet.

§ 41.

John i. 21.

**423**] We have already dealt with both parts of this verse in parr. 269–275.

### Christ addresses His Mother by the title of "Woman."

§ 42.

John ii. 4, and xix. 26.

**424**] R. Isaac remarks that Jesus here gives to His mother the title of אשה, which always means a married woman, whereas if Christians are right in believing in the Perpetual Virginity of Mary He ought to have called her בתולה.

How ridiculous a learned Rabbi can sometimes be! Besides he is quite wrong in his facts. The use of אשה proves nothing at all. For if the reader will be good enough to look at the very first passage in Scripture where the word occurs, he will find that when Eve was made, before she was brought to Adam, she was called אשה. No doubt Christ used the term as an ordinary title of respect. It is perhaps hardly necessary to mention again that the doctrine of the Perpetual Virginity of the mother of our Lord is at best only a pious belief, and not generally accepted among Protestant Christians. See par. 302.

### Herod's Temple Forty-six Years in Building.

§ 43.

John ii. 20. "*The Jews therefore said, Forty and six years was this temple in building.*"

**425**] It is asserted by R. Isaac, and many of the less instructed Jews of our own time, that this statement is wrong. For in the first place Herod the Great, who built it, reigned only thirty-seven years in all; and secondly, Josephus expressly tells us that it was built in eight years (*Antt.* XV. xi. 5, § 420).

The proof looks clear, does it not? Yet I wonder that the objectors do not read a little further, and say, also with Josephus, that the Temple itself was built in a year and a half (*Antt.* XV. xi. 6, § 421). They have, however, overlooked the fact that the former passage really refers only to the building of the cloisters and the outer enclosures, and, much more important, that Josephus also tells us that at the end of the procuratorship of Albinus (64 A.D.) the Temple was "finished" (*Antt.* XX. ix. 7, § 219). How long, then, did it take? Not a short year and a half; not only eight years; but if, as seems to be the case (Josephus, *War*, I. xxi. 1, § 401), it was begun about 20 B.C., some eighty-four years in all. This at least is what Josephus really tells us, if we take into consideration not only one or two of his passages, but all three.

**426**] It may, however, be asked, Why, then, in the Gospel do the Jews say only forty-six years, and not eighty-four? Because they were speaking at a time when only forty-six years had elapsed. Their words do not mean, do not even imply, that the Temple was actually finished when they spoke, but that it had already been forty-six years in building. The supposed difficulty then falls to the ground. Observe, by the bye, that the verse serves as an approximate guide to the date of our Lord's conversation. It must have been held in about the year 26 A.D. This agrees with the probable date of His birth. For, as is well known, the early calculators made a mistake in reckoning the commencement of the present era by some four or five years at least too late.

## The Incarnate Christ.

### § 44.

John vi. 38. "*For I am come down from heaven, not to do mine own will, but the will of him that sent me.*"

**427**] Those who have not yet accepted the Christian Faith seem to us Christians to be singularly slow in understanding what that faith is. For we must set it down to ignorance of the nature of Christianity when we find R. Isaac asking in all seriousness whether this saying of Christ's refers to the descent of His body from heaven or of His soul, and further pointing out that if it was His body then the saying is contrary to the statement in the Gospel according to St. Luke, that He was born at Bethlehem. But it would never occur to a Christian to suppose for one moment that Christ here intended to say that His body came down from heaven. It is self-evident to him that this was not the case.

**428**] Then, says our Rabbi triumphantly, it must be His soul which is said to have come down! But this is true of every man's soul; wherein then lies the superiority of Jesus? But he is mistaken again. Christians never suppose that Christ meant that His soul came down from heaven into a body which was from earth. What they affirm is this, and this is the meaning of Christ's words here, that Christ as a Person came down from heaven, and took a human soul and a human body, both of which were as truly and as completely human as those of ordinary men. In this verse, that is to say, Christ claims to have existed before He became man, and to have come down to earth in order to become man. Perhaps we Christians see the difficulty, as well as the magnificence, of this belief at least as clearly as do Jews, but at any rate let there be no misunderstanding as to what Christians believe. To remove misunderstanding is one of the principal objects of this course of studies in Jewish and Christian controversy.

**429**] Our Lord's words, however, suggest to the Rabbi another question. Christ says that He has come "not to do mine own will, but the will of him that sent me." On this R. Isaac remarks: "This shows that the sender is not one with the sent, for the will of the sent is not like the will of the sender."

With regard to this it should be noticed that Christ does not say that His will was different from His Father's, as though He Himself desired one thing and His Father another. There is no trace of such opposition here. On the contrary, He was content to do His Father's will whatever it might mean for Him in suffering.

Yet it is probable that what the Rabbi intended to say was that Jesus' words indicate the existence of two wills, His own and His Father's, and that, in the connexion in which the words were spoken, this indicates that in the Divine "Persons" (to use the only term at our disposal, imperfect though it is) there were and are separate and distinct wills, although, as we Christians believe as strongly as Jews, there is One God and One God only.

**430**] With regard, however, to the existence of a will in each of the Divine " Persons," there is little to be said, because we are on the threshold of truths which far surpass the limits of human thought. Every one acknowledges that at first it seems contradictory to affirm that in the one Godhead there is more than one will, but religious and philosophic thought soon finds itself at a loss when it endeavours to grasp the significance of expressions revealing the nature and essence of the Divine. Given a Teacher of so holy a character, so far-seeing a vision, so remarkable a power as Jesus of Nazareth, it is but true wisdom to accept His statements of the Being of God, and to endeavour to understand them as far as we can.

**431**] It must, however, not be forgotten that when Christ spoke these words He had in mind not the Son in heaven, but Himself living and working upon earth. In this case, then, it is plain that as He was fully man He had a will, distinct from that of God. And He may well have been thinking chiefly of this will, and have intended to say that it (though distinct from the will of His Father) was nevertheless always entirely given up to carrying out the desires, not of Himself, but of that Father in heaven. He claims that as man He desired nothing but what His Father willed. Even so the claim is great, but only because it transcends our own experience. Nothing less could be expected of Jesus if He was as faultless as He is described in the Gospels. True that (with this interpretation) the verse lays stress on the manhood of the Lord Jesus. But no Christian will object to this. For if Jews will only understand that for Christians Jesus Christ is absolutely and entirely man, as well as absolutely and entirely God, they will cease from adducing as arguments against Christian teaching any of those passages in the New Testament which insist on His manhood. We grant to the very uttermost that He was man, and we do but wish that our own wills were like His will, completely handed over to our Father in heaven, content to do and to bear His will. For therein lies peace and unutterable joy.

### THE UNBELIEF OF THE LORD'S BRETHREN.

§ 45.

John vii. 5. "*For even his brethren did not believe on him.*"

**432**] The Rabbi has already spoken of this in §§ 29, 32 (see parr. 385–390, 401, and also 536), and apparently returns to it here only because it gives him an opportunity of heaping up abuse on our Lord. It is sufficient to refer the reader to the discussion upon those sections.

### R. JOSHUA BEN PERACHIAH.

§ 46.

John vii. 15. "*The Jews therefore marvelled, saying, How knoweth this man letters, having never learned?*"

**433**] This again is not true, says our Rabbi, for Jesus the Nazarene was a scholar of R. Joshua ben Perachiah, and fled with him to Alexandria because of King Jannai, as the wise men of that generation testified in the Talmud, when they saw him with their eyes.

R. Isaac rightly understands the Evangelist to mean that our Lord had not received technical instruction from recognized Rabbinic teachers, and he flatly denies that statement. What is his authority for his denial? The Karaite sceptic

(כוסר), as J. Z. Lichtenstein writes in his *Chizzuk Emunath Emeth*, here appeals to the Talmud! Certainly indeed he shows that he does not know much about that famous work, for he thinks, in the first place, that its authors lived at the same time as Christ, instead of four or five hundred years later; and, in the second place, that R. Joshua ben Perachiah was a contemporary of Jesus, instead of living, as he did, some eighty years before His birth! For observe that R. Isaac informs us when R. Perachiah lived; it was in the time of King Jannæus, who persecuted the Rabbis, about 87 B.C. So we are told in *T.B. Sanh.*, 107*b*; *Sota*, 47*a*; which may be consulted very conveniently in Strack's *Jesus, die Hæretiker und die Christen*, 1910, § 8*b*, *c*. Strack further adds (pp. 33 *sq.*) that learned Jewish scholars like Z. Frankel and Grätz consider that the statement in the Babylonian Talmud is spun out of a somewhat similar statement in the Jerusalem Talmud (*Chagiga*, II. 2, p. 77*d*) (where, however, the name of R. Perachiah's pupil is not given), and is quite untrustworthy. In fact, no scholar of to-day believes it for a moment. It is a mare's nest.

**434**] Observe, however, the impression made by the Lord Jesus upon His audience. They were learned men, and perceived that His method of discussion, and the phrases by which He expressed Himself, did not correspond with those which were in favour among themselves. Yet they could not withhold their admiration at the matter of His teaching, and the far-seeing power that it revealed. For in spite of His evident want of scholastic training, He went to the root of things, and spoke with deep theological knowledge. Yes, for, after all, there is something better than that poring over the *minutiæ* of *pilpul* which is so dear to many a learned Jew; and there is something more inspiring than even the most original lectures at a great University. God is at the centre of things, and he who is most in touch with Him has the truest understanding of theology. It was this which marked the Lord Jesus throughout His course—His abiding communion with His Father in heaven, and His consequent insight into spiritual facts. The learned Rabbis around Him might well wonder; He drew His inspiration from heaven, and revealed to them the will of God, and the truth concerning Him.

### THE ADULTERESS.

§ 47.

John viii. 3-11. "*The scribes and the Pharisees bring a woman taken in adultery; and . . . they say unto him . . . Now in the law Moses commanded us to stone such: but what sayest thou of her? And this they said, tempting him, that they might have* whereof *to accuse him. But Jesus . . . said unto them, He that is without sin among you, let him first cast a stone at her . . . and Jesus lifted up himself, and said unto her, Woman, where are they? Did no man condemn thee? And she said, No man, Lord. And Jesus said, Neither do I condemn thee: go thy way; from henceforth sin no more.*"

**435**] The incident appears shocking to R. Isaac, because, in the first place, he says, the decision of Jesus is against the Law; next, it is contrary both to human laws and even to Christian practice; lastly, it would lead, if carried out logically, to the destruction of all laws, and ultimately to that of the human race.

**436**] Yet, in reality, the Rabbi is making much ado about nothing. For his whole argument is based upon the assumption that Jesus gave here a legal decision, whereas nothing was further from His thoughts.

Observe that if the Scribes and Pharisees had been really sincere in their demand that the Law should be kept, they would either have brought the guilty man with them, as well as the guilty woman, or, if that was not possible, at least would have included him in their statement of the case. For those passages of the Law to which they appealed definitely condemn the man to death as much as the woman. See Lev. xx. 10; Deut. xxii. 22. For some reason, however, they did not do this, and so they have laid themselves open to the suspicion that they did not really care about the fulfilment of the Law.

**437**] We can indeed hardly be judging them unjustly if we attribute another motive to them. Their question was a mere trap for the Teacher from Galilee. Just as on another occasion they tried to ensnare Him over the question whether it was lawful to give tribute to Cæsar or not (Matt. xxii. 15–22), in the hope that He would either appear to zealous Jews to be contradicting the letter of the Mosaic Law, or else would embroil Himself with the Roman authorities, so it was now. If He let the woman off, it was clearly against the Torah; if He condemned her to death, capital punishment was at that time the prerogative of Rome (John xviii. 31). But our Lord, it will be observed, never answered their question. He was not a judge, a legally appointed representative of justice, and He refused to act as one (Luke xii. 14).

**438**] Besides, we must remember that the work of Jesus was something much greater, much further-reaching, than that of adding to the countless number of legal decisions. His aim was not to decide questions of Law, but to convince people of their own sin, and so to bring them in humility to God. Hence it was, that, as the Scribes and Pharisees waited round Him, thinking that now at last He was in a hopeless dilemma, He solemnly looked at them and said: "He that is without sin among you, let him first cast a stone at her." Yet what tenderness He showed even to them! For when He had said this He looked down again, that He might not see their blushes, and one by one they went away, each convicted that he himself at least (whatever might be the case with the others) was not so free from sin that he could dare take the leading part in the execution of this sinful woman.

Then Jesus spoke to the woman, asking her if she had been formally condemned, and on her replying in the negative, added that neither would He, for His part, pronounce formal condemnation on her. But His last words showed plainly enough what He thought, for He bade her sin no more.

May we not hope that such a deliverance from the threatening of the Scribes and Pharisees to bring her to death, with the solemn warning of the holy Teacher, would combine to lead her to see the awfulness of her sin, and bring her to true repentance? Certain it is, at least, that the faithful and wise attitude of our Lord has not had that dire effect upon morals and law which is predicated of it by the Rabbi, and that the teaching of Jesus has always been the great incentive to purity and holiness, when His followers have endeavoured to obey it.

### Did Jesus claim to be God?

§ 48.

John viii. 40. "*But now ye seek to kill me, a man that hath told you the truth, which I heard from God.*"

**439**] One can hardly be surprised that a person seeking for arguments against our holy faith should lay hold of these words, and bid us notice that our Lord here calls Himself man, not God, but after all that we have said to our readers at different times about the reasons why the Lord Jesus called Himself man, we can hardly suppose it to be necessary to repeat ourselves now. Suffice it to say that no Christian denies for a moment that Jesus was man, and therefore fully acknowledges that it was only right for Him to use the term of Himself. See what has been said on Part I. § 10, parr. 113, 114. See also par. 200 and also the remarks on Part II. § 44, parr. 427–431, with reference to John vi. 38. As for R. Isaac's statement that our Lord never called Himself God, it is enough to refer the reader to par. 123, and to the discussions on §§ 50, 51 of this Part (parr. 441–447). The Lord Jesus knew that He was man, and knew also that He was God, incredible though it seems to our Jewish friends, and He referred sometimes to the one fact, and sometimes to the other.

## One Flock and one Shepherd.

§ 49.

John x. 16. "*And other sheep I have, which are not of this fold: them also I must bring, and they shall hear my voice; and they shall become one flock, one shepherd.*"

**440**] The vision of our Lord goes forth beyond the immediate present to the distant future, and to many other countries than Palestine, as well as to numberless other races than that of Israel, and wonderfully indeed has His prophecy been fulfilled! But our Rabbi strangely uses the verse as an occasion for an attack upon our Lord and His followers. For he not only says that our Lord here speaks the truth, in saying that there shall be one religion and one king, according to the testimony of the prophets (and so far every Christian will agree with the Jew), but proceeds to argue that this religion will be that of Israel, and the King the Jewish Messiah. Even to this, in itself, we can make no objection. But what the Rabbi means is that Christianity is not the religion of Israel, which we utterly deny, and that Jesus is not the Jewish Messiah.

But why should we trouble our readers over and over again? They will find the errors of the Rabbi's arguments exposed, as regards the one religion, in parr. 31–34, and the one king in parr. 15, 25–30, 79.

## Jesus one with the Father.

§ 50.

John x. 30. "*I and the Father are one.*"

**441**] These words of the Lord Jesus are very important, and demand our careful consideration. For from them, as

R. Isaac says, Christians deduce the oneness of essence of the Father and the Son.

(1) Against this interpretation the Rabbi brings once more his favourite text, Mark xiii. 32, but we have already considered this in parr. 114, 399 *sq*.

**442**] (2) He brings forward a more serious argument by saying, on the authority of a Socinian writer, Martin Czechowitz, who died in 1608,* that Jesus' words do not necessarily mean that the Father and the Son are of one essence, for St. Paul writes in 1 Cor. iii. 8: "Now he that planteth [St. Paul] and he that watereth [Apollos] are one," which does not mean that St. Paul and Apollos were one man, but only that they worked together with the same aim and purpose. What have we Christians to say in reply? This, that no one ever supposed that our Lord's words in themselves necessarily conveyed the usual Christian interpretation of them, but that when they are considered in their context they do necessarily convey it. For read the passage. In *v.* 28 Jesus said: "I give unto them eternal life; and they shall never perish, and no one is able to snatch them out of my hand." Then in *v.* 29: "My Father, which hath given *them* unto me, is greater than all; and no one is able to snatch *them* out of the Father's hand." There we have similarity, and, as it would seem, equality of infinite power, predicated of both the Father and the Son. Can beings possess equality of infinite power and yet be distinct in essence?

Further, how did they who listened to our Lord understand Him? This at least is certain. For the Jews were so furious with Him that they took up stones to cast at Him, and when He asked the reason, they replied, "For blasphemy; and because that thou, being a man, makest thyself God." To them His meaning was quite clear; by saying "I and the Father are one" He claimed to be God, in the highest possible sense of the term. Yet, as the words are recorded for us in the Greek, there are two points which ought not to be overlooked. First, the word "one" is in the neuter

* The reference is to his *Colloquium trium dierum*, p. 60, which was published in Latin and in Polish.

gender, not the masculine. Our Lord does not, that is to say, mean that He is identical in personality (for want of a better term) with the Father, but that He is one in essence with Him. Secondly, that along with this unity He and the Father remain distinct; He says "are," not "am." He claims, while remaining other than the Father, to be of one essence with Him.

**443**] (3) What! says our Rabbi, claim to be God indeed! That is blasphemy! Then He rightly met the fate of Nebuchadnezzar and the Prince of Tyre! Every Christian must confess that R. Isaac is right, perfectly right, if Jesus was not God. But if He was, where is the blasphemy? The fact is that a Jew never argues out, either with himself or with others, the question whether Jesus was divine. He always assumes that He was not, and endeavours to meet the Christian upon that assumption. He never looks the question fairly in the face. Can it possibly be that he is afraid to do so?

## Jesus calls Himself the Son of God.

§ 51.

John x. 33–36. "*The Jews answered him, For a good work we stone thee not, but for blasphemy; and because that thou, being a man, makest thyself God. Jesus answered them, Is it not written in your law, I said, Ye are gods? If he called them gods, unto whom the word of God came (and the scripture cannot be broken), say ye of him whom the Father sanctified and sent into the world, Thou blasphemest; because I said, I am the Son of God?*"

Compare Ps. lxxxii. 6, 7. "*I said, Ye are gods, and all of you sons of the Most High. Nevertheless ye shall die like men, and fall like one of the princes.*"

**444**] Our Rabbi devotes much space to the consideration of these passages, but we venture to think that he misunderstands both the Psalm and the purport of Christ's argument.

(1) The Psalm. R. Isaac says, rightly in our opinion, that the Psalm is directed against the judges of Israel who judged unrighteous judgment. But he goes on to state that the word "gods" in reality means angels, and that the saying means: I have reckoned you like the angels, because of your connexion with them in having a soul which is from on high (cf. R. Isaac's argument in § 96, par. 570), but seeing that you are drawn after the lower part of your nature, you shall not have continuance like them, but shall die like ordinary men.

The Rabbi's zeal, however, against the Christians has misled him. The point of the position of the judge in ancient Israel is that he represented God to the people, so that in not a few passages there is doubt whether we ought to translate *'elohim* by "God" or "judge" (Exod. xxi. 6, xxii. 8; Judges v. 8). It is to this fact that God refers when He addresses the rulers of Israel: "I said, Ye are gods," I allowed you, that is to say, to be called by this name because you enjoy the position and work which in its fulness belongs only to Me, that of judging between man and man. I called you gods, in other words, sons of the Most High, as sharing in His prerogatives, but, in consequence of your misbehaviour, you shall die like ordinary folk, and fall, as he falls who after being in a high place is utterly abased. The question of the relation of the judges to angels does not enter into the subject.

**445**] (2) We are now in a position to understand the argument of our Lord. In parr. 441–443, when we considered *v.* 30 of this 10th chapter of the Gospel according to St. John, we saw that He claimed to be one with the Father, one, not in what we call personality (for as a "person" He is distinct from Him), but in essence and true being. The Jews at the time saw what He intended, and called His language blasphemy. To this He answers that Scripture itself (He calls the Psalms "Law" in accordance with Rabbinic custom *) uses the word "gods" of Israelites summoned to exercise a specially holy

* See Bacher, *Terminologie*, 1905, i. 197 and ii. 231.

function. The Jews, therefore, cannot blame Him for employing the same word of Himself, when He, who had been set apart by the Father and sent by Him into the world, calls Himself the Son of God. If an ordinary judge could be called "God," how much more could He?

**446**] At first sight it looks as though the Lord were trying to defend His usage of the term only upon principles which are accepted by every learned Jew, for they are illustrated by almost every page of Halachic and Haggadic literature, but seem to our more prosaic Western minds to be too much akin to verbal quiddities. Yet underlying our Lord's reference there is a truth which appeals to us more strongly. The judges could not receive the name of "God" unless there were something in them which corresponded in reality to Him. That correspondence, however, was very small indeed when compared with the correspondence between Christ and His Father. Christ's claim, it is true, is enormous. He affirms that before He came into the world He had been set apart for this special work in the world, and sent into the world to carry it out. It does not seem possible to water His language down to any lower sense. He claims pre-existence, and with it express consecration and mission from the Father, and, on the strength of this claim, He urges that He cannot be blamed for calling Himself the Son of God. He does not, it will be observed, actually repeat His previous claim to unity with the Father (*v.* 30), but He does say that He stands in so unique a relation to Him that He is His Son, both His representative to the world and the concentration of His activity.

**447**] No doubt this will seem as shocking to Jews now as it did when the words were first spoken, until they turn to Jesus, but this is not the fault of the Evangelist, as R. Isaac asserts. Neither St. John nor the Lord Jesus misinterprets the words of the Psalm. These are quoted with full regard to their historical meaning, and in complete accordance with Rabbinic principles. Further, as we Christians maintain, our Lord and the Evangelist show true insight into the thought underlying God's language to the rulers of Israel: "I said, Ye are gods."

### The Son is one with the Father.

§ 52.

John x. 38; xiv. 11 and 20; xvii. 21–23.

**448**] Our Rabbi is fond of repeating himself, and therefore gives us once again his arguments against the unity of the Father and the Son. But we have more compassion on our readers, and therefore think it enough to refer to what has been said on Matt. x. 40, at § 14, parr. 339 *sq.*

### All things were given by the Father to the Son.

§ 53.

John xiii. 3; xvi. 15; compare Matt. xxviii. 18.

**449**] Here again R. Isaac reproduces the arguments which he used before, quoting certain passages from the Gospels, which, as he wrongly supposes, contradict these sayings. It does not seem necessary to do more than ask our readers to look once again at parr. 379 *sq.* They may also find it well to turn to our examination of § 50 (parr. 441–443).

### A New Commandment.

§ 54.

John xiii. 34. "*A new commandment I give unto you, that ye love one another; even as I have loved you, that ye also love one another.*"

**450**] Yet we read in Lev. xix. 18: "Thou shalt love thy neighbour as thyself"; and these words are actually quoted by Christ in Matt. xix. 19 and xxii. 39. How, then, can He say that it is new?

This question has been discussed fully in parr. 325–332, on Matt. v. 44 (§ 11). Further, J. Z. Lichtenstein, in his commentary on our present verse, points out that R. Aqiba's decision was that in cases of emergency a man's own life must come before that of his companion. See T.B. *Baba Mezia*, 62*a*: "Thy life precedes the life of thy companion, for this is the meaning of Lev. xxv. 36: 'That thy brother may live with thee'"

בא ר׳ עקיבא ולימד **וחי אחיך עמך** חייך קודמין לחיי חבירך.

Although Aqiba's verdict met with opposition, it became the accepted principle. Compared with such an opinion, our Lord's command, enforced as it was by His own example of giving His life for others (John xv. 12, 13: "This is my commandment, that ye love one another, even as I have loved you. Greater love hath no man than this, that a man lay down his life for his friends"), was indeed new.

## Jesus and God.

### § 55.

John xvii. 3. "*This is life eternal, that they should know thee the only true God, and him whom thou didst send*, even *Jesus Christ.*"

Compare 1 Tim. i. 17. "*Now unto the King eternal, incorruptible, invisible, the only God,* be *honour and glory for ever and ever. Amen.*"

**451**] Once more the objection is raised by our learned Jew that Jesus does not call Himself God, and that St. Paul distinguishes Him from God. We have, however, replied to this so often that it is sufficient to refer our readers to par. 439, and to the references there given. Briefly it may be said that the Jewish objection is very largely due to failure to understand the meaning of the Christian doctrine of the Incarnation.

### Judas and the Soldiers.

§ 56.

**452**] In John xviii. 1-6 we read that Judas led the soldiers who came to take Jesus; that when they appeared Jesus asked them whom they sought; and on their replying, "Jesus of Nazareth," He said to them, "I am *he*." "And Judas also, which betrayed him, was standing with them. When therefore he said unto them, I am *he*, they went backward, and fell to the ground." In the Synoptic Gospels, on the other hand (Matt. xxvi. 47-49; Mark xiv. 43-45; Luke xxii. 47), Judas gave a sign to the soldiers by kissing Jesus, and they took Him.

To a reader of history, and, we venture to say, much more to a writer of history, it seems absurd to argue from these verbal differences that the narrative is untrustworthy. Differences in unimportant details are rather the proof, not the denial, that the testimony of witnesses is true (cf. par. 298). Here both sets of persons testify to the all-important point that Judas was guide to them that took Jesus. Whether he actually did, or did not, carry out his proposal to kiss His Master as a sign to the soldiers, matters very little. According to John, our Lord seems to have forestalled him, and to have made the kiss which followed only an act of hypocrisy towards Himself, and no longer also a sign to the soldiers. Why blame the Synoptic Gospels for not stating this at length? It is to be feared that Jews treat the New Testament with wilful injustice. They do not accord to it the same measure of reverent study, of historical common sense, which they pay to the Old Testament. Yet every Jew will grant that when two passages of the Law speak of the same thing, one passage may be fuller than the other, without either being wrong. What says R. Nehemiah in T.J. *Rosh haShanah*, III. 5 (58*d*)? "The words of the Law are poor in one place and rich in another."

דברי תורה עניים במקומן ועשירים במקום אחר.

So, too, we find in *Bemidbar R.*, § 19, towards the end (on Num. xxi. 21)—

כל דברי תורה צריכין זה לזה שמה שזה נועל זה פותח.

"All the words of the Law need each other; for what one closes, another opens." See also *Tanchuma* on the same passage, ed. Buber, p. 129. If this be granted to the Law, why refuse it to the Gospel?

## THE CRUCIFIXION OF JESUS THE DESTRUCTION OF THE JEWISH KINGDOM.

### § 57.

John xix. 15. "*The chief priests answered, We have no king but Cæsar.*"

Cæsar therefore, says R. Isaac, was already their ruler, before Jesus was crucified, so that the argument of the Christians that the Jews lost their kingdom only after, and because of, the crucifixion, is mistaken.

**453**] Here we have yet another example of the way in which our Rabbi misunderstands the Christian argument. We must distinguish plainly between what Christians do say and what they do not. It is perfectly true to write as I have done in par. 78: "Herod the Great died about the very year that the Lord Jesus was born, and since that date the Jews have never had a king to reign over them as a united nation." But no Christian ever says that the Jews ceased to have a king because they crucified Jesus. What they do say is that the Jews by their treatment of Jesus brought about their destruction as a nation dwelling in Palestine. Is this so very wrong? Is it either inaccurate or unjustifiable? If it is, Christians err in company which every other Jew than R. Isaac will consider sufficiently good to warrant the Christian statement, that of the great Maimonides himself. See his *Hilkoth Melakim*, xi. 4 (*Yad*, Amsterdam, 1702, iv., p. 307): "He who thought he would be the Messiah and was slain by the Sanhedrin . . . caused Israel to be destroyed by the sword, and their remnant to be scattered."

אותו שדמה שיהיה משיח ונהרג בבית דין··· זה גרם לאבד ישראל בחרב ולפזר שאריתם.

This statement we Christians most heartily accept. For to our minds it is clear that if the Jews had but received the teaching of the Lord Jesus they would have remained in peace, paying to Cæsar his due (Matt. xxii. 21; Rom. xiii. 1), and therefore giving the Romans no excuse for rooting them out, and, in consequence, would, long, long since, have experienced the full delights of the Messianic age. But the teaching of Jesus was for them, as for most men to-day, whether Jews or Gentiles, at once too high and too humbling, and so, refusing the full revelation of God's nature and God's love, they took their own way, and reaped the natural product of their selfishness in an awful harvest. See further, parr. 77–80.

## My God and your God.

## § 58.

John xx. 17. "*Jesus saith to her, Touch me not; for I am not yet ascended unto the Father: but go unto my brethren, and say to them, I ascend unto my Father and your Father, and my God and your God.*"

**454**] The words show, according to our Rabbi, that Jesus confesses that he is not God, and that he is only Son of God in the same sense in which all Israelites are God's sons, as it says in Deut. xiv. 1: "Sons are ye to the LORD your God"

(בנים אתם ליהוה אלהיכם).

How it is that Jesus distinguishes Himself from the Father we have already shown repeatedly. See above on par. 439. Observe also the exact wording of our Lord's language here. He carefully does not say "our Father" or "our God," but "My Father and your Father," "My God and your God." He leaves room, that is to say, for a difference in His own relation to God and the Father from that which the disciples held. The sentence, in other words, is fully compatible with the Christian doctrine of the supreme sonship of Christ, and the comparative sonship of believers.

**455**] Lastly, may one word be added with regard to the teaching of the passage as a whole? Mary Magdalene, when she recognized Jesus after this His resurrection from the dead, fell at His feet saying, "Rabboni!" and, as it appears, was clinging to them. But Jesus saith to her: "Do not stay clinging to Me thus; there is more for thee than this. I am ascending to the Father; then thou shalt have perfect communion and fellowship." Even at that moment of blissful thankfulness at His resurrection, Jesus would draw her thoughts away from the earthly and visible to the unseen, with its promise of intercourse closer than she then enjoyed. The ascended Christ is nearer to believers than He could ever have been on earth. If Christ were reigning as king in Palestine, He would not be as nigh to His servants as He is now, when He is seated in glory.

### The Restoration of the Kingdom.

§ 59.

Acts i. 6, 7. "*They therefore, when they were come together, asked him, saying, Lord, dost thou at this time restore the kingdom to Israel? And he said unto them, It is not for you to know times or seasons, which the Father hath set within his own authority.*"

**456**] Upon this passage R. Isaac makes three remarks. First, the restoration of the kingdom of Israel will yet take place. Secondly, Jesus does not say that He will restore the kingdom, and therefore confesses that He was not the Messiah. Thirdly, it is plainly impossible, according to the words of Jesus, to know when the end of this exile will come.

**457**] As to the Rabbi's first statement we answer: Certainly; but why say so? Although some Christians deny that the kingdom of Israel will be restored, those who are better instructed do not.

It is convenient to reply to the two last arguments together, although they have already been dealt with briefly in par. 98.

The Rabbi's process of reasoning is very curious, for Jesus does not say that He will not restore the kingdom, but only that His disciples must not expect a definite answer to their inquisitive question. It is plain, in spite of the Rabbi's opinion to the contrary, that since Jesus does not refuse the claim on their part that He can restore the kingdom, He considers Himself the Messiah, by whose hands the kingdom will be established. The Restoration is in the future; Jesus, who still lives, and enjoys already power far more widely exercised than when He was on earth, will one day bring it about.

**458**] But when this will be we know not, neither are we to inquire into the date too particularly. For to do so has ever been a temptation to many. When the pressure of calamity has been felt severely, then the hearts of the Lord's servants have cried out in their agony, "How long, O Lord, how long?" And they have set themselves to study the signs of the times, and to calculate the year of the fulfilment of their hopes. No one will blame this, if it be kept within bounds. But only too often they have overpassed the limits of prayerful trust, and have allowed themselves to fix a short period of ten or twenty years, or even of one year, in which the Lord is to perform His promises. All such calculations are rightly blamed by the thoughtful, whether they be Jews or Christians.

### Gamaliel.

§ 60.

Acts v. 34–39.

**459**] This passage has already been fully discussed in parr. 81–83.

### Abraham and Terah.

§ 61.

Acts vii. 4. "*Then came he* [Abraham] *out of the land of the Chaldæans, and dwelt in Haran: and from thence, when his father* [Terah] *was dead,* God *removed him into this land.*"

**460**] What a treasure this seventh chapter of the Acts of the Apostles is to opponents of Christianity, especially to those who have only a superficial acquaintance either with our holy religion, or with the Jewish manners and methods of the time in which it was written! There are so many statements in the chapter which contradict, or seem to contradict, the plain narrative of the Old Testament, and it is very easy indeed to draw attention to these and to point out the ignorance of a writer who could make such errors! Many Jews have fallen into the trap, and our friend R. Isaac among them. In saying this, it is not implied that there are no real, or perhaps even insoluble, difficulties contained in this chapter. What is meant is that these are not inconsistent with deep knowledge of the Scriptures on the part of St. Stephen, or of the writer of the Acts, upon whom the responsibility must be laid. For we cannot imagine that he would have recorded gross errors if he had known them to be such. Thus Stephen may almost be left out of sight as we consider this chapter. The writer of the Acts, whom, with most modern scholars, we assume to have been St. Luke, must bear the brunt of any attacks that are made.

**461**] In the present case, it is asserted that he betrays ignorance of the Bible by saying that Abraham left Haran after the death of his father. Now such ignorance is so gross that in the case of the writer of the Acts it is not very probable. For, if we may judge from those many examples to which we can apply accurate tests, St. Luke was a very careful historian, and therefore it is not likely that he did not know the very elements of Old Testament history. Now it is plain that if, according to Gen. xi. 26, Terah was seventy years old when Abraham was born,* and (Gen. xii. 4) seventy-five more years had passed when Abraham left Haran, Terah was then only a hundred and forty-five years old. But we are told in the very same passage (xi. 32) that Terah was two hundred and five years old when he died. It is therefore evident to a mere child that Abraham left Haran not after the death of Terah, but sixty years before.

**462**] How, then, do we account for the statement of which complaint is made? Let us consider the effect of the sum in arithmetic which has just been made. Terah had come up

* The verse, however, is interpreted otherwise by some writers, who find themselves able to argue that Abraham is mentioned first only because of his importance, and was really far the youngest, being sixty years younger than Haran the eldest. See R. Biscoe's thoughtful Boyle Lectures on *The History of the Acts of the Holy Apostles* (delivered in 1736–1738, and his arguments there against the *Chizzuk Emunah* (edition 1840, pp. 384 *sqq.*)).

from Ur of the Chaldees, accompanied only by Abraham, Lot and Sarah (Gen. xi. 31) and Lot and Sarah went with Abraham to the land of Israel. Abraham, that is to say, left his father alone in Haran, although he was already an old man of a hundred and forty-five years of age. In other words, as the Rabbis themselves point out, he was guilty of an act of filial impiety. The Jews indeed attempt to defend him from this charge by saying that God expressly told him that he was to disregard the fifth commandment, "Honour thy father and thy mother," although no one else was to disregard it. But it is not God's way to give positive orders which override principles already accepted as binding by those to whom His orders are addressed. If indeed it be urged on the contrary that Abraham was told by God to slay his son, it may be pointed out that Abraham evidently did not know that such an action was contrary to the will of God (for doubtless he saw it often done by religious parents among the heathen round him), and also that the issue of that charge showed that it was never God's intention that it should be carried out. But here Abraham goes forth, leaving Terah in his old age. There is more, however, to be said than this. The Jews do not shrink from accusing God Himself of fraud and deceit. He is depicted as being well aware of Abraham's neglect of the primary duty of caring for his father, a duty even more esteemed by the ancients than it is to-day, and as taking means to prevent the Gentiles perceiving this dereliction of duty, by causing the death of Terah to be mentioned out of its proper place, viz. before the departure of Abraham for Canaan. A method of reading the Scriptures which accuses both Abraham of impiety and God of deceit must be viewed with suspicion. It is not likely that Abraham would have left Terah in his old age.*

* מה כתיב למעלה מן הענין וימת תרח בחרן. א"ר יצחק אם לענין החשבון ועד עכשו מתבקש לו עוד ששים וחמש שנים. אלא בתחלה אתה דורש שהרשעים קרויים מתים בחייהם. לפי שהיה א"א מפחד ואומר אצא יהיו מחללים בי שם שמים. ואומרים הניח אביו והלך לו לעת זקנתו. א"ל הקדוש ב"ה לך אני פוטרך מכיבוד אב ואם. ואין אני פוטר לאחר

**463**] In any case it is unscholarly to accuse the writer of the Acts of ignorance, when we find one of the most learned of all Jews making precisely the same remark. Philo, it is true, was not orthodox if judged by the modern standard of orthodoxy, but every one is aware that he was a man of immense learning. He says (*De Migratione Abraham*, § 32, Mangey I. 463 and 464) : "Abraham moved from the land of Chaldæa and dwelt in Haran. But after his father died there he removed from that place also, so that he now had forsaken two places." Philo, in other words, deliberately rejects the elementary calculation that Terah lived long after Abraham left him, and says that he died first. What was Philo's reason? This is indicated by the way in which he proceeds to develop the subject. For by his later statements in §§ 34, 36, p. 466, he regards Terah's death as typical of the condition of Haran, and implies that those who seek Canaan must first leave the place of death.

Does not this suggest to us a possible reason for the statement in the Acts, which at first sight is so extraordinary? Stephen, the Hellenist, speaking of the change which was brought about by Christ's teaching, may have had some such an idea as that of his great contemporary Philo of Alexandria, that the old and unrenewed life ends in death, and again, that only by means of spiritual death can we go forward into our promised land of rest.

It is, therefore, not unreasonable to ask our readers at least to give the writer of the Acts the benefit of the doubt. It is unscholarly to accuse him of ignorance unless we are prepared to accuse Philo also of ignorance, which is absurd. It is much more probable that St. Stephen first, and after him

מכיבוד אב ואם. ולא עוד אלא שאני מקדים מיתתו ליציאתך. בתחלה וימת תרח בחרן ואח"כ ויאמר ה׳ אל אברם וגו׳.

Breshith R., § 39, on Gen. xii. 1, and also Yalqut, § 62, on the same verse. Cf. the *Midrash haGadol* on Gen. xii. 1 (Schechter's edition, 1902, p. 201):

**ומבית אביך.** אמ׳ ר׳ שמואל בר נחמני אמ׳ אברהם לפני הקב"ה שמא יהרהרו עלי בני אדם ויאמרו זה שהוא מקרב את האומות תחת כנפי השכינה הניח אביו זקן והלך לו.

the writer of the Acts, to whom the Pauline thought of life through spiritual death must have been very well known, deliberately adopted that version of the relation of Abraham's departure to Terah's death which enabled them, and the more thoughtful of their hearers, to learn a spiritual lesson of such far-reaching importance.

**464**] *Postscript.*—It is no part of the present writer's duty to explain the numbers given in Genesis. The writer of the Acts has been accused of ignorance, and it has been shown that the accusation is extremely improbable, and a reason has been suggested why he made his statement. He took a different view of the verses in Genesis from that which is now received in Jewish circles. Whether at the same time he accepted one or other of the systems of chronology which differ from that which is incorporated in the Massoretic text is a further question into which there is no occasion to enter. In any case it is well known that the dates contained in the Hebrew Bible are not so universally received among scholars as the other parts of it.

## The Promise to Abraham.

### § 62.

Acts vii. 7. "*And the nation to which they shall be in bondage will I judge, said God; and after that shall they come forth, and serve me in this place.*"

**465**] "Lo, thou seest from this verse also," writes R. Isaac, "that the apostles of Jesus and the writers of the New Testament were not well acquainted with the Law and the Prophets, for the verse does not run thus in the Law, but as follows (Gen. xv. 14): 'And also that nation, whom they shall serve, will I judge: and afterward shall they come out with great substance.' But this writer, for lack of knowledge, changed the half of this verse for the half of another, and wrote: 'And after that shall they come forth, and serve me in this place.' But he took this from what God said to Moses in Exod. iii. 12, 'When thou hast brought forth the people out of Egypt, ye shall serve God upon this mountain.'"

**466**] Truly a Daniel come to judgment! R. Isaac writes like a babe, who has never read a page of Jewish literature. For even allowing for the moment that he is right in his assertion that the second half of Stephen's sentence is taken from the Book of Exodus, what does it matter? Nothing is commoner in Jewish writings than to join quotations from different parts of Scripture together as if they came from one and the same place. It is only to be expected that Stephen, as a Jew, should do as other Jews do.

**467**] Whether, however, R. Isaac is right in saying that the second half is taken from Exodus is a wholly different matter. The careful reader of the passage in Genesis will hardly agree with him. For what do we find? That in Gen. xv. 16, in the very same utterance as *v.* 14, God promises to Abraham "and in the fourth generation they shall come hither again." Bearing this in mind, does it not seem probable that, after all, Stephen is but giving the true sense of the passage in Genesis, having only shortened it a little? No Jewish scholar is likely to find fault with him for shortening a quotation, for it is in full accordance with the principle laid down in *Pesachim*, 3*b*: "Rab Huna said that R. Jehudah said in the name of R. Meir: A man should always teach his pupil the shortest way."

אמר רב הונה אמר רבי משום ר׳ מאיר לעולם ישנה אדם לתלמידו דרך קצרה.

Further, it is doubtful if a single Jewish writer of ancient times can be found who is punctilious about the exact accuracy of his quotations from Scripture. What does R. Joshua haLevi say (after 1467 A.D.) in his *Halikoth 'Olam*, II. 2? "The method of traditional teaching is to shorten the passages of Scripture, and it does not bring them forward as they are."

דרך הגמרא לקצר המקראות ואינו מביא אותם כהויתו.

Thus, for example, a Mishna-teacher of the school of R. Ishmael quotes: "and the priest shall come again, and the priest shall come in," as though one sentence followed the other, whereas in reality they are separated by four verses (Lev. xiv. 39, 44). *Makkoth*, 13*b*—

תנא דבי ר׳ ישמעאל ושב הכהן ובא הכהן.

In fact, R. Isaac's objection to this part of Nepheri's speech is frivolous and ignorant.*

### The Number of those who went down to Egypt.

§ 63.

Acts vii. 14. "*And Joseph sent, and called to him Jacob his father, and all his kindred, threescore and fifteen souls.*"

**468**] We read, however, in Gen. xlvi. 27: "All the souls of the house of Jacob, which came into Egypt, were threescore and ten." What a gross error! Stephen says seventy-five, Genesis seventy! But it is plain that before we accuse Stephen of a mistake we must be sure that he means exactly the same thing as the writer of Genesis. In fact, however, it is not easy to understand the figures of the latter. As they stand they are not consistent with themselves. For we read in *v.* 26 that there were sixty-six persons, and in *v.* 27 that there were two more, and then that the total was seventy, a curious piece of addition. That, however, the numbers of those mentioned in *vv.* 15 (33), 18 (16), 22 (14), 25 (7) do make up seventy in all is plain, so that we are not concerned to dispute the general result, viz. that Genesis says seventy and Stephen seventy-five.

* The curious reader will find several other examples of the same kind in Surenhusius, *Biblos Katallages*, 1713, pp. 45 *sq.* Let him consult also Strack, *Prolegomena Critica*, 1873, pp. 65 *sq.*, from which the reference to R. Joshua haLevi is taken.

**469**] How, then, did Stephen arrive at his number? He took it bodily from the early Jewish translation of Genesis called the Septuagint. This adds in *v.* 20 five more persons not mentioned in the Hebrew, who were grandsons and great-grandsons of Joseph, thus bringing up the total to seventy-five. The discrepancy, therefore, between Genesis and Stephen is more apparent than real.

Let us, however, not fail to notice the exactness of St. Luke. He had already told us that Stephen was a Hellenist, a Jew, that is to say, whose mother-tongue was Greek, who therefore of course used the Græco-Jewish translation, called the Septuagint. What would Jewish and other critics have said if St. Luke had made Stephen quote the Hebrew form and not the Septuagint when the latter differs from the former? Would they not then have argued, very fairly, that as St. Luke spoke of a man who knew no Hebrew preferring it to the translation which he had used from boyhood, and such an inconsistency was extremely improbable, no doubt the whole narrative was false, and due only to the imagination of an ignorant story-teller? We, however, see here an undesigned coincidence, according to which a Judæo-Greek quotes from a Judæo-Greek version, even when that version disagrees in some small point with the received Hebrew text, and our belief in the accuracy with which St. Luke reproduces the information he had received is strongly confirmed.

## Shechem.

§ 63 continued.

Acts vii. 15, 16. "*And Jacob went down into Egypt; and he died, himself and our fathers; and they were carried over unto Shechem, and laid in the tomb that Abraham bought for a price in silver of the sons of Hamor in Shechem.*"

**470**] Three objections have been brought against these verses; let us consider them one by one.

1. Some have thought that Stephen says that Jacob himself was buried at Shechem. If so, the Proto-martyr, in spite of the learning attributed to him, must have been more ignorant than a child of four or five years of age. Luke, too, in recording the utterance, must have presumed upon the ignorance of his readers. Are either of these presuppositions probable if they are considered dispassionately? But, as the true text of the passage shows, Stephen does not say that Jacob was buried in Shechem. He states the simple fact that Jacob died and our Fathers, and adds that these were carried up and buried there, without including Jacob. It is indeed possible to translate the phrase grammatically so as to include him, but we are not justified in preferring the loose construction to the strict, or, if we do adopt it, to forget that St. Stephen and St. Luke had a right to assume the presence of common sense in those who heard, and in those who read, their words. This objection is trivial.

**471**] 2. The next difficulty is of a wholly different kind, and requires consideration. According to *v.* 16 not only Joseph, but also his brothers, were carried up from Egypt and buried in Shechem. R. Isaac, however, tells us roundly that they were buried in Egypt. Were they? How does he know this? He is depending solely on the silence of Scripture, for we are told there absolutely nothing whatever about the matter. Tradition says they were not buried in Egypt, and though R. Isaac as a Karaite cares nothing whatever for tradition, when it contradicts his theories, he does not represent the bulk of his fellow Jews in this respect. *The Book of Jubilees* (between 150 and 100 B.C.) tells us that "the children of Israel brought forth all the bones of the children of Jacob save the bones of Joseph, and they buried them in" Machpelah (§ 46). *The Testaments of the Twelve Patriarchs* (written between 135 and 100 B.C.) informs us that the sons of Simeon "laid him in a wooden coffin, to take up his bones to Hebron; and they took them up secretly" (Simeon, § 8). So again the sons of Levi "laid him in a coffin, and afterwards they buried him in Hebron, with Abraham, Isaac, and Jacob" (Levi, § 19). So of Gad, five years after he died "they carried him up to

Hebron, and laid him with his fathers" (Gad, § 8). So also we read of Benjamin in particular, and his brethren in general, that they "brought up the bones of their fathers secretly during the Canaanitish war, and they buried them in Hebron, by the feet of their fathers" (Benj., § 12). Similarly Josephus, surely a man not ignorant of Jewish tradition, writes: "At length Joseph's brethren also die, after living happily in Egypt. And after some time their descendants and children took up their bodies and buried them in Hebron" (*Antt.*, II. 8, 2, § 199). The *Mekilta* on Exod. xiii. 19 says the same: "Whence do we know that they took up with them also the bones of the rest of the Patriarchs? Because it is said; hence 'with you,'" attaching, that is to say, the tradition either to the words "with you" or to the numerical value of the word translated "hence," viz. twelve.* Rashi on the same verse in Exodus answers the question by the former of the two alternatives. Lastly we are told in T.B. *Sota*, *7b*, that Judah's bones were carried about in the wilderness.†

From all this evidence it is plain that Stephen had abundance of Jewish tradition at his back when he said that the Fathers were carried up out of Egypt, the main contention of R. Isaac, that he knew nothing of that about which he was talking, being thus disproved.

**472**] Our readers, however, will doubtless have observed that the tradition quoted above speaks of burial at Hebron, not at Shechem. This is a matter of less importance, but it must be remembered that we are expressly told in Scripture that one of Jacob's sons, viz. Joseph, was buried at Shechem. It is therefore possible that Stephen was thinking chiefly of him. It is, again, possible that the well-known Samaritan tradition that all the sons were buried at Shechem existed in Stephen's time, and that, on the whole, he thought it more accurate than the tale that they were taken to Hebron. In any case our readers will have come to the conclusion, we

* מנין שאף עצמות שאר השבטים העלו עמם שנאמר מזה אתכם.

† כל אותן שנים שהיו ישראל במדבר היו עצמותיו של יהודה מגולגלין בארון.

See further, Rashi on this passage also.

hope, that Stephen and Luke cannot be accused either of mere ignorance or of devising fables out of their own head.

**473**] 3. The third objection is much the most serious of the three, and cannot he met very satisfactorily at present. "The tomb that Abraham bought for a price in silver of the sons of Hamor in Shechem!" Every one knows that it was Jacob, not Abraham, who bought land in Shechem from Hamor (Gen. xxxiii. 19; Joshua xxiv. 32). Abraham bought his ground in Machpelah from Ephron the Hittite (Gen. xxiii. 16). What is the explanation of this strange divergence? Ignorance, sheer ignorance, says the man in the street, including, alas, R. Isaac. But it would be very difficult to find any scholar of to-day, be he Jew or Christian, who would give such an answer now. Stephen's speech, and Luke's whole book, are too full of accurate knowledge for it to be at all probable that either of them made so childish an error as verbally here seems plain.

**474**] What, then, is the cause of the statement? No one quite knows, but in all probability there has been condensation so great as to become obscurity. Clearly only a very short account of the speech has been preserved, and the notes of it are doubtless intended to be more of the nature of memoranda than an accurate transcript. In all such cases of compressed reporting mistakes very easily occur. The most plausible of specific suggestions is perhaps that of J. Z. Lichtenstein, in his *Chizzuk Emunath Emeth* and also his Commentary, to the effect that Stephen really said "the tomb that he [Jacob] bought, like Abraham, for," etc., the point being that Stephen was comparing the two Patriarchs. Such a comparison is found in the *Breshith R.*, § 79, on Gen. xxxiii. 19, and the *Midrash ha-Gadol* (Schechter) on the same passage, where the three purchases, Abraham's of Machpelah, David's of the Temple Mount, and Jacob of Joseph's burying-place, are mentioned as the three spots in the Holy Land which indubitably belonged of old to Israel. It may well be that Stephen had in his mind a comparison of this kind, when he was endeavouring to show his hearers the method of God in leading His people about from place to place, and in giving them at first but little foothold in the land which afterwards was to be theirs. At most it was but two tombs! The question suggested by the remarks of Aben Ezra and Ramban on Gen. xxxiii. 19, why Jacob bought land, and that of Kimchi on Joshua xxiv. 32, why Joseph was buried at Shechem, find a common solution, if Jacob, as Stephen says, like Abraham his grandfather, bought the plot of ground for a family tomb.

### DAMASCUS OR BABYLON.

§ 64.

Acts vii. 43. "*And ye took up the tabernacle of Moloch, and the star of the god Rephan, the figures which ye made to worship them: and I will carry you away beyond Babylon.*"

Amos v. 26, 27. "*Yea, ye have borne Siccuth your king and Chiun your images, the star of your god, which ye made to yourselves. Therefore will I cause you to go into captivity beyond Damascus.*"

**475**] R. Isaac remarks here: "You see that the author writes quite differently from the words of the prophet." What if he does? Would the Rabbi have an Alexandrian Jew like Stephen quote the Hebrew Bible like a Jew of Palestine? Imagine what he would have said then! He would have been the very first to accuse the historian of fraud and deceit. But probably the learned critic forgot, when he spoke so sharply, that the Septuagint was a translation written by Jews for Jews, and that Jews, not Christians, must bear the blame of any mistakes made.

**476**] There is no need, indeed, to minimize the differences of the two passages quoted above. Those in the first part of Acts vii. 43 and in Amos v. 26 have only a philological interest. We may assume, however, that the Hebrew is right, and the Septuagint wrong—but that is not Stephen's fault; it is the fault of Jews who lived long before him. The only variation in the quotation which appears to have been made by Stephen himself is the phrase, "beyond Babylon," instead of "beyond Damascus," doubtless because it was a short way of saying that the Jews were in fact carried to Babylon, and beyond. Surely in principle it is precisely the same as the use of *al-tiqri*, so well known to every Jewish scholar.*

## Simon Magus.

### § 65.

**477**] Acts viii. 9–11. On the account of Simon Magus given in the Acts our Rabbi remarks that he finds in a Polish work called the *Great Old Chronicle*† that Simon performed many miracles by the aid of magic, and that therefore he was worshipped as a god. So, the Rabbi concludes, was it with Jesus. The Rabbi further illustrates his theory by the incident at Malta recorded in Acts xxviii. 6, when the islanders said St. Paul must be a god because he shook off the viper from his hand and was uninjured. The last comparison is of little weight. For the chance remark of the uneducated barbarian produced no belief in the divinity of the Apostle. Nor is there much point in the comparison between Simon Magus and our Lord. What force has the *Great Old Chronicle*, written a thousand years or more after the events, as a witness to the truth of Simon's doings? And even if it were true that Simon wrought miracles by magic, how does this afford proof that Jesus wrought them by the same method? Besides, is the moral difference between the two to go for nothing? Do Jews really intend to place a charlatan like Simon on the same

* See Glossary.

† This, the *Kronika polska*, to which R. Isaac refers also in his Preamble to Part I. (par. 5), was published at Cracow, 1564, and was the first historical work in Polish. Its author was Martin Bielski, a Protestant.

level as Him who has been the means of raising whole nations to the highest position in the scale of ethics? Is it thinkable that the beneficent effect of the life and teaching of Jesus of Nazareth has been due to fraud and magic? We Christians appeal confidently to the moral sense of every fair-minded and cultivated Jew, and ask if it is possible that good fruit can grow out of an evil tree? If not, it is time to have done with such unsavoury comparisons, and to recognize the unique grandeur of Jesus of Nazareth.*

### All Foods made Clean.

§ 66.

478] On Acts x. 11–16, the vision to St. Peter of the sheet filled with all manner of beasts, R. Isaac refers to xi. 5–10, 1 Cor. x. 25, and Mark vii. 15, and says that he has already considered the subject of eating unclean food in Part I. § 15, and Part II. § 18 (see also parr. 418 *sq.*). Very well; so have we at the same places. Here it is sufficient to point out that in reality the main object of the vision was not to inform St. Peter that he might eat certain food, but to tell him not to think persons unclean if they happened to be Gentiles and not Jews. He was to dare to accompany the messengers who would soon come to him from Cornelius, the Roman centurion, and, on his return with them, tell him freely of the way of salvation in Christ. He went, and admitted Cornelius to full religious privileges. It is probable that Jews are still far from having attained to such liberty of thought and kindliness as here were inculcated. On the other hand, many a Gentile needs to be reminded that Jews, after all, do not deserve to

* If there were any reason for identifying the Simon of Cyprus mentioned in the common text of Josephus (*Antt.*, XX. vii. 2, § 142) as persuading Drusilla to leave her husband, and marry Felix, with Simon Magus, the argument would be even stronger, but there is no evidence to warrant the identification, and for Simon Niese reads Atomus.

be treated with contempt. The Gospel of the Lord Jesus bids us all, whether of Jewish or of Gentile blood, receive every man freely in the name of Christ.

### The Length of the Reign of King Saul.

### § 67.

Acts xiii. 21. "*And afterward they asked for a king: and God gave unto them Saul the son of Kish, a man of the tribe of Benjamin, for the space of forty years.*"

**479**] Our Rabbi has a long note on this verse, to the effect that Saul did not reign so long as is here stated, in fact, not more than ten years at the outside. He may be right; the question is of little importance, and it may be confessed at once that so much obscurity hangs over the length of Saul's reign, that no one can make any positive assertion regarding it. For it is nowhere clearly stated in the Old Testament. Hence different opinions on the subject have always been held. Josephus, for example, in *Antt.*, VI. xiv. 9, § 378, says the same as St. Paul, affirming that "Saul reigned during Samuel's life eighteen years, and after his death twenty-two * years." But in X. viii. 4, § 143, he says only twenty years, though referring, as it seems, to the whole period of his reign. R. Isaac depends much on the curious verse, 1 Sam. xiii. 1, the text of which is very doubtful. We shall be wise if we defer coming to any conclusion upon the question of the length of Saul's reign until we possess more information about it.

* Some manuscripts read "two."

## The Second Psalm.

### § 68.

**480**] To read the long disquisition in the *Chizzuk Emunah* (long for it, we mean, for we grant that the learned author is always concise) one would suppose that no thoughtful Jew ever interpreted the Psalm of King Messiah. Nothing could be further from the truth. The Psalm has been referred by Jews to Messiah over and over again. Such an exposition is Jewish, thoroughly Jewish.

In proof of this assertion, which may appear strange to not a few readers, whether Jews or Christians, it may be well to recall some statements in Jewish works, and it will perhaps be more convenient if we take them in what may be called the reverse order, mentioning first the later, and afterwards the earlier, witnesses. Both we and our readers want only to discover the truth, and when we have seen it, to obey its behests.

**481**] What does Kimchi say in the thirteenth century? He himself thinks that it refers to David, but he is candid enough to let us know in his comment on the twelfth verse, that "our teachers interpreted this Psalm of the Messiah." * That is a general statement, but if we wish to see the kind of way in which they did so, the manner in which they explained verse after verse of the Psalm in reference to Messiah, we need only turn to the pages of the *Yalqut*, § 621, written, as it seems, in the same thirteenth century: "R. Huna said in the name of R. Idi, In three parts were the punishments divided: one for King Messiah, and when His hour cometh the Holy One, blessed be He, saith, I must make a new

* ויש מפרשים זה המזמור על גוג ומגוג, והמשיח הוא מלך המשיח; וכן פרשו רבותינו זכרם לברכה (בבלי ברכות ז.ב).

(Ed. Schiller-Szinessy.)

covenant with Him, and so He saith, To-day have I begotten thee" (*v.* 7).* Again, on *v.* 9: "'Thou wilt bruise them with a rod of iron'; this is Messiah ben Joseph." †

**482**] Maimonides himself says much the same in his introduction to *Sanhedrin*, c. 10: "The prophets and the saints have longed for the days of the Messiah, and great has been their desire towards him, for there will be with him the gathering together of the righteous and the administration of good, and wisdom, and royal righteousness, with the abundance of his uprightness and the spread of his wisdom, and his approach to God, as it is said: The Lord said unto me, Thou art my son, to-day have I begotten thee." ‡ Maimonides plainly believes that the second Psalm concerns the Messiah.

**483**] Aben Ezra (twelfth century) is of opinion that a poet composed it either with reference to David or to the Messiah. He does not, that is to say, regard the Messianic interpretation as at all impossible, although he himself does not adopt it.§ Saadiah, not Saadiah haGaon, as once was supposed, but a writer of perhaps the twelfth century, says in his commentary on Dan. vii. 14, which is printed in most Rabbinic Bibles: "And there was given him dominion. For God would give him dominion and royal power, as it is written in the second Psalm, Yet have I set my King." ‖ Rashi (eleventh century)

* רבי הונא בשם רבי אידי בשלשה חלקים נחלקו הייסורין אחד למלך המשיח וכד תיתי לו שעתיה אומר הקב"ה עלי לכרות לו ברית חדשה וכה"א אני היום ילדתיך.

† **תרועם בשבט ברזל** זה משיח בן יוסף.

v. 8, *Ask of me*, etc., is also explained in the *Yalqut* in the same way as in *Midrash Tehillim*, *vide infra*.

‡ התאוו הנביאים והחסידים ימות המשיח ורבתה תשוקתם אליו למה שיהיה בו מקבוץ הצדיקים והנהגת הטובה והחכמה וצדק המלך ורוב יושרו והפלגת חכמתו וקרבותו אל האלהים כמו שנאמר ה' אמר אלי בני אתה אני היום ילדתיך.

§ הנכון בעיני כי זה המזמור חברו אחד מהמשוררים על דוד ביום המשחו על כן כתוב אני היום ילדתיך, או על המשיח.

‖ **ולה יהיב שולטן.** שיתן לו שולטנות ומלכות ככתוב ואני נסכתי מלכי.

tells us frankly: "Our teachers interpreted the subject of this Psalm with reference to King Messiah, but according to its plain meaning it will be right to expound it of David himself, according to what is said in 2 Sam. v. 17 *sqq.*: When the Philistines heard that Israel had anointed David to be king over them, the Philistines gathered their hosts, but fell at his hands." *

**484**] It is hardly necessary to remind the learned reader that the *Midrash Tehillim* (eleventh century at latest) interprets the Psalm of Messiah. At the seventh verse the same saying is found which has already been quoted from the *Yalqut.* At the eighth verse we find the following: "R. Jochanan said, There were three to whom the Holy One said: Ask, and these are they: Solomon, and Ahaz, and King Messiah. . . . King Messiah, for it is said, Ask of Me and I will give thee." † Not much earlier, say in the early part of the ninth century of our era, the *Pirqe d'R. Eliezer*, § 28, interprets the Psalm of Messiah, for we find there that "all the nations will be gathered together to fight with the Son of David, as it is said: The kings of the earth set themselves," etc. (*v.* 1).‡ In the same way the *Breshith Rabba* (of about the sixth century, § 44, about a third of the way through) quotes the eighth verse, "Ask of Me," in reference to King Messiah, in the same words that have been cited from the *Midrash Tehillim.*§

**485**] So we come to the Talmud, which, after all, is the great source from which all later writers drew. In T.B. *Berakoth*, *7b*, it is assumed that Ps. ii. 1 refers to the war of

* רבותינו דרשו את הענין על מלך המשיח ולפי משמעו יהיה נכון לפותרו על דוד עצמו כעין שנאמר וישמעו פלשתים כי משחו ישראל את דוד למלך עליהם ויקבצו פלשתים את מחניהם ונפלו בידו.

† א״ר יוחנן ג׳ בני אדם אמר להם הקב״ה שאל ואלו הן. שלמה ואחז ומלך המשיח··· מלך המשיח שנאמר שאל ממני ואתנה.
(Ed. Warsaw, 1875.)

‡ כלם כאחת להלחם עם בן דוד שנא׳ יתיצבו מלכי ארץ וגו׳.
(Ed. Lemberg, 1874.) It should, however, be stated that the MS. translated by Mr. G. Friedlander (1916) reads "the house of David" instead of "the Son of David." Yet even that MS. is referring to events still future.

§ See also par. 481.

Gog and Magog, *i.e.* to Messianic times.* T.B. *Sukkah*, 52*a*, also understands the Psalm to refer to Messiah: "Our Rabbis have taught us in a Mishna with reference to Messiah [ben David], who is about to be revealed quickly [in our days], that the Holy One, blessed be He, saith to him, Ask [of Me something, and I will give] thee, for it is said, I will declare the decree [etc., To-day have I begotten thee]. Ask of Me and I will give thee nations for thine inheritance." †

**486**] We have now traced as far back as the Talmud the reference of this Psalm to the Messiah and His time by Jewish writers. There are, however, earlier witnesses to it in other Jewish works, which have not come down to us in Hebrew or Aramaic. The latest of these is the book called the Second, or Fourth, of Esdras, which is assigned by its latest editor, Canon G. H. Box, to a date not later than 120 A.D. The use in it of the phrase, "my Son the Messiah" (vii. 28, 29), or simply, "my Son" (xiii. 32, 37, 52, and xiv. 9), can hardly be due to any other influence than that of the second Psalm. The writer, that is to say, believed that our Psalm referred to the Messiah. But we may go back earlier, before the time of Christianity, and we still find the same reference in an undoubtedly Jewish writing, the Psalms of Solomon, written between 70 and 40 B.C. In xvii. 23, 26 the author says: "Behold, O LORD, and raise up unto them their king, the son of David . . . as potter's vessels with a rod of iron shall he break in pieces all their substance." ‡ We can hardly doubt that this is taken from *v.* 9 of our Psalm. So also in xviii. 8 the phrase, "the rod of chastening of the LORD'S anointed" is due to the first verse. Last, and perhaps earliest of all, are two passages in the Book of Enoch (about the beginning

* גבי מלחמת גוג ומגוג כתיב למה רגשו גוים וגו׳.

† ת״ר משיח [בן דוד] שעתיד להגלות במהרה [בימינו] אומר לו הקב״ה שאל [ממני דבר ואתן] לך שנא׳ אספרה אל חוק [וגו׳ אני היום ילדתיך] שאל ממני ואתנה גוים נחלתך.

The words in brackets are omitted in the Munich MS., but do not affect the argument.

‡ Ryle and James' translation.

of the first century B.C.), where in lii. 3, 4 we find the phrase, "His Anointed," used of the Son of man, and in cv. 2 the sentence spoken by God: "For I and My Son will be united with them for ever in the paths of uprightness." Both these expressions are doubtless derived from our Psalm, indicating that the Messianic interpretation of it was accepted by the author of this ancient book.

**487**] Our readers will not, we trust, misunderstand the object with which these many quotations have been adduced. They do not prove that the Psalm is Messianic, but they do show that it is folly to pretend that such an interpretation is not thoroughly Jewish. From the thirteenth century of our era, to as far back as the first or second century B.C., many Jews, and probably the majority of them, understood it to refer to Messiah. Any Jew, therefore, to-day, who sees in it a prophecy of the Son of David is but walking in the footsteps of his great predecessors.

**488**] Many, however, will reply, that although undoubtedly this is an ancient Jewish interpretation, yet it must not be regarded as expressing the literal meaning and primary reference of the Psalm, but only as an application. Now, if this were the case—that the reference of the Psalm to the Messiah was not intended by its original author, but was only an adaptation of its language—no thoughtful student of the New Testament would be in the least disturbed. Another example would be added to the long list of similar adaptations in the New Testament; that is all. But is it true that the plain and literal meaning of the Psalm favours a primary reference to David or to any other ordinary king? Many writers say so; but is it true?

**489**] Of course there are allusions to David and the things of David; no ode in honour of the Messiah could very well omit them. The "hill of Zion" was David's city, which he conquered, and where he dwelt. The nations did "rage" against him. He was the "anointed" of the Lord. More than that, God did give him a special promise of sonship. But could he ever expect "the uttermost parts of the earth" to be his possession? However much he asked, had he any right to think, or was a courtier justified in saying it of him, that he would "break them with a rod of iron," and "dash them in pieces like a potter's vessel"? Were the kings, the judges of the earth, to kiss him in humble obedience, lest they should "perish in the way"? After all is said and done, David and his successors on the throne were but petty princelings compared with the great monarchs of their time, much more with those of our own day. The countries in which their law ran, the population over whom they claimed dominion, were minute in comparison with the empires of Assyria, Babylon, and Egypt, of Alexander, and of Rome, much more with that of Great Britain. If you do insist upon the literal meaning of the Psalm, insist upon it, and see whither it carries you, far, far beyond the tiny dominion of David and Solomon, to the utmost confines of the whole round world. Such a ruler was ever the Hope of Israel. It is more in accordance with the wording of the Psalm to think that its author had such a world-wide King in view.

**490**] "The Messiah is the speaker, and the whole Psalm is composed in his name," writes Wellhausen in the Polychrome Bible, as quoted by Canon Box on *The Ezra-Apocalypse* (1912, p. lvi.), and although Wellhausen is not especially a friend of the Jews, yet he certainly is not prejudiced in favour of orthodox Christian teaching. So also Prof. Driver, perhaps the most careful of all recent Hebrew scholars, inclines to the opinion that the Psalm is ideal, and descriptive of the great coming Messianic King (*Studies in the Psalms*, 1915, pp. 69–71).

**491**] Whether indeed the author, in his delineation of the Messianic King, intended to convey the full Christian doctrine of His origin and nature, is an entirely different matter, and not to be answered offhand. The tendency of the modern scholarship in which most of us have been brought up is to deny more than a very slight knowledge of the future to those devout souls whom the LORD honoured with the breath of His inspiration. In any case, the quotations from the Old Testament by the writers of the New do not at all imply the belief that they of olden time had accurate knowledge of the details of those events which they foretold. They did not produce, as it were, photographs of persons before they lived, much less cinematographic films of the incidents of their careers. Outlines, more or less shadowy; promises, burgeoning with Divine fruitage; ideas held in solution, but crystallizing into form and substance in due course; these were the staple of their visions. The New Testament writers, on the other hand, had to do with facts. They were in front of them, before their eyes. There was no escaping their influence. And as those holy men, pious, God-fearing Jews, considered these strange facts, they could not but recall to their mind sayings and incidents related in their sacred Book, the principles of which threw light on the events they now beheld, and they quoted words accordingly.

**492**] Can we be surprised that at least two of these writers, if not three, saw in the words of this Psalm, which they, with other Jews, had long been accustomed to regard as Messianic, a description of Him whom they found to be their Saviour, the true Messiah, and that they quoted its language in reference to Him? But observe exactly how the words of the seventh verse are used by St. Paul in our passage, Acts xiii. 32 *sq.*: "We bring you good tidings of the promise made unto the fathers, how that God hath fulfilled the same unto our children, in that he raised up Jesus; as also it is written in the second psalm, Thou art my Son, this day have I begotten thee." St. Paul, it will be noticed, is not referring to the Psalm in proof of our Lord's Eternal Sonship. That is another question altogether. He quotes it in relation to our Lord's resurrection. Just as the original author of the Psalm found in the proclamation of the kingship of Messiah the proof of His Sonship, so St. Paul finds the same proof in Christ's resurrection. This, not the Eternal Generation, is the subject of which St. Paul is speaking. The resurrection, says he, shows the Sonship of Christ. The argument is similar to that of Rom. i. 4: "Who was declared to be the Son of God with power, according to the spirit of holiness, by the resurrection of the dead." For although the Apostle there writes directly of the general resurrection rather than of Christ's own, this is because he considers Christ's as the first-fruits. That Christ rose, and thus brought about the final resurrection of all, was the solemn declaration and proof that He was God's Son.*

**493**] Even in Heb. i. 5, 6 there is no direct claim to the Eternal Generation of the Second Person in the Trinity. The writer does but insist that He is called Son, and for this reason is higher than the highest angel, who is not so called. "For unto which of the angels said he at any time, Thou art my Son, this day have I begotten thee? . . . Let all the angels of God worship him." That this is consistent with the highest possible Christian doctrine of the Divine nature of the Son, His eternal Sonship in the Blessed Trinity, is evident. But it is equally evident to the unprejudiced reader that the writer did not intend his quotations from the Old Testament to do more than express the reality of His Sonship in a way higher than the highest of angels could claim. What this involved was perhaps not understood at first. It was real, it was supreme, it was far truer sonship than anything attributed to man, or Jew, or Jewish nation, or the whole hierarchy of angelic ministrants, but more was not said by the author of the Epistle, perhaps because he felt that more was not required. But human thought, in touch with things Divine, could not rest until it had reasoned out the truth that He who was so much was no less than the very embodiment of God, "the effulgence of His glory, and the very image of His essential being," Son in the highest, fullest, most complete, and perfect meaning of the word, the Second Person in the Eternal Trinity, Himself very and eternal God.†

* This seems to be the meaning of Heb. v. 5 also.

† It is hardly necessary to do more than mention two arguments adduced by R. Isaac against referring this Psalm to Christ. One is that He never ruled anywhere, and therefore has not been king. The reader will find this absurd objection refuted in parr. 15, 27, 79. The second is that to the Divine Son the Father could not say, "Ask of Me"; but this overlooks the fact that according to the Christian faith the Messiah was fully man as well as perfect God, and therefore could pray to His Father in heaven, as indeed we find Jesus praying again and again. That Messiah was expected to pray, see the quotation given above from T. B. *Sukkah*.

"To see corruption."

§ 69.

Acts xiii. 35. "*He saith also in another* psalm, *Thou wilt not give thy Holy One to see corruption.*" So also ii. 27.

Psalm xvi. 10. "*For thou wilt not leave my soul to Sheol; neither wilt thou suffer thine holy one to see corruption.*"

**494**] It will be observed that the English Revised Version of the Psalm agrees with the form in which the verse is quoted both by St. Paul in Acts xiii. and by St. Peter in Acts ii. But the argument of R. Isaac of Troki is that in each case the translation is wrong, for the word rendered "corruption" (שחת) more naturally means the "pit," and to prove his case he adduces such clear passages as Ps. xciv. 13, with Prov. xxvi. 27 and Ps. vii. 15. *Shachath,* he says, is certainly "pit" there, and it is only proper to explain it as "pit" here. It is but a synonym for "Sheol," the underworld. The Apostles, then, he implies, are mistaken in their attempt to deduce from the Psalm evidence that the Messiah's body was not to suffer corruption. Besides, David was speaking not of Messiah at all, but of himself.

**495**] Now, on the whole, it is probable that our Rabbi is right in saying that *shachath* in the sixteenth Psalm does not mean "corruption," but "pit," either as designating the grave in general, or possibly as a lower place within the boundaries of Sheol.

Yet this is not certain. For, if it were, we should not find so first-rate a scholar as König, in his Hebrew Lexicon (1910), translating it here not by "Grube" (pit), but by "Verderben, Vernichtung" (destruction, annihilation), and adducing in support of his translation several passages, in particular Ps. lv. 23: "the pit of destruction" (*be'er shachath*), where the second word *shachath* can hardly be another word for "pit." The Psalmist there, it would seem, speaks of a pit

K

which ensures the destruction of those who are thrown into it. It is, therefore, not impossible, after all, that in our Psalm the early Jewish Greek translation, which we call the Septuagint, was right in rendering the word in Pss. xvi. 10; lv. 23, by *diaphthora*, the same word which we find in Acts xiii. 35 and ii. 27.

**496**] It may, however, be argued, especially by those who are unacquainted with the Jewish mind, that even this does not justify the meaning of "corruption" evidently presupposed by St. Peter and St. Paul, for the usage of *diaphthora* points to the rendering "destruction" rather than "corruption." That is quite true, and if we had to do only with Gentile thought nothing more could be said. But the Apostles were not Gentiles but Jews, and must not be judged by a Gentile standard. What Jew is there, especially what learned Jew is there, steeped in Jewish methods of exposition, who, when he is enlarging some point in his exhortation, will hesitate to deduce from a mere word, by its etymology, or its spelling, or something else either closely or remotely connected with it, a proof for his argument? For he is well aware, all the time, that, as it is adduced by a Jew and addressed to Jews, the gist of his remark will be appreciated, while force of a kind which it was never intended to possess will not be attributed to it. A Karaite like R. Isaac, or a merely Western scholar, may think such a method strange; but not a typical Jew, speaking to Jews. The Apostles do but lay stress on the derivation (as distinct from the usage) of the word *diaphthora* (which, by derivation, is essentially "corruption"), and no student of the Talmudim or Midrashim can be in the least surprised at their doing so. The Apostles were Jewish to the backbone.

**497**] But surely, it may be said, they spoke Hebrew or Aramaic, and not Greek! Possibly, though we may be pretty certain that St. Paul, when he was preaching in the synagogue at Antioch in Pisidia (Acts xiii. 35), used Greek, for that alone would be understood by the majority of his hearers. But it may be granted that St. Peter, when he addressed the multitude at Jerusalem (ii. 27), may have spoken to them in Aramaic. Even this, however, is far from certain, for, with the numbers present from foreign lands (ii. 9–11), Greek would have been the language most generally understood. But even if it be allowed that the Apostles spoke in Aramaic or Hebrew, could they not have used the same form of argument, speaking, as already stated, as Jews to Jews, and therefore employing methods to which they and their audience were accustomed? Is it quite so impossible a thought that Jews could have taken this sixteenth Psalm to refer to the corruption of the body after death? Listen to what the *Midrash Tehillim* on Ps. xvi. 9, says: "*Therefore my heart is glad:* in the words of the Law. *And my glory rejoiceth:* in King Messiah, who is about to come forth from me; for it is said (Isa. iv. 5), 'For over all the glory [shall be spread] a canopy.' *My flesh also shall dwell in safety;* after death. R. Isaac said: This teaches us that the worm and the maggot did not prevail over him." * It is evident that the compiler of the Midrash explained *shachath* not as "the pit," but as "destruction," and, if "flesh" be taken strictly, even as "corruption."

498] To sum up, then, what we have said. Whatever may be the original meaning of the Psalm, the Apostles were quite within their rights, as Jews speaking to Jews, to illustrate their doctrine of the resurrection of the Lord's body by this passage. We ourselves may not, and probably cannot, see in it a direct prophecy of that great event. Certainly we do not believe the fact because of the words of the Psalm. But the quotations confirm the thoroughly Jewish character of the New Testament, which ought, therefore, to commend itself to all Jewish readers.

* **לכן שמח לבי**, בדברי תורה. **ויגל כבודי**, במלך המשיח שעתיד לצאת ממני שנאמר כי על כל כבוד חופה: **אף בשרי ישכון לבטח**, לאחר מיתה. אמר רבי יצחק מלמד שלא שלט בו רמה ותולעה.

## The Yoke of the Law.

§ 70.

Acts xv. 10, 11. "*Now therefore why tempt ye God, that ye should put a yoke upon the neck of the disciples, which neither our fathers nor we were able to bear? But we believe that we shall be saved through the grace of the Lord Jesus, in like manner as they.*"

**499**] Our Rabbi brings forward two objections to these words of St. Peter, the first being that in Matt. xix. 18 our Lord Himself bids the young rich man keep the commandments; and the second that He then tells him to give the whole of his property to the poor, thus showing, asserts the Rabbi, that the Gospel is a heavier yoke than the Law. For whereas the Law tells us to give away one-tenth of what we get, the Gospel charges us to bestow all. Similarly, says our opponent, Jesus' command to turn the other cheek (Luke vi. 29) is harder than the demands of the Law.

We have already shown the fallacy of the Rabbi's arguments, due to a misunderstanding of the special nature of the case in Matt. xix., and of the far-reaching character of true love to God and man in Luke vi. It is, therefore, unnecessary to trouble the reader again. See parr. 349–355, 415–417.

## The Remnant of Edom.

§ 71.

Acts xv. 17. "*That the residue of men may seek after the Lord, and all the Gentiles, upon whom my name is called, saith the Lord.*"

Amos ix. 12. "*That they may possess the remnant of Edom, and all the nations, which are called by my name, saith the LORD that doeth this.*"

**500**] Yes, the verbal difference is plain. No one denies it. *Edom* is read as *'adam*, and *yīrshu* as *yidrshu*. If, however, we may consider that Amos is interested chiefly in the spiritual, not the physical, conquest of the heathen by Israel (as surely we may), then the substance of the old Jewish translation into Greek (the Septuagint) used by St. James, is much the same as the Hebrew. In any case the variation is more of antiquarian than of practical interest. R. Isaac's curious statement that the original does not say that God's name is to be called on the converted heathen, but on Israel, cannot seriously be defended. It is preposterous to translate the relative in this passage by "because."

## FORBIDDEN FOODS.

### § 72.

Acts xv. 20, 29.

**501**] R. Isaac returns once more to his charge that modern Christians do not observe the Apostolic Decree. So much has been said in reply to him on Part I. § 15 (parr. 152-159), and also on Part II. § 18 (par. 348), that it is not necessary to trouble the reader again.

### THE MOTHER OF TIMOTHY.

§ 73.

Acts xvi. 1. "*Timothy the son of a Jewess which believed; but his father was a Greek.*"

**502**] Our Rabbi argues that she was an immodest woman, seeing that she was united to an uncircumcised Greek.

What if R. Isaac is right? In that case the Law will not have saved her from sin, but she is converted to a true knowledge of God by the power of the Gospel and the teaching of the Lord Jesus Christ. There is, however, no sufficient reason for the Rabbi's charge. Timothy had known the Scriptures from his childhood, and an ungodly mother would not have taught him thus (2 Tim. iii. 15).

### THE CIRCUMCISION OF TIMOTHY.

§ 74.

Acts xvi. 3. "*Him* [Timothy] *would Paul have to go forth with him; and he took and circumcised him because of the Jews that were in those parts: for they all knew that his father was a Greek.*"

**503**] Many readers are astonished at the circumcision of Timothy when they bear in mind the stiff attitude which St. Paul took up towards circumcision. The difficulty, therefore, which R. Isaac felt is quite natural, and deserved to be brought forward. When the Apostle writes: "I Paul say unto you, that, if ye receive circumcision, Christ will profit you nothing. Yea, I testify again to every man that receiveth circumcision, that he is a debtor to do the whole law" (Gal. v. 2, 3), how can he circumcise Timothy? And, if both St. Paul and Timothy were circumcised, why did they not both keep all the commandments of the Law?

**504**] Yet although the verbal difficulty is great, it is met by the common proverb that circumstances alter cases. For when St. Paul wrote thus to the Galatians, he was inveighing against the belief of persons who thought that there was no salvation for them unless they were circumcised, or, at the least, that they could never rise to any high standard of religious life unless they were thus joined outwardly and visibly to the ancient community of Israel. To all such St. Paul says that circumcision as a means of salvation is worse than useless, yes, that it absolutely cuts off persons from Christ. Salvation by Christ and salvation by works are self-contradictory terms; one excludes the other. St. Paul did not get his young convert circumcised in the hope that it would be a help to Timothy's salvation. It was, as we are expressly told, "because of the Jews." How could Timothy enter the synagogues, in places where he was known, and perhaps take part in preaching or expounding, as his master did, when at any time it was possible for him to be turned out, on the ground that he was an uncircumcised Gentile? St. Paul himself, we must remember, was not ashamed of becoming like a Jew, that he might gain the Jews (1 Cor. ix. 20); why should his disciple do otherwise? It was, then, no question of Timothy's circumcision being a means of salvation. "God forbid," they would both have said. Nor, therefore, of their being bound to follow it up by observing the various commands of the whole Law, as Jews still endeavour to do, if they are to attain to righteousness. Circumcision in Timothy's case was purely a matter of convenience, so that he might have unimpeded intercourse with men of his own nation, and win some of them for his dear Saviour, the Lord Jesus Christ.

### THE JAILOR'S QUESTION.

§ 75.

Acts xvi. 30, 31. "*Sirs, what must I do to be saved? And they* [Paul and Silas] *said, Believe on the Lord Jesus, and thou shalt be saved, thou and thy house.*"

**505**] Our friend argues that this is contrary to the answer given by Christ to the rich man in Matt. xix. 17; Mark x. 19; Luke xviii. 19 *sq.* The error of the Rabbi's argument has been shown in parr. 290, 352–355.

### ST. PAUL CALLED A GOD BY THE IGNORANT HEATHEN.

§ 76.

Acts xxviii. 6. When St. Paul was not injured by the viper's bite, "*they changed their minds, and said that he was a god.*"

**506**] It is sufficient to refer the courteous reader to what has been said in par. 477.

### DEATH FROM ADAM TO MOSES.

§ 77.

Rom. v. 14.

**507**] This has been fully discussed in parr. 126–130.

### Lo-Ammi.

§ 78.

Rom. ix. 24–26. "*Us, whom he also called, not from the Jews only, but also from the Gentiles; as he saith also in Hosea, I will call that my people, which was not my people; and her beloved, which was not beloved. And it shall be,* that *in the place where it was said unto them, Ye are not my people, there shall they be called sons of the living God.*"

Hosea ii. 23 (25). "*And I will sow her unto me in the earth* [or, "*the land*"]*; and I will have mercy upon her that had not obtained mercy; and I will say to them which were not my people, Thou art my people; and they shall say,* Thou art *my God.*"

Hosea i. 6. "*Call her name Lo-Ruhamah: for I will no more have mercy upon the house of Israel.*"

Hosea i. 9. "*Call his name Lo-ammi: for ye are not my people, and I will not be your* God."

Hosea ii. 1 (i. 11). "*Say ye to your brethren, Ammi; and to your sisters, Ruhamah.*"

**508**] "Behold, thou seest, attentive reader, how Paul blinds the eyes of the uncircumcised, and of all the simple fools who are enticed to follow him, by these words, which would appear to teach that the Gentiles were called of old by the name Lo-ammi, and by the name Lo-ruhamah, and that afterwards they would be called by the name Ammi, and by the name Ruhamah. But he who examines the Book of Hosea i. and ii. will understand that he referred only to the people of Israel, for they, when they turned away from following the LORD, were called Lo-ammi and Lo-ruhamah, but when they return unto Him shall be called sons of the living God, and Ruhamah." Thus far R. Isaac.

**509**] How the Rabbi must have laughed in his sleeve, as he tried to throw dust in the eyes of his intelligent readers! For if they were really intelligent they would grant what he says, and yet acquit the Apostle of any attempt to deceive his followers. For, indeed, there is no doubt that the Prophet did refer only to Israel; not, however, as R. Isaac appears to have thought, to all Israel, including the Jews strictly so called, but to Israel as contrasted with Judah, to Ephraim, the Ten Tribes, who were the objects of Hosea's address.

But let that pass; it is agreed that Hosea had not Gentiles, but Israelites, in mind.

**510**] Yet R. Isaac, as a good scholar, ought to have been well aware that to quote the passage of Gentiles was a thoroughly Jewish proceeding. Karaite though he was, he knew his Talmud, and could use it when occasion offered. He ought, then, to have remembered that in T.B. *Pesachim*, *87b*, R. Eliezer [ben Hyrcanos], in proof of the proposition that in the hour of the LORD'S anger He remembereth mercy, says: "The LORD sent Israel into captivity among the nations only that proselytes might be added to them: for it is written: And I will sow her to me in the land (Hos. ii. 23, Heb. 25). And a man sows a seah only to gather many cors [one cor contains thirty seahs]. Then R. Jochanan proves the same truth from the verse: And I will have mercy on her upon whom I had not had mercy." * Rashi's comment on R. Jochanan's quotation is: "They who were not my people clave to them, and became my people." †

Thus we have Rashi in the eleventh century, and RR. Eliezer and Jochanan in the end of the first century, explaining passages in Hosea as referring to the conversion of Gentiles, and yet St. Paul is blamed for quoting the same passages in the

* ואמר ר"א לא הגלה הקב"ה את ישראל לבין האומות אלא כדי שיתוספו עליהם גרים שנ' וזרעתיה לי בארץ כלום אדם זורע סאה אלא להכניס במה כורין ור' יוחנן אמר מהכה ורחמתי את לא רוחמה.

† **ואמרתי ללא עמי עמי אתה** אולם שלא היו מעמי דבקו בהם ויהי לי לעם.

same way in the middle of the first century, only some thirty years earlier than the sages whose words are recorded in the Talmud. Why blame the Christian Jew, St. Paul, for doing what two non-Christian Jews, almost contemporary with him, did with impunity?

Once more I appeal to my learned and intelligent readers to accept the New Testament as giving a thoroughly Jewish description of the relation of the Old Testament to the New, and of the fulness of spiritual teaching and application that the Old Testament contains for those who are steeped in Jewish lore, and whose eyes are opened to appreciate the work of the Spirit of God.

### The Stone of Stumbling.

§ 79.

Rom. ix. 32, 33. "*They stumbled at the stone of stumbling; even as it is written, Behold, I lay in Zion a stone of stumbling and a rock of offence: and he that believeth on him shall not be put to shame.*"

Isa. xxviii. 16. "*Behold, I lay in Zion for a foundation a stone, a tried stone, a precious corner* stone *of sure foundation: he that believeth shall not make haste.*"

Isa. viii. 14. "*And he shall be for a sanctuary; but for a stone of stumbling and for a rock of offence to both the houses of Israel.*"

Similarly Rom. x. 11. "*For the scripture saith, Whosoever believeth on him shall not be put to shame.*"

1 Peter ii. 6. "*Because it is contained in scripture, Behold I lay in Zion a chief corner stone, elect, precious: and he that believeth on him shall not be put to shame.*"

**511**] Our friend does not state very clearly what it is to which he objects in the quotations made by St. Paul, and afterwards by St. Peter, from the Book of Isaiah. To be sure, he tells us that St. Paul has mixed up two passages, but no one who is acquainted with Jewish writings can find fault with the Apostle for that. Nothing is commoner, and St. Paul, as a Jew, was doubtless accustomed to do so from his youth.

Is, then, the blame due to the fact that the quotations are not made with that verbal exactness which modern readers desiderate? It is quite true that they are not textually accurate, and even bear traces of connexion with the ancient Jewish-Greek Version made in Alexandria. But Jews have never shown much care in meticulous precision of verbal quotation. What, then, is R. Isaac's difficulty? Presumably it is due to his discovery, and the discovery is so easy that even a child could have made it, that the Prophet was not speaking directly of the Messiah. And yet the Apostle quoted his words as descriptive of the Lord Jesus Christ!

**512**] Yet what did the Prophet mean by this Stone which was at once so precious and a stone of stumbling? A great English scholar, Dr. Hort, writing on 1 Pet. ii. 6, says: "By the stone Isaiah probably meant the Divine king or kingdom of Israel founded in David, the true strength and bond of the nation, resting securely on the promise of Jehovah and alone capable of holding together the elements of the people in opposition to the forces tending to draw them asunder." It may, however, be still more probable that Isaiah had in mind the revelation of God, culminating in His temple on Mount Zion, which, if received aright, was indeed a sanctuary, but, rejected, became a cause of stumbling and ruin. For this is always so. Every truth taught by God is a test to those to whom it comes; if they accept it they receive blessing with it; if they reject it, they suffer. Whichever interpretation of the Prophet's words be right, can any Christian, who holds that the full and perfect revelation of God was made on Mount Zion in the person of Jesus Christ, be blamed for saying that the Prophet's language describes the two-fold effect of such a revelation? What is more natural? What more justifiable? Jesus became a sanctuary to some, and to others, alas, a stone of stumbling. The Apostles did but show their insight into the true meaning of the Prophet's language, far-reaching as it is.

**513**] It may be noted that a glimpse of the purport of Isaiah's words seems to be found in T.B. *Sanhedrin*, 38*a*: "The Son of David does not come until the two Houses of Israel have perished, namely the Head of the Captivity in Babylon and the Patriarch in the land of Israel, as it is said, And He shall be for a sanctuary," etc. (Isa. viii. 14).* The passage is obscure, but it appears to mean that Messiah is to be both a sanctuary and also a cause of harm and destruction.

**514**] Similarly we find Bechai on Exod. xiv. 31 (p. 92[c]) referring Isa. xxviii. 16 to the Messiah. The whole passage is worth quoting as a typical illustration of the use of the Old Testament Scriptures by Jewish writers: "'Unless I had believed to see the goodness of the LORD': Faith (Emunah) in the coming of the Redeemer, for this is a great cornerstone in the Law. For it is written: Behold I lay in Zion, etc. (Isa. xxviii. 16), and every one who believeth has much merit. That is what is said of Abraham, who was the root of faith (Emunah), 'and He believed in the LORD, and He counted it to him for righteousness' (Gen. xv. 6). And behold he meriteth to attain to Gan Eden, for it is said, 'Open ye the gates, that the righteous nation which keepeth Emunim may enter in' (Isa. xxvi. 2). And he merited to attain to the life of the world to come, for it is said, 'but the righteous shall live by his Emunah' (Hab. ii. 4)." †

* אין בן דוד בא עד שיכלו שני בתי אבות מישראל ואלו הן ראש גולה שבבבל ונשיא שבארץ ישראל שנא׳ והיה למקדש ולאבן נגף ולצור מכשול לשני בתי ישראל.

† **לולי האמנתי לראות בטוב ה׳.** אמונה בביאת הגואל שזה פנה גדולה בתורה זהו שאמר הנני יסד בציון אבן גו׳ וכל המאמין יש לו זכיות הרבה הוא שנאמר באברהם שהיה שרש האמונה והאמין בה׳ ויחשבה לו צדקה. והנה הוא זוכה לגן עדן שנ׳ פתחו שערים ויבא גוי צדיק שומר אמונים וזכה לחיי העולם הבא שנאמר וצדיק באמונתו יחיה.

### Neither up to Heaven nor down to the Abyss.

§ 80.

Rom. x. 6–9. "*But the righteousness which is of faith saith thus, Say not in thy heart, Who shall ascend into heaven?* (*that is, to bring Christ down*) *or, Who shall descend into the abyss?* (*that is, to bring Christ up from the dead*). *But what saith it? The word is nigh thee, in thy mouth, and in thy heart: that is, the word of faith, which we preach: because if thou shalt confess with thy mouth Jesus* as *Lord, and shalt believe in thy heart that God raised him from the dead, thou shalt be saved.*"

Deut. xxx. 11–14. "*For this commandment which I command thee this day, it is not too hard for thee, neither is it far off. It is not in heaven, that thou shouldst say, Who shall go up for us to heaven, and bring it unto us, and make us to hear it, that we may do it? Neither is it beyond the sea, that thou shouldest say, Who shall go over the sea for us, and bring it unto us, and make us to hear it, that we may do it? But the word is very nigh unto thee, in thy mouth, and in thy heart, that thou mayest do it.*"

**515**] The courteous reader will not fail to make the observation that the Apostle does not even introduce the words as a direct quotation from Scripture, although it is very evident that he makes use of a Scriptural passage. But after saying, "Moses writeth" (*v.* 5), he adds in contrast: "But the righteousness which is of faith saith thus." He means that the Christian heart which has experienced the righteousness which Christ gives says to one who is hesitating to accept the Lord Jesus as his Saviour: Raise no difficulty, for there is none. It is not a matter of going up to heaven, as though there were any need to bring Messiah down—He is come, without any activity or effort on your part! Neither is it a matter of going down into the abyss, the place of departed spirits, as though Christ were still there, weak and helpless. Nay, He has risen! And this without your aid or exertion. What is required from you is different altogether. The positive teaching of the Christian is: Salvation is close at hand for you to accept. It is a matter only of mouth and heart. And this is the Gospel which we preach. For if you confess with your mouth that Jesus is Lord (acknowledging Him as your supreme Lord and Master), and believe in your heart—I do not say that He came to earth, or even that He died, but—that He was raised triumphant over sin and death, then thou shalt be saved.

St. Paul's argument, every reader will notice, is a beautiful application of certain words and phrases found in Deuteronomy. The Apostle does not profess to quote them literally, and much less to claim that he is representing the original meaning intended by Moses.

**516**] Yet our friend R. Isaac of Troki objects to his use of them, an objection which is amazing on the part of so learned a man! For he must surely have forgotten that such an application of passages in the Bible to themes other than their primary intent is one of the most ordinary and common methods employed among Jews of all ages to illustrate their sermons and give point to their exhortations.

Did he not remember that this very passage of Deuteronomy is quoted with a far from literal interpretation of its original meaning in T.B. *Erubin*, 55*a* (compare also the *Yalqut in loco*)? "Rabba said, 'It is not in heaven': that is, It [the Law] will not be found with him who exalts his mind upon it [*or*, within himself] like the heavens, and it will not be found with him who extends his knowledge upon it [*or*, within himself] like the sea. R. Jochanan used to say: 'Not in heaven' means: It will not be found with the conceited. And 'it is not beyond the sea' means: It will not be found with pedlars or travelling merchants." * So, somewhat similarly, a

* רבא אמר **לא בשמים היא** לא תמצא במי שמגביה דעתו עליה (עליו) כשמים, ולא תמצא במי שמרחיב דעתו עליה (עליו) כים. ר׳ יוחנן אומר **לא בשמים** לא תמצא בגסי רוח, **ולא מעבר לים היא** לא תמצא לא בסחרנים ולא בתגרים.

writer also quoted in the *Yalqut* tells us that the passage means that "The Torah is not to be found with astrologers, whose faith is in the heavens." * Perhaps I may be allowed to add one further example showing how far the Jewish mind is able to go in its usage of Scripture phrases. In the *Baal hatturim* (by Jacob ben Asher; died 1340) on the passage it is pointed out that the initial letters of the Hebrew words for "Who shall go up for us to heaven" form that all-important word, "Circumcision," and the final letters the word for LORD, showing that none shall ascend near the LORD except he be circumcised.† Yet R. Isaac implies that St. Paul, here and elsewhere, shows ignorance of Scripture, because he does not quote it in its primary meaning!

**517**] R. Isaac's own interpretation of the passage in Deuteronomy is that the commandment there mentioned is that of repentance, which had been urged in the previous verse. In this he follows Seforno and Nachmanides. He says that Moses intends to show us the greatness of the command to repent, together with the easiness of fulfilling it; saying that while things esteemed precious are usually very hard to attain, repentance is not, for it is very near thee, in thy mouth and in thy heart, to do it. Thus repentance depends on confession of mouth and sorrow of heart, as the intelligent know.

**518**] The Rabbi's explanation is not impossible, but the more probable reference of the sacred writer is to obedience to the Lord generally, as made known to us in His Law. "The commandment meant," says Driver in his well-known commentary on the passage, "as Deut. xi. 22, xix. 9 show, is devotion to Jehovah, with the obligations which it involves, especially obedience to the moral and religious demands made by Him of His worshippers: It is not too difficult for thee, neither is it far off. It is nothing abstruse or incomprehensible, like the complicated structure of the human frame

* שמואל אמר אין התורה מצויה באיסטרולוגין שאומנותן בשמים.

† **מי יעלה לנו השמימה**, ר"ת מילה וס"ת הוי"ה לומר שאינו יכול לעלות אצל ה' אם לא שיהא נימול, וכן התהלך לפני והיה תמים שנאמר על המילה. (!!)

(Ps. cxxxix. 6; cf. cxxxi. 1; Prov. xxx. 18); it is nothing recondite, which can be reached only by laborious and protracted study."

**519**] It is probable that Driver's interpretation is right. But if R. Isaac's were, there is one point which he has overlooked. For it does not seem unfair to remind him (as others have already done, *e.g.* Lichtenstein in his *Chizzuk Emunath Emeth*) that repentance towards God is joined by Hosea (iii. 5) with repentance towards David their king. In other words, repentance towards God implies for its fulness sorrow at the rejection of God's manifested will, and acceptance of this when it is perceived. For just as to Hosea the repentance of the Ten Tribes involved also their acceptance of David and his line, so the repentance of Israel to-day will include the acceptance of the rejected Messiah, Jesus Christ the Son of David.

## The Deliverer out of Zion.

### § 81.

Rom. xi. 26. "*And so all Israel shall be saved: even as it is written, There shall come out of Zion the Deliverer; He shall turn away ungodliness from Jacob.*"

Isaiah lix. 20. "*And a redeemer shall come to Zion, and unto them that turn from transgression in Jacob.*"

**520**] R. Isaac blames the Apostle for completely misquoting the words of the Prophet. He implies that the quotation is not only verbally wrong, but that it does not give the right sense at all.

To be quite frank, St. Paul's words are difficult, and the whole of the explanation of them is yet to be discovered. But I hope that after our previous investigation of several of St.

Paul's quotations during the course of these studies, my readers will join with me in believing that either wilful corruption or crass ignorance on the part of the disciple of Gamaliel is incredible.

There are two or three points to be borne in mind. First, St. Paul's words very nearly correspond to the Septuagint Version, that is, to the old Jewish rendering which he found in almost universal use in his time, especially among such non-Palestinian Jews as formed part of the recipients of this Epistle to the believers in Rome. This will not quite clear up the difference between St. Paul's words and those of the Hebrew, for the Septuagint has "on account of Zion" and not "out of Zion," but the phrases are much more alike in the Greek than they are in the English, and it is not impossible that St. Paul's form may be the more original of the two. In any case the difference between these two terms is of no great importance.

**521**] Secondly, the accuracy of the Hebrew text is not above suspicion. For many critics think that where the Massoretic text has "unto them that turn from transgression in Jacob," the older and better text is preserved in the Septuagint, "He shall turn away ungodliness from Jacob." * For, after all, no one in these days thinks that the text preferred and stereotyped by the Massoretes in the eighth to the tenth centuries of our era is to be regarded as immaculate. That this is not the case has been proved over and over again. It is, therefore, not too much to ask our readers at least to suspend judgment before condemning St. Paul, until scholars are agreed what were the actual words which the Prophet wrote. Further, let us not forget that if the Apostle errs in finding a verb at this place, he has the support of the Targum for his error. For this runs: "to bring back the rebelliousnesses of the House of Jacob to the Law." † But in fact, the Hebrew and the Septuagint, St. Paul and the Targum, agree in the general sense of the passage, which is that the coming of the Messiah, His final and full coming, shall be contemporary

* See Canon G. H. Box, *The Book of Isaiah*, 1908.

† לאתבא מרודיא דבית יעקב לאוריתא.

with the removal of sin in Jacob. In this hope and blessed expectation, Christians and Jews are one.

### SATAN UNDER OUR FEET.

§ 82.

**522**] Rom. xvi. 20, with 1 Thess. ii. 18. See the discussion of this in Part I. § 12, par. 131 *sq.*

### THE INCESTUOUS MAN AT CORINTH.

§ 83.

1 Cor. v. 1. "*It is actually reported that there is fornication among you, and such fornication as is not even among the Gentiles, that one* of you *hath his father's wife.*"

**523**] Whence was it, asks R. Isaac, that the Apostle derived his knowledge that such an action was a grievous sin, save from the Law of Moses? He condemned the man therefore out of the Law, although he has said elsewhere that Christians are free from the Law. It is plain, then, our Rabbi proceeds to argue, that Christians are, after all, not free from the commandments which are written in the Law. Jesus, therefore, did not redeem them from the curses of the Law, as the Apostle supposed when he was writing Gal. iii. 13.

**524**] It is passing strange that so learned a man as R. Isaac can make such an assumption and frame such an argument, which would almost demand the pardon of my readers for its introduction, were we not engaged in studying the objections raised in the *Chizzuk Emunah* against Christianity in the order in which they are presented.

For why should the Law of Moses have been the only source whence St. Paul derived his knowledge that such an act was wrong? On the contrary, it is plain, from the fact that he says the Gentiles did not commit it, that he presupposes such knowledge in the world generally, quite apart from any revelation contained in the Law of Moses. He recognizes the existence of the moral law among the Gentiles. The Rabbi's assumption, then, is demonstrably false. St. Paul may well have condemned the man out of the moral law accepted by Jew and Gentile alike, and seems, in fact, to have done so.

**525**] Further, where does St. Paul say, or imply, that Christians need not observe the moral law, whether it is contained in the Law of Moses or not? * So far is he from doing this, that, if any one will but take the trouble to read the New Testament for himself, he will see that the Apostle urges his readers again and again to avoid sin in every form, and to strive after the utmost possible purity and holiness in every relation of life. Oh, for a little common sense in our controversy one with another! A little of it would have saved our opponent from supposing for a moment that Christians are taught that they are free from the commandments of the Law in any such sense as that they are not obliged to keep all that tend to holiness and purity. Such a supposition mistakes altogether the meaning of Christianity, whether taught by St. Paul or by any other writer in the New Testament.

Similarly the Rabbi's use of Gal. iii. 13 is equally mistaken, but it will be better to defer our consideration of that passage until we deal with it fully in its proper place, parr. 537–544.

Meantime, I may perhaps be allowed to refer to what I have said on the Permanence of the Law, in parr. 173–179, and on Christians and Good Works, in parr. 290 *sq.*, 355, 551.

* Even so learned, and so modern, a Jew as Dr. K. Kohler can allow himself to say: "Paul's opposition to the law includes the moral law, and even the Decalogue" (*Jewish Theology, systematically and historically considered*, 1918, p. 437), but Dr. Kohler's book, admirable though it is for Judaism, shows abysmal ignorance of Christianity.

## Christians are to judge Angels.

§ 84.

1 Cor. vi. 3. "*Know ye not that we shall judge angels?*"

**526**] The absurdity of this is plain, says R. Isaac, for, in the first place, the very greatest of the Prophets had fear of the angels, and, in the next, how could Paul judge between them, seeing that they are not material so that they can sin and come into judgment?

As for the greatest of the Prophets being afraid of them, why should he not be, so long as he was in mortal flesh? But will he be hereafter, when he himself is clad in the glory of the resurrection robe? There is no reason to suppose so.

**527**] With regard to the second objection, here indeed is absurdity! For the Rabbi has forgotten, as he would readily enough confess, that the angels did in fact sin. For what else are Satan, and Samael, and a host of others, but fallen angels, who not only have sinned themselves, but even tempt human beings to sin? And shall not man be able to judge such? For no one, so far as I am aware, supposes that men will be the final and supreme judges of such evil doers, but they can and will be assessors of the Divine tribunal, confirming the verdict of the omnipotent and all-righteous God, by their assent to the justice of His decree.

**528**] Besides, our Rabbi has surely overlooked the statements of Jewish scholars that hereafter the righteous among men are to be superior even to the angels who have never sinned. R. Jochanan says in T.B. *Sanhedrin*, 93*a*; "The righteous rank above the angels of service." * See also *Midrash Tehillim* on Ps. ciii. 20. R. Isaac ought to be more careful in his statements.

* אמר ר׳ יוחנן גדולים הצדיקים יותר ממלאכי השרת.

Cf. also *The Ascension of Isaiah*, ix. 38, 39 (in this part a Jewish-Christian's writings perhaps of the first century A.D.): "It is given to thee to see God, and *on thy account* power is given to the angel who is with thee."

## PERSUADING JEWS TO BECOME CHRISTIANS.

§ 85.

1 Cor. vii. 18–20. "*Was any man called being uncircumcised? let him not become uncircumcised. Hath any been called in uncircumcision? let him not be circumcised. Circumcision is nothing, and uncircumcision is nothing; but the keeping of the commandments of God. Let each man abide in that calling wherein he was called.*"

Gal. v. 3. "*Yea, I testify again to every man that receiveth circumcision, that he is a debtor to do the whole law.*"

**529**] It is asserted that these verses form a reproof to Christians because they endeavour to win the Jews to accept Christianity.

The fact, however, is very different, as I am sure the intelligent readers of these pages will readily perceive. For St. Paul had in his mind quite other circumstances than those imagined by the Rabbi. In his Epistle to the Corinthians he is not thinking of Jews at all, but of Jews who had already become Christians. There were two parties in the Church of Corinth, Jewish Christians and Gentile Christians, and these were continually endeavouring to persuade each other that their own condition was the better. The Apostle would make peace, and he therefore reminds them both that the all-important thing was faith on the Lord Jesus, with the earnest life that ought to characterize it. If this existed, nothing else mattered very much. In the Epistle to the Galatians, on the other hand, St. Paul is dealing with a more serious case. Certain Christians of Jewish birth were going round the Churches, persuading believers of Gentile origin that it was necessary for them to be circumcised. He therefore warns his readers most solemnly against any such doctrine. Gentile believers had already found full liberty in Christ, and to yield to these persuasions would involve much more than the bare act of circumcision, even bondage under the whole Law of Moses. For a believer in Christ to be circumcised would imply that he had made up his mind to be saved by the works of the Law, instead of by Christ, that he had in fact fallen away from Christ altogether.

530] We may add that if St. Paul had meant what the Rabbi thinks he meant, opposition to the opinion that Jews ought to be won over to the faith of Christ, he would have contradicted his own efforts to win them, and even the experience of his own conversion. No one had been a stricter and more orthodox Jew than St. Paul, and yet he had given up much, that he might accept the Lord Jesus as his Saviour. Would it have been natural that one who felt that he owed everything in life, all that made existence here worth living, to the Lord Jesus, should have urged his readers not to endeavour to lead other Jews to the same blessing which he had found so precious to his own soul? Of course St. Paul would have been strongly opposed to the use of any unfair influence, much more any downright compulsion, in order to get Jews to be baptized. But with this every right-minded Christian agrees. We believe in religious liberty, more sincerely perhaps than do Jews. For indeed we fear, that in places where they have much power, as in Palestine, New York, and even in the East of London, they employ no little pressure and unfair compulsion to prevent members of their race from listening to the words of the Gospel. We Christians acknowledge with shame that Jews have suffered much from persecution in the past. But we cannot help seeing signs that they themselves are beginning to persecute Christians (only Jewish Christians, so far) in the present. We sometimes wonder whether Jews, notwithstanding the terrible lessons they have received, have even yet learned the elements of toleration in the modern and Christian sense. It is easy for the few and the down-trodden to be tolerant; the test comes when they are many and strong. Then is seen the presence, or the absence, of humble and sincere faith in the God of righteousness and love.

## Accuracy in Numbers.

### § 86.

1 Cor. x. 8. "*Neither let us commit fornication, as some of them committed, and fell in one day three and twenty thousand.*"

Num. xxv. 29. "*And those that died by the plague were twenty and four thousand.*"

**531**] The discrepancy is plain; the Pentateuch says twenty-four, St. Paul twenty-three. Of course explanations have been given. One is that only twenty-three thousand died of the plague, and the rest were slain judicially by Moses (see Num. xxv. 4). But we are expressly told in *v.* 9 that twenty-four thousand "died by the plague." Another way of getting out of the difficulty is to lay stress on the phrase, "in one day," and thus to suggest that although twenty-three thousand died on one day, the rest died on the preceding or following days. But it is useless to deceive ourselves with quibbles such as these. The number as it stands is an error, and we possess no means of explaining it. Yet suppose St. Paul did make a mistake in a number, of what possible importance is it? No one to-day imagines that any single writer of either the Old or the New Testament was necessarily preserved from mistakes in trivial matters. We Christians, at any rate, are quite willing to grant that the Apostle may have made an error. Yet, after conceding this, we may not forget another possibility. For knowing what we do know of the Apostle's methods in referring to Scripture we may reasonably suspect that there was a Jewish tradition bearing on the point, and existing in his time, which has not come down to us. On the whole this is the most probable solution of the difficulty, but the whole question is of infinitesimal importance.

## Victory over Death.

§ 87.

1 Cor. xv. 54, 55. "*Then shall come to pass the saying that is written, Death is swallowed up in victory. O death, where is thy victory? O death, where is thy sting?*"

Isaiah xxv. 8. "*He hath swallowed up death for ever.*"

Hosea xiii. 14. "*O death, where are thy plagues? O grave, where is thy destruction?*"

**532**] Our Rabbi says that St. Paul alters the words of the prophecy, in order to bring biblical assistance to his false faith, for the saying he quotes comes nowhere in the Prophets; and there are only the two passages in Isaiah and Hosea, given above.

The precise nature of R. Isaac's objection is not very clearly stated, but apparently he does not find fault with St. Paul for quoting two separate passages as one (for then he would be obliged to blame most Jewish writers for doing the same thing) but for quoting inaccurately, either in language or in sense or in both. We must, then, consider each quotation separately.

**533**] In Isa. xxv. 8, we find: "He hath swallowed up death for ever" (בלע המות לנצח), which St. Paul quotes in the form: "Death is swallowed up in victory," the only difference of any importance being the words "in victory." Scholars to-day would not so translate the original, for the meaning thus assigned to נצח is post-biblical, but the Apostle cannot be seriously blamed for his translation when it is also that of Aquila, the typical Jewish translator. If R. Aqiba's pupil could render the phrase "in victory," we can hardly blame Gamaliel's for doing so as well. There is not, we may notice, any further question in this passage of the accuracy of the general sense presupposed by the Apostle, viz. that the final work of the Messiah is to destroy death and its power. This in fact is accepted in the Midrashim as a self-evident truth. See *Shmoth R.*, § 30, on Exod. xxi. 1, speaking of Pharez: "For the Messiah will come from him, and in His days the LORD will cause death to be swallowed up, as it is written: He hath swallowed up death for ever"

(שהמשיח עומד הימנו ובימיו הקב"ה מבליע המות שנאמר בלע המות לנצח).

Thus, as the language of St. Paul's quotation is sufficiently near to the original, and the general sense in which the passage is quoted is not impugned, his use of the passage may be considered justified.

**534**] The case of his employment of Hosea xiii. 14 is more complicated. In the first place, the meaning of the words in the original is far from certain. The word translated "where" is found only three times, once in the tenth, and twice in the fourteenth verse of this chapter. Many scholars, especially those of earlier days, render it by "I will be," but the majority to-day agree with those mentioned by Aben Ezra, who took it to mean "where"

(אהי. י"ש אומרים כי אהי כמו איה).

So, again, the word translated by St. Paul as "thy victory" means in the original either "thy words," *i.e.* thy cause in the law-court, or even thy words of triumph at success, or, and more probably, "thy plagues." The literal rendering, therefore, of the passage may well be, "Where are thy plagues, O death? Where is thy sting [*or*, thy pestilence], O grave?" If so, the form employed by St. Paul is indeed a paraphrase, but is not inaccurate.

**535**] But what of the sense? Is the Apostle right in using it as he does? This is more doubtful. Recall the context in Hosea: "Shall I ransom them [for the sentence is to be taken as a question] from the power of the grave? Shall I redeem them from death? Where are thy plagues, O death? Where is thy pestilence, O grave? Repentance shall be hid from mine eyes." The Lord is warning His people! He is summoning death and the grave to put forth all their powers, for He will not repent of His judgment upon those who have grievously sinned against Him. Yet the Apostle quotes this sentence as describing Messiah's supreme victory over death and the grave! But as a good Jew, accustomed to Talmudic methods, why should he not? The language fitted his thought, and the verse may well have been used in Jewish hymns long before his time to illustrate the same idea. Besides, in any case, the thought of Hosea presupposes that the LORD is the supreme master of death, and bids death and the grave act as His servants to perform His work. Thus the language of Hosea is glorious, setting, as it does, even death itself under the feet of the living God. St. Paul, intentionally or unintentionally, helps us to realize this by his method of quotation. Death shall not have the final victory, but it and Sheol shall be altogether overcome.

### JAMES THE LORD'S BROTHER.

§ 88.

Gal. i. 19. "*But other of the apostles saw I none, save James the Lord's brother.*"

**536**] The statement that James believed on the Lord Jesus is thought to be contrary to John vii. 5.

What of it? If St. Paul was referring to the same time in the life of St. James as that to which the Evangelists alluded, there would be reason in the Rabbi's objection. But he is speaking of a much later period, when St. James had long since accepted the Lord Jesus whole-heartedly, and had become one of the leading Christians in Jerusalem. What is there so extraordinary in this? The history of St. Paul himself ought to prevent any surprise at so great a change. On the fact of the early incredulity of St. James, see parr. 385-390, 401, 432.

## THE MESSIAH ACCURSED!

§ 89.

Gal. iii. 13. "*Christ redeemed us from the curse of the law, having become a curse for us: for it is written, Cursed is every one that hangeth on a tree.*"

**537**] No one can be surprised that this verse comes as a shock to every Jewish reader, for it causes every Christian the more pain and grief the more he understands it. The writer of the *Chizzuk Emunah* has much to say, and that not of a favourable kind.

**538**] In the first place, he argues that it is impossible for people to be redeemed from the curses (*sic*) of the Law, except by keeping its commands. Jesus, on the other hand, abolished these (so at least His followers assert), and therefore He has done nothing to redeem men from it. But the learned Rabbi here fails to grasp the sense of the word "redeem," although it is not uncommon in the Law itself. Surely he has forgotten that it is used in Exod. xiii. 13, and elsewhere, of the redemption of an eldest son by a sum of money. Death was the boy's portion; what part did he himself take in fulfilling the commandments of the Law? Another paid the redemption money for him, and by that ransom he was delivered. So is it with Christ! He has redeemed us from the curse of death brought upon us by the Law.

**539**] Even if so, would the Rabbi add, that does not set men free from obeying the Law. But who said it did? The Hebrew boy was not redeemed that he might grow up careless of the divine commands and neglectful of God. Far from it. His redemption was but the beginning of a life devoted to the LORD. So with the true believer. Not in spite of his redemption, but because of it, he desires to carry out the will of God, and to perform the commandments of the Law in their truest and highest sense. He is delivered from its curse that he may keep it the more (see parr. 160–165).

**540**] Secondly, the Rabbi would persuade us that the claims of the Law lie only upon the children of Israel, and not on the Gentiles. These, he says, are free from its curses, apart from any redemption, even as they have no share in its blessings. In fact, no argument is more common than this on the lips of Jews when they are disputing with Christians. And it is to be feared that none is less true.

For, after all, every educated person in these days is acquainted with the fact that the Law as it stands is drawn largely from Gentile sources, and therefore that much of it was binding on Gentiles before it had a claim on Jews. It was not given to Moses on Sinai as something brand new, brought straight down from the heavenly world without any previous contact with earth. Whatever might have been thought in the Middle Ages, no Jew, I am persuaded, believes this to-day. The Law, as we possess it, has incorporated much of what was known to Gentiles centuries before the time of Moses, as is apparent from the study of the Code of Khammurabi (Amraphel), the contemporary of Abraham. The special glory of the Law of Moses is not its absolute originality, but rather its masterly selection of the better portions of Gentile laws, and its enforcement of duties set in their highest form, and founded on the most solid basis. Thus, because there is so much in the Law which is common ground to Gentiles and Jews, the former may be condemned by it as much as the latter.

**541**] It may, however, be said that the Gentiles never acknowledged the Law, and therefore cannot be said to be bound by it, so as to incur its blame or forfeit its blessings. What! Is there no truth at all in the famous Haggada that the Law was offered to all the nations in turn before the Jews, but that they one and all refused it? I, at least, have too much respect for the earnest exponents of Judaism to believe that they told idle tales as mere catch-pieces for their serious exhortations. Occasionally, no doubt, they may have done so, but in general there was a deep truth underlying their paradoxes and Oriental hyperboles. I should be untrue to all my teachers if I had not learned at least this much from them. What, then, is the verity underlying the form of this Haggada? Is it not this, that all the Gentile nations refused the Law, not indeed formally, as the tale portrays them to us, but in heart and deed? The great principles of the Law were known to them of old, long, long before the Exodus, and they would not follow them, but refused to the supreme God the homage of their hearts.

**542**] But does a man escape a moral duty, as the Rabbi then would appear to suppose, by refusing to undertake it, or even by unwillingness to listen to the statement of what it is? The reply is obvious. By so doing he becomes doubly guilty. If so, then Gentiles, as well as Jews, stand condemned if they do not keep the Law; and Gentiles, as well as Jews, need redemption from its curse.

**543**] Thirdly, complaint is made that the Apostle does not quote the passage from Deut. xxi. 23 accurately, but has left out the words "of God": "He that is hanged is accursed of God." We have, however, so often seen the worthlessness of such complaints about inaccuracy of quotation, that it hardly seems to be worth while to spend more time in considering them. Yet it is possible that in this case the Rabbi meant to imply that he preferred another mode of explaining the text. For some Jewish scholars, as, for example, Rashi, think that Moses' words should be translated: "He that is hanged is an insult to God." Cf. Mishna *Sanhedrin*, vi. 4 end. But Nachmanides shows that, however interesting this may be as a Drash, the simple meaning is that he that is hanged is accursed by God. If so, St. Paul loses nothing of the sense by omitting the word "God"; for who can curse with any effect, but He?

**544**] Fourthly, by a sorry jest, quite unworthy of the solemnity of the occasion, R. Isaac shows that he misunderstands the subject. For the Apostle, in using so strong an expression about the Messiah, desires to point out to us the awfulness of the experience through which He passed. Now, for the first and last time in the whole of His existence, the Messiah knew the full meaning and force of sin. Sin was, in a sense, upon Him. He sacrificed Himself to the very uttermost, even to the extent of bearing sin. It rested, in some awful and inexplicable way, on Him who was in Himself sinless, that by thus accepting the burden of sin He might release us from it. He was the victim on whom the sins of the world were laid, and by whose sacrifice righteousness was satisfied. If so, then surely upon that holy sacrifice, as upon the scapegoat in olden time, the curse of God rested, though but for a moment. Almost at once the separation from Him who is "of purer eyes than to behold evil" passed away, and He was able to commit Himself to His Father's keeping in perfect peace (Luke xxiii. 46). See further the remarks on Matt. xxvii. 46, in parr. 376–378.

### ABRAHAM'S SEED.

§ 90.

Gal. iii. 16. "*Now to Abraham were the promises spoken, and to his seed. He saith not, And to seeds, as of many; but as of one, And to thy seed, which is Christ.*"

**545**] R. Isaac here repeats the arguments that he had used in Part I. § 13, and ordinarily it would have been sufficient to refer the reader to what has been said in answer to him there, viz. in parr. 137–143. But Prof. Driver was good enough to call my attention to an article written by him upon this passage in the *Expositor* for January, 1889, in which he adopted an explanation proposed by Abr. Geiger, and afterwards accepted by Delitzsch. It is to the effect that we find in the Mishna and the Targum of Onkelos derivatives of the root זרע, which must be translated "seeds," and mean successive generations of men. So in the Mishna *Sanhedrin*, iv. 5 (11), "In the case of a murderer his own blood, and the blood of his seeds (זַרְעִיּוֹתָיו), are assigned to him to the end of the world. For so we find in the case of Cain, . . . 'The bloods of thy brother cry unto me from the ground.' The text does not say 'blood,' but 'bloods'; *i.e.* Abel's own blood, and the blood of his seeds (זַרְעִיּוֹתָיו)." Similarly in the Targum of Onkelos on Gen. iv. 10, "The blood of the seeds (זַרְעִין), which were destined to spring from thy brother." *

Hence it is probable that to St. Paul the use of the plural of substantives formed from the root זרע, in the sense of successive generations of men, seemed to be nothing extraordinary, and, regardless of the usage of the Hebrew Bible, he therefore calls attention to the fact that the actual wording of the passage in Gen. xxii. 18 excluded, strictly speaking, the performance of the promise in successive generations of Israelites, and required its fulfilment in one generation, which was summed up in Christ.

This explanation is so interesting, as coming ultimately from so famous a Jewish writer as Abr. Geiger, and recommended by two such distinguished Gentile scholars as Driver and Delitzsch, that it is certain all the readers of this work will like to have it before them. Personally, however, I still prefer the explanation that was given in parr. 137–143.

## Gifts among Men.

### § 91.

Eph. iv. 8. "*Wherefore he saith, When he ascended on high, he led captivity captive, and gave gifts unto men.*"

Psalm lxviii. 18 (19). "*Thou hast ascended on high, thou has led* thy *captivity captive; thou hast received gifts among men.*"

**546**] Here again, says R. Isaac, Paul wrote the very contrary of what the Psalmist said, King David of blessed memory, in order to adduce some support for his faith. For

* See also Jastrow's *Talmudic Dictionary*, *s.v.* זַרְעִית, זַרְעִיתָא, זַרְעִי.

the Psalmist did not write: "Thou hast given gifts to men," but "Thou hast received gifts among men."

Alas! why would R. Isaac insist on writing as if he were an ignorant Gentile, instead of bringing forth his treasures of Jewish lore like the trained scholar that he was? For it is hardly credible that any one acquainted with Jewish literature should find fault with the Apostle for his Midrashic use of this Psalm. Such a use of this very verse was a commonplace among Jewish writers from early times, and every Jewish controversialist ought to say so frankly. The Targum will make this plain: "Thou, namely Moses the Prophet, didst go up to the firmament; Thou didst lead captivity captive, *i.e.* thou didst teach the things of the Law; Thou didst give them gifts, even to the sons of men."

סלקתא לרקיע (משה נביא) שביתא שביתא (אלפתא פתגמי אוריתי) יהבתא להון מתנן לבני נשא.

Rashi is equally clear in expounding the passage of Moses: "*Thou hast gone up.* The leader of his people, Moses the son of Amram, came on high. *Thou hast led captivity captive*, *i.e.* the Law. *And thou didst receive gifts*, *i.e.* from those above, even to give them to the sons of man."

**עלית.** אתה נגיד עמו משה בן עמרם למרום. **שבית שבי** את התורה. **ולקחת מתנות** מן העליונים ולתתם לבני אדם.

The Babylonian Talmud, too, refers to the verse in much the same manner. See *Sabbath*, 88*b*, 89*a*. Moses goes up to heaven to receive the Law, but the angels object, that, after God has hidden it for nine hundred and seventy-four generations before the creation of the world, He should now seek to give it to flesh and blood. Eventually there is said to Moses, "Thou hast gone up on high, thou hast led captivity captive, thou hast received gifts *b'adam*, *i.e.* as a reward because they called thee Adam."

**עלית למרום שבית שבי לקחת מתנות באדם** בשכר שקראוך אדם.

The Apostle's exposition is grave compared with this!

The *Metzudoth David*, on the other hand, interprets it of Israel. "*Thou hast gone up on high.* And with all this, thou Israel hast gone up on high! He means, thy hand is raised on high to prevail against them, to receive the Law. And *thou didst bring* it *captive* out of the hand of the angels, and *thou didst receive* it for gifts, that it should be found among the sons of man, and not among the angels above."

**עלית למרום.** ועכ"ז אתה ישראל עלית למרום ר"ל רמה ידך להתגבר עליהם לקבל את התורה **ושבית** אותה מיד המלאכים **ולקחת** אותה למתנה להיות מצויה בבני אדם ולא בין מלאכי מעלה.

**547**] It is true, no doubt, that none of these passages is earlier than St. Paul, but they show the way in which the verse was used by Jews, and it is hard to understand why non-Christian Jews may quote it so, and Christian Jews may not. But it may be replied that the Targum, the Talmud, Rashi, and the late *Metzudoth David* never intended to give a literal explanation, but only to afford their readers some homiletical pleasure and spiritual delight. Quite so. Did St. Paul intend to do otherwise? There is not a shadow of reason to suppose so. He, a Jew, quotes like a Jew, loving to find spiritual applications. Treat him fairly as you would any other Jew; he asks no more.

But Jews apply it to Moses or Israel, he to Jesus! Why not? His application is at least as legitimate as theirs. And it was but natural that, as a Christian Jew, he should quote the verse to illustrate the heavenward journey, and the life-giving influence, of Him, who, as Christians hold, has returned to the glory of His Father, in the heights above. Non-Christian Jews applied the verse to the giving of the Law; a Christian Jew to the giving of the Spirit. Why should he not?

## You and God.

### § 92.

1 Thess. ii. 10. "*Ye are witnesses, and God also.*"

**548**] "See how Paul stumbles in his language, and how confused his thoughts are, in a simple matter in which the majority of ordinary Christians would beware of stumbling! For he puts the creatures in front of the Creator! He ought to have said: God is witness, and also ye! . . . Paul's pride is brought down, and his shame exposed in the eyes of all, great and small alike!"

It is sufficient to reply that the Apostle was writing a letter, not a carefully prepared theological treatise, and that having written: "Ye are witnesses," he adds as a kind of afterthought: "Yes, and God is also." In fact, it is the very greatness of God that makes St. Paul mention Him as a climax to his previous assertion. Ye, after all, are nothing, God is supreme! Is this to belittle God? Besides, let the Rabbi blame Isaiah, who in lix. 2 writes: "Your iniquities have separated between you and your God." The charge is absurd.

## St. James and St. Paul.

### § 93.

James ii. 24. "*Ye see that by works a man is justified, and not only by faith.*"

Gal. ii. 16. "*Knowing that a man is not justified by the works of the law, save through faith in Jesus Christ.*"

Rom. iii. 20. "*By the works of the law shall no flesh be justified in his sight.*"

**549**] The Apostles do not agree, cries our Rabbi. St. James requires works, like Deut. vi. 25; St. Paul does not.

Far be it from me to deny that the verbal disagreement between the two Apostles has caused great searching of heart among Christians, but personally I cannot help thinking that the answer to the difficulty lies in the fact that they were addressing different kinds of people.

**550**] Is it not possible that two non-Christian Jewish teachers might differ as much verbally? One might insist, when speaking to those Jews, not so very few after all, who are inclined to think that because they have been circumcised all will necessarily be well with them at the last: Beware, be not so forgetful of your duties; you must, if you are to enter the courts of heaven, do your best to keep God's commandments. Yet if he were addressing people who said that it was quite unimportant what faith they followed if only their lives were straight, he might say: Nay, faith in the true God you must have, if you are to share the privileges that He gives to His servants.

So it may well have been that St. James was writing to persons who thought a bare acceptance of the Messiahship of Jesus was enough, and he says: Nay, it is not; you must show your faith by your works. On the other hand, St. Paul, as we know, was inveighing against those who would persuade Gentile believers that they must accept and practise the requirements of the Jewish Law, and he tells them plainly that a real and living faith on Christ and His redeeming work was all that was required.

**551**] That St. Paul could, and did, insist on the need of works by every professing Christian has been touched upon in parr. 179, 290, *sq.* To the references there given may be added Acts xxvi. 20: "That they should repent and turn to God, doing works worthy of repentance"; and Titus iii. 8: "These things I will that thou affirm confidently, to the end that they which have believed God may be careful to maintain good works." Further, in Gal. v. 6, St. Paul combines the two truths taught by himself and St. James, when he speaks of "faith working through love."

As for Deut. vi. 25: "It shall be righteousness unto us, if we observe to do all this commandment before the LORD our God, as he hath commanded us." I ask, Who will and can do it? Let the reader look into his own heart and life, and he will find all so full of failure that he will thankfully accept the merit won for him by Christ, the self-sacrifice of Messiah for his need.

THE EPISTLE TO THE HEBREWS.

§ 94.

**552**] This is a part of the New Testament in which Christian people take great delight, both for its spirituality, and for the insight into Old Testament truths which it displays. But our Rabbi adduces two objections against it: first, that its authorship is unknown; secondly, that its canonicity is uncertain.

**553**] Let us consider first the question of authorship. Far from me be it to attempt to prove who it was that wrote it. Briefly speaking, R. Isaac is quite right when he says that no one knows this. It was indeed thought at the end of the second century of our era that the Epistle was written by St. Paul, and this has been the favourite theory with the unlearned in all ages since, but it is given up by scholars. Neither out of all the many names proposed is there one which secures even a majority of votes among thinking people.

What of this? Is it of any real importance? No doubt, we should all like to know who was the author of so great an Epistle, but if we cannot tell, does that injure the value of its contents? Jews as well as Christians would be in a poor way if it were necessary in all cases to know the names of the authors of their sacred books. Will any Jew of learning be good enough to tell us who wrote the books of Joshua, of Judges, of Kings, or most of the Psalms, or Job, or Ecclesiastes, or Chronicles, to say nothing of those many portions of other books, the traditional authorship of which is more than doubtful in these days of critical scholarship? The value of a book to us lies in its appeal to our soul, not in its authorship. Every thoughtful Jew, I am sure, will agree with me in this.

**554**] Secondly, it is said that there are doubts about the canonicity of the Epistle. Yes, while it seems to have always been accepted in Alexandria, and was known and esteemed at Rome by Clement of Rome in the end of the first century, and in North Africa by Tertullian in the end of the second, it was not generally received as canonical in the West until the middle of the fourth. But have there never been any doubts about some of the books now contained in the Hebrew Bible? What of Proverbs, Esther, Ecclesiastes, and the Song of Songs? Jews cannot throw stones at Christians in respect of canonicity any more than in that of authorship.

**555**] But let us be quite clear and candid. A man may reject the Epistle to the Hebrews because he thinks it is uncanonical and unworthy to be included in the canon of the New Testament writings. What of it? Does he thereby imperil his own salvation? Certainly not. We have no right whatever to say so. The Epistle to the Hebrews is not even one of the most important treatises in the New Testament, and if a man does not choose to use it, he does not incur any great and awful penalty. But, to my mind, he does show this, that he has a very slight acquaintance with the historical circumstances in which the New Testament writings were composed, and has a very poor sense of what does, and what does not, reveal God to his soul. The nearer a man is to Christ, and the more knowledge he possesses of the Old Testament, and of the method of its interpretation current during the first century, so much the more gladly will he study the Epistle to the Hebrews. Who it was wrote it, I know not, but the author was some one deeply versed in the things of God. Let that suffice for the devout student, be he Jew or Christian.

## THE SONSHIP OF CHRIST.

### § 95A.

Heb. i. 5, and Psalm ii. 7. "*Thou art my Son, this day have I begotten thee.*"

**556**] The use of this Psalm has been fully discussed in § 68, parr. 480–493, with reference to Acts xiii. 33.

THE SONSHIP OF CHRIST, *cont.*

§ 95B.

Heb. i. 5. "*I will be to him a Father, and he shall be to me a Son.*"

2 Sam. vii. 14. "*I will be his father, and he shall be my son.*"

**557]** R. Isaac informs us that the use of this passage by the author of our Epistle is a mistake, for in the first place God spoke the words to David in reference to Solomon, not the Messiah, and, secondly, they cannot refer to Jesus, because the statement follows that "if he commit iniquity, I will chasten him with the rod of men, and with the stripes of the children of men," and Christians believe that Jesus never sinned at all, and thus, on their own showing, the passage cannot relate to Him.

**558]** Now let us grant at once that God's words to David referred directly, not to the Messiah, but to David's descendants generally, and, as Kimchi puts it, "to the whole seed of David, not to Solomon only." The promise was to David's descendants, even though they might, and sometimes did, require punishment for their sins.

Yet no one, probably, will deny that this glorious promise did, in fact, form a fresh starting-point for the even more glorious hope of the coming of the Messiah. It affected the whole trend of Messianic prophecy. It suggested the everlasting continuance of David's house, the descent from him of the King who should be more than a second David, and the dignity of the Divine Sonship promised to this mighty Ruler. This seems also to be the thought of Ps. lxxxix. 27–37, where the description is too great to suit any merely mortal king of David's line.

**559]** So again in the *Psalms of Solomon*, xvii. 5 (4), 23 (21): "Thou, O Lord, didst choose David to be king over Israel, and didst swear unto him touching his seed for ever, that his kingdom should not fail before Thee. . . . Behold, O LORD, and raise up unto them their king, the son of David, in the time which thou, O God, knowest, that he may reign over Israel thy servant." * And in the second century of the Christian era we find Trypho, the learned Jew with whom Justin Martyr held his discussion, appealing to this passage in 2 Sam. in support of his belief that the Messiah will be a son of David (*Dialogue with Trypho*, § 68).

**560**] But even if it were not the case that this passage in the historical books is recognized by Jews as pointing forward to the Messiah, on the ground that it referred at first to all those descendants of David who should sit upon his throne, yet surely to a Christian who was assured that of all David's seed there was none who approached Jesus the Messiah, it was allowable to use the words spoken by God to David, and to take them as descriptive of the attitude and relation in which God had promised to stand towards him. Never, writes the author of this Epistle, did God give to angels so glorious a promise as this which He gave to David's seed, chief of whom confessedly is the Messiah ; why, then, do some suppose that there are any angels greater than Messiah, and pray to them rather than to Him ? Angels cannot claim to stand in that peculiar relation of sonship to God which Scripture attributes to David's great descendant, the Messiah ! Quite apart from any question as to who the Messiah is, whether Jesus of Nazareth or not, Jews can hardly help accepting the validity of this argument adduced in the Epistle to the Hebrews.

### ANGELS WORSHIP THE MESSIAH.

### § 95c.

Heb. i. 6. "*And when he again bringeth in the first-born into the world he saith, And let all the angels of God worship him.*"

* Ryle and James' translation.

Psalm xcvii. 7. "*Worship him, all ye gods.*"

**561**] The courteous reader will not fail to observe certain points of interest about the words of the Epistle which might escape the glance of the hurried critic. In the first place, the Messiah is called the firstborn. No Jew, of course, can be surprised at this, for the title is given Him in purely Jewish writings. So, for example, in *Shmoth R.*, § 19, we read, on Exod. xiii. 2: "'Sanctify to me all the firstborn.' R. Nathan saith, the LORD saith to Moses, As I made Jacob firstborn, for it is said 'Israel is my son, my firstborn' (Exod. iv. 22), so do I make king Messiah firstborn, for it is said 'I also will make him *my* firstborn' (Ps. lxxxix. 27)." *

**562**] Secondly, if the best commentators upon the Epistle are to be any guide to us, the reference is to the Messiah when He shall come hereafter to judge the world, not to His first coming in the Incarnation. The author says: "When He again bringeth." He regards the Messiah, that is to say, as carrying out the Last Judgment. Now it will be remembered by all Jews who are well acquainted with the history of their nation that this is not primarily a Christian, but a Jewish belief. The *Book of Enoch* was not written by a Christian, but by a Jew. And the author of it says repeatedly that the Judgment will be executed, not by God as such, but by the Son of man. Christians have but identified that Son of man with the Messiah, an identification perhaps not made earlier than Christianity.

**563**] Thirdly, we have already seen in parr. 333-337 that the use of that term, "the Son of man," by a Jewish writer (and it is very similar to the term "the Man" in another Jewish book, 4 Esdras), suggests that it was chosen as a short and convenient expression for the great truth hinted at in Ezek. i., the famous vision of the Merkaba, which so few Jews dare to study. For one reason why that vision was granted to the Prophet was surely this, to remind him that in God

* **קדש לי כל בכור**, ר׳ נתן אומר, אומר הקב״ה למשה כשם שעשיתי יעקב בכור, שנא׳ בני בכורי ישראל, כך אני עושה למלך המשיח בכור, שנא׳ אף אני בכור אתנהו.

Himself there is the quality of man. The Charioteer was as a man. So it may well be that the future Judgment will be carried out by, if we may say so, those attributes of God which He shares in common with humanity, summed up for the author of the Book of Enoch in the title of "the Son of man," and expressed for us Christians in the name of Him who has taken human nature, Jesus the Messiah.

If so, the author of our Epistle surely cannot be blamed for referring a passage in the Psalms which speaks directly of supernatural powers worshipping God, to Him who unites in Himself the human attributes inherent in the Deity, and has undergone the temptations and the trials of mankind. The human character of God as revealed to Ezekiel became visible to men generally in the Person of Jesus of Nazareth, by whom God will judge the world. Regard the Christian doctrine as we may, the Christian author of the Epistle to the Hebrews was quite within his rights in his application of the Psalm. A thoughtful Jew, who had never heard of Jesus, might well have made the same application of it to the Messiah.

### "Thy throne, O God, is for ever and ever."

### § 95d.

Heb. i. 8 from Ps. xlv. 6.

**564**] Our friend says that the translation quoted by the author of the Epistle to the Hebrews is wrong, and should be: "Thy throne is *the throne of* God for ever and ever," which is, we may notice, the rendering of the margin of the Revised Version of the Psalm. Further, he says it means that the throne was an eternal one; and in summing up the passage he tells us that the Psalm was spoken of Messiah, whom God will establish, of the seed of David; also that he will be king over all Israel, and that there will be no intermission to his kingdom, the throne being for ever; for he will reign, and his son, and his son's son after him for ever.

**565**] It is clear from this that the controversy between the Rabbi and ourselves concerning the use of the forty-fifth Psalm is narrowed down to a very small issue, for he believes that it was written of the Messiah, as we ourselves do, and the only difference between us is whether or not the author of the Epistle to the Hebrews was justified in quoting the verse in the manner he does. Both he and R. Isaac interpret the Psalm of Messiah; that the former also thinks that the Messiah is Jesus has nothing to do with the immediate question.

**566**] The Rabbi says the writer is wrong in his use of the Psalm, because he quotes the verse in the form, "Thy throne, O God, is for ever and ever." Yet if he did, the Rabbi must blame not him, but rather the Jewish translator of the Septuagint, who gives exactly the same rendering. If the Greek words in the Epistle to the Hebrews are addressed to the Messiah as God, so they must also be addressed in the Greek translation made by the seventy Jews, and we may fairly ask: why should the Christian Jew be blamed for doing what the Alexandrian Jew did with impunity. But, frankly speaking, it is not at all certain that either the Septuagint or the author of the Epistle meant this. The former found in the Hebrew the word "God" following immediately upon the term "Thy throne," and imitated the Hebrew, perhaps without caring to decide what was the inner meaning of the latter. Then, in his turn, the Christian writer, finding that the Jewish-Greek translation which he used had so convenient an expression for his purpose, may have adopted it as it stood, without troubling to compare it with the Hebrew, or, if he did so compare it, have been content to leave it in the same difficult, but poetic, form which the Psalmist himself wrote.

**567**] In the interests of truth, however, it is necessary to point out that whether or not the rendering "O God" is right, it is in no way required for the argument of the writer of the Epistle. "It is commonly supposed," says Bishop Westcott in his commentary on the Epistle, "that the force of the quotation lies in the divine title, which, as it is held, is applied to the Son. It seems, however, from the whole form of the argument to lie rather in the description which is given of the Son's office and endowment. The angels are subject to constant change, He has a dominion for ever and ever; they work through material powers, He—the Incarnate Son—fulfils a moral sovereignty and is crowned with unique joy. . . . In whatever way, then, the words be taken, the quotation establishes the conclusion which the writer wishes to draw as to the essential difference of the Son and the angels. Indeed it might appear to many that the direct application of the divine Name to the Son would obscure the thought."

**568**] Thus we are not justified in finding in the words a certain and direct "proof" of the divinity of Jesus, for the writer to the Hebrews did not quote them with this object, but we have every right to insist on the fact that the Psalmist contemplates the coming of a King who shall be deemed superior by God to all other beings in the created world. The author of the Epistle believed Jesus to be this King, the Messiah, and therefore he naturally and rightly says that the promise was fulfilled in Him.

"THOU HAST LOVED RIGHTEOUSNESS, AND HATED INIQUITY; THEREFORE GOD, THY GOD, HATH ANOINTED THEE WITH THE OIL OF GLADNESS ABOVE THY FELLOWS."

§ 95E.

So Heb. i. 9 and Ps. xlv. 7.

**569**] This passage is a continuation of the former, and is only worth mentioning because R. Isaac makes the mistake of saying that the writer of the Epistle understood the first word "God" to be in the vocative, and thus to be a direct title of the Messiah. But the Rabbi must have been led astray, perhaps by the Polish version which he used, for there is no hint of this in the Greek. He has made a mistake, and no more need be said.

## THE EIGHTH PSALM.

§ 96.

Heb. ii. 6–9. "*What is man, that thou art mindful of him? or the son of man, that thou visitest him? Thou madest him a little lower than the angels; thou crownedst him with glory and honour, and didst set him over the works of thy hands: thou didst put all things in subjection under his feet. For in that he subjected all things unto him, he left nothing that is not subject to him. But now we see not yet all things subjected to him. But we behold him who hath been made a little lower than the angels,* even *Jesus, because of the suffering of death crowned with glory and honour.*" See Ps. viii. 4–6.

**570**] The explanation of the Psalm given us by R. Isaac is that it speaks of man in general, who is less than angels* because he has a body,† and yet receives such honour from God, by virtue of the soul, that God has made him rule over the animal world. But is not this a bathos? Does not the Psalm in reality suggest to us something more? Had not the Psalmist in mind the moral greatness of men, whose very children are the means of God's power being recognized (Ps. viii.)? Man indeed is a little less than angels, yet he is given honour and glory; and the phrase points to a wide vista of influence and power, in which the dominion over the beasts and birds and fishes is but a foretaste of that supremacy over "all things" which is verbally stated by the Psalmist.

**571**] If so, it will be observed that the writer to the Hebrews is not so far wrong. Man is to be exalted, and

* Whether *Elohim* here should be translated "angels" is of no immediate importance. R. Isaac accepts the rendering of the New Testament and Jewish writers generally, and I think rightly. But most moderns translate it by "God."

† Yet why is the possession of a body necessarily a mark of inferiority? Does not such a suggestion smack of Manichæism?

his argument is that we see One Man exalted already. He was made lower than the angels, but, because He suffered death, He has been raised far above them, crowned with glory and honour. He is, therefore, in such a position that angels must worship Him, as the author already wrote in the first chapter. Thus R. Isaac's further difficulty that here Christ is said to be less than the angels, whereas there He had been described as superior to them, falls to the ground.

**572**] But it may be objected that if we thus explain the passage as a tribute to the hope of the eighth Psalm by its fulfilment in the case of one Person already, how is it a proof of Christ's divinity? But who ever said it was a proof of this? Certainly not the writer of the Epistle. For he does not adduce the Psalm as a proof of Christ's divinity, or indeed as a proof of anything in the modern sense of the word "proof." He was, quite evidently, a Jewish-Christian, accustomed to turn to the sacred Scriptures to illustrate, and thus to confirm, everything he wrote (for they were permeated, as he believed, through and through with the power of God), and, convinced as he was that Jesus was the Messiah, passage after passage of Scripture came into his mind, bearing upon the subject from every possible point of view. He was a Jew, and he wrote like a Jew, for whom Scripture was like Moses' bush, all on fire with the presence of God, and if he was writing about the character of Messiah, or His nature, or His position and work, and recalled words of Scripture which suited his thought, he (like every other Jew quoted in Talmudic writings) would not hesitate to use them for his purpose. Scripture for Jews of old had such wide and manifold applications as to suit every truth. Let the Jews, then, judge the writer of the Epistle by Jewish standards. In all probability he never supposed that the author of the Psalm consciously referred to Messiah (whatever he thought the Divine Author who inspired him might Himself have intended), but he did see that it held out the promise of a greatness for Man which is yet to be, and also that already One Man, the Lord Jesus Christ, has attained to that greatness. You may deny the fact that Jesus of Nazareth is the

Messiah—that is another matter altogether—but you cannot blame the writer of the Epistle for the way in which he quotes Scripture, if only you deal out to him the same measure of justice that you allow to other Jews.

### THE NEW COVENANT.

§ 97.

**573**] Heb. viii. 8; Jer. xxxi. 31. See Part I. § 29; parr. 230–233.

### "A BODY DIDST THOU PREPARE FOR ME."

§ 98.

Heb. x. 5–7. "*Wherefore when he cometh into the world, he saith, Sacrifice and offering thou wouldest not, but a body didst thou prepare for me; in whole burnt offerings and* sacrifices *for sin thou hadst no pleasure: then said I, Lo, I am come (in the roll of the book it is written of me) to do thy will, O God.*"

Ps. xl. 6, 7. "*Sacrifice and offering thou hast no delight in; mine ears hast thou opened: burnt offering and sin offering hast thou not required. Then said I, Lo, I am come; in the roll of the book it is written of me: I delight to do thy will, O my God.*"

**574**] The general meaning of this portion of the Psalm is plain. The Psalmist, conscious of deliverance from some extreme danger, perhaps a very serious illness, comes before the LORD to offer more than mere sacrifices, even himself, for complete obedience to the will of God. For his ears, he says, have been framed for that very purpose, that they may hear the commands that God may choose to give him, and that he may carry them out to the full. This is substantially what R. Isaac says, and he is right.

**575**] But the Jews of Alexandria did not translate "Mine ears hast Thou opened," but paraphrased, "A body didst Thou prepare for me." Why they did so is not clear, but in all probability they were moved by the desire to make the meaning of the Psalmist plainer than ever, and to leave no loophole for the reader to escape from the clear duty of consecrating himself to God wholly and entirely. They wished him to understand that God formed not his ears only, but all his body, with every one of its members, that he might hear, see, think, and perform the will of God with all his powers. If so, we must say that this old Jewish rendering is certainly interesting, and is only so far wrong that it ceases to be a literal translation, and becomes a paraphrase. But this is very common elsewhere, both in the Septuagint and in the Targums. No blame can be attached to the Alexandrian translators on this score.*

**576**] Now comes the Jewish-Christian, who is writing his hortatory letter to the Hebrews, *i.e.* members of the same race and the same faith as himself, but presumably dwellers in Palestine, or even Jerusalem. He has heard that they are inclined to waver in the simplicity of their faith, and he desires to strengthen and encourage them by every means in his power. He therefore directs them once more to the Messiah, the Lord Jesus Christ, in whom they and he believe. He has now reached the point when he is speaking of the coming of the Messiah into the world, and is describing the spirit and aim with which He leaves the abodes of bliss. The Messiah, he says, would thus address His Father in heaven. I come down to earth, not to perform any mere external sacrifices, good though these are in themselves, but

* It is possible, but improbable, that the Greek word for "body" is due to a mere mistake, the misreading of the word for "ears" by some copyist. But how the common Greek text arose is of no importance to us, for in any case it represents the thought of the Hebrew.

to carry out Thy will in its entirety. Therefore hast Thou framed my ears, nay, a whole body hast Thou prepared for me, that I may carry out Thy will to the uttermost. The writer employs the phraseology of the Alexandrian Jews, and we cannot blame him.

**577**] But the Psalmist did not intend to refer to the Messiah, you say! No, I suppose that he did not. What of that? Surely the Christian may use the words of Him! There they stand in a Jewish version, ready to hand, and after all they do exactly express the work of the Messiah as the Christian understands it. If the Psalmist, David or whoever else it was, could dare to say that he himself put aside all thought of sacrifices in comparison with the blessed privilege of doing the will of God, how much more could He say it who came down to earth for men's salvation, that He might fully accomplish that will!

**578**] For, if we consider the passage closely, the use of it by the writer to the Hebrews is not merely verbal, and depends on no mere quibble of Jewish exegesis. The sentence states a great truth; that external sacrifices are insufficient, and that the accomplishment of the will of God, in one's character and life, is everything. Ordinary men, alas, fail to do this; but Messiah succeeds: "His power to do the will of God corresponded with His purpose to do it."* And because He fulfilled it, therefore salvation was procured for every one who will put his trust in Him. Thus the believer, looking to the finished work of Christ, gladly applies to Him the Psalmist's words, and cares little whether he quotes from the Hebrew, and speaks of "ears," or from the paraphrase of the Alexandrian Jews, and says: "A body didst Thou prepare for me."

## THE OMISSION OF DAN IN REV. vii. 5–8.

### § 99.

**579**] R. Isaac is very severe on the fact that the writer of the Revelation of St. John omits the name of Dan from his

* Bishop Westcott.

list of the Jewish Christians who were sealed out of the Twelve Tribes, and adds the name of Manasseh instead. But this is a misstatement. For the writer is not enumerating the sons of Jacob as such, but those who were sealed out of every Tribe. He is plainly thinking of the Twelve Tribes in their geographical distribution. But among these he includes the tribe of Levi, and is therefore bound to omit one of the others, if he is not to go beyond the number twelve. He thus has not omitted Dan, and put Manasseh instead, but he has inserted Levi, and omitted Dan. It is well to be accurate about such matters.

**580**] But even so there is a difficulty. What made the author omit Dan, rather than any other of the twelve?

Now here we must remember that this author is not alone in omitting a name, or names, from what looks at first sight like a complete enumeration of the Twelve Tribes. For Moses does the same in Deut. xxxiii. He inserts Levi, and leaves out Simeon. Did he do so, pray, because he was an ignorant person, careless even of so ordinary a piece of information as the proper names of the twelve sons of Jacob? For that is the accusation which R. Isaac ventures to make against the writer of the Revelation, well-acquainted though he shows himself to be with Jewish matters elsewhere. Surely the accusation of ignorance is preposterous in either case. Similarly with the writer of 1 Chron. ii. 3–viii. He enumerates the Tribes, and omits Dan * and Zebulon! Why does he? That I cannot say, neither is it our present business to inquire. But it is not likely to have been through that crass ignorance of the A B C of Judaism, which some attribute so lightly to the writers of the New Testament.

**581**] Yet, after all, if, as we have seen, the author of the Revelation mentions Levi, and therefore has to omit one of the others, why does he choose Dan? The reason is not far

* In 1 *Chron.* vii. 12, חשם בני אחר may have been originally חשים בני דן (cf. *Gen.* xlvi. 23), in which case אחר may have been inserted because the MS. was illegible. Or possibly אחר was used as a convenient mode of designating a person with whom there were unfavourable associations; cf. אחר as the equivalent of Elisha ben Abuyah. The margins of the Authorized and Revised Versions would read Ahiram (Num. xxvi. 38).

to seek. The Tribe of Dan had made a bad name for itself, for its unfaithfulness to God. Look at the *Targum of Jerusalem I* (the so-called Targum of Jonathan) on Exod. xvii. 8: "Amalek killed men of the house of Dan, for the Cloud did not hide them because of the strange worship that there was among them."

וקטיל גוברין מדבית דן דלא הוה עננא מקביל יתהון מן: בגלל פולחנא נוכראה די ביניהון.

Or recall *Bemidbar R.* on Num. ii. 25, "On the north side shall be the standard of the camp of Dan." "*The North.* Thence comes darkness into the world. But what has this to do with Dan? Because it brought darkness into the world by idolatry. For Jeroboam made two calves of gold. And idolatry is darkness; for it is said (Isa. xxix. 15), 'and their works are in the dark.' And Jeroboam went round over all Israel, and they would not receive his teaching, save the Tribe of Dan, for it is said (1 Kings xii. 28 *sq.*), 'Whereupon the king took counsel, and made two calves of gold . . . and he set the one in Dan.' Therefore the Holy One commanded that Dan should be encamped on the north."

**צפון.** משם החשך יוצא לעולם. וכנגדן שבט דן למה שהוא החשיך בעולם בע"א שעשה ירבעם שני עגלי זהב. וע"א חשך הוא שנאמר והיה במחשך מעשיהם. וחזר ירבעם על כל ישראל ולא קבלו ממנו אלא שבט דן שנאמר ויועץ המלך ויעש שני עגלי זהב וגו' ואת האחד נתן בדן. ולכך צוה הקב"ה שיחנה דן בצפון.

A Jewish writer earlier than the translator of the Targum, or the compiler of the Midrash, is even more severe. For writing in the first century B.C. he roundly accuses the Tribe of Dan of open apostacy in the days to come. See the *Testaments of the Twelve Patriarchs: Dan* v. 4-6: "I know that in the last days ye shall depart from the Lord . . . and whensoever ye depart from the Lord, ye shall walk in all evil and work the abominations of the Gentiles. . . . For I have read in the book of Enoch the righteous, that your prince is Satan."

**582**] This last clause comes very near to the opinion of some of the Christian Fathers that Antichrist was to appear from the Tribe of Dan,* but there is no certain evidence that the Jews themselves thought this, however likely it may seem after the passages already quoted. For these at least show that Dan was in bad odour in Jewish circles, and that therefore an early Jewish-Christian writer, like the author of the Revelation, might readily share the same opinion, and, when he had to leave out one of the Twelve Tribes, in consequence of his insertion of Levi, might easily select Dan. His action is quite in accordance with what we know of Jewish thought at the time.

**583**] With regard to the objection brought forward by R. Isaac against the mention of Manasseh, we have already shown that this is due to a mistake. But, in any case, even if he were right in supposing that the writer of the Revelation desired to name the sons of Jacob, and not the Twelve Tribes geographically considered, then, as he did not care to include Dan, Manasseh was the name that lay next to hand. For Ephraim was always so identified with Joseph in later years that it would have been absurd to name him as well as Joseph (*v.* 8). Therefore Manasseh, as the only other grandson of Jacob of whom we know anything, would naturally be mentioned. But it is not necessary to labour this point.

### Addition and Subtraction.

§ 100.

Rev. xxii. 18 *sq.*

**584**] In this last paragraph of his whole book, as in the last of his First Part, R. Isaac blames Christians for adding to their Law, and also for subtracting from it. On the general question it is sufficient to refer my honoured readers to what has been said on I. § 50, parr. 292–294. He further specifies in particular the observance of the Sunday, with reference to

* So Hippolytus, *Christ and Antichrist*, § 14. See also Irenæus, V. 30, 2.

which it will be enough to refer to parr. 166–171; and he also speaks of the Dietary laws, for which parr. 152–159 may be consulted.

We have thus come to the end of the Rabbi's work, and our task is done. But before bidding farewell to my readers, I should like to make a few final remarks as a kind of general survey.

**585**] What are the chief lessons that we have learned from the study of the *Chizzuk Emunah?*

1. Few of the writings of the New Testament are elaborate and scholarly disquisitions; the majority of them being rather the rapid outcome of thoughts of men in close touch with God, who desired to encourage their readers in their faith on Christ.

**586**] 2. None was written primarily to convince those who do not believe upon Him. None, in other words, is a treatise on Christian evidences. We must not expect, therefore, to find in any book of the New Testament direct and formal arguments that Jesus is the Messiah, much less that He is divine. The only writing of which this could be said with any truth is the Gospel according to St. John, and even this was addressed to Christians, and not to those who were ignorant of the faith.

**587**] 3. We must allow to the writers of the New Testament the same liberty of exposition that we grant to other Jewish writers. The latter used Midrashic methods; the former also. It is perfectly true that many of the passages of the Old Testament quoted by the writers of the New cannot be adduced as direct "proofs," in the modern sense of the word, of the facts and doctrines with which the New Testament writers connect them. But these never intended their quotations to be interpreted rigidly. They quoted the Old Testament with the same freedom as did their Jewish contemporaries, and we have no right to expect anything else from them.

**588**] 4. We have, I trust, also learned that both the Old Testament and the New are writings marked by a much higher standard of spirituality than anything outside them, and that we are able to appreciate them just so far as our own hearts are attuned to know and understand spiritual things, and no further.

**589**] 5. But it may be asked: Why, if the Old Testament is so good, do we need the addition of the New? Because, in fact, the New is higher than the Old. I do not mean that its ethical demands are higher, absolutely and in themselves, but it is higher in that it presents to us a Life lived in perfect accordance with these demands, and describes to us the power that He still confers on His followers from His home above.

**590**] 6. For we must continually bear in mind what the Christian doctrine of the Incarnate Christ really is, through ignorance or forgetfulness of which R. Isaac, like so many other Jews, often goes astray in his verdict upon Christianity. For he frequently assumes that statements to the effect that our Lord was hungry, tired, suffering, etc., show that He was not divine. But the essence of Christian teaching is that unless He was liable to human feeling and human pain He would not have been man. In other words, Christian doctrine insists that when we speak of the Son of God being Incarnate, we mean that He was completely human in every particular except sin, and completely divine, though the exercise and the exhibition of His Divine power were limited by the conditions of His "complete humanity." For it is evident that He would not have passed through the experience of men at all if He had employed omniscience, omnipresence, omnipotence. These in their actual use He put off during the time of His manhood upon earth. For, after all, they belong, I suppose, to the outer circle of the Divine nature, if we dare put it thus, not to its very essence. To thinking people of to-day they count for infinitely less than love. And this the Incarnate Son retained and exhibited to the uttermost, in all the actions of His life, down to His death upon the cross.

**591**] Let me add a few words to my Jewish readers in particular. You will, I think, acknowledge that I have made it my first aim throughout to be scrupulously fair and above-board. Indeed it always seems absurd when one who writes on religious subjects hides wilfully and of purpose anything which in fact belongs to them so closely that the withholding of it will give a false impression of the whole. No one wants a temporary victory in the cause of truth. We desire to win men, men themselves, not their mere acknowledgment that our arguments are better than theirs. It would never be of advantage either to you or to me if I were to draw unfair inferences or make a faulty exegesis, though, of course, in spite of all efforts, error creeps in here as elsewhere. Further, never have I intentionally said a word that can irritate you, much less one that is calculated to increase ill-feeling between Jews and Gentiles. Neither race can afford to throw stones at the other, but it would ill become a writer on religion to increase the heap of missiles.

**592**] Also a few words to my Gentile readers. Occasionally, I fear, you may have felt disappointed that I have not accepted those interpretations of passages which, on the surface, appear to you to be most natural. But it is precisely because Jewish arguments and modes of thought are often so different from our own that it has been necessary to examine these Jewish writings of the New Testament with greater care than they sometimes receive. The Apostles were Jewish Christians, and regarded the Old Testament and its prophecies with Jewish minds, and we must beware of reading into their expressions more than they themselves intended them to convey.

**593**] In any case, may we all, Jews and Gentiles, readers and writer alike, remember that controversy in itself, and as such, is painful and unedifying. For intellectual subtlety alone never yet won a heart to God, and never built up a character in likeness to Him. We want to know by ever deeper experience the true nature of prayer, and of blessed communion with God, the final revelation of Whom, as we Christians believe, has been made in the person of Jesus Christ, the Son of David, the Son of man, and the Son of God.

**594**] Finally, may we all, both readers and unworthy writer, meet hereafter in bliss, singing the song of thanksgiving for redemption from the Egypt of sin, and from the fiery trials of this ungodly world, standing upon the crystal sea before the throne of God, and saying: "Great and marvellous are thy works, O Lord God, the Almighty; righteous and true are thy ways, thou King of the ages. Who shall not fear, O Lord, and glorify thy name? For thou only art holy; for all the nations shall come and worship before thee; for thy righteous acts have been made manifest" (Rev. xv. 3, 4). And "Unto him that loveth us, and loosed us from our sins by his blood; and he made us *to be* a kingdom, *to be* priests unto his God and Father; to him *be* the glory and the dominion for ever and ever. Amen" (Rev. i. 5, 6).

אכן חלינו הוא נשא׃
לכן אחלק לו וברבים׃
ובאו ורננו במרום ציון׃

# ADDENDA ET CORRIGENDA TO VOL. I.

N.B.—*The reader is asked to consult the Indices for additional references.*

Page 11, line 4. *For* ההצער *read* ההצעה.

,, ,, line 3 from bottom. "a certain Polish Chronicle." Afterwards in this Preamble R. Isaac speaks of this as "the Great Chronicle which is printed in Polish." See further in par. 477.

Par. 10. Canon Box's arguments may now be seen more conveniently in his *Virgin Birth of Jesus*, 1916, pp. 12-15. See also *The Hebrew-Christian Messiah*, pp. 260–265.

,, 12. The *Ascension of Isaiah*, xi. 2 (probably first cent. A.D.), speaks of Mary's descent from David.

,, 23. See Driver on Deut. iv. 30.

,, 44. *For* במית *read* מבית. Perhaps a better translation is "Woe! for their lances" (with which they oppress the people). "Woe! for their secret accusations." The passage is part of a long indictment against the Sadducean High Priests. See further, Chwolson, *Das letzte Passamahl Christi, u.s.w.*, pp. 121–125.

,, 45–46. See Klausner, *Die Messianischen Vorstellungen*, pp. 99–103. He says: "Gog und Magog spielen im Talmud die Rolle eines collectivischen Antimessias."

,, 50–54. On the Shekinah, see Glossary.

,, 77 *sq.* One system of Jewish Chronology reduced the usual computation of 206 years for the period of Greek domination to 34 years, and this seems to have been (roughly) that which R. Isaac followed. See G. Margoliouth's argument with reference to the Sadducean Christians of Damascus in the *Expositor*, Dec., 1911, pp. 503–507; also the *Jewish Encyclopedia*, iv. 70.

,, 81–83. For Gamaliel's saying compare Aboth v. 20 (24): "Every dispute (or, perhaps, secession) which is for the glory of God shall at last be established, and that which is not for the glory of God shall not be." See Chwolson, *Das letzte Passamahl Christi*, pp. 96 *sq.*

,, 105–125. On the subject of the Trinity in Unity, compare *The Hebrew-Christian Messiah*, Lect. ix.

,, 144–151. In T. B. Berakoth, 57*a*, Gen. xlix. 11 is applied to Messiah.

,, 160. "The Law . . . as he!" This passage is misplaced, and should come between parr. 165 and 166.

,, 162. See *The Hebrew-Christian Messiah*, pp. 194–205.

,, 163. So Maimonides speaks of one who "hastens after the commandments" (רודף אחר מצות), *Hilkoth Tephillah*, vi. 1.

Par. 167. R. Simeon b. Menasya explains Exod. xxxi. 14, "It is holy unto you," by "Unto you is the sabbath delivered, and not you unto the sabbath."

,, 185 end. Clement of Alexandria, *Strom.* i. 19, 94, has—

εἶδες γάρ, φησίν, τὸν ἀδελφόν σου, εἶδες τὸν Θεόν σου.

,, 188. Pastor A. Jeremias has modified his language in the second edition of his book, and in any case he seems to refer to an astrological and heavenly Virgin, not to one on earth. There seems to be little or no evidence of the existence of a widespread belief that the expected Deliverer would be born of a human mother who was a virgin at the time of His birth. The meaning of Isaiah himself is very obscure, and it is possible after all that Matt. i. 22 is only a Christian adaptation of his phrase in accordance with Jewish methods.

Page 160, note. Consult also Dalman, *Jesaja* 53, 2nd edition, 1914.

Parr. 228 *sq.* See *The Hebrew-Christian Messiah*, pp. 31 *sq.*

,, 237–244. *Ibid.* pp. 26–30.

,, 274. Polish, like all the Slavonic languages, also has no article, so that R. Isaac need not have known Latin to make this mistake.

,, 276-282. See *The Hebrew-Christian Messiah*, pp. 270–272, 321 *sq.*

,, 283. In Part II., § 21, R. Isaac quotes Dan. vii. 27 of Messiah. See par. 357.

# GLOSSARY

# and

# INDICES

# GLOSSARY.*

*Aboth*, "Fathers." A treatise of the Mishna (q.v.), with no Gemara (q.v.) attached to it. To the majority of English readers it is the most interesting of all the treatises, for it contains a large number of important ethical sayings. It may be found with an English translation in Singer's *Authorised Daily Prayer Book*, pp. 184 *sqq.*, Edition annotated by I. Abrahams, 1914. The quotations in this *Manual* are generally made from Dr. C. Taylor's *Sayings of the Jewish Fathers*, 2nd edition, 1897.

*Aboth d'Rabbi Nathan.*

An enlargement of the Mishna treatise *Aboth*, attributed to R. Nathan, a Tanna (Mishna-teacher) of the 4th generation (160—220): but in its present form this treatise is post-Talmudic.

*Al-tiqri*, "Do not read."

A phrase used in the Talmud and elsewhere when a Rabbi desired to give a midrashic (q.v.) explanation of a passage. He said, "Do not read" the true text, but read something very like it, such, for example, as "r" for "d" (see par. 93).

The object was not, as has been fondly supposed, to throw doubt on the accuracy of the text, but only to deduce a lesson from it.

*Aqiba.*

One of the most famous of the teachers mentioned in the Mishna (q.v.). He was born about 50 A.D. and killed by the Romans as a leader in Barcochba's revolt about

* This short Glossary, with the accompanying explanations, may be useful to some non-Jewish readers. It is not intended to be of any assistance to Jewish people.

132 A.D. He insisted on the inspiration of every word, and even every letter, of Scripture.

*Baalshem—The*, "The Master of the Name."

The founder of the sect of Chassidim. Born about 1700 in the Bukowina, died 1761 A.D. Apparently a singularly holy man, insisting more on the religious spirit than on the observance of forms of religion. He laid great stress on the Immanence of God.

According to him a really righteous man (*Zaddiq*) stands in a special relation to God. Hence his followers regard him as the great mediator between themselves and God. The same claim (though generally in less measure) is made by and for each leader of a group of Chassidim to-day.

See the *Jewish Encyclopedia*, ii. 383—386; and especially Schechter, *Studies in Judaism*, 1896, pp. 1—55.

*Bereshith R(abba)*. An exegetical, mostly haggadic (q.v.) midrash (q.v.), on Genesis, mainly dating in its present form from about the sixth century. See Oesterley and Box, *The Religion and Worship of the Synagogue*, 1907, pp. 81 *sq.*; 1911, pp. 84 *sq.* *Shmoth R.* and *Bemidbar R.* are Midrashim of the same kind, but of the eleventh or twelfth century.

*Bible.*

The Hebrew Bible is arranged under the following heads: I. The Law (*Torah*), *i.e.* the five books of Moses. II. The Prophets (*Nebiim*): (1) Former, 1 and 2 Samuel, 1 and 2 Kings; (2) Latter, Isaiah, Jeremiah, Ezekiel and the Twelve ("minor") Prophets. III. The Writings (*Kethûbîm*): (1) Psalms, Proverbs, Job; (2) the Five Megilloth or Rolls, viz. Canticles, Ruth, Lamentations, Ecclesiastes, Esther; (3) Daniel, Ezra and Nehemiah, Chronicles. The Jews often refer to the Scriptures as "Law, Prophets and Writings," or as TNK, the initial letters of the Hebrew titles.

*Boethus.*

A Sadducean priest. His son, or perhaps he himself, was made High Priest about 25 or 24 B.C. by Herod the Great. Boethusians became synonymous with Sadducees. See the *Jewish Encyclopedia*, iii. 284 *sq.*

*D'rash*, "explanation," of a passage rather than a book (*midrash*). In contrast to *P'shat* (q.v.) it is an explanation which is either far-fetched or, at the least, does not lie within the ordinary grammatical meaning of the passage.

*Elisha ben Abuyah*, also called *Acher*, "another."

"Our Rabbis have taught, Four men went up into Paradise, and they were these, Ben Azzai, and Ben Zoma, Acher, and R. Aqiba" (T.B. Chagiga 14*b*). Ben Azzai gazed and died. Ben Zoma gazed and went mad. Acher "cut the plants," *i.e.* (as it seems) divided the Godhead. R. Aqiba alone came out unhurt. It is probable that Acher (Elisha ben Abuyah) adopted some form of Gnosticism. Some scholars are of opinion that his fault was that he disliked Pharisaism and tried to lead Jews to break its precepts. He lived from about 70 to 130 A.D. See Streane's *Translation of Chagigah*, 1891, pp. 83—89; also the *Jewish Encyclopedia*, v. pp. 138 *sq*.

*Gematria*, either "arithmetic," or "letters."

There are no separate numerals in Hebrew, but each letter has a numerical value attached to it in accordance with its position in the alphabet. Hence by adding up the letters of which a word is composed it is possible to say that the whole word equals a certain number. Not only so, but by a process of reasoning which appeals only to those who accept the inspiration of Scripture in every letter, two words which are equal in numerical value may be treated as equal in meaning.

*Gemara*, see Talmud.

*Haggada* (plural *Haggadoth*), "declaration," "narration," "telling."

A term of very wide meaning expressive of all exposition of scripture that does not deal directly with legal decision (*i.e.* that is not halakic, q.v.). Thus it includes almost, or quite, every other form of Biblical exegesis, and, in particular, illustrative stories. See especially Strack, *Einleitung in den Talmud*, 1908, pp. 5 *sq.*; also Oesterley and Box, *Religion and Worship of the Synagogue*, 1907, p. 75; 1911, p. 78.

*Halaka* (plural *Halakoth*), "walk," "rule," a legal decision determining the walk of life. Contrast "Haggada." It is applied to the legal element of the oral law.

*Karaite*, "Reader." A name given to themselves by the followers of Anan (died between 780 and 800 A.D.), who rejected the oral traditional law taught by the Rabbis, and attempted to derive all customs and doctrine from scripture (*mikqra*), *i.e.* the Pentateuch. See *Rabbanite.*

*Kōsher*, "correct," "proper."

An epithet describing food ritually correct to be eaten by Jews.

*Law.*

The Hebrew name is Torah, which, however, does not appear to be used of Law in the abstract, but only of "the Law." This was regarded as (1) Written, contained in the Pentateuch, though occasionally the term is used of other books of Scripture; (2) Oral, a traditional Law taught by God to Moses on Mount Sinai and handed down by him. The Oral Law had no fixed contents, but was continually being enlarged and modified (but only, as was claimed, in accordance with fixed principles guiding its evolution from the first) by successive generations of teachers. The first authoritative code of it was the Mishna (q.v.) of R. Judah ha Nasi. See also *Bible.*

*Maimonides.*

A very famous Jewish writer and codifier of the oral law, born at Cordova 1135, died at Cairo 1204. His principal works are the *Yad-ha-Chazāqa* or Digest of the Oral Law, and the *Môreh-Nebûkim*, a philosophical investigation of many religious subjects.

*Massora*, *māsôreth*, *massoretic*, "tradition," "traditional."

The massoretic text of the Hebrew Bible is the ordinary text, with vowel points. It represents the results of the study of the "Massoretes," the "traditionalists," who lived from the second half of the eighth century to the first half of the tenth century A.D. The most accurate edition of this text is that which is now (1918) being published by the British and Foreign Bible Society.

*Mekilta.*

A homiletical midrash (q.v.) on the book of Exodus

(from ch. 12). In its original form belonging to the first part of the 2nd century A.D., in its present form rather later; the most important and valuable of the *midrashim* (q.v.).

*Midrash*, plural *Midrashim*, "explanation," "exposition."

In particular the semi-homiletical explanations of different books of Scripture, *e.g.* the Midrash on Genesis. They are of very various ages, and generally speaking contain Haggada (q.v.) rather than Halacha (q.v.). See also *D'rash*. For an account of the different Midrashic works see Oesterley and Box, *Religion and Worship of the Synagogue*, ch. v.

*Mitzvah*, "commandment."

Any action performed out of obedience to the will of God.

*Mishna*, see Talmud.

*Moses de Leon.*

Born at Leon in Spain about 1250, died 1305 A.D. Probably the author of the present form of the *Zohar*, a strange Cabbalistic Midrash, which he pretended was written by R. Simeon ben Jochai, who died at Meron near Safed in Galilee about 161 A.D.

*Onkelos*, see *Targum*.

*Pesiqta Rabbathi.* A homiletical midrash (q.v.) on the special lessons read in the Synagogue from the Law and the Prophets. It is said to be as old as the second half of the ninth century A.D.

*Pirqe Aboth*, "chapters of Aboth"; see *Aboth*.

*Pirqe d'Rabbi Eliezer*, "chapters of R. Eliezer."

A midrashic (q.v.) narrative of the more important events recorded in the Pentateuch, attributed to R. Eliezer ben Hyrcanus, who lived in the end of the first century A.D., but in its present form not earlier than the ninth century; translated into English with copious notes by G. Friedlander, 1916.

*P'shat*, "simple."

The explanation of a passage derived solely from a study of grammatical and lexical meaning of the words in their context. Contrast *D'rash*.

*Rabbanite.*

A nickname given by the Karaites (q.v.) about 800 A.D. to their adversaries the orthodox Jews, as "the partisans of authority" (see Grätz, *Geschichte der Juden*, 1871, v. 181. English translation 1892, iii. 136), "Rabban" ("our teacher") being a title of the president of the Sanhedrin from the time of R. Gamaliel the Elder, teacher of St. Paul.

*Saadiah.*

Head ("*Gaon*") of the Rabbinic academy at Sura in Babylonia. Born 892, died 942 A.D. His book on the Articles of Faith and Doctrines of Dogma ("*sepher Emunoth w'Deoth*") was written in 933.

*Sabbathai Zebi.*

Born at Smyrna 1626, died in Albania 1676. When he was twenty-two years of age he claimed to be the Messiah, at first more or less privately. In 1665, however, he claimed the position openly, and multitudes of Jews believed in him, including many prominent Rabbis of the time. But after being imprisoned by the Sultan he became a Moslem in 1666, and persuaded many of his followers to imitate him. See the *Jewish Encyclopedia*, xi. pp. 218—225.

*Shekinah*, "dwelling" (in the abstract sense).

A term used to express the thought of God's dwelling with men, more particularly of His Presence as in some way making Itself visible. See Oesterley and Box, *The Religion and Worship of the Synagogue*, 1907, pp. 191—195; 1911, pp. 217—221; and J. Abelson, *The Immanence of God in Rabbinical Literature*, 1912, pp. 76—149, 377—382; also C. Taylor, *Sayings of the Jewish Fathers*, 1897, pp. 43 *sq.*

*Talmud*, plural *Talmudim*, "study," "teaching."

A summary of the oral traditional law with discussions and illustrative tales. It is in two parts: (1) the Mishna, "repetition," a comparatively short collection made about 190 A.D. by R. Jehuda ha Nasi. It is composed of many treatises known by the names of the principal subject in each. (2) The Gemara, "completion" and "learning," which takes the form of a commentary on the Mishna. Strictly speaking the word "Talmud" is used of the Gemara alone. The Gemara is two-fold: (i.) the Palestinian or Jerusalem Gemara, of the fourth and fifth centuries, containing the opinions of Jewish scholars living in Palestine, cited as T(almud) J(erushalmi). (ii.) the Babylonian Gemara, mostly of the sixth century, containing the opinions of Jewish scholars living in Babylon, cited as T(almud) B(abli). Of these an edition of the Mishna interwoven with the Babylonian Gemara is "the Talmud" *par excellence*. Hence quotations from a Talmudical treatise without either of the prefixes T.B., T.J., refer to the Babylonian Gemara.

*Tanchuma*. Perhaps the oldest Haggadic collection of homilies extant, of the fifth century. Oesterley and Box, 1911, p. 92.

*Targum*, plural *Targumim*, "translation."

Aramaic translations of the Hebrew Bible frequently so far from literal as to be rather paraphrases.

I. *On the Pentateuch:* (1) *Targum of Onkelos*, apparently an Aramaic form of "Aquila," of the second century A.D., generally literal. (2) *Targum of Jerusalem I.*, often called by a mistake the Targum of Jonathan. In its present form not older than the second half of the seventh century A.D. Often paraphrastic. (3) *Targum of Jerusalem II.*, or "Fragment Targum," so called because it exists only in many pieces, often quite short. It seems to be of about the same date as the Targ. Jer. I., and is of much the same character.

II. *On the Prophets* (Former and Latter, see *Bible*). *The Targum of Jonathan ben Uzziel*, because attributed to him. He was a pupil of Hillel, at the beginning of the Christian era, but the Targum in its present form is of about the fifth century A.D. It is not so literal as the Targum of Onkelos, especially in the prophecies.

III. *On the Holy Writings* (see Bible). The Targums on these are by many writers, of about the same date as the Targums of Jerusalem; that on Chronicles is later.

On the whole subject see especially Strack, *Einleitung in das alte Testament*, 1906, § 84; also Oesterley and Box, *The Religion and Worship of the Synagogue*, 1907, pp. 44—50; 1911, pp. 46—52.

*T.B.*, see Talmud.

*T.J.*, see Talmud.

*Torah*, see *Law*.

*Yalqut*, "scrip" (1 Sam. xvii. 40), "collection."

A large collection of materials from various midrashim (q.v.), many of which are no longer extant, covering the whole Hebrew Bible. It is similar in character to the patristic *catenae*. The Yalqut *par excellence* bears the name of Simeon. It is not earlier than the middle ages. Who the Simeon was is unknown.

*Yiddish*, Jüdisch, "Jewish."

A language of which the basis is mediæval High German, into which have been wrought many Hebrew words and phrases, and, in addition, not a little of the language of the country in which any Jew who uses it happens to live. Its German basis forms the real distinction from the *Ladino*, or Jewish-Spanish, of Levantine Jews, which is a fairly pure mediæval Spanish, with the addition of a certain amount of Hebrew. Both forms of "Jargon" are of extreme interest philologically. The dialects of Yiddish are innumerable, their differences depending on the amount of the third ingredient, non-German and non-Hebrew words. Hence if in a company of Yiddish-speaking Jews from various parts of the world the question "What is true Yiddish?" is asked, a satisfactory answer is seldom received. Each person naturally supposes that his own form of it is the best. Mr. Leo Wiener, the chief authority on the vast Yiddish literature, says in the *Jewish Encyclopedia* (vii. 305) that the dialects "may be conveniently grouped in three divisions: (1) the southern, spoken in the south of Russia, in parts of Galicia, and in Roumania, and corresponding more closely to a variety of Bavarian; (2) the Polish, the dialect of Poland and parts of Lithuania and Galicia; and (3) the Lithuanian, the dialect spoken in the greater part of Lithuania, and bearing strong resemblances to the dialects of Henneberg and of parts of Saxony." The best dictionary of Yiddish is by A. Harkavy, New York, 1901, 1905.

# INDICES

*The numbers refer to the paragraphs, not to the pages, unless expressly stated.*

## i. GENERAL

# ii. HOLY SCRIPTURE, AND OTHER EARLY LITERATURE

*Large type indicates that the passage is examined at length.*
*The Old Testament books are in the Hebrew order.*

(*a*) OLD TESTAMENT.

### (*b*) Apocrypha and Pseudepigrapha.



### (*c*) New Testament.

(*d*) HELLENISTIC AND PATRISTIC LITERATURE.

(*c*) Rabbinical Literature.

THE END